Reforming American Politics

A Christian Perspective on Moving
Past Conflict to Conversation

Harold Heie

Front Edge Publishing

For more information and further discussion, visit
http://www.respectfulconversation.net

Published by
Front Edge Publishing, LLC
42015 Ford Road, Suite 234
Canton, Michigan

Front Edge Publishing specializes in speed and flexibility in adapting
and updating our books. We can include links to video and other
online media. We offer discounts on bulk purchases for special events,
corporate training, and small groups. We are able to customize bulk
orders by adding corporate or event logos on the cover and we can
include additional pages inside describing your event or corporation. For
more information about our fast and flexible publishing or permission
to use our materials, please contact Front Edge Publishing at info@
FrontEdgePublishing.com.

Dedicated to Jim Skillen who woke me from my apolitical stupor by helping me to see that God intends to redeem all of Creation, including the political realm. During our many years of friendship, Jim consistently exemplified respectful conversation as founder and president of the Center for Public Justice, partnering with God in sowing seeds of redemption within American politics.

Contents

Christianity is love of neighbor, or it has lost its way.
—**Michael Gerson**

In an age of flaming rhetoric, fractious politics and fissiparous ideology, Harold Heie exemplifies a much better way. The discussions he moderates in this book treat red-hot issues like immigration, health care, economic inequality and money in politics, as well as more general considerations of Christian principles, Christian prudence and Christian practice. The marvel for readers will be to see believers airing their differences frankly, but doing so with Christian friendship preserved and Christian wisdom to the forefront. It is hard to imagine a better book for times like these.
—**Mark Noll, co-editor of** *Religion and American Politics*
(Oxford University Press)

* * *

At a time when public discourse has devolved from disagreement to partisanship to tribalism, Harold Heie has determinedly promoted "respectful conversations." As evident in this, his latest summation, Heie does not settle for bromides or platitudes. He insists on thoughtful, theological, informed discussions, and he points us, all of us, toward a better way.
—**Randall Balmer, John Phillips professor in religion, Dartmouth College and author of** *Redeemer: The Life of Jimmy Carter*

* * *

Reforming American Politics not only provides important principles for Christians to use when engaging in political discussion and engagement, but it models those principles through the use of real discussions between Christians who disagree politically. In an era within American politics in which Christian political engagement on both sides of the political divide is driven more by partisan loyalties than Christian values and in which Christians of all political stripes exhibit far more political self-righteousness than political humility, this book can help us as Christians not only to envision, but to practice, a way forward out of the mire in which we presently find ourselves.
—**Corwin E. Smidt, research fellow at the Henry Institute, Calvin College**

* * *

In an era of increasing social polarization, thoughtful conversations across the political divide are becoming less and less common. For Christians, navigating this terrain can be dicey, especially with regard to the complicated issues of the day. *Reforming American Politics* offers a helpful critique of and corrective to the status quo, showing that it is possible for thoughtful people of faith to differ on matters of substance in a way that dignifies and respects competing perspectives. Conversations such as those highlighted in this book are more important than ever. Harold Heie has done a great service here.

—Daniel Bennett, associate professor of political science, John Brown University and president, Christians in Political Science

* * *

Harold Heie practices what he preaches—which is civil conversation, from a serious Christian theological perspective, amid a context of brutal division. He doesn't just theorize about this essential challenge—he creates contexts that model the way forward. This book is an impressive example of what Heie is about. I strongly recommend it—and the practices it embodies.

—the Rev. Dr. David P. Gushee, distinguished university professor of Christian ethics and director, Center for Theology and Public Life, Mercer University

* * *

In Reforming American Politics, Harold Heie exhorts Christian citizens to adopt new practices and conversations to ensure, as much as we are able, a more just political order. Refreshingly, he does this while resisting the temptation to merely recount well-known examples of our past failures to do so. What could easily be a book of indictments is instead an invitation, filled with practical examples for those of us who aspire to live faithfully into our God-given calling as Christian citizens in pluralistic political communities.

—Stephanie Summers, CEO Center for Public Justice

* * *

The bitterly divided state of current political culture in the U.S. has been widely recognized and lamented. Unfortunately, Christians, rather than bridging political divides and modeling charitable discourse, have often been agents of division and incivility themselves, and many churches have been racked by political controversy. Harold Heie has long been a voice for calm, respectful conversations among Christian over controversial issues. In *Reforming American Politics*, he advances the countercultural notion that loving your neighbor might actually involve *listening* to your neighbor. This volume is a valuable resource calling for Christians to be Christians first and political activists second, and its contributors model charitable Christian discourse throughout. Individual Christians, churches, Christian colleges and other organizations will greatly benefit from the timely wisdom found in these pages.

—**Rick Ostrander, vice president for research and scholarship, Council for Christian Colleges and Universities**

* * *

In *Reforming American Politics*, Harold Heie beckons us to his laboratory of discourse, an eCircle he created by inviting scholars and public figures to engage in respectful conversation with people who disagree with them, on some of the most taxing political issues of our time. One part extended illustration and another part theological and moral analysis, *Reforming American Politics* wonderfully models good conversation, as it elucidates essential ingredients for navigating political disagreement in healthier ways than we currently manage. This book is a great resource for Christians (and others) who are concerned about destructive political discourse in the United States, and who are eager to know what we can do to effect real change.

—**James Calvin Davis, professor of religion, Middlebury College and author of *In Defense of Civility* (WJK) and *Forbearance: A Theological Ethic for a Disagreeable Church* (Eerdmans)**

* * *

Many faithful Christians are longing for a way forward in the midst of our divisive political culture. In *Reforming American Politics*, Harold Heie offers an approach to political engagement defined by grace, empathy, love, civility and justice. He challenges Christians to acknowledge the dignity in those with whom we disagree, seek out respectful conversations across

party lines and serve as agents of healing in our broken democracy. I can think of few books that are more relevant in our current moment.
—John Fea, Professor of History, Messiah College,
Author of Believe Me: The Evangelical Road to Donald Trump

* * *

Harold Heie once again draws together a rich collection of thoughtful, strong-viewed Christians to engage our most divisive topics in uncommonly productive ways. Following Heie's commitment to respectful disagreement as a deep expression of love leads away from meaningless, mutually uncomprehending posturing and toward the kind of disagreement that changes the world. As Heie and his conversation partners chart an audaciously and obviously better way forward for Christian political discourse and action, the challenge left with the reader is to choose to take up this model, and go and do likewise!
—Rob Barrett, director of forums and scholarship,
The Colossian Forum

* * *

While many voices have been uplifted, deploring the "polarization" of public discourse in the U.S. (somehow it always turns out to be somebody else's fault), Harold Heie—for years now, without fanfare—has been convening "respectful conversations." Please note: "respectful" doesn't mean "reduced to pious generalities." No, what happens in these conversations is genuine give-and-take. The result, as this latest volume shows, is a blessed alternative to the routine mud-slinging and hand-wringing.
—John Wilson, Englewood Review of Books

* * *

Harold Heie offers a rather timely contribution to American politics. He asks: What ails American political practice and how might we remedy it? Heie suggests political inequality—defined loosely as the unequal possession of political power—disempowers the vulnerable and thus, weakens America's biblical promise. As such, Heie offers political equality as a richer envisioning of political engagement, for it affords us means through which

one may humanize *the other*, giving voice to the voiceless, via a recognition of our shared personhood. Overall, this instructive and innovative approach is a must-read for practitioners and scholars of Christian political engagement. A courageous undertaking no doubt, one not without risks or criticisms. But that may very well be the point!
—**Derefe Kimarley Chevannes, Ph. D. Candidate, Political Science, University of Connecticut**

* * *

Dr. Heie invites the reader to a respectful conversation on politics. I can't think of a more important subject at a more essential moment in our history. My hope for the students that I teach is that they learn to consider multiple perspectives and they listen well—this book demands both, as deep expressions of the "love for neighbor" to which Jesus calls those who profess to be his followers.
—**John Fernstrum, South O'Brien School, Paullina, Iowa, JH-HS Social Studies**

Foreword

By Richard J. Mouw

I LIKE THE word "reforming" in the title of this book. In my younger days as a social activist I was more inclined to think in terms of "radical change" and even "revolution" (although I never endorsed the violent variety). But these days I am happy with the idea of "reform."

More specifically, the "form" part of it has come to loom large for me as I think about faith-guided engagement with political matters. In recent decades, there has been a strong emphasis on "spiritual formation" in the Christian community. And I have become convinced that a key factor in finding remedies for the problems addressed in this fine book has to do with the failure in spiritually "forming" believers for our participation in the public square. The late Ronald Thiemann of Harvard Divinity School identified an important need when he wrote, in his book *Constructing Public Theology* that local congregations should serve as "'schools of public virtue,' communities that seek to form the kind of character necessary for public life."

We seem to be especially virtue-deficient in the Christian community these days, particularly when it comes to political matters. Much is needed in discovering remedies for our inability to talk to each other in productive ways about our political differences. Nor is it enough simply to pledge to be "nicer" in our arguments. We must also clarify what the basic disagreements are *about*. This book does that in effective ways, looking, for example, at how we see some of the structural issues differently in our conceptions of what a healthy society would look like. On political topics, we cannot easily work at forming the right kind of character—nurturing the appropriate virtues—without also exploring together what it means to seek *justice* in a God-glorifying manner.

In convening the discussion in these pages, Harold Heie has once again shown himself to be a gifted leader in promoting the cause of "respectful conversations." And Harold has been willing to take some significant personal risks in this regard. He has not only brought scholars and other Christian leaders together again to explore difficult topics respectfully, but he has done his own grassroots homework on the political version of this venture, by attempting to have respectful conversations in local contexts. Harold has some painful stories to tell in this regard, but he has not given up—for which we can all be grateful.

Harold and I can both remember a time when evangelicals had a reputation for being unconcerned about political concerns. Things have changed significantly in this regard over the past half-century—to the point where now American evangelicalism is widely viewed as intensely "politicized."

There is an important lesson to be learned from this history. It is not enough for Christians simply to care deeply about political matters. We must also learn to approach these matters wisely, and with the clear awareness that in this time before the return of the true King we have an obligation to treat our neighbors—including those neighbors with whom we seriously disagree about fundamental matters—"with gentleness and respect" (I Peter 3: 16).

May this book serve to promote that important cause.

Preface

THE PREMISE BEHIND this book is uncomplicated and easy to state. (It isn't rocket science, at least to *say*; it is much harder than rocket science to *do*.)

> **Jesus has called all his followers to love their neighbors. Providing someone who disagrees with you a safe and welcoming space to express that disagreement and then talking respectfully about your disagreement is a deep expression of love.**

To express love in this deep way requires that you first listen carefully to the other person, trying to understand why she holds to her beliefs. By first giving her a "voice," you can build the trust needed for her to also listen to you. This foundation of mutual understanding and trust will enable you to then talk respectfully about your agreements and disagreements, not knowing beforehand where that conversation will take you. Hopefully it will lead to a better approximation to the "truth" about the matter at hand or a desirable course of action.

To commit to such engagement with another person is hard work that is counter-cultural. Quick text messages, tweets, Facebook postings or sound bites will not suffice. But it is the loving way to address disagreements. Such arduous work will require healthy doses of humility, courage, respect, patience and hope—Christian virtues that seem to be in short supply these days, even among those who give lip service to these virtues as among their "religious values."

This book is a report on the results of my attempt to facilitate such a challenging process for various aspects of the contentious topic of American politics. More specifically, the purpose of this book is twofold:

1. To model "respectful conversations" among Christians who have strong disagreements about:

    - How Christians and others should talk to one another about political issues (Part 1).
    - The meaning of politics and the appropriate scope of political activity (Part 2).
    - Selected public policy proposals that are hotly debated (Part 3).
    - How churches and Christian para-church organizations should proceed, or not proceed, relative to political activity (Part 4).

2. To recommend a "Way Forward" for Christians (and others) to seek to reform American politics that presents a stark contrast to current ways of doing politics, drawing on the results reported in Parts 1-4 and foundational Christian values.

Chapters 1-10 (Parts 1-4) consist of my distillations of the highlights of the postings from 23 "conversation partners" on my website http://www.respectfulconversation.net for 10 pre-announced monthly subtopics around the general theme, "Reforming Political Discourse," that took place from September 1, 2017 through July 2018. This electronic conversation (eCircle) attracted 18,823 page views. For each of these 10 subtopics, I posed one or more leading questions to two or more conversation partners, carefully recruited based on my expectation that their responses would reveal significant disagreements.

For those readers of the book who are not faint of heart, I highly recommend that you go to my website and read all of the 66 pieces (each about 3,000 words in length) that were posted during this conversation.

This recommendation is based on the unavoidable fact that when I sought to distil these many postings in this book, my own biases and preconceptions may have been given preferential treatment despite my careful attempts to be fair and balanced.

In the concluding chapter (11), I present my views on a possible "Way Forward" for Christians (and others) who wish to consider and, hopefully, embrace a way to do politics that differs significantly from the way that most Christians currently engage in politics; and reflects my understanding of timeless Christian virtues and other Christian values. While the content of this chapter draws heavily on what I have learned from the many postings of the conversation partners, I take full responsibility for the content of this chapter due to my many embellishments and additions.

Relative to my goal of modeling respectful conversation among Christians who have strong disagreements regarding contentious political issues, the reader will have to judge whether my conversation partners attained this goal in the midst of some strong disagreements. My view is that they modeled such respectful conversations to an admirable extent, stating their views with clarity and deep conviction, yet with grace-filled kindness, while also recognizing and acknowledging the deep Christian commitment of those with whom they disagreed. For example, one of my conversation partners Matthew Soerens expressed this significant accomplishment well in his reflection about his conversation partner, Robert McFarland, with whom he had some major initial disagreements about hotly contested immigration issues.

> ... what I'm grateful for [is] Robert's tone in this discussion: Whether we ultimately agree or disagree, we can do so respectful that the other's views are genuinely based on our respective desires to love our neighbors in fulfillment of Jesus' commands.

Robert returns the compliment:

> ... allow me to express my appreciation for the content and tone of Matthew's second essay. I appreciate his effort to highlight our many points of agreement. Our conversation thus far reveals our agreement that the common good depends on willingness to move beyond rhetoric.

I close this preface with a few suggestions as to how readers can most profitably navigate the content of this book.

First, as the reader will soon find out, all of the 10 subtopics dealt with in this book are extremely complex. Those readers looking for simple answers that will fit on bumper stickers will be very disappointed. You may find your "head spinning" as you attempt to sort through the intricacies of competing perspectives on a given subtopic, all of which are cogently presented. In light of that, my modest navigation tip is that after you read this preface, read the concluding chapter (11) before diving into Chapters 1-10. That may help you to observe some "flow" and coherence in this book (my hope being that such coherence does not only exist in my mind).

My second suggestion is directed at anyone who would like to initiate a conversation about the content of this book in a small group setting (possibly in a church or college or seminary). Given the current brokenness of political discourse, in which too many Christians are deeply complicit, it will be foolhardy to attempt to jump into conversation about the thorny subtopics presented in Parts 2-4 until your group has struggled with the prior issue of how you are going to talk to one another about these other thorny subtopics.

Your attempts to discuss these difficult subtopics will hit a quick dead end, at best, or will prove to be totally antithetical to the call of Jesus for Christians to love one another, if your group resorts to name-calling, questioning of motives and demonization of those whose disagree with you that now seems to be the norm in political discourse.

Therefore, before your group jumps into discussion of the challenging subtopics in Parts 2-4, I strongly recommend that you facilitate an initial group discussion of Part 1 (Political Discourse). I will be encouraged if in your discussion of Part 1, your group comes to agree with my position (reported in Chapter 2) that giving someone who disagrees with you a safe and welcoming space to express and discuss that disagreement, is a deep expression of love for that person. But, of course, you should provide your group with a safe and welcoming space to disagree with me about that.

Talking Past Each Other or Worse

CAN THE CURRENT appalling state of political discourse be reformed? Such a dream seems hopeless. But that dream animates this book, which will conclude with some recommendations for improving political discourse that emerged from 10 months of conversation with 23 conversation partners who have sought to identify common ground.

Since you cannot attempt to fix something unless you first understand what is broken, we start this daunting task with suggestions from Republican Jeff VanDerWerff and Democrat Kim Van Es as to some of the problems with current political discourse, which will give some initial hints toward possible directions for reform.

Rather than talking about existing problems in the abstract, Jeff and Kim start by reflecting on two YouTube video clips taken from political reports on cable TV. The first is a CNN roundtable, hosted by Kate Bolduan, that focused on the legitimacy, or not, of using unnamed sources in a story in the spring of 2016 about whether President Trump inadvertently or carelessly divulged classified information to two Russian diplomats visiting the White House Oval Office.[1] The second clip is a FOX News report

---

1 http://youtu.be/67zEy_hgRPw

from Sean Hannity regarding his interview with Donald Trump Jr. about his June 2016 meeting with a Russian lawyer and others.[2]

Some Problems With Current Political Discourse

It should be noted up front that despite the fact that they sit on opposite sides of the political aisle, Jeff and Kim expressed few disagreements in their postings about the nature of current political discourse (the vital significance of which will be elaborated later). In Jeff's words: "While my conversation partner and I each claim partisan and ideological commitments that render us on separate sides of many issues, it would seem our approach to engaging democracy as well as our attitude towards political discourse is quite similar. That's good to know." Relative to their analyses of the two video clips, Kim says: "Given the egregious nature of both video segments, I found little in Dr. Jeff VanDerWerff's response with which to disagree."

Here are some of the problems with current political discourse about which Jeff and Kim agree; problems that are evident when TV pundits and citizens engage one another and when politicians interact with one another (noting Jeff's suggestion that "unsurprisingly, it matters not whether this discourse originates from the left or right of the partisan and/ or ideological spectrum. Both sides are culpable and complicit in the current state of affairs").

Personal attacks

Kim regrets the extent to which "personal attacks" are prevalent in political discourse. Jeff concurs: "The politics of personal destruction ... is clearly on the rise."

Examples of such personal attacks abound in the YouTube video clips. Kim notes that when Sean Hannity lays out his argument for the hypocrisy of the Democrats and mainstream media who expressed concern over possible collusion, he says, "What a bunch of phonies. What a bunch of hypocrites." Kim suggests that such "name-calling lowers the level of argument to that of mean kids on the playground." Jeff suggests that what Sean

2 http://youtu.be/I1vvzxf8PIA

Hannity says "captures nicely what U.S. Sen. Ben Sasse has aptly dubbed 'weaponized distrust.'"

CNN is not to be spared from such criticism. Jeff says that "the CNN roundtable discussion was, at best, a three-on-one debate that is better described as a shouting match." Kim says the following about the "yelling" in the CNN clip: "After [Carl] Higbie attacks the anonymous sources and mocks the CNN reporters, host Kate Bolduan can't hold it in any longer. She yells, she points in Higbie's face, and at times she is trying to talk over two or three other people. At this point the show becomes more like the worst of reality TV than news programming." While recognizing that anger may sometimes be called for, Kim rejects the view that such anger should be expressed by "yelling."

> Then there was yelling, the default tactic in so many battles. Clearly, there are things that make us so angry that many of us want to yell. The Bible includes the story of Jesus overturning tables in the temple (Mark 11; Matthew 21). The writers do not say that he yelled, but his expression of anger was very clear. But what I have learned as a teacher, a parent, and a political activist is that yelling does not foster healthy discourse. I regret the few times when I was angry: There are many situations in which anger is an understandable and even righteous response. But I *do* regret some instances of yelling, instances that only proved my lack of self-control. Yelling turns conversation into drama (in the worst sense of the word)—a soap opera in which the focus turns from the subject at hand to the actors' reactions. How far will the enraged person go in his or her language and behavior?

Kim also criticizes the "shaming" in the CNN video clip, observing that "guest Keith Boykin, former aide in the Clinton White House stayed controlled in his tone [like Higbie]. But as he disagreed with Higbie, he used shaming language/personal attacks, which, again, may attract viewers but distracts from the issue being discussed. Boykin said to Higbie, 'Carl, you're embarrassing yourself. You're embarrassing yourself, your party and your country. You should not be doing this; you are a better person than this. I'm ashamed for you.' This public shaming made me uncomfortable and did not seem professional."

Market-driven entertainment

Why are personal attacks so ubiquitous in political news coverage? A hint is given by Kim's comment above that the personal shaming in the CNN video clip "may attract viewers." Jeff puts it more forcefully.

> Not only has the 24/7 news cycle given rise to a need—airtime must be filled—but the increased competition for eyeballs, page views and/or click-throughs clearly heightens an understandable temptation to highlight those who are willing to say the most outlandish and controversial things.

Personal attacks seem to do well in the "competition for eyeballs" because they are forms of entertainment that attract viewers, as suggested by Jeff's take on the two video clips: "In many ways, they've each in their own way become, sadly, a form or kind of entertainment."

Both Jeff and Kim then hit the nail on the head by pointing out that the bottom line is the dollar: "We must not forget that the media is an economic enterprise, a business with a bottom line" (Jeff); "It is especially understandable that news networks do whatever they can to gain viewers because they are commercial entities" (Kim).

But both Jeff and Kim provocatively suggest that the ultimate fault lies with the citizens who decide to watch such "drivel": "Truth be told, those who tune in to such drivel deserve to be admonished too; without an audience, there'd be no market" (Jeff); "I don't have to like their style, and we can choose to get our news elsewhere" (Kim).

Blurred lines between news and commentary

A derivative problem flowing from the desire to attract viewers by offering entertainment is that it is difficult to distinguish between "news" and "commentary." Kim and Jeff describe this problem in the following ways.

> So, we have these so-called news networks. What does that label mean? In the olden days, the 'news' was Walter Cronkite or Ted Koppel reporting, as objectively as they could, the events of the day. But today's 'news network' includes not

only reporting but much commentary—commentary
from invited 'expert' guests but also from employees of the
network itself ... It is problematic for consumers when it is
not clear what is news (presented as objectively as possible)
and what is commentary (a certain take or opinion on the
news) (Kim).

There is no question that the line between fact and opinion has
been blurred beyond distinction. ... those who are charged
with informing us often make things more complicated by
conflating news and commentary (Jeff).

To be sure, it is questionable whether anyone can report the news in
a way that does not reflect in some way the interpretive framework of
the reporter. But the extreme extent to which "news" and "commentary"
are conflated today is what makes it challenging for viewers to determine
when a news report is indeed "fake."

Kim makes the extremely important point that any form of human
discourse, political or otherwise, is inhibited if no distinction is made
between "fact" and "opinion": "For true discourse to happen, we must
understand the difference between fact and opinion and own up to what is
what." While expressing her belief that "the unwillingness of some members of the Right to acknowledge climate change is a loud case in point,"
Kim observes that "both conservatives and progressives are guilty of presenting misleading information to advance their causes."

My own view is that the word "misleading" is too mild. The tenuous
relationship with "truth" that characterizes much current political conversation is tragic and may be the greatest obstacle to any hope for reforming
political discourse.

Redirection

Redirection is "diversion from the topic at hand," or "changing the
subject" in popular parlance. Both Jeff and Kim find redirection to be
prominent in the CNN and FOX News video reports, with particular criticism directed at Sean Hannity's monologue.

Hannity's monologue epitomizes a classic example of an argument based on redirection. Not wanting to take on squarely the poor judgment, if not ethical lapse, displayed by Donald Trump Jr. in agreeing to meet with a Russian attorney who supposedly had dirt to dish on his father's presidential campaign opponent, Hannity shifts his audience's attention to the alleged malfeasance and misdeeds of Hillary Clinton as well as those working on her behalf (Jeff).

Rather than exploring the concerns many Americans had about this meeting [of Donald Trump Jr. with a Russian lawyer and others], Hannity quickly turns to past perceived improprieties of the Democrats: a DNC operative working with Ukrainian officials to boost Hillary Clinton; money from the Obama state department used by an Israeli political group against candidate Benjamin Netanyahu; and a uranium deal brokered by Clinton with the Russians that was followed by large Russian donations to the Clinton Foundation (Kim).

Kim quickly adds that while she does "not have enough information to know whether election interference or other types of illegal deeds happened in the Trump-Russian contact or any of these other situations," all she knows is that "when the topic at hand is muddled by deflecting to other events, truth-pursuing political discourse is unlikely to occur." This astute observation points to the extreme obstacle that "redirection" presents to the hope for reforming political discourse.

In Kim's view, such redirection was also rampant in the presidential debates prior to the 2016 election.

> The presidential debates of last year's election showcased each candidate's ability to swerve away from an uncomfortable question or topic. One practiced move involved ignoring the question and instead highlighting their own party's achievement on a related matter. Another polished move involved ignoring the question and instead attacking the opponent. The two sides are like fighting spouses coming

back at every charge, 'Yeah, but **you** ... ' Both moves make true political discourse or honest debate nearly impossible.

Listening only to an echo of yourself

The more academic descriptor for this problem with current political discourse is "confirmation bias." Kim defines "confirmation bias" as "our mind's tendency to absorb only that which confirms our preconceptions," giving the example of our picking out "the statistics that support what we already believe to be true." Kim finds "our biased cable news channels and our targeted social media" to be "confirmation bias on steroids" that "just keep our home fires burning, stoking them with news and perspectives we will like."

Kim asserts that the primary problem with such confirmation bias is that "many of us aren't even exposed to opposing political ideas."

Jeff presents the same concern about confirmation bias in his reflections on the CNN and Fox News video reports: "As far as the target audience of these two video clips, both the CNN and FOX segments seem primarily focused on viewers who are of like mind. This suggests the goal of these efforts may well be one of affirmation or reinforcement; it is clearly not one of persuasion." The point Jeff is making is that "Americans are choosing to associate, more so than ever, with people who are largely like themselves."

Jeff adds an interesting report on the surprise experienced by Carl Trueman, a faculty member from Westminster Theological Seminary who is a native of Great Britain, when he received the advice from many of his newfound American friends "that there was only one place to get the unvarnished truth." Jeff reports that: "Eager to see and hear this for himself, Trueman soon discovered otherwise and subsequently argues: 'Not that Christians abandon one biased news channel for another; rather it is Christians above all people [who] should take seriously their responsibility as citizens and make every effort to find out as much as they can about the issues that matter.'" Jeff concludes that "this requires more than a single source or vantage point."

Social media and politicians talking to each other, or not

The problems with the political discourse identified above reflected an analysis of two cable TV news video clips. Do things get any better on social media, like Facebook or Twitter? Not a chance! There is ample evidence that the problems get worse on social media. Jeff says that "our social media habits or practices may be making matters worse by inadvertently fueling extremism." He adds that "it does seem to me that too much of what passes for disagreement on Facebook or other social media platforms masquerades as thinly veiled attacks as opposed to genuine arguments," because "the digital age and cyberspace has provided an opportunity for the shrillest voices and most unhinged among us to easily communicate their message."

As for his own attempts to generate "respectful conversations" about political issues on Facebook in his "rural corner of Iowa" since the election of President Trump, Jeff says, "I've largely failed." This leads Jeff to ask, "Can a healthy dialogue take place on social media?" Although Jeff says that he "persists" with his Facebook endeavors, a limitation as to what can be expected is embedded in Jeff's own assertion that the root problem with current political discourse is that "we are not talking to or with each other." (More about that later.)

This failure to talk to and with each other is not only rampant on social media, it is also ubiquitous in much of the blogging that takes place on the Internet. If you examine the "comments" on blog postings, you seldom find much that advances the conversation. Rather, it is common to find very cryptic comments that either praise the blogger or excoriate him or her (often resorting to personal attacks) without really engaging the substance of the blog in a thoughtful, in-depth way.

The question remains as to whether the abject failure of pundits and citizens to genuinely talk to one another about political issues on cable TV news and through social media is also prevalent when politicians engage one another. When that engagement is on cable TV or through social media, their discourse seems to do no better than the pundits and citizens who are bashing each other (with the exception, sometimes, of carefully orchestrated debates on public television). But what happens in the halls of Congress and state Legislatures? It appears to me, in theory at least, that politicians could genuinely talk to one another in such legislative settings, if it were not for a totally inadequate process for political deliberation, as the next section will reveal.

No time for nuance and deliberation

Jeff hints at this problem when he identifies "time limitations" as one of the structural problems for media coverage of politics. Since Jeff does not elaborate, I will add my reflections on this problem.

The attention span of many consumers of political news coverage appears to be very short. And, besides, a long, nuanced debate about a complex public policy issue (e.g., health care or tax reform) is not found to be entertaining by most listeners. Therefore, we receive a steady diet of short sound bites or news articles that cannot do justice to complexity and nuance. As a result, many listeners form positions on public policy issues that do not adequately address the complex issues being considered.

Such a penchant for "quick answers" on the part of citizens is unfortunate. But this tyranny of time constraints becomes especially problematic when it pervades the halls of Congress and other legislative bodies. I am reminded of a question we used to ask when I worked in the aerospace industry, "Why is there never time to do it right the first time, but always time to do it over again?"

A case in point is what transpired relative to the Graham-Cassidy health care amendment proposed in September 2017. Senate GOP leaders initiated a process by which GOP leaders bypassed the usual steps of public hearings and committee deliberation, relying instead on a "task force" that met privately to produce a bill. To make it worse, a decision needed to be made within a week or so of proposing the bill. Due, in part, to the call for "regular order" from Sen. John McCain, the 50 votes required for approval were not obtained.

The "regular order" Sen. McCain called for is very time-consuming, including a proposed bill being assigned to a committee, or more than one. Public hearings are scheduled in coordination with the ranking (most senior) member of the opposition party on the committee. After the hearings, the chairman brings forward a version of the bill he or she likes and schedules a "markup" to consider amendments. The members of the committee from both parties offer amendments, debate them and vote on them. If the committee approves the amended bill, it is bought to the floor of the legislative body for consideration.

I am attracted to this time-consuming process because I am process-oriented to a fault. It's genius in legislative bodies in that it allows for at least some degree of bipartisanship; the lack of which is the major cause of current political gridlock. After the demise of the health care bill, President Trump assured the American public that health care reform was not finished, sounding like Congress will find the time to do it all over again. As of this writing, that remains to be seen.

Feeling is good, but so is thinking and credibility

One of the "leading questions" posed to Jeff and Kim pertained to the "rhetorical tools" used in political discourse. This raises an important distinction relative to "methods of persuasion" that can be traced back to Aristotle, a distinction between ethos, pathos and logos, which has been described as follows: Ethos is an appeal to ethics, and it is a means of convincing someone of the character or credibility of the persuader. Pathos is an appeal to emotion, and is a way of convincing an audience of an argument by creating an emotional response. Logos is an appeal to logic, and is a way of persuading an audience by reason.

Jeff's take on the CNN and Fox News video clips is that "the rhetorical tools employed in each of these video clips appear to emphasize pathos, almost to the exclusion of logos and ethos. Emotion, characterized by anger or hate, seems to drive much of the discourse as opposed to logic or expertise."

Jeff then invited Kim to comment on the "ideal balance or proper relationship between logos, pathos and ethos." Kim's very thoughtful response about the relationship between logos and pathos includes the following:

> First, an argument with no logos should be viewed skeptically. Logos is an appeal to our minds, to our sense of rationality. If a political speaker fails to engage our intellect through the fair use of facts, he or she may not understand an issue well enough to explain things properly. ... A shallow understanding is not something I want in my elected officials.
>
> Another reason that a politician may fail to include facts is that the facts do not bolster his/her argument. ...

Quentin Schultze's helpful book on public speaking[3] argues that when we speak publicly, we define reality for our listeners. What a grave responsibility this is. Defining reality requires the use of solid information and an appeal to logic. It is absolutely unacceptable when politicians speak on a topic without understanding it. It is even worse when they lie or tailor the truth. Of course, candidates on all sides fudge the facts. … lying in presidential campaigns [is] a practice going all the way back to Adams vs. Jefferson.

I would much rather hear politicians say, 'I don't know' than guess on the facts or state an ignorant opinion. …

For some of us audience members, logos is enough to shape our thinking and move us to action. But for many of us, pathos is also needed—an appeal to our emotions. … Pathos helps us feel as well as think.

However, too many political speeches or political rants rely solely on pathos (e.g., Facebook posts, online comments responding to newspaper editorials). They appeal to (or prey on) recipients' fear, anger, prejudice or self-interest. Whereas this approach often works to persuade, a speech should not be judged based on audience impact only. In my mind, the best speeches combine logos and pathos to present the speaker's best understanding of reality.

Note especially Kim's argument for the importance of *both* logos and pathos, which reflects the fact that human beings are not disembodied intellects (what Peter Gomes has called "brains on a stick") nor should they succumb to a mindless emotionalism. However, Kim shares Jeff's concern that a problem with media political coverage is an excessive reliance on pathos; methods of persuasion that "appeal to (or prey on) recipients' fear, anger, prejudice, or self-interest."

But what is the role of ethos? Kim's response is nuanced and complex:

---

3 Schultze, *Essential Guide to Public Speaking.*

But what I want to spend more time discussing is the mode of persuasion known as ethos. Ethos is our impression of the speaker him/herself—what we perceive to be the person's character. Here is what Aristotle, the father of rhetoric, had to say about ethos: 'Persuasion is achieved by the speaker's personal character when the speech is so spoken as to make us think him credible. We believe good men more fully and more readily than others: this is true generally whatever the question is, and absolutely true where exact certainty is impossible and opinions are divided ... his character may almost be called the most effective means of persuasion he possesses.'

Looking at the people we have elected as our political leaders, on what basis do we judge their character? What character traits are we actually looking for? Kim adds:

I am very much afraid that the ethos qualities that attract us in politicians may not always result in the best people to represent us in executive or legislative branches of government. My other observation is that we as an electorate disagree about the character qualities we find admirable.

Let's look at the contrasting *ethe* (plural of ethos) of the previous and current presidents. Barack Obama was generally cool and calm (especially important for a black man, unfortunately). He weighed his words. He was quick to laugh, especially at himself. His smile seemed attractive and genuine. For some people previously disengaged, Obama represented them in some way—youthful, optimistic, a person of color, someone from modest means who had worked his way up. The fact that he was running for president represented hope and change.

In contrast, Donald Trump was a celebrity star long before he made a serious run for political office. His persona as a firm, successful businessman on *The Apprentice* suggested to some that he could steer a big ship, like a country, for example. His no-nonsense approach seemed like the perfect antidote to D.C. stalemate: 'Trump isn't afraid to say it like it is.' And by appearing sympathetic to the electorate's concerns (about immigrants, the corrupt political establishment, the neglect of the working class), he garnered trust and allegiance.

In the most recent presidential election, there is no doubt who was more knowledgeable and experienced in matters of state. But in my opinion, ethos, coupled with pathos, ruled the day on November 8, 2016. And now we have what we voted for.

Kim has given all of us a lot to think about. Of particular importance, in my estimation, is her insight that "we as an electorate disagree about the character qualities we find admirable [in the politicians who represent us]." As an evangelical Christian, I am concerned that many evangelicals have chosen to ignore the question as to whether the character traits of politicians they support comport well with the character traits that are consistent with the Christian faith, such as love, joy, peace, patience, kindness, generosity, faithfulness, gentleness, self-control (Galatians 5: 22-23), humility and truthfulness.

Are Christians Part of the Problem?

It is tempting for Christians to think that the above extensive litany of problems with political discourse applies only to those who do not share their Christian faith commitment. But the evidence suggests otherwise.

Jeff raises two important questions: "Are evangelical Christians more likely to be considered part of the problem or part of the solution today when it comes to engaging democracy? Are we known by our love or have we let the world press us into its political mold?"

Based on the experience of her friend Jaci, Kim notes that Christians have developed a "reputation" for being part of the problem with political discourse, whether that is "fair or not."

I am afraid that political discourse from some American Christians has left a very bad taste in the mouth of the world (those who don't share our faith tradition).

My friend Jaci was a marketing director for a software solution company. She had worked with the same business people for several years—individuals of diverse backgrounds and faiths. Over dinner one evening, it came out that Jaci was a Christian. Her comrades couldn't believe it. They couldn't believe that someone who was respectful, reasonable, professional and fun was part of that demographic of 'American Christian.' Instead, they associated the label of Christian with someone who was bigoted, sexist, homophobic and judgmental. Fair or not, Christians have developed this reputation, partly due to our political discourse.

In a response to his own questions, Jeff says that "evangelicals seem to have let the world press them into its mold of political practice." He amplifies by suggesting that too many evangelicals have let the world press us into its political mold by substituting loyalty to a political party for our "ultimate loyalty" to "the Kingdom of God," noting that such overemphasis on party loyalty is not limited to Christians.

Too many citizens it would seem, evangelicals included, exhibit a 'malleable innocence' whereby party largely trumps (no pun intended) all other commitments or convictions and results in a rather telling tribalism.

This is problematic, not the least because of American evangelicalism's increasingly close ties to the Republican party. What does the logic of collective action currently say about where we place our ultimate loyalty?

... partisan loyalties and ideological convictions may need to be sacrificed on the altar of Christian commitment to the Kingdom of God. ... there may be times, for instance, where an individual is called to confront their own party specifically or the governing authorities generally, but it is equally possible where collaboration with someone from another party or partnering with the state is entirely appropriate.

... Evangelicals have failed to maintain a proper or critical distance from power and it has clouded our judgment as well as the ability to offer a critique of our own side.

Jeff provocatively suggests that resorting to "culture wars" rhetoric amounts to "employing the same sort of (political) weapons as the world," which may call for a "cease-fire."

If winning the culture wars on the world's terms is the only viable means or reasonable way to engage public life, there is little doubt then that evangelicals are captive to a contemporary pagan corruption.

Waging rhetorical war with our enemies, or political opponents, has resulted in an untold number of battle-worn casualties, both intended and unintended. If, in fact, evangelicals are paying too high a price for this participation in a culture war it seems prudent, even wise, to issue a cease-fire. In doing so, the church will be granted the requisite independence for assuming its witness in public life by engaging democracy in a way that maintains a faithful presence on behalf of God and the kingdom of heaven.

But Jeff is quick to add that "this, of course, does not mean that evangelicals must remain silent or avoid entering the public square, but it does suggest that at a minimum they think more carefully and thoughtfully about why and how hot-button social issues are addressed when engaging democracy through public life." The next two sections of this chapter and the entire next chapter will address the open question of the best means for Christians to "engage democracy through public life" that is deeply informed by Christian values.

What We May Discover if We Talk
to Our Political Opponents

The above extensive litany of problems with current political discourse, for which many Christians are complicit, could lead to despair. A common element for all of these problems is **a lack of genuine conversation among political opponents**. Whether on cable TV, through social media or in the halls of Congress, political opponents typically choose to avoid talking to each other about their disagreements using strategies like attacking their opponents, "changing the subject," venting their feelings by yelling, and associating only with people who will echo their views.

This overarching problem is captured by Jeff in his response to the title that I gave him and Kim for their conversation, "Talking Past Each Other or Worse." Jeff titled his first posting "Without Question, It's Worse." Elaborating he says, "It's worse than simply talking past each other. There's little question we are not talking to or with each other."

There are two underlying erroneous assumptions that fuel our inability to have genuine conversations with our political opponents that can be detected if one digs beneath the surface of an exchange that Jeff had with reader Wayne, who is a friend of Jeff and a friend of mine. Wayne responded in the following way to the first postings from both Jeff and Kim: "Both of our conversation partners dislike President Trump and feel many evangelicals are misguided, misinformed or blindly loyal. Do we really have both sides of the aisle represented here?"

A first hidden assumption in Wayne's response is that because Jeff and Kim "agree" in their views of President Trump and evangelicals (as well as their beliefs about some problems with current political discourse, as enumerated earlier) they are not fairly representing both sides of the political aisle (Republicans and Democrats). This points to a bigger hidden assumption: Republicans and Democrats need to disagree about everything.

Jeff sniffs out these hidden assumptions in his response to Wayne: "If the evidence for having both sides represented means we have to disagree on everything, well, I'd suggest that is what is, in part, wrong with our politics and why, among other things, we need to reform our political discourse."

Jeff then suggests that if people on opposite sides of the political aisle would actually talk to each other, then they may uncover some areas of agreement.

> If those holding differing positions on some of our most pressing or contentious problems never encounter or interact with anyone on 'the wrong side' ... in other words, if the two sides don't talk, aren't in relationship, how will either one ever discover that on many issues they are not as far apart as they've been led to believe or have assumed all along?

But, there may be a catch here. Is it possible that Republican Jeff and Democrat Kim have found many areas of agreement because they do not represent the extremists in their respective parties? Jeff suggests that this may be the case.

> I can't speak for Kim, but I suspect she may be a center-left Democrat and I'm a center-right GOP member. That leaves us closer to each other than some of today's most active partisans and on occasion it means we're more likely to find common ground.

Jeff adds the provocative suggestion that the idea of a "polarized America" characterized by "culture wars" may be overplayed. There may not be as much polarization as is assumed because those "moderates" in either party (like Jeff and Kim) do not get as much press as those extremists who can't agree on anything. Of course, with the "hollowing out of the middle" that appears to be taking place in both parties, those on both sides of the aisle who are willing to talk to each other for the purpose of finding some common ground may be a dying breed. This suggests the need for electing more "moderates," which is much easier said than done since the momentum, as a function of our electoral system, is in the other direction.

In any case, all politicians need to be encouraged to talk to one another. There is no other hope for finding the common ground needed to foster the common good. And finding such common ground will require that **we learn how to disagree.**

Jeff brings home this point about the need for all of us to learn how to disagree with his reflections on the controversial question of whether President Trump "is the problem" relative to the current dismal state of political discourse. Jeff emphatically asserts that this is not the case.

> Truth be told, at the end of the day, *Trump is not the problem!* ... He clearly is not the cause of our current state of affairs or the increasingly suspect quality of contemporary political discourse. No, Trump is the consequence of what plagues us. Removing him from office, then ... would not address that which has given rise to Trumpism. For that to happen, to begin the arduous process of diagnosing root causes and not just symptoms, we must learn once again to engage one another and to enter into relationships and conversations with those who do not share our political views, especially when they are our brothers and sisters in Christ.

The key exhortation here is that "we must learn once again to engage one another and to enter into relationships and conversations with those who do not share our political views."

More Hints Toward Reform of Political Discourse

In addition to their insightful critiques of current political discourse, both Jeff and Kim can envision a better way, starting with the suggestion above that politicians, pundits and citizens who disagree about political issues need to start talking to one another.

Kim says, "I long for a more excellent way" and Jeff says, "It seems to me engaging democracy, not just participating in politics, but doing so in a way that makes public life more attractive or appealing is an expression of the more excellent way my conversation partner longs for." But they do not settle for wishful thinking. In addition to the call for political opponents to start talking to one another, they provide more hints as to the contours of "a more excellent way," which I will only briefly point to in this chapter (with much elaboration to come in succeeding chapters).

Don't hesitate to "speak up"

Remaining silent about your political views will obviously negate the possibility of finding any common ground with someone who holds differing views as you seek to foster a common good. You must "speak up" with clarity and conviction, especially if you believe that those who disagree with you are playing loose with the "truth."

> From my perspective as a reformed Christian, I am called to speak out when false information is presented as true. We are called to be agents of knowledge (Kim).

> I'd ... like to second Kim's call to 'speak out when false information is presented as true.' Obviously, we should do so as respectfully and thoughtfully as possible, keeping in mind that we may have misunderstand or misread something we've heard or seen, but speaking out is as necessary as it is perilous. Few people like confrontation (and it is probably wise to avoid those who revel in conflict), but I'd contend it is required if we truly love others. I'm often shocked at the easiness with which friends or family members pass along misinformation and falsehoods via email or Facebook. Many times, the story or "news" item seems to me too fantastic to be true—and yet it does appear to confirm the predisposition or bias of the sender/poster as well as many of the recipients/readers presumably (Jeff).

But at this point I would like to add a special warning. It is all too easy to speak up with clarity and conviction about your own beliefs in a confrontational manner that doesn't provide a welcoming space for the person who disagrees with you to express his or her differing beliefs with clarity and conviction. You need to exemplify that very rare combination of deep commitment to your own beliefs and openness to carefully considering the contrary beliefs of others, even to the point of being willing to acknowledge that you may be wrong and should refine your views based on the best insights of the other person. That will require an overarching commitment to seek the "truth."

Pursue the "truth"

As Kim notes relative to our callings as Christians to be "agents for knowledge": "The kicker is that I too need to accept the truth whether or not it bolsters my position." She adds that such a commitment to pursuing the "truth" is rare in "today's political climate."

> In today's political climate, to concede a point is not in the list of rhetorical options. Noting the value of an opponent's claim could be fatal—like dealing a death blow to one's self. Should this be our mentality? Isn't part of growth and the pursuit of truth acknowledging when you haven't considered a point or may need to alter your perspective?

A pre-condition for seeking after the "truth" is a willingness to "listen well" to the contrary beliefs of others as to what that "truth" is.

Listen well

Jeff proposes that "Learning to listen as well as engage those in the other [political] party is essential."

One of our readers, Kevin, insightfully points us to the importance of having "wise ears" (not just "wise tongues"), noting the example of Jesus.

> Perhaps it's not only 'wise tongues' that our world desperately needs, but 'wise ears'?

> As this latest exercise of respectful discourse gets rolling, the quality of our discipline to hear can't be overemphasized. It seems to me that the human condition, likely amplified by our privileged Western individualism, biases us toward expressing/defending our own rights and voice, too often failing to exercise and strengthen our underdeveloped senses of hearing, seeing, feeling others. So, of course, we get an endless series of shouting matches ... as if talking louder and listening less helps us to be heard. This seems particularly true when the 'conversation' attempts to span disparate identities, ideologies and degrees of social power.

The story of Jesus' response to 'a woman caught in adultery' in John 8 reminds me that Jesus chose silence rather than debate, doodling instead of immediate response, and question instead of accusation to turn the tide of this nearly fatal lynch mob (aka the 'court of public opinion'?) back to reflect on its own absurd inadequacy to pronounce judgment, or to question the true nature of God's justice as manifest in the Christ. Before it is about any 'them' it begins with 'us' and our utter and perpetual failure to see, call forth, and be changed by the *Imago Dei* among us, particularly those counted most wretched.

Start at home

It should go without saying (but that isn't the case) that each of us needs to examine how we engage others in political discourse and, if found wanting, take steps to do better. But, in addition to such self-examination, Jeff suggests that if we are affiliated with a particular political party, we should start by examining and, if need be, criticizing the weaknesses of our own party before addressing what we believe to be the shortcomings of those on the other side of the aisle.

> It has always seemed to me that the beginning of a healthy discourse must start with me or my side. Removing the plank from our eye before zeroing in on the speck in someone else's eye, seems prudent if not wise, not to mention biblical (Matthew 5:7).

> Criticism should be lodged primarily with one's own party first and foremost.

Jeff adds, "Maintaining a critical distance, or independence, from either party is necessary."

Develop personal relationships with those who disagree with you

Jeff expresses dismay at how often it is the case that "if someone happens to be on the 'wrong side' or in the 'other party' then that apparently disqualifies them from being in any sort of relationship with me," adding the following question, with his own response: "Are those with whom we disagree no longer our neighbors or our colleagues or our friends? I really don't think so."

On the positive side, Kim reports on her good experience of having "friends who not only tolerate disagreement but even welcome it, even on Facebook," adding, "These mature friends possess intellectual humility, realizing that they see through a glass darkly. They appreciate hearing other points of view when those positions are expressed respectfully. They don't cover their ears and start chanting nonsense to avoid exposure to an opinion that might challenge their own." This suggests the possibility that developing personal relationships, even close friendships, with those who disagree with you may be the best starting point for political discourse because, in doing so, we come to understand the reasons for disagreements that flow from differing social locations.

Model within the Christian church

Sad to say, individual Christians have often failed to exemplify respectful conversations in their engagements within their Christian communities and with those who do not share their faith commitments when it comes to dealing with political issues. In fact, too many Christians have gladly contributed to the toxic political discourse. That needs to change. But how?

First, Jeff asserts that "evangelicals ... should start with a willingness to recognize and concede that there is, in fact, political disagreement within the body of Christ." Not all evangelicals are Republicans.

Jeff adds that given the disagreements among evangelicals regarding political issues, we must "learn how to disagree well," not with just those who do not share our faith commitment, but "also—maybe especially—with fellow believers who happen to hold a different position or belong to another party." Jeff's punchline, however, is that while "there is nothing inherently wrong with disagreeing ... how we go about doing so matters to our witness." Therefore, "the church and its members should be modeling for the wider world how to better disagree."

What will characterize such modeling? Jeff says, "It starts with how we speak to and about others. Not only must the tongue be tamed, but our tone needs to reflect the fruit of the spirit, not the tenor of the times" (referring to the "fruit of the spirit" enumerated in Galatians 5:22-23: "love, joy, peace, patience, kindness, generosity, faithfulness, gentleness, and self-control").

Of course, such virtues as the "fruit of the spirit" cannot be legislated. As Jeff notes in his view that while "virtue ... remains a vitally important element in this grand experiment of American democracy," it is "not the responsibility of government to make its citizens good." This assertion comports with my own view that in our pluralistic society, where different people and groups hold to different conceptions of what is "good," government should not be legislating one particular view. But the various segments of our civil society, like churches, should be able to foster their own conceptions of the "good" within their communities (provided they do not unnecessarily impinge on the ability of other segments of society to do likewise). Therefore, the Christian church needs to be proactive in cultivating the virtues needed to promote respectful conversation in the political realm.

As to the "witness" to the larger society referred to above, Jeff reminds us that "a wary world ... is closely watching us."

Insist on guidelines for respectful conversation

"Plain Conversation" is an educational series hosted by the Sioux County Democrats that, under Kim's leadership, holds periodic face-to-face conversations about contentious political issues at a local coffee shop in Sioux Center, Iowa. A recent conversation focused on a discussion of funding for women's health, which included guest speakers from Planned Parenthood. Kim's announcement at the beginning of the meeting was:

> 'Plain Conversation' is a place where we become more educated about a topic affecting government and politics. We ask that you respectfully listen to the speakers who have traveled and given of their time to be here tonight. We will let them share their prepared remarks uninterrupted, and

then there will be a time for questions. When that time comes, we ask that people raise their hands and wait to be called on. Then please limit your question or comment to no more than one minute. We in this room may have some differences of opinion, but our goal tonight is to have intelligent, respectful discourse about our topic. Thank you in advance for following these guidelines.

Kim reported on this meeting as follows:

The expectations were clear. And for the most part, these rules were followed. During the Q&A, I tried to go back and forth between the raised hands of conservatives and progressives. A few times I needed to stop people from dominating the floor. Once when a man became angry because he was not allowed to continue speaking (saying, 'I know my legal rights!'), I was able to calmly tell him that after speaking to the local police chief earlier today, I knew that I could ask him to leave if he didn't respect our rules for discourse. Then I proceeded to invite the next person with her hand up to ask a question.

… during that 'Plain Conversation,' opposing sides had no choice but to listen to each other. They had to hear each other's questions and concerns and stories. Now I know that some people left angry that night. But that evening proved to me that everyday citizens participating in civic life can attempt to model and even insist on respectful discourse.

Note that up front, before the conversation started, Kim made clear her guidelines for "respectful discourse" and her attendees, by and large, abided by those guidelines. I have similarly stated up front my "guidelines for respectful conversation" during this present eCircle and my previous eCircles, and my conversation partners have abided by these guidelines to an admirable degree, at least to date. In the best of all worlds it would not be necessary to insist up front on such guidelines for talking respectfully to one another. But, alas, we are not living in the best of all possible worlds.

It won't be easy

The various hints enumerated above toward reforming political discourse are much easier said than done. Engaging in respectful conversation with those who disagree with you strongly about political issues may actually alter some of your views, leading to uncovering some common ground for governing well. As Jeff points out, following this path will not be easy.

> Finding common ground or a middle way is much more challenging than simply 'going with the flow' or categorically rejecting everything out of hand. Instead, the more difficult task might involve exercising discernment, employing imagination, or even being willing to compromise.

Choose Generosity Rather Than Bellicosity

In summary, to reform the current toxic nature of political discourse, Christians, and all other citizens, must choose generosity rather than bellicosity (remembering that to be "bellicose" means "favoring or inclined to start quarrels or wars"). Therefore, it is fitting to close this chapter with Kim's powerful call to "generosity."

> The opposite of bellicose may be generous, as in generous of spirit. [Jeff's] response to my first post would be an example. Even though we are on opposite sides of the aisle, he still looked for points of agreement. A politician with this spirit will look for commonalities, ways that legislators in different parties can work together.
>
> Sadly, an ethos of generosity does not seem to be widely admired at this time in our country's history. There is common ground, but few dare to venture there. For example, why can't pro-life and pro-choice acknowledge that we all want to see fewer abortions? Why can't the "our" in "our streets" refer to African-Americans, store owners, the police—the entire community?

Can a person characterized by a "generous spirit" get elected in our present political climate? Kim is "skeptical," but she would like to see more "generous people" try, reminding those of us who claim to be followers of Jesus that he exemplified such a generous spirit.

> Can a person with a generous spirit (e.g., Jeff) get elected in this climate? I am skeptical, but I would like to see more people with this ethos try. Whether we are running for office or not, we can try to arrest the bellicosity and instead present a generosity of spirit that comes through in so many stories about Jesus (his response to the adulterous women; his words to the robbers on the cross; his welcoming of children; his inclusion of tax collectors). It's crazy how this first-century man still has so much to teach us in our 21st-century world.

2

What Does Christian Love Demand?

THE FIRST CHAPTER identified toxic problems with the nature of political discourse in America, with the word "discourse" used in the narrow sense of "conversations" among those politicians and their citizen supporters who have strong disagreements about political issues. After noting that Christians are often part of the problem, recommendations were presented as to steps Christians can take to ameliorate these problems.

In this chapter, originally titled "A Proposed Christian Approach to Political Discourse" (the title has been changed for reasons that will soon become apparent), a much more expansive view of the nature of political discourse is presented that, rightfully, goes beyond the question of how we should talk to one another about our political disagreements to also deal with the question of what other types of political engagement are demanded of Christians in light of the call of Jesus for his followers to love others.

I am one of the two conversation partners for this topic. My partner is Greg Williams, a Christian who is a doctoral student at Duke University Divinity School.

Upon a first reading of our respective postings, readers may conclude that my proposal and Greg's proposal have little in common. In what follows, I will first present, in our own words, the major contours of our two proposals without evaluative comments, followed by my evaluations in the form of my perceptions of our agreements, disagreements and remaining unanswered questions. To give the reader fair warning, some (many?) of you may find some radical elements in both of our proposals.

Heie Proposal: Christian Love Requires That I Engage in Political Conversations With Humility, Courage and Love

My proposal is limited to the issue of "how" Christians, and others, should talk to those who disagree with them about political issues. This is my starting point because whatever issues need to be addressed and whoever should be addressing these issues, we cannot proceed until we grapple with the foundational question of how we should engage in conversation with those who disagree with us about these issues.

My starting point takes literally the dictionary definition of "discourse" as the "formal and orderly expression of thought on a subject," which, as will soon be seen, is a narrower view of the meaning of "discourse" than the one Greg is using. (What Greg calls "political discourse" I would call "political engagement"—much more about that distinction later. In the meantime, I will use the phrase "political conversation" rather than "political discourse" in presenting my proposal.)

My proposal is meant to present a stark alternative to the brutal coarseness of current conversations among politicians and their supporters that was reported on in Chapter 1. I begin by pointing to some of the structural problems with the American political system that cause political enmity.

> There is room for disagreement as to the causes of political enmity. A primary reason, in my estimation, is that for too many politicians and their supporters doing politics is about winning rather than about governing well. And this focus on winning has led to pernicious political structures and practices that militate against genuine political conversation. These include closed primaries that attract more ideologically extreme voters who have little interest in dialogue, gerrymandering of voting districts that protect politicians from having to engage opposing views, and the

inordinate role of financial support from donors at the extreme ends of the political spectrum. The net result is a hollowing out of the middle that militates against politicians reaching across the aisle in search for common ground.

But I want to dig deeper by focusing on some foundational reasons for the brokenness of political conversation; the attitudes (enduring dispositions) that underlie such questionable political structures and practices. Although it will sound quaint, I maintain that the root causes of political rancor are lack of humility, lack of courage and lack of love.

Ask yourself when the last time was that you heard a politician or staunch supporter of a particular public policy position say "I may be wrong." As Scripture teaches, we all "see through a glass darkly" (1 Corinthians 13:12). As human beings, the particularities of our social locations inform our views on public policy. The position taken by someone who disagrees with me may be deeply informed by his/her gender, socioeconomic status, sexual orientation, his/her race and elements of his/her personal biography, which may enable him/her to see things that I miss. Likewise, my particularities may enable me to see things that he/she misses. And since we are both finite and fallible human beings, we cannot claim that either of our partial glimpses captures the full truth on the matter, as only fully understood by God. In addition, I can be blinded when I succumb to the temptation to sin by thinking *it's all about me and those who agree with me.*

It is hubris and a gross failure to exemplify an appropriate attitude of humility for me to assume that I have a God's-eye view of the truth about a given policy issue. It takes genuine humility for me to express my beliefs with clarity and conviction while acknowledging that "I may be wrong." The ideal of "humility" that I call for can be summarized as follows:

> **Humility: The acknowledgement that however strongly I hold to my beliefs and express them with deep conviction (and, yes, even with deep emotion and passion), I may be wrong.**

Exemplifications of courage are also often missing in the political realm. Too often, politicians do not express their deepest convictions for fear of what their constituents will think and the possibility that they may be punished for such honesty on the next election day; another symptom of the inordinate focus on winning in politics.

I have personally witnessed such lack of courage in face-to-face conversations I have had with some local elected officials as I have advocated for the well-being of my immigrant neighbors, documented or undocumented. A specific example involves my advocacy for Iowa state legislation for temporary driver's licenses for all immigrants, which, in my estimation is a win-win-win situation (good for public safety, employers and immigrant families). The response of one member of the Iowa legislature was, in effect, that he agreed with the need for such legislation and would support it if it were proposed by others (jumping on a bandwagon), but it would be too politically risky for him to take the initiative to propose such legislation.

Relative to the August 2017 tragedy in Charlottesville, I am not in a position to know or to pass judgment on the motives of others. But I encourage politicians who have remained silent about President Trump's equivocation regarding the moral culpability of the protestors and anti-protestors in Charlottesville to examine their motives. Is it possible that such deafening silence reflects a failure in courage? My ideal of courage can be summarized as follows.

Courage: The willingness to 'speak out' my understanding of the 'truth' relative to the issue at hand, even if negative consequences result from my doing so.

In addition to failures to exemplify humility and courage, I believe that lack of love is the primary attitudinal cause of the current coarseness of political discourse.

Starting with an area of agreement among Christians, I know of no Christian who denies that Jesus calls his followers to "love others" (Mark 12:31). But there is much disagreement as to how to express that love. My proposal for a Christian approach to all human conversation, in the political realm or anywhere else, focuses on one expression of love for others that I find to be too rare in Christian circles. I am loving another person when I abide by the following guidelines for respectful conversation:

- I create a safe and welcoming space for her to express her perspective on the issue at hand.

- I listen carefully, seeking to empathetically understand the reasons she has for her perspective.
- I express my perspective, and my reasons for holding that perspective, with commitment and conviction, but with a non-coercive style that invites conversation about disagreements.
- I explore whether we can find some common ground that can further the conversation. But, if we cannot find common ground, I conclude that "for now we agree to disagree"; yet I will do so in a way that demonstrates respect for the other and concern for her well-being and keeps open the possibility of future conversations.
- I aspire to be characterized by humility, courage and patience.

There is an extremely important element that pervades these steps: "getting to know" the person who disagrees with you. Those politicians, pundits and citizens who bash each other on cable TV, talk radio or in their local newspapers have typically not taken the time to get to know each other very well. When you take the time to get to know the person who disagrees with you, you may uncover new insights from her reasons for her perspective and you may discover that she too wants the best, although you may differ as to what is best. In politics, this often means that you may find agreement on ends (e.g., the needs of those living in poverty must be addressed); with your disagreements being primarily about the best means to accomplish those ends (e.g., emphasizing free-market mechanisms or governmental interventions). During this process of getting to know her, you can build the mutual understanding, trust and respect needed to continue your conversations.

While recognizing the excesses of nostalgia, this suggests the need for politicians to go back to the days when Tip O'Neill and President Reagan developed a friendship that made it possible for them to work across the aisle in the midst of their deep political disagreements.[4]

Although it appears trivial on the surface, a current problem in Washington is the virtual elimination of adequate time for socialization among

---

4 See reflections by Thomas O'Neill, Tip's son, in an essay aptly titled, "Frenemies: A Love Story." The most telling reflection is, "What both men deplored more than the other's political philosophy was stalemate, and a country that was so polarized by ideology and party politics that it could not move forward."

politicians on opposite sides of the political aisle brought about, at least in part, by the inordinate amount of time spent on fundraising.

What are my arguments for the importance of Christians expressing their love for others in this conversational mode? I appeal to both personal experience and Scripture.

In my former life as a vice president for academic affairs at two Christian colleges, I have seen some positive results from my attempts to live out these guidelines for respectful conversation in proving leadership for my faculties, which has been likened to herding cats. But there was one notable exception, when my commitment to a collaborative leadership style led to my being fired for "lack of deference to the president and board of trustees," who exemplified a top-down approach to leadership.[5]

As if the pain of being fired was not enough, it was magnified considerably when I was not provided a welcoming space to present my point of view; when I was silenced, rendered voiceless. But one day, a member of the board of trustees who apparently was not involved in the decision that this governing body made came to my home because he wanted to hear my side of the story. Finding someone who was willing to listen to my perspective on what had transpired brought joy to my whole being. It was like coming across an oasis on a journey through a desert. As he left my home that sunny morning in South Central Pennsylvania, I knew that I had been loved.

But I don't wish to make my experience normative. What light is shed by Scripture? I will limit my reflections to one passage, 1 Peter 3:15 (in Today's New International Version):

> Always be prepared to give an answer to everyone who asks
> you to give the reason for the hope that you have. But do this
> with gentleness and respect ...

Richard Mouw, the former president of Fuller Theological Seminary, on whose shoulders I stand since his book *Uncommon Decency*[6] has inspired me and supports my proposal much more eloquently than I can, once expressed an unusual take on this verse.

---

5 For those readers interested in all the gory details, I refer you to Chapter 14 ("Fired") in my book *Learning to Listen*, 68-75
6 Mouw, *Uncommon Decency*.

Paraphrasing generously, Mouw reported that in his Christian upbringing, great emphasis was placed on the first sentence in this verse (express the reasons for the hope that is in you "with commitment and conviction"—to use my own words); but virtually nothing was said about the second sentence ("do this with gentleness and respect").

This failure to heed this entire exhortation points to the scarcity of a rare combination pointed to by Ian Barbour in his definition of "religious maturity."

> It is by no means easy to hold beliefs for which you would be willing to die, and yet to remain open to new insights. But it is precisely such a combination of commitment and inquiry that constitutes religious maturity.[7]

As quoted by Jeff VanderWerff in our September conversation, Richard Mouw draws on Martin Marty in highlighting the importance of "civility" in living out this rare combination of commitment and inquiry, calling for a "convicted civility."[8]

> One of the real problems in modern life is that the people who are good at being civil often lack strong convictions and people who have strong convictions often lack civility. ... We need to find a way of combining a civil outlook with a 'passionate intensity' about our convictions. The real challenge is to come up with a *convicted civility*.

Openness to the beliefs of others without commitment to your own beliefs too easily leads to sheer relativism (I have my beliefs, you have yours; end of conversation). Commitment to your own beliefs without openness to listening to and respectfully discussing the beliefs of others too easily leads to fanaticism, even terrorism. (As C. S. Lewis has observed, to which past and recent world events tragically testify, "Those who are readiest to die for a cause may easily become those who are readiest to kill for it."[9]) *One of the most pressing needs in our world today is for all human beings, whatever their religious or secular faith commitments, to embrace,*

---

7 Barbour, *Myths, Models, and Paradigms*, 136.
8 Mouw, *Uncommon Decency*, 12, drawing on Martin E. Marty, *By Way of Response*, 81.
9 Lewis, *Reflections*, 28.

and hold in tension, both commitment and openness; giving living expression to "convicted civility."

In response to the question as to what is at stake if Christians don't model a better alternative to the brutal rancor of current political discourse, my answer is: "The credibility of the prophetic witness of the Christian church is at stake." It is tragic that many Christians have been silent in the face of the current broken nature of political conversations that directly violates Christian teachings regarding humility, courage and love or, worse yet, gladly contribute to such pernicious conversation.

I conclude my proposal by noting that it is my "quest for truth" that is the foundational reason for my passion for seeking to orchestrate respectful conversations among people who have strong disagreements, in the political realm and elsewhere.

> This passion has emerged from a continuous integrative thread in my life since my early teaching days: my insatiable 'quest for truth' at the cognitive level and my aspiration to live out that truth one day at a time. The ultimate authority to which I am committed is not to be found in the pronouncements of church leaders, the pope or anyone else, or to the interpretations of Scripture and doctrines of any particular Christian tradition or denomination, for no person or Christian tradition/denomination has a corner on God's truth. Rather my ultimate authority is the truth as God fully knows it. The fact that I am not God presents a considerable challenge. Since I only have a partial glimpse of the truth, at best, it is important for me to engage with humility, courage and love in respectful conversations with those whose glimpses differ from mine, so that, together in conversation, we can gain better approximations to that truth.

I anticipate at least three objections to my proposed Christian approach to political conversation.

First, are there not limits to my call to respect others? Should I respect those white supremacists, neo-fascists, and members of the KKK who marched in Charlottesville chanting "Jews will not replace us"? It depends on what you mean by "respect."

Stephen Darwall has made a distinction between two kinds of respect.[10] **Appraisal respect** is a positive evaluation of somebody's achievements or virtues. **Recognition respect** is elicited by the worth someone has simply because she is a person, independent of her achievements or virtues. From my Christian perspective, all persons are of worth because they are "beloved by God" and have been created in the image of God, however distorted that image has become. Therefore, I recognize the worth of those who practiced bigotry while marching in Charlottesville at the same time that I believe that their beliefs and actions are deplorable. And that means that I would be willing to engage them in respectful conversation about our disagreements, if they so desire.

The above reflections on the marchers in Charlottesville leads to my response to the third leading question that Greg and I have been asked to address: What does it mean for Christians to love their enemies in politics? Starting with a definition of an "enemy" as someone who is "antagonistic to another"; someone who is "seeking to injure, overthrow or confound an opponent," then, from the outside looking in, I may have my share of enemies. But my proposal for how I should engage others in political conversation does not depend on whether they consider themselves to be my friends or enemies; whether they seek my well-being or not. When I engage anyone who disagrees with me, I am to love him/her by engaging in conversation according to the guidelines that I enumerate above. But I must say that even if she considers herself to be my enemy, I do not consider her to be my enemy since he/she is "beloved by God."

A second possible objection is that my proposal allows Christian perspectives on public policy issues to gain a hearing in the public square. Should particular religious perspectives be allowed in public discourse in our pluralist society? The substance of my perspectives on political issues will be deeply informed by my value commitments as a Christian. Some argue that this is impermissible in the public square. Political discourse should be value-neutral. But that is impossible. No one comes from nowhere. Every person brings their values to public conversations. For some, these values flow from particular religious commitments. For

---

10 Darwall, "Two Kinds of Respect," 36-49.

others, they flow from differing religious commitments or from secular views about the nature of reality and our place within that reality.

This means that political discourse should be characterized by a "level playing field," where all perspectives, religious or secular, should be given a hearing; an approach that has been called "dialogic pluralism," where each perspective is not evaluated on the basis of its genesis (e.g., did it come from a Christian, a Muslim, an atheist or from a Republican, Democrat or Independent?), but, rather, on the basis of the extent to which the perspective being proposed can lead to public policy that fosters the common good.

A third possible objection to my proposal is that it has absolutely no hope of being "successful." I can only imagine some of my readers rolling on the floor laughing: "Harold, you are living in la-la land; totally out of touch with political reality." It is hopelessly naïve to think that a significant number of politician and their supporters will soon be embracing the virtues of humility, courage and love in their engagement with political opponents. Such virtues are in short supply, even among those, like Christians, who pay them considerable lip service. I will address this objection in some detail at the end of this chapter.

Williams Proposal: Christian Love Requires That I Actively Seek to Foster the Flourishing of Poor, Marginalized and Oppressed Peoples

Greg affirms the importance of giving expression to the virtue of love in the realm of politics: "I could not agree more [with Dr. Heie] on the importance of love for the practice of politics." He adds:

> The New Testament is clear that this [love] is the sum of all the virtues. As 1 Corinthians 13:13 states, 'And now abideth faith, hope, and charity, these three; but the greatest of these is charity.' I do not quote the King James Version only because it is still the most eloquent rendering of the text in English (though I believe that it is). I also want to highlight that Christians affirm a specific sort of love—caritas, charity, the kind of self-giving love that moved the Son of God

to take the form of a slave (Philippians 2:7) and which powers the two most important dimensions of Christian practice—care for the poor and care for one's enemies. In the Incarnation, God does both ... In assuming human flesh to Himself, the Word of God, Jesus Christ, allows us, as human beings, to do His works, too, and thereby calls us to solidarity with poor and oppressed people everywhere (work that solidarity starts, but does not end, among the poor and the oppressed themselves) and to the work of active peacemaking for the sake of a common life with and for meaningfully diverse others. In this way, God makes us ambassadors of reconciliation (2 Corinthians 5:20), and heralds of God's commonwealth of peace and freedom, in which there is no poverty, no degradation, no war.

Note Greg's assertion that God especially calls us to solidarity with poor and oppressed people everywhere and to the "work of active *peacemaking* for the sake of a common life with and for meaningfully diverse others" (italics mine).

Greg reinforces in even stronger terms the need for Christians to express Christian love on behalf of "the exploited and the oppressed" as follows: "It is absolutely crucial to stress that Christian love is unequivo-cally partisan. With the God who took the form of a slave, it stands on the side of the exploited and the oppressed and against their exploiters and oppressors."

Greg also affirms a broad definition of "doing politics" as not only deal-ing with the "search for common ground that seeks the common good" (as I originally proposed). Rather, "doing politics" also includes our col-lective attempt to find ways for persons who don't share the same views as to a "common good" to, nevertheless, "come together to make a common life." In his own words:

... the goal of political life is not to make everyone else look, think, and act like oneself, but to negotiate the terms of a common life with people who are meaningfully different. Politics happens because people disagree on how to go about achieving basic goods. How are we going to raise our kids?

How are we going to take care of our elders? How should
we work to avert the coming of a climate catastrophe that is
already here for the poorest and the most vulnerable? What
should education look like? What should our food system
look like? The goal of politics is not to get everyone to give
the same, pre-prescribed answers to these questions but to
enable people who have radically different answers to those
questions to live together in such a way that every person is
able to participate in that common life and, in that context,
to flourish.

Drawing on the work of one of his professors at Duke Divinity School,
Luke Bretherton (who I should report, in the interest of full disclosure,
was extremely helpful to me as a consultant as I was shaping the agenda for
this eCircle), Greg says that, "While Dr. Heie speaks of political opponents
coming together to discover a common good, I prefer, together with Luke
Bretherton, to speak of diverse communities coming together to make a
common life."

Given this view of the "public sphere," the pressing question is whether
the poor, marginalized and oppressed play a meaningful role ("have a
voice") in the doing of politics in America. Greg answers with a resound-
ing "**No!**" He elaborates as follows, first drawing on the writing of Jürgen
Habermas to describe the genesis of the idea of a "public sphere": "The
birth of the public sphere was a key part of the creation of the modern,
bourgeois state, because it guaranteed one of that state's key features: limited government. The public sphere, as a place where private individuals
could gather and discuss matters of common significance, created 'the
public' as such, a body that could limit the scope and authority of the state
and to which the state could be held accountable." Greg adds that it is necessary to "create a public sphere that is for everyone, one not dominated by
the one, the few or the many."

Greg then points to two problems that have evolved relative to this idea
of a "public sphere": the "decline in the number of genuinely public spaces
where people can come together" and certain marginalized groups have
been denied entry.

Greg cites Robert Putnam's book *Bowling Alone*[11] as a text that tracks the decline of the number of genuinely public spaces, noting Habermas' argument that "as membership in labor unions, churches, mosques, and synagogues, rotary clubs, debating societies, amateur sporting leagues and other voluntary associations continues to plummet, ... we can expect the quality and quantity of 'civil discourse' to continue to fall."

Greg elaborates on the problem of marginalized groups being denied entry into the "public sphere."

> The public sphere is, by definition, a sphere for anybody and everybody. But the 'everybody'—the 'everyman'—that it includes has never really been all human beings. Rather, the bourgeois public sphere has always primarily served as a meeting place for the paradigmatic bourgeois subject— propertied, white, male and heterosexual.

Therefore, while "workers, women, people of color and LGBTQ people have contested the scope of the bourgeois public sphere and thus broadened it, countervailing forces have also sought to narrow it." Greg attributes these countervailing forces to the "neoliberal capitalist order."

> As common spaces have cropped up where exploited and oppressed people can appear publicly to one another and organize and contest their immiseration, the neoliberal capitalist order has responded with strategies of enclosure and containment. In this light, we can reconceptualize the decline of public spaces tracked by Habermas and Putnam. It is not something that has happened naturally, but something that has been engineered, a basic feature of neoliberalism.

Greg adds that "the state and the market have many ways of enclosing common spaces to prevent the entry of subaltern voices into the public sphere and shut down subaltern counter publics," further asserting that "it is clear that contemporary neoliberalism would rather destroy the public sphere than allow these groups [working-class people, queer people, people of color] the opportunity to appear as genuine public actors."

---

11 Putnam, *Bowling Alone.*

In response to these countervailing forces, marginalized groups have responded as follows:

> The commons, the demos (the last, the least, and the lost whom Jesus Christ came to serve and to save) have always sought to seize space within the public sphere, or to make public spheres of their own—at union halls, gay bars, pride centers, anarchist infoshops, punk venues, black churches and alternative religious spaces—in order to meet one another, to identify common concerns, to organize and fight the ruling classes and/or just to survive.

Greg is particularly concerned with the diminishing role of the working class in American politics. Starting with the broad view of politics as including ways to live together in the midst of our differences, Greg expresses this concern as follows: "Employers and workers ... may well actually have nothing in common—thanks to the inequalities created by capitalistic modes of production." As Greg's bio reveals, he is actively addressing his concern in his work with the Industrial Workers of the World organization.

Greg asserts in unambiguous terms his conviction that because the working class and other marginalized groups do not "share a common good," attempts at "persuasion" during a conversational stage of political engagement, while "part of the political equation," will not suffice. Rather, when dealing with "workers and employers," more overt "force" and "conflict" will be required. In order to not diminish the strength of Greg's conviction on the matter, I present his entire quote.

> If the goal of politics is to identify and seek a common good, something that everyone shares regardless of their social location, then politics will be, primarily, about persuasion. If you and I share a single, identifiable common good, then all our differences of opinion can be explained as differences in how to seek that good. My task, then, will be nothing more and nothing less than to try to convince you that my way of seeking our shared good is more effective, and vice versa. In that context, the norms of respectful conversation that Dr. Heie has laid out make perfect sense as universal rules

for how Christians should conduct themselves in politics. If the goal is to persuade my adversary, then I should try to do so with love, and that means doing so respectfully and with an open mind, from a posture of active listening. But if we don't share a common good but nevertheless have to figure out how to live together, how to make a common life, then persuasion, while it will, surely, still be part of the political equation, will not be the sum total of political discourse. To return to the example of class, if workers and employers have basically opposing interests, if, as the preamble to the constitution of my union says, 'the working class and the employing class have nothing in common', then, while the process of making a common life may involve persuasion, it will, surely, involve force as well. Workers will not just attempt to persuade their bosses to pay them a living wage with moral arguments; they will also, often, have recourse to strikes, slowdowns, boycotts, occupations, blockades, sabotage and all other manner of mass and covert action to force their bosses to comply with their demands. In such a world, in which the common life that people create together is made not only through persuasion, but through conflict as well, Christian love demands that we be militantly partisan for the working class, for colonized people, for racial, religious and sexual minorities—in short, for the last, the least and the lost with whom Jesus Christ revealed God's unwavering solidarity in becoming incarnate in the form of a slave. Christian love in politics will be lived not only at the podium, but on the picket line, not only in televised debates, but through the tear gas and the gall of militant street actions.

Greg also points to the need for the "institutions" of civil society to play a major role in doing politics in America. Citizens participate in many institutions of society (besides government), such as families, businesses, churches, synagogues, mosques, schools, unions, journalistic outlets, service organizations, professional organizations and other voluntary associations. Any consideration of doing politics in the broad sense of finding ways to live well together must give serious consideration to the role of these many mediating institutions. Greg elaborates on the role of these various institutions, again drawing on the writings of Jürgen Habermas. He first affirms the centrality of "institutional existence" for any kind of discourse: "... 'civil discourse'—or any other kind of discourse—does not arise out of the blue. It does not and cannot happen between individuals with nothing standing between them and the state and the market. Rather, 'public discourse' and 'the public' itself needs to have an institutional existence." He goes on to point out what he considers to be "free speech's most basic precondition."

> ... free speech's most basic precondition [is] physical and institutional space where people can appear to one another as public actors—particularly if they are marginalized along the lines of race, class and gender.

It is on this basis that Greg asserts that the conversation I have orchestrated for this present subtopic ("Why is political discourse on the decline and how can we revive it?") is "the wrong question." Greg points us to what he believes is the "correct question."

> The correct question is: 'How is the public sphere in crisis and how can working-class people organize to seize and reinvent it as a commons?' The desire for a civil society, one in which people can genuinely talk to and listen to one another about issues of common concern, cannot be separated from the economic and political processes by which civil institutions are produced. These institutions are in crisis, but there also exist, now as ever before, countervailing forces that seek to create a public sphere that genuinely is for everyone, one not dominated by the one, the few, or the many.

Finally, Greg makes the radical proposal that for the poor, oppressed and marginalized to have an influence in the political process, the virtues of humility, courage and that aspect of love that focuses on conversation (my "guidelines for respectful conversation") may have to be suspended.

> Alternative spaces for political discourse, whether anarchist infoshops, punk venues, black churches, gay bars, freedom

schools or popular assemblies continue to grow, and to spawn a new form of political discourse, a new sort of public life, a commons rather than a public in any ordinary sense of the term. Alternative institutions of this sort house a different kind of speech because they serve different people ... Different sorts of discourse arise in the context of different sorts of politics, as different sorts of people try to have different sorts of conversations.

Note especially Greg's proposal that there may be need for "a different kind of speech" because different people are being served. He provides the following example:

... queer black and black feminist authors like James Baldwin and Audre Lorde have shown that the exclusive focus on reason in enlightenment European discourse comes from the presumption that the subject of that discourse owns his body and is therefore able to control his body and, with it, his emotions (emotions, here, are construed with passions—the link between controlling the body and controlling the emotions is the commitment to disciplining sex; slavery and heteronormativity are, for both Baldwin and Lorde, inextricably linked), in order to focus on pure ideas. The suppression of emotion in political discourse, under the guise of making that discourse 'rational,' is rooted in a commitment to controlling the body, a commitment that presumes that human bodies can be owned and that the paradigmatic subject of rational discourse owns his body, among others. In other words, enlightenment claims about the universal norms for what good comprises good discourse are not universal at all: they come from the heteronormative commitments required to reproduce a genocidal, slaveholding society. In response, Baldwin, Lorde, and other queer black and black feminist authors have proposed different sorts of discourse, which give full play to the body, to the emotions, and, as Lorde famously argued, the power of the erotic. Far from being disembodied and rationalistic, good ways of thinking and speaking together are embodied and passionate—if, that is, you think that good ways of thinking and speaking together are ways of thinking and speaking that resist colonization, enslavement and other sorts of capitalist regimes of enclosure.

Therefore, Greg gives an emphatic "**No!**" to the idea that "no matter who speaks, there is a need for shared norms for how speaking is to take place," adding that "instead of starting with a normative definition of 'speech' to which we can then adduce 'political,' I wish to start with a normative definition of 'politics' and then figure out what kinds of norms of speech go with it."

Greg closes with his conviction that the realization of his proposal will provide a "fleeting glimpse" of the full Kingdom of God to come.

> ... We need to reject politics as given, utterly, by naming it as politics according to the logic of Empire, the logic of slavery, the logic of death which our Lord Jesus Christ came to destroy by his glorious resurrection and ascension to the right hand of God the Father! We need to hold out hope for a different sort of politics, a politics of life and freedom, a politics that is about having enough for everyone, about beating swords into ploughshares, about loosing the bonds of injustice and breaking every chain, a politics that is about the business of making every ditch and valley to be raised up and every mountain and lofty hill to be made low, the crooked places straight and the rough places plain—a politics, in short, that is about all flesh seeing and sharing and loving the glory of the Lord together!

> ... I do want to submit that, in the contemporary American context, these sorts of freedom struggles are an essential place to look for a fleeting glimpse of the Kingdom's advent.

> ... we should ask, 'where are the politics of God taking shape in the world? And what is political speech like in those places?' You can't just model respectful conversation and

then ask those engaged in political struggle to join you. You must take up the struggle, and, from that place, which is the place of Jesus Christ, you must ask what sort of speech makes sense, and build the institutions to go with it.

Agreements

At first glance, it would appear that Greg and I inhabit two different worlds—that our respective proposals are incommensurable. To be sure, we have some fundamental disagreements. But before elaborating on areas of disagreement, I will point to some common ground.

Christians are called to love others

Greg and I agree that the virtue of love is central to any Christian ethic. We are not alone. I know of no Christian who denies that Jesus calls his followers to "love others" (Mark 12:31: "The second [commandment] is this, 'You shall love your neighbor as yourself'"). Greg notes the importance of giving expression to the virtue of love in the realm of politics: "I could not agree more [with Dr. Heie] on the importance of love for the practice of politics."

Loving others requires seeking the flourishing of the poor, marginalized and oppressed

Greg and I agree that Christians should express Christian love on behalf of "the exploited and the oppressed." This shared belief comports well with numerous biblical teachings throughout both Testaments of the Bible. Consider especially the meddlesome words recorded in Isaiah 8:6-7, expressed in terms of the need for "justice."

> Is not this the fast that I choose: to loose the bonds of injustice, to undo the things of the yoke, to let the oppressed go free, and to break every yoke? Is it not to share your bread with the hungry, and bring the homeless poor I into your house; when you see the naked, to cover them. And not to hide yourself from your own kin?

Jesus is equally meddlesome in his call to those who claim to be his followers to address the needs of the "least among us" (the hungry, thirsty, naked, sick, and the prisoners and "strangers" in our midst), as recorded in Matthew 25.

Political engagement involves more than conversation, but not less

I was wrong when I originally stated that "politics, at its best, is only the search for common ground that seeks the common ground." Although I believe that politics should start with conversations that seek common ground, Greg helped me to see that that is not the end of political engagement. I now embrace, along with Greg, that a more adequate view of the purpose of politics is the broader view that "doing politics" also includes our collective attempt to find ways for persons who don't share the same views as to a "common good" to, nevertheless, "come together to make a common life."

The voices of the poor, marginalized and oppressed are not adequately represented in American politics

Greg and I share this belief, although our firsthand experiences with groups we believe to be marginalized differ. Greg is especially concerned with the diminishing role of the working class in American politics. I believe that the weakening of the influence of labor unions in America lends credence to Greg's concern.

My experience in northwest Iowa leaves no doubt in my mind that my Latino neighbors are a marginalized group in local politics and beyond. In meeting with them and with elected politicians who should be representing them, I am struck with how "voiceless" my Latino neighbors are in the public sphere.

My listening to the stories of LGBT Christians in my local community and beyond convince me that they have not been adequately included in conversations about how we can all live well together.[12]

So, while there is room for disagreement about the extent to which certain groups have been left out of the political conversations in America, and how that inequity should be addressed, which begs for ongoing

12 For extensive elaboration regarding this claim, see my book *Respectful LGBT Conversations*, which presents a synthesis of my recent eCircle on "Christian Perspectives on Human Sexuality."

conversation, I believe, along with Greg, that there are many instances of such marginalization.

The institutions of civil society need to be more engaged politically

I agree with Greg's concern that the "institutions [of civil society] are in crisis," in two ways: First, participation in many of these institutions ("in which people can genuinely talk to and listen to one another about issues of common concern") is on the decline. Secondly, where these institutions are alive and well, their "voices" are not adequately represented in the American conversation (such as it is) on how to live well together.

Christian love demands more than respectful conversation

Greg astutely notes that "You can be open and respectful when advocating for cuts to social benefits or against police accountability just as much as when struggling for labor rights and immigration reform."

This insightful observation points to another area of agreement: The political engagement of Christians needs to include expressions of love that *go beyond* modeling respectful conversations with those who hold to differing political views. I frame this "going beyond" respectful conversation in terms of the need to do "justice": Our political engagement must strive to foster justice for all peoples, starting with the poor, marginalized and oppressed among us.

Christians need to be agents for justice

Here I believe Greg and I are on the same page, since Greg proposes that we need to create "just institutions" and that Christians engaged in politics should work at "loosing the bonds on injustice." In brief, I believe that a portion (not all) of what "Christian love demands" is that Christians work toward "doing justice" for all peoples.

To introduce the concept of "justice" into the conversation is fraught with potential for misunderstanding since this multifaceted concept is too often reduced to justice that is "retributive" ("punitive") as in the criminal justice system. I am using this word in the "distributive" sense of an equitable allocation of the goods of life. This fits with the previously noted teachings of Scripture (e.g., Isaiah 8, Matthew 25) that Christians should seek to foster the flourishing of the poor, marginalized and oppressed. This aspect of justice also includes the requirement that all persons should have the opportunity to participate in the political process.

But this aspect of justice also raises the question as to what it means to "do justice" to the many non-governmental institutions of society mentioned above. For starters, I believe this means that all of these institutions need to be given the opportunity to contribute to the "doing of politics" in the broad sense of forging a way for all of us to learn to live well together. Chapter 4 of this book that extends a comprehensive call for political activism will address other aspects of what it means to "do justice" to the various non-governmental institutions of our civil society.

Christians love demands that Christians be agents for the Kingdom of God

Here, a kernel of agreement between Greg and I will also be the seed for a major disagreement. Greg asserts that "in the contemporary American context, these sorts of freedom struggles [that he describes in his proposal] are an essential place to look for a fleeting glimpse of the Kingdom's advent."

But Greg also suggests that my proposal about how Christians should talk to their political opponents is "not speech for the Kingdom and politics for the Kingdom,"

> My argument with Dr. Heie's attempt to 'save' U.S. political discourse is that it confuses temporal things for eternal things. It seeks to define norms for 'speech' as such and 'politics' as such—not speech for the Kingdom and politics for the Kingdom.

I must say emphatically that I agree with Greg's exhortation for Christians to provide a "fleeting glimpse of the Kingdom's advent." But we have some differing beliefs about how Christians should be agents for the Kingdom of God. This will be one of the areas where Greg and I disagree; a topic to which I now turn.

Disagreements

I will be happy to have future conversations with Greg, and others, about my perceptions of areas of agreement, as outlined above. But where do we disagree?

You will recall my earlier acknowledgement that my original view of the scope of politics (searching for common ground that seeks the common good) was "wrong" in being too narrow and that Greg's broader view of politics (as also including the attempt to forge a flourishing common life together in the midst of lack of agreement about a common good) was "right." In that same spirit, I now lay bare two areas of disagreement where I respectfully suggest that I am "right" and Greg is "wrong" (as a precursor for possible future conversations).

Both questions are important

Greg asserts that I am asking the wrong question when I ask how Christians should talk to those who disagree with them about contentious political issues. Rather, the "correct question" is, "How is the public sphere in crisis and how can working-class people organize to seize and reinvent it as a commons?"

As noted above, I reframe his view of the "correct question" in terms of the "doing of justice," and broaden it to extend beyond "working-class people": "How can Christians work to foster justice for the poor, marginalized and oppressed in America?"

But, whatever the best framing of these two questions may be, I believe that both of these questions are important. It should not be the either/or choice that Greg seems to suggest. A broad view of the demands of Christian love calls Christians to *both* engage those who disagree with them about contentious political issues in respectful conversation *and* work tirelessly to foster justice for the poor, marginalized and oppressed in our society (one aspect of which is to make sure that such groups are adequately represented in our conversations about political issues).

The Christian virtues on which I focus are normative

My second disagreement with Greg is very significant and apparently irreconcilable (in the spirit of my proposed fourth guideline for respectful conversation, we may just have to "agree to disagree for now"). In brief, I believe that the Christian virtues of humility, courage and love are normative for Christians in all circumstances. It appears to me that Greg disagrees. I will seek to elaborate.

Recall my proposal that when engaged in conversations about contentious issues, the Christian virtues of humility, courage and that aspect of love that creates a welcoming space for listening to and talking respectfully about disagreements should always be exemplified. Greg answers with an emphatic "**No!**" by rejecting the idea that "no matter who speaks, there is a need for shared norms for how speaking is to take place." He elaborates by suggesting that I have things upside down.

> In essence, what Dr. Heie seems to me to want is to construct a shared project of political speech, the purpose of which is to 'save' U.S. political discourse from its current state of decline, to stand it back up on itself, and then, baptizing that project as Christian, to invite different political actors to join it, including the poor and the marginalized. He wishes, in short, to construct a normative definition of speech and then fit all sorts of different politics into it ... I propose to turn Dr. Heie's proposal on its head. Instead of starting with a normative definition of 'speech' to which we can then adduce 'political,' I wish to start with a normative definition of 'politics' and then figure out what kinds of norms of speech go with it.

I couldn't disagree more. While agreeing with Greg's proposal that the broad purpose of politics includes finding ways to "come together to make a common life" and that (in my own words) this requires that justice be done for all peoples, with particular concern for the poor, marginalized and oppressed, I strongly disagree with the idea that when engaged in conversations about contentious political issues, a Christian should violate any of the Christian virtues of humility, courage and that aspect of love that creates a welcoming space for listening to and talking respectfully about disagreements.

I argue for the normativity of these virtues fully realizing that there is no "one-size-fits-all" approach to talking about political issues or most anything else. A conversation about any political issue can take many unexpected twists and turns depending on the issue at hand and who is talking (witness my electronic exchanges with Greg). But I believe that in attempting to navigate these unexpected twists and turns, a constant should be a commitment to exemplifying humility, courage and love. And, it is important for the reader to remember my proposal, that in the very process of practicing these virtues, you will "get to know" the other person better, which will, hopefully, build the mutual understanding, trust and respect needed to continue your conversations toward the goal of collectively gaining a better approximation to the "truth" about the issue at hand.

But what is a Christian to do when such respectful political conversations have been exhausted and have hit a dead end? That is a good question, to which I will now respond.

Peaceful Resistance to Injustice

Greg and I agree that injustice should be resisted. But how?

In the brief bio that Greg submitted for my eCircle, he identified himself as an "anarcho-communist." My partial understanding of what that means is to call into question free-market capitalism and, relative to employer/worker relations, either advocate for common ownership of the means of production or for employer/worker relations to be guided by a network of workers' councils (or possibly both).

To be more specific, Greg is explicit about actions that workers may have to take to ensure that "their bosses pay them a living wage," as follows:

> ... if workers and employers have basically opposing interests, if, as the preamble to the constitution of my union says, 'the working class and the employing class have nothing in common,' then, while the process of making a common life may involve persuasion, it will, surely, involve force as well. Workers will not just attempt to persuade their bosses to pay them a living wage with moral arguments; they will also, often, have recourse to strikes, slowdowns, boycotts, occupations, blockades, sabotage, and all other manner of

mass and covert action to force their bosses to comply with their demands.

What do I make of this list of possible uses of "force" on the part of workers? As an introduction to my response, I first acknowledge the excesses of unfettered "free-market capitalism," a major symptom of which is the growing inequality between the rich and the poor.[13] So, I have no problem with resistance to injustice in the workplace, *provided that the means of resistance to injustice are peaceful.* That is where I draw "a red line in the sand," recognizing that it may sometimes be difficult to know exactly where this line is.

For example, a peaceful strike of workers as a protest against unjust wages or working conditions is appropriate. But I see the use of "occupations," " blockades" and "sabotage" as crossing the line into violent behavior. And for a number of other cases outside the category of employer-employee relations, like responding to a business that makes an egregious moral decision, strategies such as peaceful boycotts are appropriate.

In addition to my assertion that the means of resistance to injustice should be peaceful, I also believe that, with rare exception, such means of resistance to injustice should abide by the laws of the land. For those readers who may be concerned about my "rare exception" clause, I remind you of the 1960 sit-in at a Woolworth department store in Greensboro, North Carolina, carried out by four young black men. They were denied lunch at the counter, in accordance with store policy and within the "law of the land" at the time. This sit-in was a potent "force" within the civil rights movement that eventually led to the civil rights legislation of 1964 that made it unlawful to practice segregation in public accommodations.

But this action and similar actions that were led or inspired by Martin Luther King Jr. (one of my heroes) were examples of peaceful resistance to injustice. It appears to me from Greg's postings that he does not draw the same line in the sand as I do between violent and peaceful means of

---

13 Given how most U. S. citizens now look with horror at the scandal of slavery about 150 years ago, I was once asked what I thought citizens 150 years from now would judge to be the most prominent scandal of our day. My answer was "the inequality in wealth between the rich and the poor."

resisting injustice, although he does call for "active *peacemaking* for the sake of a common life with and for meaningfully diverse others" (italics mine).[14]

To be even bolder, I believe, contrary to the position that I understand Greg to be taking, that the virtues of humility, courage and love should be normative for Christians, and all other persons,[15] not only during the conversational stage of political engagement, but also while pursuing all peaceful means for resisting injustice. My primary exemplars for the centrality of this claim are Martin Luther King Jr. and Nelson Mandela.

The Peaceable Kingdom

As already noted, Greg and I agree that Christians should provide a "fleeting glimpse of the Kingdom's advent." But it was painful for me to read Greg's assessment that my proposal was neither "speech for the Kingdom" nor "politics for the Kingdom," since the primary motivation for my proposal is my belief that it provides intimations of the Kingdom of God. It appears to me that Greg and I have differing views as to how the Kingdom of God will be fully realized and how Christians should be agents for God's Kingdom.

To begin sorting out this possible disagreement, I return to the third possible objection (just mentioned in passing above) to my proposal that "Christian love requires that I engage in political conversations with humility, courage and love," which is that my proposal has absolutely no hope of being "successful."

As I said before, I can only imagine some of my readers rolling on the floor laughing: "Harold, you are living in la-la land; totally out of touch with political reality." It is hopelessly naïve to think that a significant number of politicians and their supporters will soon be embracing the virtues of humility, courage and love in their engagement with political opponents. Such virtues are in short supply, even among those, like Christians,

---

14 I realize that my suggestion that non-violence should be a norm for all Christians will raise many unanswered questions in the minds of some readers, the consideration of which is not possible in this brief chapter (e.g., Is war never justified?). For my response to such vexing questions, I refer interested readers to Chapter 21 (Tragedy, Just War and Peacemaking) in my book *Learning to Listen, Ready to Talk*.

15 Since these virtues are expressions of "human values," not just "Christian values."

who pay them considerable lip service. It is also hopelessly naïve for me to think that attempts to foster justice for the poor, marginalized and oppressed will lead to any "success" if I preclude a resort to violent means.

I acknowledge the force of this objection. But "success" is not uppermost in my mind. My aspiration is to be faithful to my understanding of how a follower of Jesus is called to engage someone with whom he/she disagrees in the political realm and every other area of discourse and my understanding of the limits that the norm of nonviolence places on my attempts to foster justice for all. I entrust the possibility of success, or not, into God's hands. In my numerous attempts over many years to facilitate respectful conversations about contentious issues and my modest attempts to seek justice for some marginalized populations, I have been sustained by the parable of the mustard seed told by Jesus, as recorded in Matthew 13:31-32.

> The kingdom of God is like a mustard seed that someone took and sowed in his field; it is the smallest of all seeds, but when it has grown it is the greatest of shrubs and becomes a tree, so that the birds of the air come and makes nests in its branches.

In ways that far exceed my limited understanding, the "Kingdom of God" inaugurated by Jesus "is here but not yet." In our broken world, we see only faint intimations of the eventual fullness of the Kingdom of God to come, something like the early morning sunrise provides a hint of the full noonday sunshine to come. In the meantime, I am called to plant tiny seeds of redemption, entrusting the harvest to God. Therefore, it is only through the eyes of faith that I can envision my trying to live well in the political realm bearing any redemptive fruit.

And it is conceivable that the redemptive fruit will only come by the way of a "cross." There is ample historical evidence that persons who believe that the peaceable Kingdom will not be brought in by violent means may be crushed by people in power who are only too happy to resort to violence (ask Martin Luther King Jr., Nelson Mandela, Gandhi or Jesus).[16]

16 As a theological aside, my proposal and my responses to Greg's proposal are deeply informed by the tension I experience between my dual commitments to basic tenets of both the Reformed and Anabaptist theological traditions. In brief, my immersion in the Reformed tradition taught me that God wishes to redeem all aspects of the created order and I am called to "partner with God" in that redemptive work and my immersion in the

More Unanswered Questions

Alas, the month of October 2017 ran out before the questions did (so many questions, so little time!). Fortunately, a number of these questions will be addressed in later chapters.

Are there limits to free speech and civil discourse?

We must consider the possibility that there are limits on pursuing respectful conversation because the call for such dialogue can be a means of control by those in power, or a way to marginalize those who will not be invited to the conversation. Furthermore, there is disagreement as to what the constitutional limits are, if any, on "free speech" in such conversations, as witnessed to by the current turmoil on a number of university campuses as to who can be invited to speak to the campus community. The next chapter on the subtopic "Are There Limits to Free Speech and Civil Discourse?" will begin to address these thorny issues.

When is respectful conversation exhausted?

Both Greg and I agree that when attempts at persuasion and respectful dialogue have been exhausted, more overt actions to promote justice are called for. In Greg's words: "When all attempts at persuasion and respectful dialogue have been exhausted, you put on a gas mask, take up a flag, a shield or a hard banner, and prepare to stand against them [Nazis marching in the streets]."

But this leaves unanswered the question as to when to decide that all attempts at respectful dialogue have been "exhausted"? My perception is that all too often attempts at respectful dialogue about contentious political issues have not even been tried, no less "exhausted."

A related problem is the tendency of those calling for respectful conversation to set pre-conditions for such conversation, stating before the conversation what at least some of the results must be. This violates the truth that you cannot predict beforehand the results of a respectful conversation. This problem is evident in the current turmoil over whether

---

Anabaptist tradition taught me that I need to choose peaceful means for planting tiny seeds of redemption.

America should "negotiate" with North Korea and, if so, what the ground rules should be for such negotiation.

More discussion of these issues is necessary.

In what ways can the institutions of civil society become more engaged politically?

Both Greg and I agree that many of the institutions of civil society are not adequately represented in the American conversation (such as it is) on how our diverse citizens can live well together. What is the appropriate role in American politics for the non-governmental institutions of our civil society, such as families, businesses, churches, synagogues, mosques, schools, unions, journalistic outlets, service organizations, professional organizations and other voluntary associations?

The two aspects of the meaning of "justice" that have been emphasized in this chapter are: 1) All relevant voices must be included in political conversations, especially those marginalized populations that have been systematically excluded from conversations that could have a significant effect on their well-being; 2) The doing of justice includes promoting the flourishing of the poor, oppressed and marginalized in our society.

But another dimension of "justice" needs to be addressed: What does it mean to "do justice" to the integrity of non-governmental institutions? This question will be addressed in Chapter 4 as a portion of extending a comprehensive call for political activism and in the Chapter 10 presentation of three case studies: two on Christian churches that have differing views as to the extent to which they should, or should not, be involved in political activities, and one Christian para-church organization. Chapter 5, on the subtopic "Party Politics and Beyond," will also be relevant since it will deal with the possibility that politics is more than what the political parties do.

How can the structural problems with the American political system be ameliorated?

Much more conversation is needed to address the structural deficiencies in our current political system. Not being a political scientist, the best I could do was to point to what I perceive to be some of those deficiencies, such as closed primaries, gerrymandering of voting districts and the inordinate role of financial support from donors at the extreme ends of the political spectrum. Greg expresses appreciation for my at least pointing to these structural problems, saying that we need to create "just institutions." But neither of us say much about how to do that. And when I read books like *It's Even Worse Than It Looks*,[17] I get depressed about the possibility of ever effecting positive structural changes in our political system, due to the existence of so many vested interests.

Much more conversation is needed to address these huge and apparently intractable structural problems. Chapter 6 on "The Role of Money and Special Interests in Politics" will include some of the broader conversation that is needed. My own sense is that such future conversations need to address a common characteristic of most, if not all, of these structural problems: the "hollowing out of the middle" caused by favoring the extreme elements of both parties. For politicians and their supporters at the extremes, it is too often "my way or the highway." There is a notable lack of that modicum of humility required to acknowledge that those on the other side of the aisle may actually have some good ideas that can be incorporated into bipartisan legislation—another example of the need for both/and thinking rather than either/or thinking.

---

17 Mann, *Worse Than It Looks*

.

3

Are There Limits to Civil Discourse and Free Speech?

CIVILITY IS NOT the first word that comes to mind when one thinks about the pathetic state of political discourse in America today. Why is that? Is there a Christian perspective on addressing that problem?

These and other related questions were the focus of a conversation between Mark Douglas, a seminary professor of Christian ethics, and Tony Carnes, a journalist and publisher working in New York City. Mark and Tony were asked to respond to the following set of leading questions:

- Are there limits to civility?
- Is the call for civility a means of control by those in power?
- Is the call for civility a means to marginalize those "who have no voice"?
- Are there ideas so repugnant and dangerous that they shouldn't be allowed to be uttered in public?
- If colleges and universities are committed to the quest for "truth," what are the limits, if any, on free speech?

What Are the Problems With Public Discourse?

As reported in Chapter 1, Jeff VanDerWerff and Kim Van Es have identified a number of problems with public discourse in America, especially in the political realm, including personal attacks that demonize persons who disagree; blurred lines between news and commentary/opinion; redirection (changing the subject); confirmation bias reflecting an us/them tribal mentality (listening only to an echo of yourself); and no time for nuance and deliberation. Tony and Mark add to or elaborate on this litany of problems.

> I feel like compassion is very out right now. Curiosity is out. What's in is condemnation and punishment. Now is not the moment for nuance; people do not want it (Tony, quoting Young Jean Lee).

> ... the need to produce heat/stir up energy may not have much to do with the actual significance of a topic for those doing the yelling. Maybe those who are yelling aren't quite so convinced by their positions as they are anxious about their significance in a very big, very complex world and yelling is a way to get attention. And maybe audiences—which really aren't the same as conversation partners—aren't quite so driven by the desire to have their own thoughts confirmed or, less often, challenged, as they are looking to be entertained by a good fight (Mark).

But there may be legitimacy in the attempt to "get attention." Possibly the call for civility in public discourse is merely a disguised attempt for those in power to maintain oppressive structures in society that benefit them and disadvantage those who are marginalized. As Mark reports, this possibility causes some students in his seminary classes to ask why the "rules for good communication" that he stipulates for his classes (to be enumerated later), that are intended to "reinforce civility," are "actually good."

Those rules help reinforce civility in my class. It doesn't take long, though, for my students—who being encouraged to ask questions about the moral and theological bases for rules, among other things—to ask about why these should be the rules. And, as criticisms of civility grow increasingly common (based, as they are, on either concerns about efficacy during turbulent times or the way some arguments for civility reinforce unjust power dynamics and oppressive structures in society), they ask whether such rules are actually good.

As noted by Tony, this ambiguity as to the value, or not, of adhering to "rules of civility" cause many to believe (erroneously, Tony would say) that there is a forced binary choice: "withdrawal from society or ... revolutionary movements." And, as Tony adds, some then reject withdrawal from society, choosing "transgressive behavior" as the "only way to get a fair hearing."

Recall that, as reported in Chapter 2, such "transgressive behavior" was called for by Gregory Williams as the only way for marginalized groups to "gain a voice," as a counter-point to my proposal that all human engagements regarding disagreements should be characterized by commitment to the normative Christian virtues of humility, love and courage.

However, Tony points out the potential fatal flaw of such "transgressive behavior," the temptation "to suppress" the voices of those who disagree.

> ... transgressions that try to stifle other people's speech are
> no longer attempts to gain voice but to suppress someone
> else's voice. The authoritarian character of such an endeavor
> is rejected by the good Samaritan as a way of being that
> builds bad character.

Readers may be unclear as to the significance of Tony's reference to the "good Samaritan." As will soon be seen, it is the parable of the Good Samaritan told by Jesus that will be the basis for the alternative that Tony presents to the false forced choice of withdrawal from society or revolutionary movements. But to prepare the readers for Tony's proposal, it will be necessary to clear some underbrush by considering what the word "civility" may mean.

Two Views on the Meaning of "Civility"

As will soon be seen, Mark and Tony point us toward two possible views as to the meaning of "civility," what I will call micro and macro perspectives. But we must first consider Tony's views as to what "civility" is **not**. Drawing on the teachings of Jesus, Tony asserts that "civility" is not "politeness" or "tolerance," which lead, at best, to a "civil co-presence."

> The framework of tolerance and civility is not adequate to Jesus' teachings. He didn't say, 'Be polite to your enemies,' or 'Tolerate your enemies.' He said something much stronger and more disturbing. His teachings were 'Love your neighbor as yourself,' 'Bless your enemies,' and 'Do good to them who despitefully use you.' Toleration leads to a civil co-presence, while doing good to your enemies leads to love. Which kind of a national household do you want to live in? A peaceful but basically disconnected group or a group with hands-on love? What a difference if we start our discussions with love, not in the realm of tolerance and civility!

> Imagine that you are in a room at a college campus party with your enemy. You may be civil, say hello, and shake hands, but you probably will stay on the other side of the room. If you follow Jesus, you would pick up some hors d'oeuvres and take them over to the one who has despitefully used you ...

Much more will be said later about the framework of love that Tony proposes. Suffice it to say for now that it doesn't settle for coexistence with those with whom you disagree (what Tony calls "co-presence"). Rather, it calls for active engagement, which can take two forms, both of which give expression to a type of civility that goes beyond politeness or tolerance.

The first form of civility (what I will call "micro civility") focuses on the *mode* of engagement with someone who disagrees with you. I have proposed "respectful conversation" as a civil mode of engagement, to be governed by the "Guidelines for Respectful Conversation" that all conversation partners for my eCircle agreed to abide by (which they did to an admirable degree). But Mark has expressed guidelines for such "civil conversation" more eloquently than I by means of the "reasons" for civility he presents in "the syllabus of every class [he teaches] … at Columbia Theological Seminary" under the title, "Hints, Tips, and Rules for a Good Ethics Class," as follows:

Because seminary classes regularly deal with matters that are both personal and potentially divisive, we all need to keep several points in mind as we communicate with each other in this class. Among these are:

1. *We are unified in Christ, not in opinion. There is no special reason to think that we all must agree on an issue in order to be part of Christ's church. Christians have been disagreeing with each other at least since Peter and Paul, and there is no reason to think that will change this side of eternity. In fact, as a general rule of thumb we ought to be suspicious about any issue about which we all agree. When all heads nod in the same way, we are either exerting illegitimate control over other persons' heads or we have stopped using our own.*

2. *Disagreement can be many things: intellectual, heated, productive, mild, etc. Our burden is to keep it from being destructive or splintering. Toward that end, there are three rules for disagreement within this class:*

   a. *Always remember that the person with whom you disagree is, like you, a finite creature created in the image of God who is no more or less likely to sin than you and no more or less capable of being redeemed than you. Demonizing others based on their positions is disrespectful to persons, contrary to the faith and in poor taste.*

   b. *You should be able to state your opponent's position so clearly and fairly that your opponent would say, "Yes, that is what I mean." Only then can you rightly give a critique of that position.*

   c *You have the responsibility of following your thought through to its logical conclusions. If you don't like those conclusions, back up, figure out where you went wrong, and then either clarify or qualify your thought accordingly.*

This marvelous statement makes me wish I could take one of Mark's ethics classes. In my estimation, it beautifully captures the meaning of the micro aspect of "civility" that focuses on the preferred mode of engagement between those who disagree about any given issue.

But Mark also points us toward a broader macro sense of "civility" that focuses not on an engagement between individuals who disagree, but rather on what it means to be a "civil society."

> If ... being civil means participating in the creation and expansion of a society that is honest, caring, open, and respectful for all persons (that is, if being civil means working to construct a just *civitas*), then the pursuit of civility is among the most important things we do.

Mark elaborates in a number of ways. First, such a "civil society" requires that all persons in society have "equal standing" when involved in "verbal intercourse over matters of common concern," suggesting that such "equal standing" is exemplified in this eCircle.

> In the instance of these essays in 'Respectful Conversations,' the context in which neighbor-love is expressed is that of American public life—a context in which, at least in theory, rights-bearing citizens who have equal standing vis-à-vis each other are engaged in verbal intercourse over matters of common concern but shaped by varied and seemingly incommensurable perspectives.

Mark also asserts that working toward a "civil society" requires "maintaining epistemic and rhetorical humility," which "supports the right of others to speak," and "committing oneself to relationship," where "unity is not the same as unanimity."

> **Maintaining epistemic and rhetorical humility.** Neither democratic discourse nor Christian vision can be sustained where ideological fervor or fundamentalist certitude trump commitments to listen to and speak with those different from oneself. Whether humility takes the form of a commitment to the type of Emersonian experimentalism that multiplies perspectives in order to figure out which ones can advance

a society or the recognition that our thoughts are not God's thoughts and our ways are not God's ways (from Isaiah 55), such a posture favors both critical and charitable engagement with others. Civility and freedom of speech are manifestations of this posture in that they constrain one's own inclinations to dominate conversations and they support the rights of others to speak.

Committing oneself to relationship. Democratic discourse and Christian vision are both undergirded by the convictions that we can be stronger together than we can be when separated and that unity is not the same as unanimity. Whether this commitment manifests in a motto like *e pluribus unum* or a verse like "different gifts but the same Spirit" (1 Corinthians 12), this value not only honors the actual diversity of persons but shapes a teleological vision of reconciliation. Maintaining civility and supporting freedom of speech become ways that persons express their hope that we need not leave others behind (let alone knock others down) in order to move closer to the beloved community of which Martin Luther King Jr. spoke.

Finally, Mark asserts that such a "civil society" requires that "those who are most affected by decisions should have a voice in making them."

If one accepts the idea that there is a macro sense of "civility" that pertains to what it means to be a "civil society" (a "just *civitas*"), the question looms as to the most appropriate means to foster such a civil society. Mark and Tony suggest that two approaches are possible, one that places a negative emphasis on "restraints" on free speech and one that places a positive emphasis on expressing "neighbor-love," topics that we will now consider in that order.

Promoting Civil Society by Imposing
Restraints on Free Speech

Mark appeals to the "obligations of public discourse for democratic citizenship" proposed by John Stewart Mill in his book *On Liberty*,[18] which includes Mill's three reasons for "listening to people with whom you disagree: 1) You could be wrong; 2) Even if you are (mostly) right, engagement with someone who thinks differently from you will help you shape your own arguments; and 3) If you don't listen to people who disagree with you, you won't be able to distinguish the basis for your arguments from unexamined prejudice."[19]

At this point, Mark points to the "tensions" between the Millian approach to the obligations of public discourse for democratic citizenship and the "obligations of revelatory discernment for faithful [Christian] living," while noting overlap between the two approaches, which includes "Maintaining epistemic and rhetorical humility" and "Committing oneself to relationship" (as described above) in addition to "Treating civility and freedom of speech as necessary but instrumental goods," which he describes as follows:

> **Treating civility and freedom of speech as necessary but instrumental goods.** The goals of civility and free expression are not being civil or expressing freedom. Instead, they are part of a collection of strategic goods to be inculcated in the pursuit of some greater good. That good in democratic polities is the creation of a society in which all persons can participate in the governing structures that allow for a robust and resilient state. That good in the Christian faith is the Kingdom of God that has been inaugurated but not yet consummated. In either instance, the wager implied in treating civility and freedom of speech as necessary but instrumental goods is that they are more likely to lead to these greater goods than are any alternatives.

---

18 Mill, *On Liberty*.
19 Mark also presents a "more theological argument for listening to those with whom you disagree," drawing on the story of Baalam recorded in chapter 22 of the book of Numbers in the Old Testament.

I will later suggest that "civility and free speech" are not just "instrumental goods"; they also have "intrinsic value." But, in the meantime, I present Mark's important proposal that his three points of overlap between democratic citizenship and faithful Christian living "hint at where civility and free speech may find their limits in either regulation or prohibition."

Restraining free speech to avoid violence

Mark notes that "treating civility and freedom of speech as necessary but instrumental goods recognizes that, historically, one of the dominant alternatives to speech in the projects of pursuing a *summum bonum* is violence," adding that:

> The temptations toward violence are endemic to human existence and have been expressed in projects having to do with either creating a better state (e.g., the French Revolution, the U.S. Civil War, Mao's cultural revolution) or bringing about the Kingdom of God. Both moral vision and long experience, though, show that using violence to bring about such ends is neither good nor, in the long run, effective.

Mark concludes that **"Where speech is used to incite, encourage, or valorize violence, it can be restricted or prohibited."**

Restraining free speech to avoid silencing critics

Mark notes that "maintaining epistemic and rhetorical humility recognizes that language is contextual, that contexts change, that responding to such changes requires a kind of social resilience, and that pluralizing perspectives is a precondition for such resilience," adding that:

> The temptation to treat one's own opinion or one's own place in time as the most important point in history (and, therein, to treat one's own concerns or the current moment as carrying a level of urgency based on the premise that if we do not get things right now, all is lost) has not only led to violence but tended to produce results antithetical to the goals of desperate projects. Again: Moral vision and long experience show that those who have treated their own perspective or any particular moment in time as singularly

and overwhelmingly important have lost both their moorings in history and their imaginations for the future— and then haven't been able to move into the moments that come next.

Mark concludes that: **"Where speech is used to end conversations, to silence critics, to shout down unpopular positions, to harm through deception, or to reject the diversity of voices, it can be prohibited or restricted."**

Mark adds the caution that "appeals to humility can be weaponized against those who face structural injustice," and we need to be attentive to that dire possibility.

> ... when those on the top tell those on the bottom to be humble, they regularly mean for them to stay in their places at the bottom. Contemporary disquiet and disgust with the virtue of civility by many of those on the political left are driven by such an awareness. Any appeal to civility that is inattentive to the reality of the structures and flows of power in social systems should be called to account for such inattentiveness and made aware of the history of deleterious consequences that follow from such naïveté.

Restraining free speech to avoid tribalism

Mark notes that "committing oneself to relationships recognizes that the kinds of othering that lead to people being treated as less than or other than human begin by separating 'us' from 'them' and building barriers between 'us' and 'them,'" adding that:

> The temptations to divide, to cordon off, and to otherwise dream up categorical differences between people have funded chattel slavery and genocide, not to mention racism, sexism, classism and the other -isms that plague societies. Where they have flourished, so have many of the deepest injustices and most horrific events of human history.

Mark concludes that: **"Where speech is used to categorize people, to generalize and then demean people, to reject and then to dehumanize people, it can be restricted and prohibited."**

Mark is quick to add, however, "that this is, perhaps, the most complicated set of restrictions or prohibitions to negotiate, if only because such restrictions and prohibitions struggle to address matters of tone, nuance, intent and context," asking the difficult question as how to tell the "difference between the same word used in either a derogatory or empowering way." He gives the example of "the way the term 'queer' with reference to LGBTQ+ persons has changed." The problem is that "the way a word is seemingly innocuous when used by one group and never innocuous when used by another."

In summary, Mark notes that in proposing these three possible restraints on free speech, he has "tried to at least to begin to do two things: 1) To offer a defense of the way the proper limits to free speech are built into the very purposes of speech in democratic discourse and Christian vision; and 2) To attend to the complexities of those limits."

However, Mark also acknowledges that "the vision of civility and free speech I am offering here comes from the perspective of someone whose social location and status (white, male, upper-middle class, educated, able, cisgender, heterosexual, Christian) is as likely to inoculate me from the most deleterious consequences of that vision as many of the things that I might actually say, write or think," which leads him to two concluding claims, the first of which is that those who have access to power and resources [such as him] need to avoid harming others who do not have similar access.

> ... the same virtues and practices that sustain the visions of democratic engagement and Christian living I am espousing here mandate that those like me whose positions provide access to power and resources have an obligation to give special and specific attention to the way language (and especially our own speech) harms others and then to oppose such use of language and mitigate its consequences as we are able through our own use of words.

Mark's second ("harder") claim is that in our broken world his proposed "restraints" on speech will not be able to eliminate the abuses of speech; the best we can do is to "manage, minimize or ameliorate" these abuses, which is an element of the human condition that has to be endured.

> The harder claim is this: In the Augustinian vision I am promoting here—one in which the 'city of God' and the 'city of man' are inextricably blurred—many of the concerns I have tried to name above are not problems to be resolved so much as they are conditions to be borne. Perhaps bearing them can mean working to manage, minimize or ameliorate them; it will not mean attempting to end them because such attempts will make things worse. In this, concerns about civility and free speech are like much of the rest of life: matters to be endured more than problems to be solved. So far as I can see, the virtues that inhere in civility and freedom of expression are the very virtues that can help us endure those concerns because they help us bear each other.

Going Beyond "Restraints" to "Neighbor-love" to Promote Civil Society

While appreciating Mark's call for "restraints" (a negative aspect of law) on free speech for the purpose of fostering a civil society (it at least keeps "civil peace"), Tony calls for "inching toward a new paradigm of the public law in democracies" that focuses on "positive law"; the "demand to do good," as exemplified by the parable of the Good Samaritan told by Jesus.

> ... Most modern discussions of civility start with a negative sense of the law in how it restricts the individuals, groups, administrations or governments from interfering with free speech and conscience, the John Stuart Mill emphasis on legal or ethical restraints.
>
> The parable of the Good Samaritan ... is pure New Testament. It emphasizes what we can call positive law; the demand to do good. Here, Jesus' focus was not primarily

on highlighting the advantages of the law's restraints. His
emphasis was on how an overly high focus on the restraints
of the law can cause us to miss what the outcast, the lowly, or
the heretic can teach us on how to do good. It is not enough
to restrain from doing evil.

Tony elaborates in some detail. Here are a few highlights.

First, in this parable, Jesus clearly teaches that loving your neighbor
goes beyond following a "set of rules" (like rules for when free speech
should be restrained, I would add). Recall that what precipitated the telling of this parable was a lawyer asking Jesus who his neighbor was. As
Tony points out:

> His interrogator obviously wanted a set of rules to determine
> what is a neighbor—just tell us what to do and to whom, the
> legal scholar said facetiously. This is where Jesus told the
> lawyer that he needed to look beyond the law to the lawless
> as his neighbors and to their example of love.

However, Tony recognizes that civility and love are not mutually
exclusive.

> The parable of the Good Samaritan teaches that before you
> can practice civility, you must practice love. Before you can
> practice love, you must have the civility to pause and look at
> the good in your neighbor.

But Tony proposes a priority order: "You need love first; then you need
civility." His reason for proposing that order is that you cannot sustain
civility without love.

> The approach that one must be civil and tolerant first may
> indeed create a peace. But it doesn't provide the emotional
> or social resources to build trust and sustain civility.

> A breach of civility is obnoxious to the orderly mind and a
> threat to civil peace. However, it probably doesn't destroy
> the social bonds as much as lovelessness.

> In the long run, civility won't last if you can't love your
> enemy as yourself. Doesn't it pain you if you see marriages
> that are civil but where there is no love left? These marriages
> very often lose their civility, too.

Tony presents an example of the priority of love by reflecting on Mayor
Ed Koch's expression of a "generous spirit toward the graffiti writers of
New York City" in the 1970s and 1980s.

> In the 1970s and 1980s, the city was awash with crime, graffiti
> and hatred. The city was going broke and was championed
> or condemned as the secular Sodom and Gomorrah on the
> Hudson ...

> One of the problems, in many people's eyes, was that the
> public order had become so chaotic that too many people
> just wanted to stay away from New York ...

> Koch was trying to balance out a love for the kids with the
> need for order. Many people would say that he didn't quite
> get the balance right, but what he did is instructive.

> He told an interviewer that the kids were creative and
> admirable, but were aiding a culture of lawlessness with
> their graffiti. He said he believed in the three strikes rule: if
> the police caught the kids *in flagrante 'graffitis'* three times,
> then the kids would be in jail for five days. He joked that
> he believed in the death penalty for murder but observed
> that 'these are kids' just throwing up a little trouble on walls.
> Of course, the trouble was expensive to clean up, and many
> New Yorkers, including one of the chief detectives on the
> anti-graffiti squad who had to run after the miscreants at
> night along the subway tracks, dismissed the writing as not
> art 'but a crime.' Koch was trying to balance out his affection
> for the kids with the needs of civility ...

Tony concludes that "If we start with love first, trust is built, ears are
unplugged, eyes are opened, and some civil conflicts can be much more
easily settled. Not all can be resolved, but all can be loved."

Mark expresses appreciation for Tony's insights, especially his proposal that "Christians should be shaped by/act out of neighbor-love," adding that he is "actually embarrassed that he [Mark] didn't raise this point in [his] ... own essay [first posting]." For emphasis, Mark goes on to say:

> Tony's ... most significant point is that the Christian obligation to 'love thy neighbor as thyself' is both unconditional and foundational for any ethic that would call itself 'Christian.' Not only is it a deeply theological claim (coming, as it does, on the heels of and linked to the first great commandment, to love God), it is the type of claim that manifests depth beyond facile understandings of those five simple words. The command to love neighbors invites us to rethink our conceptions of love. (Love can be commanded rather than only arising naturally? Love can be directed at a wide range of persons rather than only the natural objects of our affection? Love can be task, virtue, and inclination all at once? Love is a social as well as a personal thing?) The commandment calls us beyond tolerance, civility and even respect for others—though, as I'll suggest below, it also shapes how and why we value tolerance, civility and respect.

Note, however, from the last sentence quoted above, that Mark sees a more synergistic relationship between civility and love than that proposed by Tony. He states that more emphatically as follows:

> ... It seems to me that civility isn't what comes after neighbor-love (contra Tony's suggestion that, "You first need love, then you need civility"). Civility is the way neighbor-love expresses itself ... *Civility is a form of neighbor-love* (italics mine).

Mark then draws out four implications of his proposal that "civility is a form of neighbor-love."

> So what are the implications of thinking of civility as a form of neighbor-love? At least these: First, to the extent that neighbor-love includes attention to intention, being civil must mean more than being polite. Politeness can

be motivated by many things; the kinds of civility that count here are those that are motivated by love. Second, to the extent that neighbor-love sits as a high standard for behavior, it offers a means for judging calls to civility. If those calls are used in defense of the maintenance of unjust power structures or illegitimate relationships, neighbor love judges them and finds them wanting. Third, to the extent that neighbor-love is something that we can get better at through practice, civility is something we should aspire to, not something we should think we've got right. And, fourth, to the extent that neighbor-love is made possible by the prior love of God, those interested in promoting civility ought to be looking for signs of the work of God in the world.

Mark adds a reflection on why these "four implications" can "help explain why social media (or at least Twitter) can feel so uncivil." (We will return to problems with social media later.)

And what do these implications get us? At an obvious level, they help explain why social media (or at least Twitter) can feel so uncivil. One simply cannot give much expression to neighbor-love in 280 characters so as people take shortcuts to get to their point, they eliminate the things that are hardest to convey: intention, integrity, depth, and naming whatever desires are motivating them. Moreover, and perhaps at a less obvious level, social media distorts not only those we interact with (and it's hard to love neighbors that we've abstracted), but it distorts us (and it's hard to love neighbors as we love ourselves when we aren't honest about who we are).

To conclude this section, I will reflect on how the above report fits, or does not fit, with the position I took as reported in Chapter 2, that the Christian virtues of humility, courage and love are normative for Christians in all circumstances (with which Gregory Williams emphatically disagreed) and that the often-ignored "aspect of love that creates a welcoming space for listening to and talking respectfully about disagreements [that micro-aspect of civility that deals with our "mode" of engagement with others] should always be exemplified."

This position that I have taken does not comport with Mark's assertion that "civility" is only an "instrumental" good. To be sure, I agree with Mark that being civil in "democratic politics" can lead to the good result of the "creation of a society in which all persons can participate in the governing structures that allow for a robust and resilient state." But I believe that even if that good result does not materialize, Christians are called to be civil, in both the micro and macro senses described above, as a deep expression of the love of neighbor to which Jesus calls all who claim to be his followers.

It's Both Civility and Neighbor-love, not Either/Or

Despite any disagreements as to the relationship between civility and neighbor-love, including whether one takes priority over the other, Mark and Tony agree that *both* should be embraced by followers of Jesus and their combination is required to foster *both* democratic discourse *and* the "Christian vision."

However, there are some Christians who would argue that Christians should refuse to "engage" questions about "the wider body politics" (avoiding "democratic discourse").[20] Mark does not find "such an approach" to be "theologically coherent," elaborating as follows:

> As a Christian standing within the Reformed tradition, it's not so much that I distrust this approach (though I do); it's that I don't find such an approach theologically coherent. If God is at work in the world, then looking out, discerning what God is doing beyond the walls of the Church, and aligning one's work and life with what one discerns God doing seems pretty fundamental to a life of Christian discipleship. All that work takes Christians out into a world that benefits from and calls for civility and a defense of free speech. Discerning what God is doing and aligning one's life to God's work is no easy set of tasks, but then Christians aren't called to do easy things.

---

20 See, for example, Dreher, *The Benedict Option.*

Based on the teaching in Micah 6:8 that "proper worship involves doing justice, loving mercy and walking humbly," Mark even asks us to "imagine" such "faithful public engagement" to be an "act of worship."

But anyone who aspires to live out this combination of civility and neighbor-love needs to squarely face some very radical elements in the teachings of Jesus as to the nature of neighbor-love, a topic to which we now turn.

The Radical Nature of Neighbor-love

It is well known that Jesus' call for Christians to love others includes the exhortation to "love your enemies" (Matthew 5:44). Tony makes the radical suggestion that such love for enemies may call for trying to understand "how your enemies may help you at times."

> A democracy is not sustainable just on the basis of tolerance of competing viewpoints or understanding of the arguments of the opponents. A rational understanding is not an emotional connection to another person or an audience, though it may lead to one. A democracy flourishes when the fractious groups see some hint of value-added in what each other do. 'Bless your enemies' becomes much easier to do over the long run in a democratic society when you see how your enemies help you at times.

The radical possibility Tony points to that there may be some "value-added" in what someone who disagrees with you does, including what he/she says, reminds me of a proposal that the Mennonite scholar Michael King has made that "genuine conversation" takes place between persons who disagree when there is a "mutual quest for treasure in our own and the other's viewpoint."[21]

In her commentary on King's proposal, another Mennonite scholar, Carolyn Schrock-Shenk, suggests that the quest for "mutual treasure" may be unrealistic when dealing with very contentious issues. But, she adds, a "minimum requirement for genuine dialogue is a readiness to change or modify one's perspective about the *person or persons* holding the opposite

---

21 King, "Conversations on Homosexuality," 153.

point of view."[22] This suggestion points to the critical importance of establishing a "personal relationship of mutual understanding and trust" with the person with whom you disagree, a topic to which I will turn in the next section.

But I first leave you with what may be Tony's most radical suggestion as to what constitutes loving someone who disagrees with you: "If we are going to criticize someone, then first we should consider if we have ever looked for the good in that person." When is the last time you have done that?

The Centrality of Establishing Personal Relationships of Mutual Understanding and Trust

Recall Mark's stress on the importance of "committing oneself to relationship" as one seeks to promote a "civil society" (a "just *civitas*"). In my own words, drawing on the reflections of Carolyn Schrock-Shenk, there is no "Way Forward" in engaging someone with whom you disagree until you first build a personal relationship of mutual understanding and trust by taking the time and effort to "get to know" the other person. And the place to start is to carefully listen to the reasons she has for her beliefs, which are inevitably informed by the particularities of her social location such as her personal biography, the religious or secular faith tradition in which she is embedded, her socioeconomic status, her sexual orientation and her race and gender.[23]

Mark has a very interesting take related to the importance of establishing personal relationships in order to arrive at "good disagreements." He starts with the counterintuitive suggestion that "actual disagreement" is an "achievement."

> Confusion, delusion and bias are parts of the human condition. They make actual disagreement an achievement. Not agreement: that, often, is too much to ask (and history suggests that attempts to either achieve or enforce agreement end in suffering). Working toward clear, honest

---

22 Shrock-Shenk, "Foreword." 15.
23 For an elaboration on this point, see Heie, *Respectful LGBT Conversations*, 279-282.

and substantive disagreement is hard. It is, I think, also necessary in societies that would endure over time and at least attempt to be just.

In other words, Mark is saying that "genuine disagreement isn't a condition of human existence; it's an achievement of human charity," adding that:

> My suggestion was premised on the idea that much of what passes for disagreement these days—at least in the public sphere—is actually people talking (or yelling) past one another or spouting catch-phrases and slogans meant to substitute for thought. It was also premised on the idea that we human beings—especially those of us who are both citizens of a democratic society and children of God— actually have the capacity to do the hard work of learning to disagree and to disagree better (or do so more lovingly, as Tony would argue).

Mark observes that "figuring out another person's arguments (not to mention one's own arguments) and discovering points of connection and divergence takes time, energy and practice, not to mention honesty, humility and charity," noting the critical role that "relationships" play in such engagement.

> ... good and important disagreements only exist in contexts where the parties involved have a relationship, value that relationship, and are willing to stay in that relationship.

I cannot emphasize enough that the starting point for developing a relationship of mutual understanding and trust with someone with whom you disagree is to "listen well." That presents a major challenge to many Christians. As Tony quotes a "Haitian-American lady pastor" from Brooklyn: "We Christians are not very good at listening." Tony elaborates on the need for "listening well" for journalists in particular; "Our self-restraint on our own opinions in the reporting process is commitment to listening well, particularly to new ideas, practices and criticism." (Much more about journalism later).

Examples: Obama/Gates and
Shaming Sarah Huckabee Sanders

The above reflections about the importance of developing personal relationships of mutual understanding and trust with those with whom you have disagreements (which starts with "listening well" as a first step toward "getting to know" the other person) may seem too abstract. To get beyond abstractions, we will now consider how this "personal approach" was or was not used, with good and bad results, in two high-profile concrete cases that drew some considerable news coverage.

Obama and Gates having a beer

You will probably recall a much publicized incident, described by Tony as follows:

> In July 2009, noted African-American scholar Henry Louis Gates Jr. arrived back from a trip and couldn't get into his house. He started to try to force the stuck door open. A neighbor, fearing a house break-in, called the police. Sergeant James Crowley and other Cambridge, Massachusetts police confronted Gates on suspicion of breaking and entering. They also feared that a confederate of his was lurking upstairs and could come down belligerent at any moment. Gates was incensed, saying that they were picking on him as a black man. The dispute increased in volume leading to Gates' arrest for disorderly conduct.

Tony describes President Obama's initial questionable response and his later corrective approach as follows:

> The affair was sorted out after a couple of hours but started to spiral into prolonged racial conflict. Obama at first associated the police response with the long history of racism in the nation. The president soon regretted his ill-tempered remarks and changed tack by inviting the professor and police officer to the White House to sort out differences over a cold beer. Vice President Joe Biden joined

them at the July 30th get together. The result was a healed breach and a lesson in Good Samaritan thinking to see the good in each other. Gates later told *The New York Times*, 'I don't think anybody but Barack Obama would have thought about bringing us together [...] the president was great—he was very wise, very sage, very Solomonic.'

Tony adds that "it was refreshing to the nation when President Barack Obama invited a policeman and a harassed Harvard professor to sit down over a beer to discuss their conflict."

Sanders shamed at a public restaurant

As noted by Tony, in the highly publicized recent incident involving Sarah Huckabee Sanders, she "thought she would take a respite with family and friends at the Red Hen [restaurant] in Lexington, Virginia." She was denied service and asked to leave the restaurant. Mark describes this event and its aftermath as follows:

> Recently Sarah Huckabee Sanders was (privately) asked to leave a restaurant in Virginia because the owner of the restaurant and that restaurant's employees were offended by SHS's complicity in supporting policies they deemed immoral (including on the treatment of LGBTQ+ persons), her willingness to demean the press and her consistent duplicity as the press secretary to President Trump. This act, itself, was a kind of private shaming—and the restaurant covered the costs for what SHS and her party had already eaten. As word about the act spread on social media, though, a private act became more public and a private shaming became a series of public/online shaming, including by SHS, who tweeted about the event on her official press secretary Twitter account and by President Trump, who never seems to miss an opportunity to make things worse. The restaurant owner was, by all accounts, civil—and so perhaps the private shaming could have been motivated by neighbor-love. The snowballing accounts and effects of the private act as it became public, though, grew increasingly uncivil.

It is important to note the distinction Mark makes between "private shaming" and "public shaming," which we will now try to sort through as we seek to draw out lessons from these two incidents.

Expressions of neighbor-love or not?

First, we all need to acknowledge that we do things, from time to time, about which we need to be "ashamed." As Mark says:

> At least in principle, I can imagine a defense of shaming as an expression of neighbor-love. The capacity to feel shame is premised on the ability to make moral distinctions and the ability to make moral distinctions is grounded in the existence of complex psychological componentry. There is, therefore, a peculiar backhanded compliment paid to those who, upon being shamed, feel shame: It recognizes their humanity. Done thoughtfully and lovingly, it may even help enhance their own sense of their humanity. There are, after all, things we might do that we should feel ashamed of.

So, there can be a place for "private shaming," where I go to a person with whom I have established a relationship of mutual understanding and trust and point out what I perceive to be a problem with something that they have done, not from a perch of supposed superiority, but out of a genuine interest in their personal growth.[24]

But a severe problem emerges when "private shaming" morphs into "public shaming." As Tony points out, "Not since Hester Prynne got her scarlet 'A' for adultery has public shaming been such a hot topic." He adds:

> ... The current uproar is the result of a 'shaming' campaign by pugilistic Liberals that involves aggressive public harassment of Trump officials and their families. Democratic United States Congresswoman Maxine Waters told supporters that

---

24 In my previous life as a vice president for academic affairs at two Christian colleges, I sometimes had to be the bearer of "bad news" after an evaluation of a faculty member's performance relative to promotion or tenure. I always started out with the "good news," applauding the faculty member for his/her strong areas of performance. But it was also my responsibility to point out areas where improvement was needed. I always tried to do so in a manner that made it clear that I was primarily concerned about his/her growth. I may not have always lived up to that aspiration. But I remember one faculty member, as he left my office, thanking me for my honesty.

'if you see anybody from that Cabinet in a restaurant, in a department store, at a gasoline station, you get out and you create a crowd and you push back on them!' She revels in the example of an owner kicking Sarah Huckabee Sanders and her family out of a restaurant in Lexington, Virginia.

Mark proposes that "social media" is the primary source of the growing problem of "public shaming," drawing on the writings of Jon Ronson[25] and Jennifer Jacquet.[26] Mark notes that while both Ronson and Jacquet "see value in shame," they "both also recognize how easy it is to get shame wrong: to let it be driven by spite or envy or vengeance or any other of a wide range of things-that-are-not-neighbor-love," as happened in the Sarah Sander's case where it was social media that brought about out-of-control public shaming. Mark explains why it is so "difficult" to "negotiate shaming on public media."

If one of the reasons it is difficult to negotiate shaming on social media is that we are not our full selves when we're acting through our avatars, another reason is that the viral qualities of social media allow things to explode so rapidly. It's doubtful we ever would have heard of the Red Hen restaurant without social media ... Social media is a tool of 21st-century communication, but as singer/songwriter Ani DiFranco reminds us in her song 'My I.Q.,' 'Every tool's a weapon if you hold it right.' And social media is especially easy to weaponize. As this example reveals, one of the ways that social media get weaponized is when they drive the collapse of public/private distinctions. And the maintenance of civility in open and free societies is predicated on the maintenance of that distinction: Civility in public life works because we maintain private spaces to retreat to when the anxieties, frustrations and angers that come with living with others in pluralistic contexts become onerous. The safe spaces necessary for intimate relationships and individual development disappear when it is so easy for private to become public.

25 Ronson, *Publicly Shamed*.
26 Jacquet, *Is Shame Necessary?*

Mark points to another "real danger" when "shaming goes viral": "We are less likely to treat shame as the punishment for bad behavior than to treat it as justification for allotting further punishment." He illustrates relative to "actions that reveal racism."

> A more complex set of illustrations have come with those whose actions reveal their racism: the white woman who calls the police on black families barbequing in the park; the white woman who calls the police on a black child selling water without a license; the white man who calls the police because he doesn't believe that the black family in the community's swimming pool belongs there; the list of such events is growing depressingly long. As they were all videotaped doing something both racist and dumb and those videotapes all went viral, they were, I think, quite properly shamed. Yet the consequences of their shaming have included the loss of employment and the sundering of relationships. Were those appropriate consequences? What is the limit to the penalties incurred through/with shaming? It seems to me that one of the real dangers in shaming when it goes viral is that we are less likely to treat shame as the punishment for bad behavior than to treat it as the justification for allotting further punishment. Recognizing that shameful behavior is shameful behavior, social media seem to feed the mob mentalities that keep us from maintaining a sense of proportion about how to respond to those who have behaved shamefully. That was the case for Hester Prynne as she dealt with Puritans; it is even more the case when shaming can go viral and be passed along by avatars who do not love but do enjoy the thrills of punishing others.

Despite Mark's concerns about social media; especially the destructive effects of "public shaming" in social media, Tony is not yet ready to give up completely on such media. He reminds us of the revolutionizing effect that Mr. Rogers had on "the mass broadcasting of television."

I am reminded of Mr. Fred Rogers' response to the mass broadcasting of television. He saw this new (at that time) media as an immense opportunity to reach children and to build neighborliness, but was stunned that the most popular way of doing kids' shows seemed to feature people throwing pies into each other's faces. He thought that there could be a better way, based on the parable of the Good Samaritan. What if we could see our neighbor in everyone? What if we could realize that the day is special just because every stranger is a human being with something to teach us about compassion and love? What if social media could build a real community through the entire country?

With the example of Mr. Rogers as a precedent, Tony radically suggests that social media could conceivably "carry the Samaritan approach forward also."

There is a problem of entering into these social media fights. It is so easy to make mistakes of emphasis, omission, facts and fairness. It is so easy to dip one's toe into the troubled waters of social media, only to hit a rock before one hardly gets into the water. It doesn't have to be that way. Social media can carry the good Samaritan approach forward also.

Frankly, in light of the problems with social media that Mark enumerates, it is hard for me to imagine such media ever being a vehicle for viewing other as "human beings with something to teach us about compassion and love." In my own words, an inherent problem with most social media is that, with rare exceptions,[27] it is not conducive to persons who disagree "getting to know one another" well enough to build the relationships of mutual understanding and trust needed to sort through their disagreements. This leads me to suggest the most important lesson to be learned from a comparison of the Obama/Gates and Sanders incidents: Obama and Gates eventually took the time to "get to know one another" (even "seeing the good in each other," over a cold beer); Sanders and Stephanie

---

27 I like to think that the electronic format that I used in my eCircle is such an exception. Although my preference would have been for my conversation partners to engage one another face-to-face, their electronic postings did give considerable evidence of their being able to build relationships of mutual understanding and trust from a distance.

Wilkinson, the owner of the Red Hen, did not build such a relationship. Tony describes this difference as follows:

> I appreciate that both Sanders and Stephanie Wilkinson, the owner of the Red Hen, were polite and stood up for their values. But did they handle the mad in themselves in the right way? Should the restaurant in Virginia have refused service, and should the member of its staff have created a firestorm by posting on social media its '86' whiteboard notice, a restaurant code that it had denied service to Sanders? Should Sanders have issued a tweet in reply later that morning? Would it have been more meaningful if Wilkinson had taken the opportunity to get to know Sanders and talk through the restaurant crew's complaints? Maybe, the owner could have invited Sanders back to the restaurant for a private chat and lunch with her and the staff. Sanders could have given an invitation to the Red Hen crew to come to lunch at the White House.

> It may be hard to consider the actions and words of the Red Hen restaurateur or Sanders as Solomonic. Certainly, neither hailed Jesus' parable of the Good Samaritan. It would have been so much better for the nation if Sanders and Wilkinson had sat down over a drink and dinner at the Red Hen or the White House. We here in New York City would be happy to host them at the Columbia University dining room. We would try to make the social space between them a holy ground of uninterrupted interaction.

Going beyond consideration of the Obama/Gates and Sanders incidents, Tony suggests another lesson that can be learned from the insidious nature of much current public discourse: You shouldn't respond to every "ill-chosen word" in a manner that draws you into the "narrative" of your interrogator.

> A tacit decline to enter into a specific argumentative conversation may be the act of grace that we call 'tact.' Not

every mistake, ill-chosen word or stupid idea should be pounced upon. You learn quite quickly in New York City that civil inattention may be a necessary survival skill and certainly helps to maintain the peace. We have loud mouths on every corner ...

In today's public square, one should quickly learn not to be drawn into the contentious world that arises from a question from your interrogator. Arguers can be relentless in trying to force an answer to a specific question. Don't do it! Don't let someone force you into their narrative. Sometimes, you just have to decline the conversation that is being offered. This particularly applies to social media. At least, answer the question that you think that they should have asked. You should prep the battle ground with the framework that is most likely to bring the good Samaritan attitude forward.

As another lesson to be drawn from another incident involving Sarah Huckabee Sanders, Tony provides an excellent example of his earlier assertion that "if you are to criticize someone, then first consider if we have ever looked for the good in that person"; an example that brings us full circle to the distinction between settling for a view of civility that is limited to "restraints" or choosing to exemplify "neighbor-love" (remembering that these two views are not mutually exclusive).

We can learn from an imbroglio that the *Los Angeles Times* writer David Horsey created last year by his very insulting portrayal of Sanders' looks. He did have the decency to apologize for his crude remarks. The paper published Horsey's apology on November 1, 2017: 'I want to apologize to *Times* readers—and to Sarah Huckabee Sanders—for a description that was insensitive and failed to meet the standards of our newspaper. It also failed to meet the expectations that I have for myself ... I've removed the offending description.'

Notice that the *Times'* writer only fesses up to violating the ... principle of restricting his speech where appropriate.

But Horsey has nothing to say about any appreciation of Sanders. As a result, the apology ends up all about him and restoring his reputation but nothing to restore the reputation of Sanders. He doesn't say that his personal insult was false, that Sanders has any good aspect, or offer any other positive kindness to her. He doesn't even admit that she has a pleasant personal appearance (perhaps because it would seem so insincere). Horsey kept his cartoon with a chunky Sanders and a slit trench of a mouth. This is like saying that one is sorry for calling the polecat an ugly stinky critter. His boundary maintenance to ward off his own fault reveals a problem of the [Restraints] ... approach without the positive kindness of the Good Samaritan parable.

A final lesson that Tony draws from the "public shaming" of Sanders is that rather than being quick to offer "opinionated comment," we should work on "opening up the public square to more people, particularly to our opponents," providing an example of what local newspapers could have done relative to the "Red Hen controversy."

In regard to the Red Hen controversy, a local paper can expand the public square and enhance our democratic process by not rushing to take sides but by reporting on what local restaurateurs should have done.

This suggestion from Tony as to the role of local newspapers relative to the "Red Hen controversy" raises the broader issue as to the role of journalism in the public square, a topic to which I now turn.

A New Paradigm for Journalism?

It is no doubt fair to say that "criticism" plays a major role in the current paradigm for journalism. In commenting further on David Horsey's "insulting portrayal of Sanders' looks," Tony likens an exclusive preoccupation of journalists with criticism to tearing off "scabs."

You might defend the columnist by saying that his job is to go ugly on opponents. That columnists don't necessarily have any pretension to a commitment to civility or kindness. They are there to tear the scabs off. As a former editor of one of our best papers said to readers, don't consider us your friend. We are not your friend when we come reporting on you.

Tony allows that there may sometimes be room for such severe criticism, but "general support for such an approach" calls into question the journalist's "profession and credibility."

Well, maybe there are occasions for the stiletto. But a scholar or journalist enters into general support for that sort of approach at the peril to his or her profession and credibility.

As his bottom line, Tony calls into question the current "investigative journalism paradigm," which is based on an "oppositional model of journalism" and uses the "journalistic triad" of starting with "criticism," moving onto "objectivity," and concluding, hopefully, with "sympathy/empathy."

The old way of doing journalism is based on the idea that a journalist is the prosecutor and judge of the people being covered by the news media. It is rooted in the investigative journalism paradigm.

The usual method of journalists is to start with skepticism in order to arrive at an objective picture, then to add sympathy toward the end of the reporting process. Over time, the reporter's skepticism can harden into cynicism about their informants and, at worst, about life itself. The public, too, has become cynical about journalists. The public believes that journalists tactically fake sympathy at the beginning of the interviews in order to advance their reporting. So, it would appear that an important source of the distrust between the journalists and their public lays in the philosophy and training of modern journalists. Objectivity, investigation,

check on power, cultural criticism/war and snark are all
based on an oppositional model of journalism.

Each of these approaches is rooted in an attitude of
superiority and distance between the journalists and the
audience. Is it any surprise that an enterprise that starts with
a judgmental attitude creates hostility in its audience?

While valuing "investigative reporting," Tony proposes a new paradigm
for journalism that reverses the order of this journalistic triad" based on
his belief that "most reporting in democratic society should be rooted in a
concern for building social trust and community well-being."

While we also highly esteem investigative reporting, we
don't think it is the primary paradigm for journalism. Rather,
most reporting in democratic societies should be rooted in
a concern for building a healthy social trust and community
well-being. Journalism should flip the journalistic triad
and start with genuine sympathy and empathy, move to
objectivity, and then if called for, add criticism.

Tony offers a practical, radical suggestion for starting the implementation of this "reversed triad."

The reporter should start with an affirmation that the person
whom he or she is interviewing has a great story to tell about
his or her life or organization. That if communicated, the
story could enrich the whole community. This involves a
sympathy with the interviewee's life, hopes and struggles
and an empathy so that you can almost feel the other's
mindset in your mind. As one goes through the process of
objectively weighing the value of the claims, a journalist
may discern a need for skepticism.

Tony reports that his own current journalism ventures seek to implement this new paradigm for doing journalism and, after some initial
hesitation, some of his critics "are won over."

Our journalists at *A Journey Through NYC Religions* have
already presented 'sympathetic objectively' to a number of

journalism schools and gatherings of editors and journalists. The typical reaction is 'that's not journalism' (by the well-known writer at a national news weekly) or 'that's not what I learned in journalism school.' However, upon further reflection, they have found that the critics are won over. A former editor at a big city newspaper confessed, 'It was caring for the community that was why I originally went into journalism.' This was the motivating reason for many of his colleagues. Sympathetic objectivity gives them a paradigm and language that fits their original hopes.

Tony concludes that this new paradigm for doing journalism "seems consistent with what Mark does in 'helping students develop virtues associated with critical and charitable engagement.'"

But Mark disagrees with Tony's proposal for a "sequential" triad. Based on his assumption that "the first task of journalists is to inform," Mark says that this task demands "accuracy," which suggests that "empathy and criticism ought to grow together rather than occur serially."

> ... Tony writes, 'Journalism should flip the journalistic triad and start with genuine sympathy and empathy, move to objectivity, and then if called for, add criticism.' I begin with a question: Why treat empathy, objectivity, and criticism sequentially (and the third, potentially, optionally)? Bypassing the conceptual cul-de-sac of questions about the possibility of objectivity, it seems to me that the first task of journalists is to inform. This task is so vital in democracies that the nation's founders enshrined freedom of the press in the First Amendment right after the freedoms of religion and speech. That task mandates accuracy. And giving accurate accounts of events and, especially, perspectives, involves both being empathetic enough to understand those perspectives and critical enough to place them in context for readers. Said differently, empathy and criticism ought to grow together rather than occur serially: We assess best when we understand well and we understand well when we have delved deeply and

critically. To return to the wisdom of Tony's first post, being
accurate is how the press expresses neighbor-love.

For what it may or may not be worth, my personal reflections on this
disagreement between Tony and Mark regarding the "journalistic triad"
are as follows, not based on any direct experience in journalism, but based
on my own attempts, not always successful, to balance criticism and empathy in dealing with college faculty as their "boss" (chief academic officer).
I have found that it is generally not best to start any conversation with
criticism. I always tried to start with some valid positive affirmation of the
person who deserved criticism, as a way to "ease into" (set the stage for)
the needed words of criticism. But although I started my conversations
that way, I seldom followed a rigid "three-step" sequence, since the conversation often moved in unexpected directions and I had to improvise.

Higher Education as a Crucible

To set a context for consideration of the limits, if any, on civil discourse
and free speech on college campuses, a much debated topic these days,
I note Tony's reminder that the teachings of Jesus about neighbor-love
demand that we give a voice to the "least of those among us," which Tony
compellingly describes as "making space for the bruised reeds."

> Jesus said that how we treat the least of the people among us,
> the weakest, the most bruised and the man or woman most
> far down in society, is a test of our goodness. So in a debate,
> we always need to keep in the forefront of our mind who
> are the least. More toleration and mercy goes to the man or
> woman furthest down, and the least allowance for public
> discourse mistakes go to the elites. This rule of thumb may
> force us to notice actors among us who need more space to
> speak and to learn how to speak up.

Who are the "least among us" on college campuses? Tony asserts that
"on most college campuses, the people least represented in the power
structures and the professorate are the political and religious conservatives," suggesting that "this means that we need to increase their numbers

and to give them proportionally more leeway in campus debates" while acknowledging that "In the few predominately conservative campuses, the Liberals need similar affirmative action."

Tony suggests that for either type of campus (predominately Liberal or predominately Conservative), "the campus minorities need a little helping hand with 'safe spaces' to tell their stories and learn how to participate in campus public affairs," adding that "the principle of not bruising the weakest is to make sure that everyone has space to speak and learn how to speak in the public square whether it is the small venue of a classroom or a big one like a town hall meeting."

However, Tony suggests that the problem with this idea of creating "safe spaces" for campus minorities, whoever they may be, is that "loudmouth Liberals and Conservatives dominate the discussions so that the more soft-spoken and less aggressive students and professors have little voice."

Mark has a different point of view than Tony on the dynamics of conversation on college campuses, no doubt reflecting his exposure to "incivility" on the part of his "Conservative" student peers in seminary, which motivated his "move toward liberal perspectives."[28] He describes his seminary experience as follows:

> ... the more I talked with my fellow conservatives, the more I came to see them as ... well, ... as real (*insert appropriate vulgar epithet here*). In private, they spoke belittlingly of many of our fellow students and condemningly of some of our more vulnerable classmates. In public, they seemed to revel in proving others wrong. In worship, their prayers sounded pharisaical. And they weren't above being sneaky

---

28 As an interesting aside, Mark describes how his movement toward "liberal perspectives" involved his embracing both/and positions rather than either/or positions. For example, he says that "I still believe in the power of free markets to solve economic problems—though now I also recognize the need for regulations and government resources to deal with the uneven distribution of the negative effects of free market solutions. I still believe in limited government—though I don't think that "limited government" and "small government" are the same things and think those who spend their energies attempting to shrink government have a dangerously anarchic sensibility. I still believe in personal responsibility—though I see how unjust social structures can inhibit the development of personal responsibility and access to power can be used to escape personal responsibility. I still believe in a strong defense—though perhaps we might only spend as much as the next five countries combined? And I still don't like paying taxes—though I'm learning to see how many ways those taxes make my comfort possible and other peoples' lives more possible.

or disingenuous in order to get their way on things ...
Cruelty may not have been at the center of that conservative
world but it rarely seemed wholly absent. The more I was
around my Conservative colleagues, the less I wanted to be
like them. And the less I wanted to be like them, the more
open I was to hearing other perspectives. As I became better
able to hear those perspectives, I was increasingly changed
by them.

Mark adds a qualifier that "I am not saying that my story is the case
everywhere. Nor am I saying that Liberals couldn't be (*repeat above vulgar
epithet*) themselves." His point, in addition to noting how this incivility
on the part of conservative students "motivated his move toward liberal
perspectives," is that "academic institutions have complex and fluid ecol-
ogies in which there are many forces at work." But he also notes that his
seminary experience shaped his current classroom practice, where "my
classrooms are not meant to be comfortable spaces and certainly not safe
spaces," reflecting his conviction that "higher education" ought to be a
"crucible." That will take some explanation.

Mark's punch line about higher education is that "each year during
commencement exercises, the most disparaging thing that my colleagues
and I can say about a new graduate is, "He/she went through unscathed."
He arrives at that conclusion in the following way:

As a card-carrying member of the Liberal academy, I value,
above almost all other things, the pursuit of truth and
the passing along of wisdom. When I teach, I do not care
whether my students agree with me. Not only do I try to
reserve revealing my perspectives until asked (preferably at
the end of a discussion), but I'm an ethicist: I argue for a
living and like doing so. I do care—a great deal—that my
students come to understand things in greater complexity
and with an ear to a wider range of perspectives. I ask them
to question old verities. To argue from perspectives they do
not hold. To name strengths and weaknesses in their own
arguments. To recognize the incompleteness of their own
understandings and identities. To attend to the complex

movements and poolings of various forms of power and the way power both distorts and makes advancement possible. To see doubt as a spiritual discipline. To recognize that truth isn't determined by vote. My classrooms are not meant to be comfortable spaces and certainly not safe spaces.

Mark observes that "some Conservatives" as well as "some Liberals" find his "classroom environment troubling." But he adds the crucial observation that neither his "Conservative" students nor his "Liberal" students report that they are "being singled out or persecuted for the positions they hold."

Mark notes that, "None of this is to say that 'loudmouth Liberals and Conservatives' are not a problem in the academy nor to disagree with the idea that *everyone* has the obligation to love the neighbors they have as well as the colleagues they like. The rules of civility still apply."

But "it is to say the only site I can think of where there is a greater likelihood of individual transformation, where one must negotiate more contending forces pushing against you, and where there is closer attention to the potential for growth and the reshaping of relationships than the academy is the birth canal. Those of us who teach at institutions of higher education think this is a good thing: It shapes personal character, it builds social resilience and it sustains a thoughtful citizenry. Those of us who teach in institutions of higher theological education think this is a faithful thing: It reinforces the spiritual practices through which our students work out their own salvation with fear and trembling as God works in them (Philippians 2:12). All the more reason to emphasize both civility and free speech."

Here is my attempt to make coherent sense out of the somewhat differing reflections from Tony and Mark as to what should take place on college campuses relative to civil discourse and free speech, factoring in Mark's earlier reflections on the "restraints" that civility calls for and their agreement that Christians ought to practice "neighbor-love" in all that they do.

Everyone on a college campus ought to be able to express his/her beliefs on any issue, within the boundaries proposed by Mark that "restricts or prohibits speech" used to incite violence, silence critics or foster tribalism (granting that it takes the wisdom of Solomon to reach judgments as to when such destructive outcomes are likely to occur).[29] But the expectation for "neighbor-love" requires that you go beyond "negative restraints" by demonstrating respect and love for a person who disagrees with you by providing a welcoming space for him/her to express a contrary point of view.

But, a perceptive reader may ask: Isn't there a contradiction between Mark saying that his classrooms are "certainly not safe spaces" and the premise behind this entire book that providing a "safe and welcoming space" for disagreement is a deep expression of neighbor-love? I don't think so because I believe Mark and I are using the words "safe space" in different ways. If what you mean by a "safe" classroom is that you will not be challenged to critically examine your beliefs, then neither Mark nor I believe that a college classroom ought to be a "safe space." But, if what you mean by a "safe" classroom is that you will not be silenced because you hold to beliefs that represent a minority perspective, then both Mark and I believe that a college classroom ought to be a "safe space."

Are We Only Talking to People Who Already Agree With Us?

I close this chapter, almost, with a legitimate concern that Mark expresses about his month long conversation with Tony, which, I believe can be expanded to a concern, possibly a fatal flaw, in this entire eCircle project.

> ... I want to offer two brief observations about the topic as it is being hosted on the 'Respectful Conversations' website. First, this conversation is very 'meta.' That Tony and I are attempting to have a conversation on the topic of respectful conversations on a website called 'Respectful

29 I recognize that many would argue that an institution of higher education can place "restraints" on free speech that reflect particular institutional commitments, as in the case of "evangelical Christian colleges," like the four colleges at which I served. To consider that argument would take far beyond the scope of this book. My own reflections on that topic can be found in "Evangelicalism and Higher Education" in Heie, A Future, 108-134. Suffice it to say here that if I could start my own evangelical Christian college, which I will probably not be able to do (thankfully, my critics would say), I would limit the college-wide institutional commitment to, "We all aspire to be followers of Jesus," allowing for wide-ranging respectful conversations about what that may mean relative to any issue.

Conversations' is so reflexive as to feel vaguely hall-of-mirrors like … The result, I fear, is that the types of people that will read, (hopefully) appreciate, and (helpfully) pass along the writing that Tony and I are doing are likely to be the types of people who like the po-mo sensibilities involved in such reflexivity, appreciate attempts to promote respectful conversations, and therein reveal that they share values that overlap with Tony's and mine. The danger in this is that far from expanding the range and significance of civil public discourse, the effect of our writings actually manifests as a symptom of the problems we want to address: that we're feeding the energies and funding the perspectives of our tribe(s) rather than expanding the conversation to reach new people with other perspectives. That I'm getting ready to post my second essay and nobody has posted a comment thus far in response to either Tony's or my first essays is at least one piece of evidence in support of this problem.

This concern needs to be seriously addressed. It fits with the failure of some of my other attempts to orchestrate respectful conversations among Christians who have strong disagreements about contentious issues.

In a nutshell, I have found it to be extremely difficult to get Christians who disagree about contentious issues in the same room together, or on the same website. So many Christians are so convinced that they and their "tribe" (those who already agree with them) already know "God's truth about the issue at hand" (allowing no room for the possibility that they "may be wrong") that they see no point in talking to those who disagree with them (beyond, possibly, trying to coerce others to agree with them).

So, what to do? My own modest attempt is to use my website and the books that emerge from my eCircles to model "respectful conversations" among those Christians who disagree, with the hope and prayer that readers will see that "it can be done," and that when it is done, some progress can be made toward finding some common ground that gains a better approximation to the "truth" of the matter, as only God fully understands that truth.

But I realize that those who are convinced that they already know "God's truth" about the issue at hand may not have the slightest interest in what I am trying to do. My only hope is that others can convince them that "they are not God"—that the God-given human condition is that all of us are finite and fallible. Therefore, there are many things about which we may be "wrong"; opening up the possibility that we can learn from those who disagree with us if we are willing to engage them in respectful conversation.

But, here is a closing reflection on Mark's legitimate concern. I think it is fair to say that Tony and Mark did not have a lot of significant disagreements about the topic at hand, and that fact, combined with the dearth of comments from readers, means that this particular month long conversation did not reflect the diversity of perspectives that Christians hold about the limits, if any, on civil discourse and free speech. But remember that I envision each of my month long conversations (some of which revealed many stark disagreements) to be only the "beginning," not the "end," of a series of ongoing conversations about the topic at hand. And I believe that the rich exchange between Tony and Mark has laid a good foundation for such ongoing conversations, that will, hopefully, include more dissident points of view. It appears to me that Mark shares this hope when he says the following after his and Tony's final third postings: "I suspect that these third essays would make excellent starting points rather than conclusions."

A Big Question Yet to Be Addressed

As with any good conversation, the exchange between Mark and Tony reported in this chapter may leave the reader with a host of new unanswered questions, which, again, beg for ongoing conversation. After setting a context, I will note one such unanswered question.

Using my own words, I think it is fair to say that both Mark and Tony agree on a two-pronged approach relative to civil discourse and free speech that reflects their commitments to the Christian faith. They support the constitutionally guaranteed right to "free speech," but recognize that this "right" is not without boundaries. Certain "restraints" must be placed on "free speech" to enable all citizens in a democratic society (Christians and everyone else) to "have a voice" on an "even playing field."

But there is a second prong to which Mark and Tony give even greater emphasis, the call for Christians (at least) to live faithful to the "Christian vision" by expressing "neighbor-love" in their engagements with all fellow citizens, which goes far beyond only living within "restraints" on free speech that are needed to give everyone a "voice." (Remembering, again, that these two prongs are not mutually exclusive.)

Given that context, the looming unanswered question is: *Who in our pluralistic society decides on public laws and policies relative to civil discourse and free speech?*

Responding to this question here would take us too far afield. But here are a few considerations that I believe need to be included in this future conversation. (I do not speak for Mark or Tony.) First, we should not assume that every American citizen embraces the teachings of Jesus (and other great religious leaders) regarding the need to love our neighbors.

Second, in our pluralistic society, Christians (and other religious folks) should not seek to impose their "Christian vision" (or other "religious vision") on those citizens who do not share that vision.

Having said that, however, I believe that some of the values that underlie civil discourse and a properly restrained free speech, such as the quest for truth, humility, concern for the well-being of others, and, yes, love, are "human values" (not just values embraced by Christians and other religious folks). Therefore, on an "even playing field" of democratic discourse, where "everyone has a voice," we should engage in respectful conversations about establishing appropriate public laws and policies relative to civil discourse and free speech.

Obviously, the above preliminary reflections beg for ongoing conversation.

4

A Comprehensive Call for Political Activism

THIS CHAPTER DEALS with the foundational question of the very meaning of the word "politics." When is one engaged in political activity? Harry Boyte, who engages Jim Skillen in conversation about this subtopic, calls for a reframing of the scope of political engagement.

> I argue the need to reframe politics by shifting the center of politics, from politicians and parties at the center to citizens at the center.

Harry presents us with an either/or choice as to the "center" of politics: Either focus on "politicians and [political] parties," or focus on "citizens." I will eventually argue that this is a false binary choice (it is both/and, not either/or). But I first need to address the confusion that can arise from the fact that Harry and Jim use the word "citizen" in different ways. It will be difficult to sort through the agreements and disagreements that Harry and Jim have as to the nature of political activism without first clarifying the differing ways in which they use the word "citizen." This illustrates the obvious, albeit, often neglected point that no conversation will get very far if the conversation partners are using the same word(s) in differing ways.

When Is One Acting as a "Citizen"?

Harry's view as to what it means to act as a citizen is succinctly stated as follows:

> Citizen politics is citizen-centered, not state-centered. It recognizes the importance of elections and constructive roles of government, but the focus is not on 'governing well', Heie's emphasis, which puts politicians at the center.

Note that Harry acknowledges the "importance of elections and constructive roles of government" which allows a role for "politicians and parties" (what he calls a "state-centered" role). But, he seems to say that when persons are carrying out this "state-centered" role, they are not doing so as "citizens." Rather they are acting as "citizens" only when they carry out non-governmental roles.

Note also that Harry refers back to the initial disagreement that Greg Williams and I had, reported in Chapter 2, about what it means to do politics; my initial view being that to do politics means to govern well by seeking common ground for the common good (the responsibility of politicians and political parties) and Greg's broader view (which I eventually embraced) being that doing politics also involves seeking to forge a common life together in the midst of a lack of agreement as to a common good (which in the terminology of this chapter includes both the responsibilities of politicians and political parties and what Harry calls "citizen politics").

Jim's criticism of Harry's view on what it means to act as a citizen is that he is "using the word 'citizen' in a broad and undifferentiated way" that does not adequately distinguish between the many differing roles and responsibilities that persons carry out, both within government and outside of government. In Jim's own words:

> I think the way you [Harry] have addressed the question of 'what citizens are citizens of' is too undifferentiated. In other words, *what I take from your comments is that citizens are citizens of society in general.* In my view, that doesn't sufficiently take into account the distinctions among social institutions and organizations, and it doesn't clarify

the relation of American citizens to the constitutions and governments of the states and the United States.

Jim elaborates further:

> ... in distinction from the argument for electoral and governing reforms, the case I am making for recognizing the differentiated identities and responsibilities of families, corporations, voluntary associations, and many other types of institutions and organizations is precisely to take into account important human responsibilities that are *not* governmental and that entail different kinds of agency. My reason for **not wanting to use the word "citizen" when referring to the exercise of those other social responsibilities** is that doing so hides from view or dissolves the differences among them, doing injustice to the rich diversity of human capabilities and agencies (emphasis mine).

> ... families, schools, businesses, churches, hospitals, the media and many other such institutions and organizations should *not*, in my view, be identified as *parts* of the political whole. Instead, those arenas of human responsibility have their own irreducible identities and should not be thought of as *parts* of a polity. We can speak of parents and children as *parts* of a *family whole*. And we can speak of trustees, administrators, professors, students and supporting staff as *parts* of a *university whole*. That's why **I believe it's a mistake to refer to the members of any of these non-political institutions or organizations as functioning in their capacity as *citizens***, because that word does not get at the distinctive kind of responsibility that is exercised by parents and children or by professors and students (emphasis mine).

In summary, Harry wishes to reserve the word "citizen" for when persons act politically though non-governmental organizations, while Jim wishes to reserve the word "citizen" for when persons act politically through governmental organizations (which he describes as involvement in "legislative, executive or judicial … machinery," which, I would add, can take place at the local, state or national levels). This difference as to the meaning of "citizen" presents a challenge as one seeks to identify areas of agreement and disagreement in their various electronic postings. In what follows in this chapter, a reader must be mindful of this difference when reading direct quotes. In my commentary, I will avoid use of the word "citizen" in the following way.

Using the words "political activity" in the broad sense of "seeking to forge a common life together," I will distinguish between **governmental** *political activity* and **non-governmental** *political activity*, laying bare my grasp of the agreements and disagreements that Harry and Jim have in these two categories. As you work through the complexities of what follows, keep in mind that I am aiming for a comprehensive view of political activities that embraces both "non-governmental" political activities and "governmental" political activities.

Problems With a Technological Paradigm in Government and Elsewhere

Harry presents a scathing critique of the "technological paradigm" that appears to reign in governmental circles and elsewhere in contemporary American society.

> Today people in every group feel devalued, victimized, powerless and hopeless about making broader change. Such sense of diminishment and hopelessness grows from what Pope Francis calls 'the technocratic paradigm,' a way of thinking which privileges a narrow understanding of science and scientifically trained experts as the authoritative decision-makers and problem-solvers.

In elaborating on this problem in government, Harry draws on the perception of John Lukacs[30] that "in the 1950s America came to vastly *underestimate* people's capacities as it shifted from a democratic order to a bureaucratic state dominated by experts. Virtually every institution—the

30 Lukacs, *Outgrowing Democracy*.

media, schools, higher education, foundations, businesses embodied the pattern. Most people were undervalued." Harry faults excessive use of the "efficiency principle" that is "detached from the civic life of communities."

> Human diminishment is accelerating in the age of Big Data and Artificial Intelligence, whose promiscuous uses are justified by the efficiency principle, employed by professionals detached from the civic life of communities, aimed at reaching narrowly defined and usually unexamined goals faster and faster.

Harry asserts that this "technocratic paradigm also tends to dominate economic and political life. The economy accepts every advance in technology with a view to profit, without concern for its potentially negative impact on human beings."

Harry also asserts that the "technological paradigm" eviscerates non-governmental "mediating structures such as religious congregations, schools, union locals, local businesses and civic groups of all kinds" that are turned into service operations to customers and clients, leading to an "erosion of the civic fabric."

Finally, and possibly most devastating for "governmental political activity," Harry asserts, is that the "technological paradigm" leads to "Manichean politics," which "objectifies 'the enemy', radically erodes common citizenship, and communicates that politics is warfare," in which any issue is framed as "a struggle of heroes against villains." He illustrates his assertion with the observation that such Manichean politics leads to "political canvassing" methods similar to "selling encyclopedias."

> The efficiency creed has shaped conventional understandings and practices of politics in elections and citizen activism. In 1974, Citizens for a Better Environment invented the modern canvass powered by a formula. The canvass involves staff going door to door on an issue, raising money and collecting signatures. The formula identifies an enemy and defines the issue in reductionist, good-versus-evil terms. It is *efficient* because hatred and anger are relatively uncomplicated emotions to manipulate. 'We've discovered

how to sell progressive politics door to door, like selling encyclopedias,' was the boast.

"Public Love" as an Alternative to the Technological Paradigm

Harry's proposal

To address the perceived "devaluation" of persons under the technological paradigm, Harry proposes the need for a "nonviolent philosophy of 'public love'" that is centered on the "needs, values and aspirations of citizens." While acknowledging the need to "democratize government," Harry focuses on the need to "democratize, schools, colleges, health settings, professions." This proposed focus is based on his own extensive experience in community organizing, including "experiences … in the freedom movement of the 1960s, working for Martin Luther King's organization."

Harry interprets the teachings of Pope Francis in *Laudato Si*[31] as affirming that "humans [are] … meaning-makers and storytellers, not reducible to the categories of the sciences," Harry notes the "*limits* of scientific and technological modes of thought," proposing that, rather than prioritizing "informational approaches for dealing with human problems" ("Big Data"), we need to take "relational and cultural approaches" to addressing human problems.

Harry, like Gregory Williams (see Chapter 2) calls for "free spaces" where "powerless groups develop civic agency" ("settings where people have room to self-organize, to develop intellectual life, and to learn relational and political skills"). But Harry questions Greg's focus on such free spaces being "resistance spaces."

It is important to note Harry's commitment to a "nonviolent approach" to the agency of non-governmental groups, as exemplified by Mahatma Gandhi and Martin Luther King Jr. Drawing on the writing of King,[32] Harry especially notes the positive effect that the "nonviolent approach" has on "those committed to it" and the way in which nonviolence is an expression of love to "opponents."

---

31 Pope Francis, *Laudato Si.*
32 King Jr., *Stride Toward Freedom.*

'The nonviolent approach ... first does something to the hearts and souls of those committed to it,' he [King] said. 'It gives them new self-respect. It calls up resources of strength and courage they did not know they had.'

King argued for seeking to understand opponents, not to defeat or humiliate them and to separate the sin from the sinner. He insisted that nonviolence is a kind of love aiming at 'a neighborly concern for others,' whether friend or enemy, recognizing their aspiration 'for belonging to the best in the human family.'

Such expressions of public love add a third dimension to the meaning of "respect for others" that I noted in Chapter 2 (drawing on the writing of Stephan Darwell). In Harry's own words:

Such love can be distinguished from *appraisal* respect, appreciation for achievements or character, or *recognition* respect, the intrinsic value of another human being, which Harold Heie espouses. Public love teaches a *possibility* respect for the *immense potential* of others including our enemies, for co-creative work that builds a world of shared material and cultural goods. Others have contributed to what I call public love.

Drawing on the experience of community organizing carried out by the Mexican-American community organization Communities Organized for Public Service (COPS) in San Antonio, Texas, Harry elaborates on his call for "co-creative work" as "public work" that focuses on the "civic possibilities of work and workplaces."

This [the work of COPS] required ... inventing a new concept of public life in which the point of action is not intimacy or personal friendship. Rather, public life is an arena for creating productive working relationships across radical differences among those who may dislike each other for the sake of building a more just and flourishing community. I see this concept as a great political invention and a way to operationalize public love for disadvantaged groups and others.

Over time, public work emerged ... as a framework which sees *citizens as co-creators, not simply voters and volunteers.* Power involves ideas and cultural dynamics, not only 'people and money.' Public work emphasizes civic possibilities of work and workplaces. It involves efforts by citizens working across differences to solve common problems, advance justice, and create community wealth, from schools, public spaces, libraries and local businesses to art, music and healthy lifestyles—a commonwealth of public usefulness and beauty.

Jim's response to Harry

Unsurprisingly, since Jim has already stressed the importance of "recognizing the differentiated identities and responsibilities of families and corporations, voluntary associations and many other types of [non-governmental] institutions and organizations," he asserts that he "couldn't agree more [with Harry] that practical training of citizens is urgently needed in the United States. To encourage people to realize that citizenship requires more than passive acquiescence in the decisions of others is crucial. To gain a sense of agency—the acceptance of active responsibility—in public life is necessary if there is to be a change in our society and culture toward greater humility, justice and public love."

Jim also notes that he is "sympathetic with many of the important influences that have shaped ... [Harry's] approach, such as the work of Jane Addams, various streams of community organizing, Catholic social teaching, theology of the people and more," adding his own appreciation for other "community organizing efforts" of the civil rights movement, the Industrial Areas Foundation, the Communities Organized for Public Service (COPS) in San Antonio and the work of Saul Alinsky, Ernesto Cortes and Paulo Freire.

Relative to the example of the civil rights movement that both Harry and Jim have cited, it is important to comment on Harry's reflection based on his own extensive personal experience within that movement.

As mentioned before, when I was a young man I was schooled by citizenship schools in the freedom movement. These prepared people to fight for 'first-class citizenship' across the South. They also gave people skills to build local communities, civic construction and conveyed the nonviolent philosophy of seeing often hidden potentials even in one's enemies, what can be called public love. People debated what citizen meant. A rough consensus usually emerged: *Citizenship wasn't mainly legal status, though all agreed on the importance of full civil and voting rights for black people.* The citizen is someone who solves problems, takes responsibility for building better communities, and spreads democracy as a way of life. This is conveyed in the song, 'We Are the Ones (We've Been Waiting For)' (italics mine).

Note carefully that although Harry focuses on the activities of non-governmental groups in the civil rights movement, he does agree on the "importance of full civil and voting rights for black people," which were brought about by means of governmental activity (legislative action). This is a hint at the viability of the comprehensive view of political activity for which I will be arguing.

However, Jim "wants to say both no and yes" to Harry's "criticism of the 'technological paradigm' as the root cause (or one of the chief causes) of the devaluation of people that causes them to feel powerless." Jim elaborates:

While I agree with you, Harry, that the technocratic paradigm of instrumental reason has infiltrated nearly every sector of society, including schools, businesses and government, I do not believe it is the chief culprit undermining the sense of agency on the part of citizens. The deeper root is the new faith—a widespread faith—that honors autonomous individuals in their quest for freedom by way of the mastery of nature.

That leads to my reason for wanting to say no to your critique of technocratic control and your proposal to push against it in order 'to transform the logic that gives primacy to efficient technological systems.' Isn't your focus, then, both too narrow and somewhat naïve in making the technocratic paradigm the lead antagonist of active citizenship. The Enlightenment's secular 'religion' of human freedom and mastery is not first of all the 'logic' of technocratic administration and control. It is deeper and more encompassing than that. Consequently, it seems to me, what is needed is to call adherents of that way of life—both those in control and those feeling powerless—to conversion, that is, to turn away from that way of life to a way of life that entails your 'nonviolent philosophy of public love.'

Jim illustrates his disagreement with Harry by addressing Harry's objection to "the consolidation of schools to gain greater efficiency," as follows:

I agree that there are many examples of the use of misplaced criteria in today's institutions, including schools, due to the adoption of technocratic norms of judgment. Think just of those who believe that if government were only run as a business enterprise it would be more efficient and less costly. However, the consolidation of schools in districts across the country, as I understand the process, was also motivated by declining populations in rural areas and by *the desire to integrate schools to achieve greater equality in education.* Those motives were very people-centered, leading members of democratically elected school boards, for example, to debate the issues intensely (italics mine).

You quote a research report approvingly that says the loss of a school [through consolidation] erodes a community's social and economic base—its sense of community, identity and democracy—and the loss permanently diminishes the community itself, sometimes to the verge of abandonment.' However, when communities were (and are) already eroding for economic and other social reasons, it was (is) not technocratic experts who manipulated passive citizens to agree to school closings. The motives and concerns of many parents, teachers and communities were *directed toward how to give their children greater schooling opportunities, and/ or to try to overcome racially segregated neighborhoods and schools*, and/or to build a sense of community in anonymous suburbia by means of the schools. I am not now advocating the consolidation of schools without qualification, and there have been many failures in public policies and education programs. You are right, in my opinion, about some of those failures. But I am simply calling for attention to the complex diversity of motives, institutional aims, and inter-institutional networks that come into play in public governance at local, state and federal levels (italics mine).

It is important to note that the italicized portions of the above quotes from Jim point to the need for political activism to go beyond equipping non-governmental groups for action. The tasks of "integrating schools to achieve greater equality in education," "providing children with greater schooling opportunities" and "overcoming racially segregated neighborhoods and schools" cannot be accomplished solely by the actions of non-governmental groups. Appropriate governmental initiatives will have to be taken to realize these laudable goals. The fact that Harry does not seem to allow significant room for such governmental initiatives leads Jim to pose some penetrating questions for Harry.

What criteria for good government and public administration do you want to encourage 'citizens' to adopt? What kind of free spaces are needed that don't exist now? Aren't families and schools and churches and associations of activists such places? Which authority should guarantee the openness of free spaces? Is it government, the courts and the First Amendment, churches, colleges or voluntary associations?

Do you have a normative idea of a polity? For example, when you speak of nonviolence, do you intend that force should not be used even by governments? Or do you mean only that citizen movements for political change should act nonviolently and work for a government that uses its force accountably, under law, to overcome oppression like slavery and to protect the innocent? Is there anything about the design of our Constitution—its federal structure, system of representation, or something else—you encourage citizens to try to change?

Therefore, in addition to (not in place of) the political activism of non-governmental groups to which Harry calls us, which Jim also embraces, Jim is proposing that a comprehensive view of political activism must also include a legitimate role for government (politicians and political parties) in fostering the well-being of communities. We now turn to what Jim considers that legitimate role of government to be, starting with his perceptions of the current problems with governmental initiatives.

Current Problems With Government

Jim notes the ambivalence that Christians in America have about the role of that aspect of politics carried out by governmental entities: "For some Christians, politics is the devil's playground. For others it's the means of protecting life, liberty and property, and in some circles a vehicle for promoting policies to help those in need." He traces at least some of that ambivalence to their being "two major ideals of the nation in play and they are at odds with one another in a curiously interdependent way." The first is the "founding ideal" of "America as God's chosen people," which morphed into the ideal of America being an "exceptional nation."

> The ideal I first want to introduce was the founding ideal that remained dominant until early in the 20th century. This was the nation of white Anglo-Saxon Protestants (WASPs) united in their covenant with the god who led them to this promised land. The nation in this inspiring myth is an Americanized derivation of Israel's exodus story (originating with the New England Puritans). A new Israel was led across

the Atlantic Red Sea, through the wilderness, and into the new promised land.

By the mid-20th century, the ideal of America as God's chosen people was boiling down, for wider secular appeal, to the 'exceptional nation', still considered unique among all nations. The nature of that ideal and its disconnect from the processes of governance helps to explain our odd American divide between 'loving America' and 'belittling government'. Ronald Reagan promised in campaign speeches to get *government* off the backs of the people in order to save the *nation*. Government, especially too much of it, threatens individual and market freedoms. So most white Americans love the nation but distrust (and in some quarters even hate) government.

The second ideal that Jim points to is "the African-American ideal of a free, equal and all-inclusive nation dependent on a strong federal government and judicial system to act on the promise of the Declaration of Independence that all humans are created equal." Jim describes the genesis of this ideal as follows.

There is a second ideal of the nation little noticed by most Americans until around the end of World War II, though anyone paying attention to what led up to the Civil War and followed from it would be aware of it. This American ideal also derived from the biblical exodus story and began to take shape long before 1776, emerging from the songs of slaves praying for God to free them from their pharaoh— the white slave master. They too looked ahead to freedom in a promised land, but they were not looking for an exit from this land in order to cross the sea to another place. Rather, they wanted to become full and free participants right where they were, within America. But, of course, for them to be free would require elimination of the slave master's right to own human property and inclusion of non-white people in all the privileges of WASP-controlled America.

Jim suggests that it is the tension between these two ideals that "makes cooperative governance nearly impossible."

> ... to the degree that these two exodus stories are mutually exclusive, they pit Americans against one another in all-or-nothing conflict that makes cooperative governance nearly impossible. This is why I would argue that most of our battles over government policies and judicial cases are at root battles over the ideal of America. They are battles for monopoly control of the power to establish the true ideal of the nation to the exclusion of all un-American ideals.

Jim asserts that this near impossibility of "cooperative governance" is fundamentally due to lack of consensus in responding to the question "**What** do governments govern?"

> *One of the central problems underlying American politics and government is that the **what** is undefined or overlooked.* For this reason, I believe: 1) the American political system is not functioning well; 2) making a case for what should be done to overcome the malfunctions is very difficult; and 3) charting a course for constructive Christian political engagement is almost impossible.
>
> The **what** to which I am referring is the polity, the public thing (a *res publica*), the political community, which is not a family thing, or an educational institution, or a business corporation, or a faith community. It might more specifically be called a public-legal community whose members are related to one another as 'citizens-in-law,' not as members of a family, or a university, or a business or a church. Citizens-in-law and their government together constitute a polity.

Jim adds that "A major reason why the **what** of our American polity remains largely undefined or overlooked is the understanding or doctrine of governance that controls our thinking and action," which is the "liberal tradition."

There is no doubt that an American federal republic (*res publica*) exists. But the Liberal tradition of ideas and beliefs, which undergirds the entire spectrum from Conservative to Liberal, from Right to Left, obscures or denies the republic's identity as a *community* of obligations in its own right. The presupposition of liberalism is that the United States is the product of a contract among free individuals who have agreed to hire a government to protect their lives, freedom and property. The government, in this view, is a means to the end of individual freedom, a servant of individuals who are the government's originating sovereigns. The contracting individuals do not recognize that as citizens in relation to a government that has the power to make and enforce laws they are bound together as a public-legal *community* that is quite different than a private contractual relationship.

Jim notes that the problems created by the "liberal tradition" exist at both ends of that ideological spectrum.

At the far right of this ideological spectrum libertarians believe that since the autonomy of the contracting individuals is the first principle of government, a government that collects taxes and acts for any purpose other than to protect the life, freedom and property of free individuals is engaged in theft and overreach. At the far left of the spectrum the first principle of government is to do whatever its sovereign creators want it to do to enhance their lives and try to ensure equal freedom for all individuals. Politics, then, consists of bargaining and brokering among contracting individuals to achieve what each one wants.

Jim adds to his critique of the "liberal tradition" by noting that it leads to our "representative legislators" becoming "little more than interest group brokers," resulting in the devastating result that, "Today there is, for all practical purposes, no common legislative, executive or judicial focus of attention on the well-being and justice of the national polity as a whole."

By this time in American history, life, freedom, property and private contracts have expanded to include everything from stock ownership to the right to define one's gender, from Social Security income to a corporation's right to act as a legal person; from a rancher's grazing rights on public land to food stamps and crop price supports; from restrictions on polluting industries to taxes on property, consumption and income. In a political system shaped by liberalism we should not be surprised to find that our representative legislators (those elected to stand in for sovereign individuals) have become little more than interest-group brokers. Nor should we be surprised that our civic discourse is scattered incoherently in all directions as various groups of individuals try to advance innumerable causes and desires. The words spoken and the laws passed have less and less meaning as individuals and government alike descend into confusion, frustration, paralysis and the feeling of powerlessness. Today there is, for all practical purposes, no common legislative, executive or judicial focus of attention on the well-being and justice of the national polity as a whole. The words 'polity,' 'political community,' 'republic,' 'commons,' 'public trust' are seldom used. There is no **what** there.

To this grim portrait of the problems with our current system of government, Jim adds two additional problems: constitutional inadequacy and electoral representation.

Constitutional inadequacy: Jim suggests that a problem with the Constitution of the United States is that it "was built on the presumed priority of state government and states' rights."

The U.S. Constitution was built on the presumed priority of state governments and states' rights. The federal system was constructed from the bottom up, not from the top down. The founders, wanting maximum autonomy for the states, granted to the federal government only two major responsibilities: defense and the regulation of interstate commerce. Responsibilities for the governance of schooling, corporations, family life, health, transportation, welfare and much more were, and still are, held by the states. The federal government was granted no authority to initiate legislation or take executive action in any of those areas.

As a result, with the exception of the "Bill of Rights," there is inadequate recognition in the Constitution "of the fact that the United States has become a national polity and is no longer merely a coalition of state polities."

> Today, few of us would deny the fact that the United States has become a national polity and is no longer merely a coalition of state polities. Yet the Constitution continues to operate on its founding purpose of serving state polities, defending the nation from foreign enemies, and regulating interstate commerce. The one exception to that fact was (is) the Bill of Rights, which was included to protect free individuals in all states from *federal government* overreach.

However, even "the Bill of Rights was not intended to encourage direct federal governance of a national polity" and "with amendments added to the Constitution after the Civil War, those civil rights became enforceable on the states by the federal judicial system. That is why today a high percentage of *state and national* struggles over social, economic, familial, educational and other matters lead to legal battles over civil rights that often reach the Supreme Court."

Electoral representation: Jim asserts that "another important element contributing to the inadequacy of the Constitution is its system of representation for Congress (both House and Senate) and the office of the president."

> Because the federal government was created to serve the states, not to govern a national polity, our system of elected representatives is designed to represent the states. Every elected representative to the House of Representatives and the Senate is chosen by local elections in each state. We

have no representatives or senators elected by a nationwide electorate even though Congress is our national legislature.

Even the U.S. president is not elected directly by a nationwide vote but by an Electoral College made up of electors chosen from each state. That is why Donald Trump could lose by nearly three million votes to Hillary Clinton in the national popular vote yet still win the election in the Electoral College. As strange as it might sound, American citizens *as constituents of a national polity* have no opportunity to elect and hold accountable members of Congress and the president by a direct vote of the nationwide constituency. Consequently, what we witness in Washington is seldom a deliberative legislative and executive process but rather one of bargaining among state-dependent representatives whose first obligation is to the people in their states or smaller voting districts. In addition, when members of Congress work on legislation, they are typically bargaining with powerful national interest groups (bankers, farmers, businesses, labor unions, insurance companies, defense contractors and many, many more). Today, those interest groups have a far greater influence on most members of Congress than do the voters in their districts. This further helps to explain both the reduction of Congress to a collection of interest-group brokers and the growing sense of powerlessness among voters that is evident in low turnout for elections.

Addressing Current Problems With Government

Jim's proposal

Jim is not optimistic about the possibility of finding solutions to the severe problems he perceives relative to that aspect of politics carried out by government.

> I should state frankly here that I do not believe the changes necessary to address the critical conditions of American government and politics will be made. The liberal and civil-religious ideologies are too deeply rooted and the Constitution too highly prized to allow most citizens even to contemplate the fundamental reforms I recommend below. The American republic is, in my estimation, falling farther and farther away from being a healthy polity on its way to becoming an increasingly conflicted and unstable plutocracy. On its present course, concentrated wealth will gain increasing control of *government* while battles over competing ideals of the *nation* will continue to fuel culture wars. Our *res publica* will decline into little more than a market in goods and labor to the advantage of those who call the *governing* shots, and elections will function as sideshows of cultural conflict over the true identity of the *nation*.

However, even though Jim does not believe there are "quick fixes for our predicament," he does propose three recommendations as to what must eventually be done.

Conversion to a vision of the nation as a governed polity that reflects a "growing civic commitment to the work of building a shared public trust."

> The first change necessary for reform is a conversion at the deepest level of American political culture, conversion to a vision of the *nation* as a *governed* polity. American civil-religious nationalism must be displaced by a growing civic commitment to the work of building a shared public trust, a just republic. This will mean acceptance of a more modest understanding of what a nation can and should be, namely,

a civic community in which the diverse citizenry work to achieve and uphold a shared public trust. For the majority of citizens this will entail relinquishing the belief that the future of their lives and of the world depends on America being **No. 1** in the world and the model for all nations. For many Christians it will mean giving up the deeply held belief that the Christian way of life and the American way of life fit together hand-in-glove as God's light to the world.

Commitment to equitably balance multiple needs for the sake of a common good as a replacement for the dominant liberal ideology.

Closely related to the first change must come the replacement of our dominant liberal ideology with a publicly minded, public-commons understanding of politics and government. Without such a change, government will continue to be thought of as simply a means to an end of individual autonomy and economic, scientific and technological progress. A sound and stable polity must instead be a community whose aim is to equitably balance multiple needs and demands for the sake of the republic's common good. Without constitutional, governmental, and popular commitment to the priority of upholding a just polity, interest-group politics will continue to dominate and eventually bury any idea that government officials are supposed to be public servants committed to wise statesmanship for the common good.

Reforming the electoral system to make it possible for the federal government to "govern [the nation] directly."

The third change we need is a significant rewriting of the Constitution to make it fit for the governance of a nationwide polity. The governments of states and localities can certainly be retained, but the federal government must become representative of the nationwide political community and capable of governing it directly. To achieve the accountability under law of members of Congress and the president directly to American citizens, and to make possible the meaningful representation of all citizens in Congress, a reform of the electoral system is required. Elsewhere I have proposed a system of proportional representation for the House of Representatives that would eliminate all gerrymandering, help to build disciplined national parties, and subordinate interest groups to the parties so they can no longer fund candidates and directly lobby members of Congress.

In response to Jim's lack of optimism that his proposed solutions to the problems of "governance" in America, a reader asks, "What's the stumbling block?"—"What is it in your view that … hinders you [Jim] from an optimistic confidence that your three changes will be taken up by repenting Christians?" This reader resonates with Jim's suggestion that the hindrance may be that "for many Christians it [pushing for these three changes] will mean giving up the deeply held belief that the Christian way of life and the American way of life fit together hand-in-glove as God's light to the world." At the same time, this reader asks Jim, "Why have you not given up?" That is a good question that should be pondered by all Christians who have not "given up" on reforming government in our country.

Harry's response to Jim

Harry agrees with Jim that a "core problem with our politics" is "the liberal framework which holds individual freedom to be the ultimate goal of politics." But, Harry adds, "we have disagreements about the solutions."

My response to Harry (and Jim) is that as I read and reread their postings, their disagreements as to solutions to our political problems are not irreconcilable; they reflect differences in "priorities," not "mutually exclusive" approaches to doing politics. That this may be the case is even suggested by the following assertion from Harry.

> I agree with Jim Skillen that we need a revitalized sense of 'civic community,' but am convinced that this requires devolving authority and developing citizens' agency, *not mainly* cultivating support for a 'sound and stable polity whose aim is to equitably balance multiple needs and demands for the sake of the republic's common good,' as he puts it. Today people of every group feel hopeless about

redressing our mounting problems and reversing civic unraveling. Many feel devalued and victimized. Politicians and government are not going to fix this problem (italics mine).

The key words here are "not mainly." They suggest that Harry is not precluding efforts to reform government. But that should not be our "main" focus. He says this elsewhere when he "challenges the proposition that reform of public governance should be *the first priority*" (italics mine). He goes on to suggest that the reason that efforts to reform government should not be our "first priority" is that you cannot address what is "wrong with politics" without first addressing the prior question of what is "wrong with the civic culture," citing Barack Obama, Yuval Levin and David Brooks.

> Former President Barack Obama's new [Obama] foundation is founded on this alternative [to the proposition that 'reform of public governance is the first priority']: 'The moment we're in right now, politics is the tail and not the dog,' Obama argued in his speech[33] to the summit launching the foundation ... 'What's wrong with our politics is a reflection of something that's wrong with the civic culture, not just in the United States but around the world.' Conservatives like Yuval Levin and David Brooks share Obama's primary focus on culture. Naked Liberals of the Right and Left assume that if you give people freedom they will use it to care for their neighbors, to have civil conversations, to form opinions after examining the evidence,' wrote Brooks, 'Our Elites Still Don't Get It.'[34] But 'if you weaken family, faith, community and any sense of national obligation where is that social, emotional and moral formation supposed to come from?'

So, Harry is not discounting attempts to reform government. Rather, he is saying that before such changes can be effected, we must first address the deeper cultural problems that prevent non-governmental entities, like families, churches and communities, from breaking out of the prevalent individualistic "liberal framework" to embrace alternative ideals like

---

33 Dovere, "Obama."
34 Brooks, "Our Elites."

caring for one another. My view is that Harry's proposal for prioritization does not preclude simultaneous efforts on both fronts (it's both/and, not either/or) by Christians who sense differing callings that fit their particular gifts and abilities.

Harry supports his argument for the priority of fostering political activism on the part of non-governmental entities by pointing to two other biblical narratives that go beyond the exodus narrative that Jim has focused on, because "there are ... limits in the exodus narrative and its politics which lead people to look to 'particular persons' for rescue."

> I agree with Skillen that the exodus narrative has played an important role in Americans' self-understanding and that there are two contending variants. Co-existing with the concept of a nation shaped by WASP assumptions, which he calls 'an Americanized derivation of Israel's exodus story originating from New England Puritans,' the other exodus story involves 'the African-American ideal of a free, equal and inclusive nation,' linked to a strong federal government. The latter exodus narrative was an important thread of the freedom movement and I know its merits.

> But there are also limits in the exodus narrative and its politics which lead people to look to 'powerful particular persons' for rescue. As Marie Ström (full disclosure: my wife, as well as a public theologian) puts it, 'The "struggle against oppression" paradigm forms the basis of many Christian efforts to promote justice. It conveys the belief that salvation is not only about individual religious experience, but affects every aspect of life, including sociopolitical issues.' This narrative holds the danger of conceptualizing other problems in Manichean terms, 'as a fight of the innocent and the forces of good against the evil-doers.' It also relies on rescue by outside powers whether divine or human saviors like Moses.

Harry notes that there is a third relevant political narrative in the Bible, which he calls the "public work story" of Nehemiah.

There is another political narrative in the Bible. It can be called the public work story. The Nehemiah story, about the Jewish leader who led the Israeli people in the rebuilding of the walls of Jerusalem, is a striking example. Nehemiah held together a motley crew—40 different groups are named, including merchants, priests, governors, members of the perfume and goldsmiths' guilds and women. Nehemiah participated in the work himself. At one point he organized a great assembly to call to account nobles making excessive profit from the poor. As the Jewish people rebuilt their walls, they renewed their purpose and identity. The Nehemiah story has been an inspiration in recent decades for many minority, low income and working class communities seeking to revitalize their spirit of community as they 'rebuild the walls.'

Harry also suggests that a fourth relevant biblical narrative is the "wilderness narrative that comes after the exodus," which is a "great example of public works projects."

... as Marie Ström [says] ... 'Gradually the Israelites are formed into a people, with new institutions such as a decentralized system of governance and new systems of sacrifice and worship that demand the full participation of everyone.' The process is full of ambiguities and setbacks. 'During the wilderness journey, the Israelites oscillate between moments of obedience and constructive activity, and moments of disobedience and apostasy.' But the wilderness story is also full of great examples of public work projects, like building of the tabernacle. Men and women 'whose hearts made them willing' (Exodus 35: 29)—the text places special emphasis on the contributions of women— contributed their skills and resources for the construction of God's dwelling place and their own place of worship. Bezalel, the organizer of the work, was filled 'with the divine spirit, with skill, intelligence and knowledge in every kind of craft' (Exodus 35:31).

Harry shares Marie's report of how she "found in Africa that using the concept of democracy as the public work of the people in building communities and a democratic society transforms people's sense of themselves from victims to agents of change." In her own words, "The tremendous energy that animates these [biblical] narratives is exactly the same energy I saw in often the poorest of the poor, dehumanized by apartheid in South Africa, brutalized by civil war in Burundi and Mozambique, disillusioned by the failures of democracy in Zambia and Malawi, as they developed the skills, confidence and power to unleash their own innate capacities, access resources within their communities and beyond and work collaboratively with fellow citizens, government departments and other institutional partners."

In summary, Harry defines "public work" as follows:

> **Public work highlights citizens as builders of a common world, not simply voters, deliberators or consumers who take the common world as a given. Public work can be defined as self-organized efforts by a mix of people who create things, material or cultural, of lasting public value, determined by deliberation.**

Harry concludes that "the public work paradigm points to a new role for the church amidst the crisis in civic culture" (more about that later).

It's Both/And: Needing Jefferson and Madison

Jim is quite clear that he is not "pitting 'elected officials' over against 'the general citizenry,'" taking a both/and position that emphasizes "joint responsibility."

> ... you won't find me pitting 'elected officials' over against 'the general citizenry' ... My argument for a healthy polity emphasized the joint responsibility of citizens and government (or governments) that constitute any polity; never would I suggest that the 'building of a just republic' is independent of 'citizens' agency.'

In fact, Jim goes beyond "not pitting" the activities carried out by government "against" activities carried out by non-governmental groups to noting the "interdependence" of activities within these two realms.[35]

> ... the exercise of responsibilities in each institution will have a bearing on all of the others. Healthy child-rearing, good schooling, the development of entrepreneurial habits and more can all contribute to strong citizen agency [in governmental activities]. By the same token, government laws and agencies responsible to protect public health, regulate food and drugs, maintain a healthy environment, uphold open markets, protect the innocent and overcome oppression and much more—all of this should have a positive impact on families, schools, businesses, and so forth.

As reported above, Harry allows for governmental political activism, but he believes the main focus (the "first priority") should be on activism on the part of non-governmental groups like families, corporations and voluntary associations. My understanding of Jim's position, reflected in his work as founding director of the Center for Public Justice (CPJ), is that there is no "first priority": the responsibilities of "elected officials" and the "general citizenry" are equally important (and CPJ has gone to great lengths to describe this "differentiation" of responsibilities).

On this point, I personally concur with Jim's position.[36] For those readers who share my commitment to the Christian faith, my agreeing with Jim is based on my understanding of biblical teachings regarding the "Body of Christ."[37] God's redemptive purposes are fostered by the collective

---

35 Jim Skillen has written extensively on the relationship between government and non-governmental groups, based on the principles of "structural pluralism" and "confessional pluralism," summarized by Jim as follows: Structural pluralism refers to Government's constitutional obligation to recognize and do justice to the variety of non-governmental responsibilities that belong to humans by virtue of their created identities, which requires constitutional limits of governmental jurisdiction so that it does not subsume non-governmental institutions and associations under its direct authority; Confessional Pluralism refers to Government's constitutional obligation to protect with equal treatment under the law the variety of religious communities, recognizing that government's jurisdiction does not include the responsibility to determine "right religion." For elaboration, see Skillen, *Recharging*, 83-86 and Skillen, "The Bible and the State," 15-28.
36 In the interest of full disclosure, I should report that I have been affiliated with CPJ for many years, serving a term as chair of their board of trustees.
37 See I Corinthians 12.

activism of all Christians, with each Christian contributing according to his/her particular talents and gifts. Therefore, some Christians will be best suited to exercise their gifts in governmental circles; some will be best suited to be activists with non-governmental groups, and some will be well suited to do both—it is all needed. We should not judge one type of endeavor to be more or less important than the other.

My both/and position can be viewed as drawing on the respective foci of both Thomas Jefferson and James Madison—a comparison that both Harry and Jim address.

Harry draws heavily on Jefferson's focus on governance by "we the people."

> My ... view comes from the tradition of political thought which sees government as the *instrument* of 'the people.' The people, as Thomas Jefferson famously put it to William Jarvis in 1820, are the only 'safe depository of the ultimate powers of the society.' Jefferson was not naïve about the people. Like Madison, he saw people as usually narrowly self-interested. But he was convinced that if the people are 'not enlightened enough to exercise their control with wholesome discretion, the remedy is not to take it from them but to inform their discretion.'

Harry expresses concern that Jim's position is too Madisonian, based on Harry's perspective that "He [Madison] believed that elected officials, not the general citizenry, were the best guides for the nation, contrasting a 'republic,' which he championed, with a 'democracy,' which he thought both inferior and unworkable in a large society."

Jim demurs, saying "Madison is not my guide," elaborating as follows: "To whatever degree I can appreciate Madison's ideas of federated government, the constitutional arrangement established at the founding is, in my view, now out of date in important respects. The United States today has a nationwide citizenry and is no longer merely an association of state polities." Recall that the problem that Jim perceives with not adequately taking into account this "nationwide constituency" is that "our current system of representation ... [makes] it impossible for citizens to hold members of the House and Senate directly accountable to the nationwide citizenry."

Nevertheless, it appears to me that the both/and position for which I am advocating still has "shades of Madison" in that it goes beyond the "direct democracy" on which Jefferson focuses, calling for a significant appropriate role for "elected officials" to avoid potential abuses of "direct democracy."

Although the above may not do justice to disagreements that remain between Harry and Jim, the following observation from Harry at the end of their month long conversation suggests that their perspectives may be close enough to form the basis of a "political alliance."

> I appreciate the invitation to join this conversation over December, and in particular am pleased to have the opportunity to discover Jim Skillen and the work of the Center for Public Justice. His center shares with the public work approach and civic studies broadly a concern to sustain and enhance civic life, beyond the 'market versus state' forced choice which now dominates in public policy. Makings of a 'political' alliance!

Issues Needing Further Conversation

Although further conversation is called for relative to all of the above, there are two other particular areas that Harry and Jim briefly address that especially beg for ongoing conversation.

Science and science education

Harry asserts that in recent years, science has "shriveled" because scientific endeavors have been thought of as "value-free techniques."

> Science, as it developed in the last 60 years, has shriveled to the view that it produces 'the answers' to complex public problems through Big Data. ... This shriveling grows from a shift to the concept of science as value-free techniques.

In addition to the problem with assuming that scientific activity is value-free, Harry notes a problem with an assumed "norm of detachment" and a university bias "against public engagement," as revealed in interviews with "several dozen senior professors across colleges [in the University of Minnesota system] and disciplines."

> ... I interviewed several dozen senior professors across colleges and disciplines. We asked if they went into their fields with any desire for public impact. The question surfaced hidden discontents with the norms of detachment which hold 'value neutrality' to be constitutive of scholarly excellence. Many leaders in their fields told me that they would not be able even to discuss their discontents given the university biases against public engagement.

These problems result in a "missing action dimension in conventional academic life," as pointed to by Philip Nyden, co-chair of the American Sociological Association's Task Force on Public Sociology.[38]

> As he [Nyden] puts it, every sociology department has a course called 'social problems' but he hasn't found one with 'social solutions.' He says, 'Academics may be well trained in methodology and theory, but they are not always trained or experienced in ... the political process of bringing about change' ... [their] "problem-oriented" approach—which assumes that the community has a deficit—obscures that fact that *academic researchers themselves may have a deficit* that needs to be corrected by experienced community leaders and activists.

Harry's suggestion is that this "deficit" of scientists [relative to the "political process of bringing about change"] can best be overcome by "collaborative work" with non-scientists that will require "skills of relational action" that will require "learning respect for others' talents"; which he refers to as doing "civic science."

> Civic science constructively addresses the knowledge wars by stressing the need for multiple kinds of knowledge to meet the large challenges facing our nation and the world —climate, energy security, health care, a sustainable and just food system, income inequality, to mention a few.

---

38 Nyden, *Public Sociology.*

Civic science stresses the work of scientists as potentially democratic public work. ...

It [civic science] holds promise to overcome the misunderstanding between scientists and the general public. Scientists believe that their work is not valued by citizens who may have last encountered science in high school. Lay citizens often feel that scientists' approaches invalidate their experiences, condescend to their intelligence and neglect skills of relational action.

Civic science is a framework for transcending knowledge wars while producing knowledge that enhances collective capacities for effective action, what we call civic agency. ... People act in their capacity *as citizens*, prioritizing deliberative and collaborative work, learning respect for others' talents.

Harry's proposal for scientists to collaborate more with non-scientists in solving societal problems points to a deficit in the formal education of scientists. He cites the research of Erin Cech[39] indicating that the technocratic paradigm has had a negative effect on "professional preparation," especially for engineers.

... in 'Culture of Disengagement in Engineering Education,' published in *Science, Technology, and Human Values*, Erin Cech reports on a study of the impact of engineering education programs, ranging from MIT to Smith College. She finds that despite strong statements of the profession that engineers are 'to hold paramount the safety, health and welfare of the public in the performance of their professional duties,' in fact "students'" public welfare concerns *decline* significantly over the course of their engineering education. In her view, 'engineering education fosters a culture of disengagement that defines public welfare concerns as tangential to what it means to practice engineering.' She traces this culture to three invisible 'ideological pillars' including

39 Cech, "Culture of Disengagement."

the idea that engineering is apolitical; that assumption that
technical knowledge is far superior to 'soft' skills of human
interaction; and meritocratic models of success.

While my own formal education in engineering borders on being
ancient history (1953- 1963), my experience comports with the results of
Erin Cech's research. Despite the high quality of my training to "do engineering," I cannot recall any conversations in my engineering courses as
to potential desirable or undesirable effects on "public welfare" of what we
were highly trained to do. It appears that the "technological imperative"
was generally operative: Being capable of doing something is sufficient
reason for doing it (an imperative that I now reject).

The above barely scratches the surface relative to the education and
work of scientists. Further questions remain. For example, is science "value-neutral"? Consistent with the work of Thomas Kuhn,[40] I believe that
science is **not** value-neutral (every action that a human being takes is
informed by one or more value commitments). But others will disagree.
Much more conversation is obviously called for.

Civic ecclesiology

Harry levels a strong criticism at members of the clergy who cater to
their parishioners perceived needs as "consumers" rather than empowering them.

> Lay citizens are mostly treated as demanding consumers and
> needy clients by clergy and other professionals, who have
> been trained to 'help' and to 'rescue' but not to empower.

Drawing on the work of Marie Ström, Harry argues for an alternative
"civic ecclesiology" that empowers church members to "play an active
transformative role in the life of the church and society."

> ... rather than treating pastoral care as an end in itself, from
> the perspective of a civic ecclesiology caring for members is
> a way of assisting them to play an active, transformative role
> in the life of the church and society ... The goal is to develop

---

40 Kuhn, *Scientific Revolutions*.

an internal public sphere and a culture of agency that can be projected out into the world through hopeful work.

Her [Marie's] thesis makes a compelling case for the relevance of the role of congregations as centers for civic repair as well as social and economic justice in affluent societies like the U.S. where civic unraveling is a crucial concern. 'For the church and its citizens to begin to play this civic role requires a new way of thinking and acting,' she argues. 'It involves congregations becoming sites of democracy education and organized citizen action [and] a new language of citizenship to describe their work of co-creation in the world, skills to do this work well, and a new habit of mind: to choose hope over victimhood and despair, shifting from an exodus mentality [which looks for salvation from outside] to seeing themselves as people of the covenant.'

At first glance it may appear that Jim's view of the role of the "goal of the church" differs from Harry's vision. In Jim's own words:

… the goal of the church as a community of faith, I believe, should be to worship and glorify God and to strengthen members of the body of Christ so they can learn to practice more fully what it means to be Christ's disciples in the service of God and their neighbors. I don't believe the church has a primary responsibility to strengthen public governance. However, I do believe that the church and its congregations should be communities that encourage one another in following the way of the cross in the service of Christ. And that should mean the strengthening of members in the realization that they are servants of God and neighbors in all spheres and capacities of life. Members of churches are also family people, working people, consumers, artists, scientists, engineers, and more. And certainly they are also citizens. The primary responsibility for training citizens, therefore, as I see it, belongs to people, including Christians, in their capacity as citizens and public servants. And that activity requires distinctively political modes of organization and agency, not ecclesiastical, familial or academic modes of organization and agency.

Unpacking this lengthy quotation brings us back full circle to the differing ways in which Harry and Jim are using the word "citizen." But those differences should not camouflage the possibility that they are "on the same page" as to ecclesiology. That is my understanding, which I will now summarize in my own words.

Jim, like Harry, believes that church members should be "strengthened … in the realization that they are the servants of God and neighbors in all spheres and capacities of life" (which certainly includes "empowering" church members to carry out this public role and can be viewed as an important aspect of worshipping and glorifying God). The difference between Harry and Jim may only be in terminology, based on Jim's call (described above) to adequately "differentiate" between the responsibilities of "government" and the responsibilities of "non-governmental" groups, like families, corporations, *churches* and voluntary associations. In a nutshell, Jim wants to differentiate the role of "government" from the role of "churches" (and other non-governmental groups), reserving the words "citizen activism" for the role that Christians play in "government." But that does not preclude churches (and other non-governmental groups) from empowering its members for their public roles as "transformers of society" in churches and other non-governmental groups. In fact, Jim points us to the "interdependence" of the activities carried out in the "governmental" and "non-governmental" realms.

> … the exercise of responsibilities in each institution will have a bearing on all of the others. Healthy child rearing, good schooling, the development of entrepreneurial habits and more can all contribute to strong citizen agency [in governmental activities]. By the same token, government laws and agencies responsible to protect public health, regulate food and drugs, maintain a healthy environment, uphold open markets, protect the innocent and overcome oppression and much more—all of this should have a positive impact on families, schools, businesses and so forth.

So, my overarching conclusion is that Harry and Jim both see a valid role for Christians in attempting to transform society through both governmental and non-governmental activities (like church activities) despite apparent disagreements as to whether activity in one of these realms should be a "first priority" (my reading of Harry's perspective being that non-governmental action should be the "first priority"; with Jim saying that activities in both of these realms are equally important). Despite this apparent disagreement, both Harry and Jim extend to us a "comprehensive call for political activism," if one accepts the broad view of "politics" as including the attempt to forge a common life together in the midst of lack of agreement as to a common good.

But a significant question about ecclesiology still remains: In addition to empowering its members to be "transformers of society" in their "non-governmental" roles, should churches ever take a "churchwide" position relative to a public policy issue being debated in the "governmental" realm? Differing responses to this outstanding question will be reported in Chapter 10.

5

Party Politics and Beyond

IN THE LAST chapter, Harry Boyte and Jim Skillen present differing views about the "center" of political activism. Harry focuses on the political activities of non-governmental groups such as families, businesses, churches and voluntary associations. While embracing an important political role for non-governmental groups, Jim also values highly the role of politicians and government (the executive, legislative and judicial branches at local, state and national levels). However, neither Harry nor Jim view these sets of political responsibility as mutually exclusive. Harry acknowledges the role of government, but gives "first priority" to the political activities of non-governmental groups. Jim argues for "joint responsibility" between government and non-governmental political actors without suggesting any priority.

This chapter continues the conversation started in the last chapter by focusing on the role of the Democratic and Republican political parties for government carrying out its responsibilities, and, as a continuation of Harry Boyte's focus, exploring further the nature of political activities "beyond" party politics.

In contrast to my typical use of two conversation partners for other subtopics, I recruited four conversation partners for this particular topic of "Party Politics and Beyond," asking each partner to focus on one particular theme in their first (of three) electronic postings.

Doug Koopman, a political science professor from Calvin College who spent 15 years in Washington, D.C. working for Republican members of both the House and Senate was asked to present a perspective on the priorities and values of the Republican Party at the present time (in theory and in present actuality, if these differ) and the extent to which these priorities and values comport with Christian values.

Jim Talen, who is serving a ninth two-year term as a Democrat on the Kent County (Michigan) Commission was asked to present a perspective on the priorities and values of the Democratic Party at the present time (in theory and in present actuality, if these differ) and the extent to which these priorities and values comport with Christian values.

Kevin den Dulk, executive director of the Henry Institute for the Study of Christianity and Politics at Calvin College, whose political party leanings are unknown to me (I didn't ask and he didn't tell) was asked to elaborate on his position that party politics is an inevitable (and, in principle, welcome) part of a democratic future, but the parties as we know them will have to adapt to some new political, economic and social realities, such that in 20 years we may not recognize them.

Angela Cowser, associate dean of Black Church Studies and the doctor of ministry programs at Louisville Presbyterian Theological Seminary was asked to elaborate on her position that party politics is not the politics of the future. Rather, we need to focus more on renewing grassroots democracy than on party politics.

The reader must be careful to not use the above brief descriptions of assignments given to my four conversation partners for their initial postings to put the four of them in "neat boxes." As the following narrative will reveal, their various postings reveal many nuances that defy simplistic categorization. Doug prepares us for this complexity when he reflects on the way in which his StrengthsFinder assessment revealed that his "leading strength" was "individualization," which he elaborates as follows:

> My leading StrengthsFinder strength is individualization. In
> brief, people strong on Individualization intentionally take
> people one at a time, and resist putting people in boxes or
> categories because such generalization and labeling reduces
> artificially and harmfully the complexity of each individual

and unique human being. To these Individualizers, to categorize folks is to disrespect their individuality, which is far more complex than even a long list of socioeconomic and demographic boxes. Individualization advocates, when they are part of a work group, are likely to be good at figuring out how people who are different from each other work together productively, as they believe differences and individuality are strengths to be encouraged even on a tightly knit and production-oriented team.

The description of persons with this strength goes on to state two special obligations such persons bear toward the good functioning of the group and respect for the individualization perspective. The first is to help others understand that true diversity is found in subtle characteristics of each individual and those differences among all individuals, and not just in big categories such as race, gender, denominational affiliation, college of graduation, age or national origin. The second obligation for people with this strength is to press to treat each individual in a distinctive way. From their view, it is both more just and more effective in a work environment to treat each person differently because the differences among people means 'the same' treatment is essentially unfair to everyone.

I quote Doug at length here to prepare the reader for Kevin's eventual claim (with which I strongly concur) that putting those in the "other party" in a particular type of "neat box" is the most fundamental pathology evidenced by politicians on both sides of the aisle. But all of our conversation partners first point out some other prevalent pathologies of political parties that emerge from what these parties view as their "functions" ("purposes").

What Is it That Political Parties Do?

Doug points out that "political parties in America have at least four different centers of activities—elected officials, full-time employees (employed directly by a party group at some level or indirectly as full-time consultants of one type or another), core grassroots activists who are dedicated but essentially volunteers, and then fairly passive voters who typically vote for one party." He then provides a thorough list of "a dozen political party functions undertaken by one, some, or all of these four activity centers," summarized as follows:

> ... to help: 1) **socialize** people into the political system ... 2) **mobilize** voter blocs on election day ... 3) **educate the public** about the political process and the issues and candidates that align with the party ... 4) **formulate policies** that are targeted to keep long-standing voters or to attract and reward new voter blocs ... 5) **conflict resolution and compromise skill identification and development** often takes place ... 6) [provide] **stability** in electoral choices which helps to provide continuity and a measure of assurance to the political system ... 7) **recruit candidates** to run whom they believe can win and serve well... 8) **simplify voter choices**, because few voters have deep or broad interest in issues or candidates and appreciate decision making shortcuts ... 9) **legitimate change** by claiming mandates for a new policy course ... 10) **encourage accountability** by rewarding cooperation and punishing dissent ... 11) **link the different branches of government and various levels** as well, to enact the policies that they have developed to attract voters and promised to pursue if voters gave them the influence to do so. When it works well, this linkage 12) **makes government more responsible and responsive** to public opinion as expressed through the common simple act of voting.

Kevin presents a more abbreviated view of the function of political parties that repeats a number of Doug's suggestions, but in a manner that hints at the danger of creating societal divisions by means of "group polarization."

> Today, parties are a potent means to mobilize segmented groups under a relatively coherent umbrella of leaders and

ideas. They serve as key 'linkage institutions,' a way for elites to rally the electorate and for the electorate to influence elites. Parties also bring structure to decision-making in Congress and state legislatures, with their dozens—even hundreds— of individual members clamoring for the interests of their home districts. Moreover, while the majority rules the halls of power, the opposition has influence and legitimacy because it speaks with a collective voice. For these reasons, among many others, political scientists and theorists often insist that modern democracies, with their extended territories and diverse populations, could not thrive without the existence of political parties. To say that we are bedeviled by the mischief of Republicans and Democrats or saddled with tired political structures is not an argument that we should abandon parties altogether.

... By using elections as a springboard for control, parties are democracy's unlikely partner. They are built to compete for blocs of voters, which is another way of saying they are designed to divide the body politic into a small range of groups that are easier to identify, target, segment and mobilize. In the process parties sharpen and amplify differences, real or imagined, with the goal of presenting stark contrasts among alternatives. The formation of a partisan entails both ascent and rejection. Parties thrive not only when you know where you belong; they also want to remind you that you don't belong somewhere else. The wider the chasm between your group and 'theirs'—the greater the group *polarization*—the deeper and more durable your identification with the group.

In brief, Kevin's concern is that "parties are *built* for competition, not reconciliation. They are designed to mobilize division" for the purpose of attracting "blocs of voters." Angela is more blunt in expressing her perception of the "political priorities of the Republican Party in 2018," which boils down to "winning elections."

The political priorities of the Republican Party in 2018 are to raise money, find and provide financial and strategic support to candidates who can win elections (no matter how ethically odious they may be), build a variety of media platforms for propagandistic purposes (Fox News, Breitbart, TBN, CBN), and use whatever means are necessary—including gerrymandering, allowing foreign powers to 'meddle' in U.S. elections, and sustained, systematic suppression of minority and poor voters, etc.)—to win elections.

Angela extends her critique of the Republican Party to the Democratic Party, suggesting that Democrats also focus on winning elections.

The political priorities of the Democratic Party in 2018 include raising money, fielding candidates who can win elections, supporting the gerrymandering of districts, satisfying mega-donors (Harvey Weinstein, George Soros) and national constituency groups (NARAL, unions), and building (and supporting) media platforms that undergird their positions and constituencies (MSNBC, *The New York Times*).

As I understand it, the purpose of political parties in America—Democratic, Republican, Green and Constitution—is: 1) to raise money to fund local, regional, state and national campaigns to elective office; 2) to choose presidential nominees; 3) to promote winning candidates for elections; 4) to organize and execute voter turnout or voter turnout suppression; 5) to win elections; in 2012, the average cost of a House race was $1.7 million and of a Senate race was $10.5 million, with minimum-maximum costs ranging from $110,000 (American Samoa) to $42 million (Massachusetts).

The concerns expressed above about an inordinate focus on winning elections (at the expense, often, of governing well, I would add) are only the tip of iceberg of the pathologies of political parties that our conversation partners point to. That litany now continues.

More Pathologies Within the Political Parties

Kevin prepares us for this further litany of political party pathologies by observing that "many citizens" believe that "American political parties are making a mess of democracy."

> American political parties are making a mess of democracy—
> or at least many citizens seem to think so. The percentage
> of Americans who view both major parties unfavorably has
> risen steadily for nearly two decades. Today, only one-third
> say that the two parties adequately represent the public; 60
> percent suggest a third party is a needed corrective. Public
> evaluations of party leadership in the U.S. Congress have
> reached record lows. As many as 1 in 3 party *members* have
> serious reservations about their own team.
>
> And is it any wonder? Parties in government appear
> hopelessly divided and hampered by encrusted leadership;
> their legislative efforts are riddled with pointless gridlock
> and other dysfunctions; the ceaseless pursuit of money
> often blinds party elites to the needs of the rank-and-
> file. We could hope for change, but the odds are long.
> The reform-minded citizen faces a deck stacked with
> obstructions—gerrymandering,   ballot   and   funding
> requirements, winner-take-all voting rules—that protect
> the party duopoly of Republicans and Democrats. We seem
> stuck with a system that channels diverse preferences to
> merely two alternatives, both of them subpar. It's easy to be
> alienated by it all.

Jim concurs with Kevin's observation of a "mess" in party politics based on his on-the-ground experiences in the trenches of party politics in Kent County, Michigan.

> Right off the bat, I love Kevin's assertion that 'American
> political parties are making a mess of democracy. ... ' Oh
> my, yes! He goes on to say, 'As many as 1 in 3 party members

have serious reservations about their own team.' Even a partisan officeholder like me has serious reservations about my team! In my community we have a demonstrably weak local Democratic Party organization. It is fraught with bickering and infighting. I'm often amazed that people can fight so hard. ... and over what? A Democratic candidate hasn't won a county-wide election in 35 years! It's the same old arguments and fights, year after year—what does the old saying suggest about doing the same things over and over again and expecting different results? I try to avoid local party meetings because there is so much dissension and I'm reluctant to suggest that any newly excited partisan attend for fear that they'll be totally turned off and lose interest. I've also seen the state and national Democratic Party come into town during presidential election years, try to totally take over local campaign efforts, and instantly disappear a few days after election day, leaving a host of hard feelings and bitter tastes.

Later on, Kevin suggests that 'parties in government appear ... hampered by encrusted leadership.' My own local Democratic Party was controlled for years by an 'elite' group of local labor leaders. They controlled local party elections to ensure their continued control of the party. (Again, one would wonder why, in the absence of any election successes.) When some like-minded non-union activists tried to expand the party base, the efforts were met with stiff resistance. I'll never forget trying to set up at a caucus site to sign up new party members, in the 1984 presidential caucus, and being evicted by the party chairperson. In my opinion, the local situation has improved but there is currently a somewhat similar situation in which Bernie Sanders supporters are accusing local party leadership of not being open to new ideas and participation. I suppose some things never change. ...

Angela adds the following scathing criticism of political parties.

> Political parties do not build democratic practices and
> good citizens; they develop ideologues, partisans and
> party operatives and apparatchiks. They seek winnable
> candidates for communities that have gerrymandered
> districts where outcomes are predetermined and settled.
> These predeterminations harden partisanship, ideological
> divisions, diminish healthy conversation and disagreement,
> increase tribalisms that stifle democratic practices of deep
> listening, understanding, conversation and relationships
> across race, class, ethnicity and location, and embolden
> partisans and single-issue people to make narrow decisions
> on single issues, and a decrease in decisions made for the
> good of the whole.

Angela elaborates by specifically pointing to the pathology of the
"outsize influence" of a "rarefied group of mega donors," resulting in the
interests of persons in dire need being "minimally attended to."

> In the normal warp and woof of daily life, I find—generally
> speaking—that a rarified group of mega donors exert an
> outsize influence on the ideological positions and legislative
> agendas of candidates and politicians. To the Democratic
> National Committee (DNC): Tom Steyer, $91 million; Paul
> Singer, $26 million; and Michael Bloomberg, $23 million.
> To the Republican National Committee (RNC): Sheldon
> Adelson, $82 million; Robert Mercer, $25 million; John
> Ricketts, $15 million (among many others). These persons
> and their singular interests hold inordinate sway over the
> legislative and political agendas of the two major political
> parties. Meanwhile, the interests of parents whose children
> are addicted to drugs, alcohol, technology are minimally
> attended to; the safety and security needs of persons who
> want to live gun-free are suppressed and mocked; the need
> for affordable housing for middle and lower-class workers
> is subverted by race and class biases that ultimately increase
> homelessness, poverty and suffering.

Kevin says he agrees "that parties have many of the pathologies that Cowser identifies," to which he adds what he believes is the most destructive pathology of all: "partisan tribalism," a topic to which I now turn.

The Ultimate Pathology of "Partisan Tribalism"

While acknowledging that "ideology or policy preferences on hot-button issues push partisans [Republicans and Democrats] apart ... and these are important concerns" (much more about that later), Kevin asserts that "the most consequential divisions are more basic," reflecting "tribalism."

> ... We often bemoan how ideology or policy preferences on hot-button issues push partisans apart, and indeed these are important concerns. But today's most consequential divisions are more basic—they operate at the level of *identity*. Political scientists call this pattern *affective polarization*, a deep emotional resonance with a party—the in-group; and visceral reaction against the opposition—the out-group. Our partisan divide isn't merely about Liberals versus Conservatives, pro-life versus pro-choice. Our lives as partisans have become downright tribal.

As Kevin elaborates, he notes that "affective polarization" is "basic" in the sense that "ideology and policy views" are "largely derivative," a "reflection of deeper and more visceral emotional attachments to political groups." Quoting Christopher Achen and Larry Bartels, Kevin adds that such "affective polarization" causes much of our political thinking to be "rationalization" rather than the formulation of a "rationale."

> ... political scientists Christopher Achen and Larry Bartels show that, contrary to our 'folk theories' of democratic citizenship, citizens rarely survey the landscape of ideologies and policy preferences, conduct a well-informed cost-benefit analysis, and make a choice to join groups that align most closely with the result of their calculus. They *start* with group attachments that fundamentally shape how they understand and act toward political ideas and

institutions. Much of our political thinking isn't rational; it's a *rationalization*. Scholars often compare the phenomenon to sports loyalists. Very few of us give our loyalty to the team most likely to 'maximize our expected utility,' determined after consideration of metrics in a spreadsheet. We generally come to that loyalty as a family inheritance, a passing down of a commitment that we didn't choose.

But Kevin suggests that it is a "next step" that makes such tribalism so destructive: an unwarranted extrapolation from a belief that the "other" is "wrong-headed" to a belief that the "other" is "untrustworthy, immoral and dangerously threatening," a common extrapolation identified by researchers at the Political Communication Lab at Stanford University.

If mere ideology or policy views were the bases of inter-group attitudes, partisans would simply describe the opposition as wrongheaded. But instead, partisans overwhelmingly label their opponents as untrustworthy, immoral and dangerously threatening. The researchers also noted that the negative evaluations across partisan lines were more intense than attitudes across other identity groups (e.g., race, gender or religion). It's a result corroborated in other studies that use 'feeling thermometers' to gauge a person's emotional response to specific groups. The 'warmth' gap between partisans is higher than any other set of groups. This is partisan tribalism, the translation of in-group identity into a marker of human worth.

As Doug cogently and humorously points out, this unwarranted extrapolation from believing that that the person from the "other" political party is "wrong" to believing that he/she is "immoral" enables adherents to either party to overlook "incompetence" because at least we are not "evil."

Both national political parties today have essentially the same message: 'We may be incompetent and flawed, but our intentions are good and the other party's candidates and those who vote for them are evil. Vote well-intentioned incompetence over evil.'

Kevin adds that "one of the reasons this tribalism cuts deep is that it's colonized areas of our life that we do not ordinarily imagine as "political," extending to television, print media, social media and entertainment.

> Facebook might seem an innocuous place to share cat pictures or the latest family news with Grandma, but recent network analysis suggests it also has become the most important hub for partisan-tinged news and in-group communication. The loss of rhetorical boundaries on Facebook—and perhaps more acutely on Twitter—reinforces the gaping political chasm. Media analysts have thoroughly chronicled how deeply our tribalism has penetrated nearly every platform (television and print, social media, etc.) and form (not only news, but also entertainment).

Kevin further notes that such partisan tribalism even affects "housing patterns" and the likelihood, or not, of "marriage across party lines."

> The [tribal] patterns go well beyond the virtual world as well. Housing patterns are increasingly correlated with partisan attachments (there are now companies that will help you find a match between neighborhoods and your partisan loyalties). Marriage across party lines, just like race and class, is increasingly rare.

Jim concurs with Kevin's observation about "partisan housing patterns" based on his own experience in western Michigan.

> Until our recent move to a condo a few blocks away, my wife, Pat, and I lived in the same house for 40 years. We often reflected about the 'bubble' that we seemed to live in. While there may have been a few closet independents in our neighborhood, you would hardly know it from conversations or election-year yard signs. The one staunch Republican on our block eventually stopped coming to neighborhood social functions. Now, the population of the 30-unit condo that we eventually moved to seems to be similarly Left-leaning.

This pernicious tendency to "live in bubbles," or, as I like to call them, "echo chambers," where we only engage with those who already agree with us on political issues (and many other issues) reflects a rampant tribalism that does not bode well for the future of political parties (or for the flourishing of society in general).

White Evangelical Complicity in Partisan Tribalism

Kevin notes, "The Christian church is not immune to partisan tribalism," suggesting that "the recent experience of white evangelicals is a prominent case study."

> If I were to put the power of partisan polarization to the test, I'd want to observe the response of white evangelicals to a GOP standard bearer who divorced twice, owns casinos, has a reputation for philandering, and thinks repentance doesn't apply in his case ... what did [social science research] reveal? Not only that partisan polarization persists under those conditions, but also that it has the potential to reframe how the faithful understand their own basic convictions.

> That partisanship among white evangelicals persisted is not a difficult story to tell. We have heard a great deal about how this election was profoundly different in its populist or authoritarian or racial undertones, that it was a historical disruption. Yet in many ways it was ordinary; the story is as much about continuity as change. The line-plot of the Republican's share of the white evangelical vote over the last five presidential election cycles is flat. The exit polls showed 79 percent of the white evangelical vote for Bush in 2004 and Romney in 2012, for example; in 2016 it was 81 percent for Trump, no different statistically from those early contests. Better surveys suggests slightly different numbers but a similar pattern.

Those trends lead me to read the news headlines about the 81 percent as less about continuity than a candidate. The question seemed to be: How could white evangelicals vote for him? But that question assumes white evangelicals were voting simply *for* a man, rather than *out of* a (partisan) identity. The strength of their attachments apparently even reshaped longstanding moral convictions, most notably the full U-turn in how white evangelicals assess the importance of presidential character. In a 2001 Public Religion Research Institute (PRRI) poll, white evangelicals were the most likely among all religious groups to think private character is important in a public leader; in 2016, just before the election, they were the least likely of all religious groups to hold that view. It is hard not to see the change as a textbook case of partisan rationalization. Yes, it is possible that some white evangelicals were nose holders who overlooked Trump's foibles in favor of higher priorities (e.g., abortion). But recent analysis by Paul Djupe and others suggests that subset of white evangelical voters was quite small. Polarization was at the forefront.

Kevin challenges Christians to examine the ways in which they may be complicit in partisan tribalism.

The faithful should pause to wonder whether and how they're caught up in those partisan practices. Are Christians engaging parties as critical insiders, advancing important goals while speaking out against the parties' manifold problems? Or have they been co-opted by the rituals that shape partisan identity, succumbing to the instincts of the political tribe?

The above compendium of pathologies of political parties, especially the emerging prevalence of partisan tribalism, may lead you to call into question the legitimacy of such parties. But, despite the scathing criticisms enumerated above, our conversation partners do not push for obliteration of political parties. That will take some explanation.

Political Parties Are not Dispensable

Kevin observes that "amid the frustration with party elites and calls for reform, there is this curious fact about political parties: *Most citizens identify with one*," as corroborated by research from the Pew Research Center.

> The Pew Research Center reports that at least two-thirds of registered voters are solid party identifiers; add in the 'leaners'—people with an affinity for a party but a hesitancy to embrace the label—and the number surpasses 90 percent. Over 60 percent of *all* citizens identify with a party and most of the others say they are closer to one party than the other …

Why is that? As already suggested above, political parties do carry out a helpful function, which Kevin has summarized as follows: "Parties are foundational to modern democracies—they link the electorate and elites, and they help bring order to governing." He elaborates further:

> Parties perform crucial functions as linkage institutions in electoral democracies by connecting elites to the electorate and bringing structure to the lawmaking process. They might do this work poorly—again, Cowser and I agree about that—but it's hard to imagine other organizations fulfilling the same functions.

The above reference to Angela agreeing with Kevin that political parties may do their work "poorly" is not the full story as to the possible agreements and disagreements that Kevin and Angela may have as to whether political parties are dispensable. Consider the following exchanges:

> … while Cowser rightly calls our attention to a host of deep-seated problems with parties today, she takes those problems as evidence that party politics are dispensable—*or at least that* grassroots faith-based organizing is preferable as a way to do justice in the world (Kevin, italics mine).
>
> Moreover, as long as that hope for change is alive—as long as we can imagine a feasible possibility for reform—I'd argue

that we have an obligation to pursue it. This brings me to my second reason for seeing Cowser's contrast between faith-based grassroots organizing and party politics as misplaced. We disagree about what parties ought and ought not do, especially in comparison to the grassroots work that Cowser describes. Indeed, that disagreement appears to be as basic as whether parties are largely dispensable to advancing public justice in electoral democracies (Kevin).

Political parties are still important because they remain—transactionally, but not relationally—the central vehicle through which ideological and political intent is exercised and measured. They exist to find, develop, fund and get elected winnable incumbents and challengers. They raise money and organize conventions, rallies and various media platforms. The elected leaders who represent the two major political parties in government are the instruments through which legislatively relevant political will is advanced and/or repressed (Angela, italics mine).

In the normal warp and woof of daily life, I find—generally speaking—that *civic (civil, NGOs, non-profits, foundations) groups are far more important* to the vitality and dynamism of the larger polis and to the development of an educated citizenry than are traditional political parties. I think, for example, about the (sustained) power and efficacy of the NAACP and the NAACP Legal Defense Fund to advance and protect the interests of African-Americans; American Legislative Exchange Council (ALEC) for strategically advancing the conservative interests of corporations, politicians and groups; Southern Poverty Law Center for educating the nation about hate groups and terrorists in our midst; and Emily's List for finding, developing and helping viable female candidates win elective office (Angela, italics mine).

Here is my attempt to sort through these reflections from Kevin and Angela. Despite Angela's view that political parties do their work poorly, she clearly says that "political parties are still important." She is not saying that political parties are "dispensable." Therefore, I believe it is fair to conclude that while Angela believes that political parties are not dispensable, she does believe that grassroots faith-based organizing **is preferable to** the work of political parties as a way to do justice in the world (which Kevin allows for in his "at least that" phrase in the first quotation above). We will later come back to the implicit suggestion from Angela above that a reason for grassroots faith-based organizing being "preferable to" the work of political parties in the quest for justice is that such grassroots organizing is "relational" in contrast to the "transactional" work of political parties.

Note also from the above exchange between Kevin and Angela that Kevin has "hope" for the possibility of "reform" on the part of political parties. Whether such "hope" is realistic is certainly debatable, an issue to which we now turn.

Can Political Parties Remake Themselves?

Contrary to the view that the two major political parties are "fixed" entities over time, Doug points us to "the overwhelming pragmatism and constant changeability" of the two parties (parenthetically noting how "frustrating and annoying" such changeability is to "those with moral certainty"). He attributes such pragmatism to the need for each party to attract "allies" ("voters") to "help them achieve their political goals," which leads to each party "always growing and changing."

> ... I make the obvious point that political parties are essential
> to democratic politics, and healthy political parties help
> politics achieve its ends in nations where voters matter.
> From the early years of the republic, government leaders
> looked for allies inside and outside the formal government
> structure to help them achieve their political goals. Parties
> were created to help in this task. In an electoral democracy,
> political majorities are always changing composition as
> historical events shape expectations and demands on

government, and as the voter pool changes over time. As such, in a healthy political system well-functioning political parties are always growing and changing, always seeking new allies while trying to hold on to what and whom they have.

To be blunt, Doug suggests that the primary motivation behind the "changeability" of the political parties is the goal of "attaining governing majorities" (again pointing to the inordinate focus on winning elections).

> The two national political parties, Democratic and Republican, are structured and led a bit differently from each other, but still each are federations of state parties held together by a few common and often vague principles and interests. Each divided by geography, ideology, class and other ways, the party federations unite every four years to select presidential candidates. The high profile of presidential contests exaggerates party unity. In fact, party coalitions shift, sometimes quickly and drastically, particularly if party professionals despair of attaining governing majorities.

Doug presents an extended example of how the Republican Party has changed since its "founding in the late 1850s," some of the highlights of which are as follows:

> Since its founding in the late 1850s, a mostly consistent GOP theme has been individualism. Founded largely to oppose American slavery and early on supporting women's suffrage, Republicans encouraged Prohibition, aided individualized Protestantism over the hierarchical Catholic Church, and blessed government 'nudges' to create private wealth over more redistributive ideas. At times in its first 70 years, the GOP was progressive, such as when it advanced abolition and women's suffrage and led electioneering reforms. Since the 1920s, however, the national GOP has been usually the more conservative party, resisting government encroachments on local governments, private activity, and charitable and religious institutions ...

Today's new dynamic began in the mid-1960s, when LBJ and the national Democratic Party leadership chose to use their large congressional majorities to expand the limited New Deal welfare state into a more ambitious Great Society and to advance voting rights for African-Americans. Originally strongly supportive of some of these items, particularly African-American voting rights, the GOP's establishment by the late 1960s began to see a counter opportunity in a 'suburban strategy' that might be particularly effective in the Democrats' previously 'Solid South.' The three themes of the suburban strategy were: 1) a strong military (defined by increasing spending on defense and veterans programs), 2) general economic growth (defined by resistance to government regulation and support for global trade agreements without much compensation to displaced American labor) and 3) limits on the national government, articulated in support for religious liberty (defined by support for traditional religious faith expression and linked social issues such as private schools, traditional marriage and opposition to abortion) and invocations of the Second, Ninth, and 10th Amendments.

The suburban strategy paid large dividends to Republicans, ... The "Reagan trinity" of economic, social and foreign policy conservatism in 1980 catapulted him into the White House and brought other strong GOP gains. The new president and Congress enacted the economic and military parts of the Reagan program—large defense spending hikes, smaller domestic spending growth and major tax cuts. ... The suburban strategy seemed successful. The 12 years of Republican presidents and more uniform GOP conservatism was adding more GOP support from the Solid South than the party was losing elsewhere. Conservatism and Republicanism became what Reagan presented— appreciation for free markets, muscular patriotic nationalism, and traditional reliance on self and locality rooted in religion.

But then, as Doug notes, the "Trump reversal" took effect, as follows:

He [Trump] took on each suburban-strategy plank, criticizing the wars in Iraq and Afghanistan, attacking as unfair the recent and pending global free-trade agreements, and largely ignoring expected religious gestures while bottom-line pledging to appoint pro-life federal judges. Further distinguishing his candidacy, Trump's immigration position was radioactive to party leaders and his call for huge infrastructure spending was more reminiscent of New Deal Democrats than a GOP whose Tea Party-infused Congress had just outlawed earmarks. Intentionally or accidentally, Trump's campaign showed how little street-cred much of the Reagan-era conservative trinity had by 2016 to even GOP primary voters. Muscular foreign policy had produced wars with no end games, free global trade had produced wealth for too few and pietistic expressions had not reversed cultural decline. Trump poked the establishment in the eye, and promised tangible results. As difficult as it was for much of the established GOP leadership to accept, Trump drove Republican primary voter enthusiasm and successful crossover appeal by revealing the sagging credibility of the Reagan trinity, while his contrary policies and crude style drew support, attractively and offensively, from the same voter pools.

This "reversal" was highlighted in President Trump's 2018 State of the Union address, when he proposed policies that could be lifted from the Democratic Party playbook: infrastructure investment, paid family leaves, subsidized job training, reducing drug prices, reform of America's prisons and providing ex-convicts with better opportunities to reintegrate into society.

Kevin seconds Doug's views on the "changeability" of political parties by noting how "the party system in the United States ... has often remade itself," citing as an example the problem of "gerrymandering" as brought up by Angela (and Jim, when he observes that his "current district [in Michigan] is the local poster child for gerrymandering[41]).

> Consider one of those problems [with parties today]: gerrymandering. Cowser claims that partisan redistricting fosters noncompetitive districts, deepens partisan divides, and impoverishes civic conversation. While some political scientists disagree about these effects (especially compared to other causes), let's accept her assertions for sake of argument. What follows from them? Like Cowser, we could issue a plausible moral indictment against parties, especially at the state legislative level, for using their cartographic machinations to devalue the power of the vote. But should we take the next step and condemn the party system *itself* as irredeemably broken? Is reform a hopeless and quixotic dream? From both her posts, I infer from her treatment of gerrymandering, as well as campaign finance and other features of American electoral democracy, that Cowser would probably say 'yes' to both questions. Better to use the more effective and edifying strategies of grassroots organizing freed from partisan shackles.

> But I'd suggest that we should answer 'no' to both questions. The party system in the United States, from its formative years to the Civil War to the Progressive Era to the 1960s, has often remade itself. Sometimes the change has been for ill, but often for good as well, and that latter fact speaks to redemptive possibilities. And those possibilities are not lost to history. Gerrymandering is an intriguing example. Many states today are introducing or considering redistricting strategies that eschew partisan mischief. In addition, that party reform has emerged from the grassroots itself, precisely the same source of moral authority that Cowser champions. Doug Koopman, our fellow conversationalist

41 Jim reports that "over the three decades that I've campaigned for elected office, despite not having moved during that period, I've been in four different district configurations," with his district "sometimes referred to as the 'snake district' because of its unusual shape."

in this series, is involved in just that sort of mass-based campaign to reform Michigan's gerrymandered regime—and it looks like that effort might bear real fruit. Now, I'm not a Pollyanna about prospects for change; in fact, my optimism about a movement for reform is cautious to the point of skepticism. But I still see in our history and current moment the opportunity for electoral reform that enhances competition and pulls candidates back from tribal extremes.

If one accepts the assertions of both Doug and Kevin that the major political parties can "change," this raises the huge question as to which future changes will best address the pathologies of the current political system, a topic that is addressed by all four of our conversation partners, to which I will add some of my own reflections.

A "Way Forward" Toward Reforming American Politics

There is no Way Forward toward reforming American politics until Americans address the ultimate pathology pointed to by Kevin: *partisan tribalism*, a pernicious form of "identity politics" that separates "us" from "them"; fueled by the unwarranted belief that because "we" believe "they" are wrong about a given public policy issue, they must be immoral or evil; which precludes respectful conversations about the "truth" of the matter.

Therefore, to lay a foundation for proposing a Way Forward, it is first necessary to expose the ways in which the rhetoric of the political parties is often disconnected from their legislative initiatives.

Moving beyond symbolism

The manner in which President Trump is proposing initiatives that sound like they are coming from the Democratic Party and other examples noted above of how the major political parties have changed over the years in order to attain "governing majorities" should make one wary of taking official party platforms too seriously. But if you will humor me for a while, here is what we are led to believe about the "values" of the two major parties, as revealed by their "ideological" platform statements.

Jim points us to "some of the strongest Democratic values [that] can be found in the preamble of its platform."

- "We believe that today's extreme level of income and wealth inequality ... makes our economy weaker, our communities poorer, and our politics poisonous."
- "And we know that our nation's long struggle with race is far from over. ... race still plays a significant role in determining who gets ahead in America and who gets left behind."
- "Above all, Democrats are the party of inclusion. We know that diversity is not our problem—it is our promise."
- "We are proud of our heritage as a nation of immigrants."
- "We believe in ... guaranteeing civil rights and voting rights, women's rights and workers' rights, LGBT rights, and rights for people with disabilities."

My own perusal of the preamble to the 2016 Republican platform reveals the following highlights:

- "We believe in American exceptionalism."
- "We affirm—as did the Declaration of Independence: that all are created equal, endowed by their Creator with inalienable rights of life, liberty and the pursuit of happiness."
- "We believe in our constitutional system—limited government, separation of powers, federalism and the rights of the people— must be preserved uncompromised for future generations."
- "We believe political freedom and economic freedom are indivisible."
- "We believe that people are the ultimate resource—and that the people, not the government, are the best stewards of our country's God-given natural resources."
- "... we wish for peace—so we insist on strength."

Of course, a looming question is how these abstract "ideological commitments" get translated into public policies. Angela presents her perception of how the values of the Republican Party have been expressed in public life.

The values of the Republican Party in 2018 are the same as they have been for as long as I've had a consciousness about it: the symbolic and substantive suppression and oppression of minority citizens and immigrants around issues of race, ethnicity, citizenship, and gender; a close melding of the goals and aims of the Republican Party and most conservative Christian fellowships in the U.S.; ... the militant and unrepentant elevation of (male, heterosexual) whiteness and white norms; and the political satiation of Republican mega-donors to the exclusion of and denigration of the material lives of white, working class and poor Republican voters.

But Kevin raises an insightful issue relative to how Angela has experienced the public expression of "Republican values." Consistent with his concern about the pathology of "partisan tribalism" (described above), he notes that Angela's perception is that the "longstanding 'values' of the GOP are *relentlessly identity-based*—having to do with one's race, ethnicity, gender, religious affiliation" (italics mine). But Kevin wonders "why Angela didn't lay quite the same kind of challenge at the Democrats' feet," since "the Democratic Party has its own history with exclusivist symbolic strategies that identify who's 'in' by defining who's 'out.'"

My own attempt to make sense of Kevin's reflections on Angela's experience of the public expression of Republican values starts with what Kevin calls "symbolic politics," which he defines as follows:

The idea of symbolic politics is that citizens join with others in political groups based on markers of identity (e.g., class, race, gender, religion), rather than substantive agreement over ideology or policy (though the symbolic and substantive may converge).

How is Kevin's concern about doing "symbolic politics" related to the party platform statements with which I started this section? My take is that these platform statements are used to distinguish between "us" and "them" (partisan tribalism); a mere "war of symbols of identity" that keep politicians from the primary legislative task of formulating public policies that foster the well-being of all Americans. But what possibilities lie beyond doing "symbolic politics" that constitute a Way Forward? Here are some steps that can be taken (in no particular order).

Step 1: go beyond symbolism to substance

Doug issues a clarion call for both major political parties to get beyond "blaming the failures of government on the other political party and its candidates."

> Polls showing declining trust in institutions, including government institutions, illustrate that most Americans doubt that politics or government can do much to solve ... anxiety and fear. Both political parties have responded in essentially the same way—not by trying to address the underlying issues but by accepting the widespread doubt and cynicism of government and blaming the failures of government on the other political party and its candidates.

Doug suggests a "new path" for both Republicans and Democrats: "to clarify their views of the scope and purpose of government and parties, and show voters real plans to address substantive and material issues, not merely symbolic ones."

Doug then elaborates on some of the substantive policy issues that he wishes those who campaigned for the presidency in 2016 had focused upon to attract voters based on their "interests" rather than their "fears and prejudices."

> ... the winning GOP candidate, or another party candidate, could have stuck to promises to rework free trade agreements for fairer terms, to rebuild traditional infrastructure such as roads, bridges, rails and shipping lanes, to start new infrastructure such as universal Internet access for rural areas and small towns, to propose other new rural and small-town development programs, to promote ideas for strong local schools, health care facilities, churches, and the like, and to advocate for other matters that would create a financial and economic infrastructure to help non-urban areas. These would have been substantive policy ideas aimed at attracting the non-urban voter, particularly in the

South, in ways and through means in which government is competent. Instead, the campaign was characterized by attracting these voters by appealing to their fears and prejudices, not their interests.

Now that President Trump has been elected, Doug suggests that what he must do as president to "keep Trump voters voting for the party" is to consider substantive ways "to improve the material condition for all individuals in the nation" rather than to continue an "offensive communication strategy that demonizes as evil the other party."

> After his [Trump's] successful election … the establishment GOP is now faced with a difficult choice in its strategy to keep Trump voters voting for the party. One choice is to alter significantly the standing Republican view of the role of the federal government in local economic development and in the material strains on the non-urban working class and their communities. This position proposes real, constructive, and appropriate ways to attract Trump voters over the longer term. In general, it is the road I believe should be taken. The other choice facing all three elements of the GOP establishment is to continue to tolerate, or at least acquiesce to an offensive communication strategy that demonizes as evil the other party and the more varied socioeconomic and demographic groups that tend to support it in elections. It will be interesting to see which path is taken. The choice Republicans make will interact in some ways with what Democrats choose; but one could do worse than have a debate between the two major parties on how best to improve the material condition for all individuals in the nation.

Note that while Doug does point to the need to foster the economic and material well-being of all Americans, his concern, and mine, is broader than that, calling for legislation that promotes human flourishing in all areas of life, including the strengthening of schools and healthcare.

Step 2: get non-governmental groups involved in doing politics

Kevin expresses grave concern that partisan tribalism/identity politics that is so prevalent in the current political realm will have a deleterious effect on the "institutions within civil society that have pushed against partisan tribalism," suggesting that this is particularly true about churches (more about that later).

> For my part, the greatest concern about the ways parties use the symbols of identity to divide and mobilize is that mediating forces have weakened. The institutions within civil society that have pushed against partisan tribalism, often by bringing citizens together in diverse groups, have eroded in their influence. Doug mentions that trust and confidence in institutions has declined, which comprises a crisis of *authority* of these institutions. The loss of the church's moral authority is perhaps the most profound illustration. What's more, as I noted in my early post, many of the institutions of civil society—unions, media, family, neighborhoods, and even churches themselves—are increasingly shaped *by* partisan forces, and so they are less likely to be countervailing. So it's a double-whammy: At the same time the authority of civil society has declined, its partisan colonization has enlarged.

Doug shares Kevin's concern about the eroding of the influence of the non-governmental institutions within civil society, adding that this results in a loss of our "rootedness" in such institutions, which leads to "anxiety and fear," especially "among the working class with high school educations or less."

> I believe we are at a moment in the nation's history where most Americans are rightly and deeply anxious and fearful about the nation's future health ... We have lost our rootedness in neighborhoods, local schools, nuclear families, local congregations, tight-knit voluntary associations, vocational expectations, and the like ... My purpose is merely to note,

as many scholars such as Robert Putnam have documented, that our human and geographic social networks, or spheres as Abraham Kuyper might say, are fraying. It is not a coincidence that the crisis of rootedness, and anxiety and fear about it, is particularly acute among the working class with high school educations or less.

These concerns expressed by Kevin and Doug are very much related to the conversation between Harry Boyte and Jim Skillen reported in Chapter 4. Recall that while Harry acknowledged the importance of the work of politicians and political parties, he argued that the "first priority" for political activism should lie with non-governmental mediating institutions like families, businesses, churches and other voluntary organizations (with Jim arguing that political activism in both the governmental and non-governmental sectors are equally important). Whether you side with Harry or Jim, it is a serious blow to the efficacy of political activism in either sector if the role of the mediating institutions within civil society are weakened by the pathology of partisan/identity politics.

Step 3: focus on "relations" not "transactions" in doing politics

Angela calls our attention to an important distinction between "transactional" and "relational" modes for doing politics. She views "transactional politics" as the typical practices of political parties, arguing that a "richer and more relational alternative" is modeled by those engaged in "grassroots democracy."

> As they are currently structured, political parties are not the answer to teaching good citizenship practices and deepening grassroots democracy. Their purpose is to raise money (small donors, mega-donors, PACS), distribute money to viable candidates, test and refine political ideas, field candidates, develop them through the rigors of fundraising, find/mobilize eligible voters, getting those voters to the polls on election day. After election day, partisans have little use for voters. The best organizers understand this transactional, highly narrow process and offer a richer and more relational alternative.

Some aspects of a "relational" approach to doing politics are captured by Angela and Jim (in my italicized portions of the quotes below).

> ... I find that—generally speaking—grassroots organizing groups are actually performing the work of developing an informed and active citizenry through their *regularly scheduled intensive training sessions*, through finding and *developing leaders* and potential leaders, through *forming relational rather than transactional models of power, and through the time and labor-intensive process of moving from problem to issue to winning on those issues* (Angela).

> It's in the hard work of organizing and reorganizing communities that concrete changes that materially improve lives happen; it's where leaders, followers, and potential leaders are *mentored face-to-face and in real time* (Angela).

> ... it seems like we have lost an historical focus on local politics ... Angela talks about *building economic, faith and social community* (Jim, in commenting on Angela's statement directly above).

Angela suggests that these local, grassroots, "relational" approaches to doing politics enable activist groups to "develop [the] trust and ...[build the] community" that is needed to "work across difference to do justice and ... [transform] the world," while acknowledging that such relational work is "laborious."

In further commenting on Angela's emphasis on the need for "relational" approaches to doing politics (which Angela calls "laborious work" compared to a transactional approach), Jim makes the interesting and provocative suggestion that such "focusing on relational meetings" is a good idea not only for churches (and, I would add, other non-governmental organizations), but is also good for the "healthy existence" of "government." The idea of having "relational meetings" among elected politicians seems far-fetched in our highly polarized political climate. But, as I have argued elsewhere,[42] and have reported on briefly in Chapter 2, I believe that "building relationships of mutual understanding and trust,"

42 Heie, *Respectful LGBT Conversations*, 279-282.

which can be the result of a "relational" approach to doing politics, is the place to start in attempting to sort through disagreements. Do we dare believe that this relational approach to the work of the various branches of government will one day become more prevalent in our highly polarized political culture? Hope springs eternal!

In concluding this section, I note that Angela agrees with Harry Boyte, as reported in Chapter 4, that focusing on grassroots democracy within the non-governmental organizations within civil society will be more efficacious than seeking to reform how politicians and political parties currently function.

> ... I find—generally speaking—that civic (civil, NGOs, nonprofits, foundations) groups are far more important to the vitality and dynamism of the larger polis and to the development of an educated citizenry than are traditional political parties. I think for example about the (sustained) power and efficacy of the NAACP and the NAACP Legal Defense Fund to advance and protect the interests of African-Americans; American Legislative Exchange Council (ALEC) for strategically advancing the conservative interests of corporations, politicians and groups; Southern Poverty Law Center for educating the nation about hate groups and terrorists in our midst; and Emily's List for finding, developing and helping viable female candidates win elective office.

But keep in mind that whereas Angela and Harry Boyte assign "first priority" to mobilizing activists to work with non-governmental organizations, rather than through politicians and political parties, Jim Skillen and I, as reported in Chapter 4, reject such a proposed prioritization. Political activism through both governmental and non-governmental organizations are equally important. Christians need to become more involved in both arenas of political action.

However, also keep in mind the possibility suggested by Angela that political activism at the grassroots non-governmental level may be an "incubator" for initiatives for reforming government.

We need to reform how campaigns are financed, we need to organize new political parties—beginning in the states, and we need to radically expand the idea and practices of citizenship—up to and including running for elective office. Grassroots organizing groups are incubators for these kinds of initiatives and movements.

Step 4: explore possible "cures" for "partisan tribalism"

As suggested above, the primary current pathology in the political realm is a "partisan tribalism" that leads to extreme polarization between "us" and "them" where not only are "they" *wrong*, but "they" are *immoral/ evil*. Is there any hope for overcoming such tribalism? Kevin suggests two possible "cures."

Institutional Cures:
the Wisdom of the Founding Fathers

Kevin suggests that "the American founders were on to the threat of partisan tribalism long before contemporary social scientists." In particular, Kevin notes that "when James Madison referenced the 'mischief of faction' in his argument for constitutional ratification, he especially worried that unbridled democracy might let loose the scourge of majority parties." In Kevin's own words, "The concern about affective polarization rooted in in-group/out-group conflict over identity and fueled by political entrepreneurs [is] all there in Madison's diagnosis of the problem of faction" and his "institutional prescription" for dealing with that problem.

> Madison's prescription was largely institutional. Extend the republic so that factions increase in not only numbers but also range of interests; structure political access through the separation of powers and federalism so that factions are divided and dispersed; and then force those separated institutions to share power so that factions compete and counter each other's ambitions ('checks and balances,' as we often say). It was a brilliant and counterintuitive move: To protect the body politic from the thing you fear, create *more*

of the thing you fear, and then build mechanisms to control them.

Doug seconds Kevin's appreciation for the "checks and balances" that our Founding Fathers built into our Constitution, while recognizing that this will be "frustrating" to those who believe their political views should be accepted by all because they are on "God's side."

> ... the genius of the American systems of federalism and separation of powers illustrate the practical limitations of political power, reinforcing the moral limitations. Even the most confident and uniform political ideology, buttressed by firm religious conviction that God puts one in the right, will be frustrated under our system. This is fortunate. Every week in my church attendance and every day when I reflect as I should, I am reminded of the fallen state of both my will and my intellect. I do not always want what is best, and even if I did I probably would not know how to get there. I expect the truths about my own limits are true of others, including those with political power. It is providential that we have a system of government that prevents any one person's will from being realized. Even the most politically skilled, ideologically pure, and religiously self-assured person will have a hard time imposing his or her will through politics and government for very long or to extend it very far.

> ... To my mind, a government limited in both reach and ambition and dispersed in its administration is both morally wise and practically expedient.

Kevin suggests that we ask "whether the Madisonian instinct for a structural fix could serve us today in addressing polarization." Kevin then asks us to "consider two possibilities, one feasible in the near-term, the other a much longer project, at best."

Kevin's proposed short-term solution is to "crush the gerrymander." He first describes the nature of gerrymandering:

> State legislatures generally redraw the lines of legislative districts in response to the reapportionment of seats

after each Census. That means the party in power has an opportunity to craft district borders to maximize the number of seats that party will win in a given election— an opportunity they have seized with abandon through the process of "gerrymandering." Not surprisingly, the resulting seats are almost always 'safe'; very few campaigns for the House of Representatives are competitive. Because incumbents don't need to moderate their views to cast widely for votes, they are liberated to govern from one side of the polarized extremes.

Kevin sees some hope for eliminating, or at least diminishing the negative polarizing effects of gerrymandering by drawing on "independent commissions" or "even a computer algorithm," conceding that it will be "difficult" to institute such reforms, but they are "not unprecedented."

Shifting the line-drawing to an independent commission or even a computer algorithm might push legislators to greater moderation by drawing lines that force them to compete for their seats. These reforms are difficult but not unprecedented. Some states have moved to commissions, and over half the states have some kind of reform initiative underway in anticipation of the 2020 Census.

Kevin's proposed long-term solution to the problem of "partisan tribalism" is more radical: "Open the door wider to new parties"; what Madison might call "increasing the number of factions." Kevin elaborates as follows.

A variety of mechanisms protect the party duopoly, but few have as much impact as our system of single-member districts with first-past-the-post voting. In nearly every legislative district, the candidate with a plurality of votes (the most votes, not necessarily the majority) wins the lone seat in that district; the losing party (or parties) goes home with nothing. It's easy to see why this favors two-party systems by comparing to legislatures with proportional representation (PR), in which parties win seats in proportion to the vote they receive. In a hundred-seat legislature, for example, a party with only 5 percent of the vote would still have 5 percent of the seats in a PR system. As a result, smaller parties have a place in legislative processes, especially when no party garners a majority and the parties must form a coalition government.

But Kevin sees the possibility of such a radical reform as being "quite dim."

> But the reforms prospects here are quite dim. The U.S. Congress, using its power under the Constitution's Elections Clause (Art. 1, sect. 4), could take action in favor of PR (it has in the past on single-member districts). But the parties have little incentive to make a change that challenges their position, and there's virtually no knowledge and tepid interest in the public about the PR alternative.

Kevin suggests that there may be other structural ("institutional") fixes to the problem of partisan tribalism, such as: "rules for presidential primaries; ballot requirements; campaign funding." But, appealing once again to the wisdom of James Madison, Kevin acknowledges that such structural changes will not be "enough." We also need citizens having "sufficient virtue."

> ... return to Madison's analysis for a moment. He placed great stock in institutional 'precautions,' but he reminded his peers that structure wouldn't be enough. To meet the threat of factions, he said, we would still need citizens imbued with 'sufficient virtue.' His message to us: *Partisan tribalism will not diminish merely by tweaking institutions. We need a civic culture that nurtures change* (emphasis mine).

Cultural Cures: the Example of Martin Luther King Jr.

Doug reminds us that "political culture is downstream and dependent on the broader social and popular culture of the nation," pointing us to an example that is very pertinent to this entire eCircle project: the coarseness of current discourse between politicians and political parties is a "reflection of the state of American culture today."

> It is common to 'hate on' the vulgarity of politicians and political parties, but I believe that understandable hate is largely misplaced. Much of what we hate about politics and parties is not the fault, in a causal way, of politics, but a reflection of the state of American culture today. The coarse elements of politicians and parties are largely a function of these same elements within American culture generally.

Locating the root of the problem of partisan tribalism with "we the people" requires a change in "heart" (my word) which obviously cannot be legislated. As Kevin points out, this "cultural cure" will require "practices [of "We the people"] that reorient and habituate our purposes."

> What would it mean, then, to build a civic culture that pushes against the prevailing practices that generate and reinforce polarization? We should not be so naïve to think that we can simply demand that our leaders get along. We shouldn't even have such a hope in *ourselves*. A change in civic culture requires practices that reorient and habituate our purposes.

Kevin then presents the marvelous example of Martin Luther King Jr.'s "insistence on the practice of non-violence" as an instance of "culture-making."

> Martin Luther King's rhetorical flourishes were inspiring, but his insistence on the practice of non-violence was the nitty-gritty work of culture-making. It was not simply a

tactic of influence; it was also a formative ritual oriented around the hopeful convictions of a disciple of Christ.

In conclusion, Kevin then challenges those of us who claim to be followers of Jesus to use our professed commitments to "community" and "serving others across all lines of difference" as a starting point to model a cultural change that rejects the "idol" of partisan tribalism.

> It's no coincidence that King's fight against the racial tribalism of his day took root in the church of Jesus Christ. Christian worship is filled with practices that can't coexist with polarized minds. We are called to worship in community; urged to confess our breaking of shalom; invited to a table together; and sent out to serve others across all lines of difference ... Church leaders often worry about bringing the political into the sanctuary, and there are compelling reasons for that concern. But is there anything churches should be better equipped to tackle than disciples who turn their tribes, partisan or otherwise, into an idol? Partisan polarization requires a multifaceted response that matches its complexity. But perhaps seekers of shalom should start when they gather.

Kevin is here suggesting the possibility that the Christian value of "shalom" may inform the attempt of Christians to present an alternative to "partisan politics" in the political arena. But in addition to that raising the question of exactly how commitment to the value of shalom can ameliorate partisan politics, it raises the broader question as to what other Christian values (besides shalom) may inform Christian involvement in politics and the role that the church can play in the political process in light of these Christian values—two challenging questions to which I now turn.

The Role of Churches in Politics
in Light of Christian Values

Chapter 10 will deal in-depth with the controversial question of the role that churches should, or should not, play in the political process. As preparation for this in-depth consideration, it is important to attempt to identify the "Christian values" that might inform any such political involvement. In that light, our four conversation partners were asked to reflect on the extent to which the values and priorities of the Republican and Democratic Parties in the early 21st century comport, or not, with their understanding of "Christian values." As will now be seen, that question is easier to ask than to answer.

No consensus on Christian values

Angela says that "there seems to be no universal consensus on what 'Christian values' are" noting that some of the values that Christians embrace lead to a wide range of practices within differing Christian "fellowships," from emphasizing "prohibitions against certain behaviors: no smoking, drinking, dancing, abortion, or premarital sex"; to exhortations: "teach the truth, feed the hungry, heal the broken, and welcome strangers."

Consistent with his previously expressed concern about putting all Republicans or all Democrats in neat categorical boxes, Doug expresses his frustration with my even asking the question about the extent to which the values embraced by Republican or Democrats comport, or not, with "Christian values." His call for talking about "individuals" rather than airtight "categories" fits with Angela's observation that there is no consensus about the values to which Christians are committed.

No consensus on translating Christian
values into public policies

Assuming, for the sake of argument, that a group of Christians can reach consensus as to a particular "Christian value." There is little chance of reaching consensus as to how to translate commitment to that value into public policy. Based on his own Christian value commitments, Doug suggests that "Christians should acknowledge ... that persons leading sovereign nations have a primary obligation to preserve, protect, and defend that nation ... Christians can hope that political leaders engage with other nations respectfully and realistically, understanding both the possibilities and necessities of global cooperation on items of common concern, as well as the inevitable limits that nation-states will put on such cooperation. Christians can also hope, and perhaps expect and even loudly demand, that political leaders create and preserve political conditions so that Christians as individuals and in Christian organizations and institutions (and individuals and institutions of other faiths) can exist, survive, act, speak, grow and even flourish."

Doug adds that "we can nudge the party's elected and professional elites to address all potential Republican voters, and all Americans, with greater substantive respect by eschewing racist, sexist and other demeaning messaging. We can push them to move beyond rhetoric to offering more substantive plans for ... a more genuinely diverse and tolerant[43] nation."

But even if a significant number of Christians agree with these exhortations from Doug, the vexing questions remain as to how to attain these goals, about which Christians who agree with these exhortations will have significant disagreements. Consider, for example Doug's call for "leaders of sovereign nations to preserve, protect and defend the nation." Does that call suggest the need for bans or strict limitations on immigration from predominately Muslim nations? I think not. But a number of other Christians disagree.

A further complication concerning the lack of consensus among Christians regarding Christian values and their translation into public policy, is that two Christians may share the same value commitments and agree upon the best way to translate those values into public policy, but they may have differing "priorities." Consider for example, Jim's explanation for his "personal preference" for the Democratic Party over the Republican Party.

> You may have gathered, by now, that, while I'm not particularly enamored with either of our political parties, my personal preference is for the party whose platform emphasizes economic and social justice over the one that emphasizes preserving, protecting, and defending the

---

43 It is important to report on Jim Talen's preference for the word "affirmative" rather than "tolerant," because, "The Kingdom that we help usher into this world should be one that does more than just tolerate our diversity. It should affirm and celebrate its divine beauty."

nation. The former themes are woven throughout Scripture and the latter is hard to find or even extrapolate.

Given this lack of consensus among Christians as to "Christian values" and the manner in which an agreed upon Christian value can best be translated into public policy. I will limit myself in the following section to reporting on three Christian values that some of my four conversation partners agree upon, acknowledging upfront that my focusing on these three values is deeply informed by my own value commitments. Consideration of these three values will be my entry into consideration of a possible role for churches in politics.

Three Christian values that have the potential to inform politics

Justice

Jim reports that it was his "commitment to political, social and economic justice, grounded in biblical and creational discernment, [that] came to be the lens through which [he] eventually viewed [his] role as an elected official," adding that such work is "gut-wrenching."

> Being grounded in principles of justice for all, and discerning how those principles should guide decision-making that benefits everyone in society, can be gut-wrenching work.

Angela also emphasizes the important of the Christian value of justice:

> ... justice ... is at the center of God's will.

Along these same lines and in anticipation of the next major section, Angela expresses deep regret that churches don't pay adequate attention to the need to "repair the people and structures that are broken by our injustice."

> ... what we actually ask people to do in congregations is teach, give money (tithe?), fundraise, maintain buildings and grounds, and organize worship; and to attend worship, Bible study, and festival celebrations. Our congregations are for the most part domesticated; our response to structural injustice often reduces down to handouts, coat drives, and

food basket giveaways, especially around holidays. We pray for the poor, the tortured, those living and dying in war zones, victims of injustice. We do not repent and we don't repair the people and structures that are broken by our injustice.

Since the concept of justice is multifaceted, it is important to situate the sense in which Jim and Angela are using the word "justice." First, to set a context, a general definition of "justice" is to treat everyone "fairly" or to give everyone his/her "due" (recognizing room for disagreement as to what is "fair" or what a person is "due" in a given situation).

The call for "fairness" has at least the following three sub-categories: Commutative Justice (protecting the rights between one individual and another individual, as in the expectation that both parties to a contract will honor that contract); Retributive Justice (punishment for a wrongful act that is proportional to the magnitude of the offense); Distributive Justice (fair allocation of goods to all members of society).

In that context, it appears to me that both Jim and Angela are using the word "justice" in the distributive sense, as testified to by the following assertions:

Disparities between white and non-white populations, in wealth, health, education, income, employment and access to power are significant, disturbing, and unacceptable (Jim).

Lives are transformed when safety and security, education and housing, health care, clean food and water are secured for all people (Angela).

Doug is also talking about distributive justice when he calls for "a financial and economic infrastructure to help non-urban areas," such as "universal Internet access for rural areas and small towns."

But there is another more subtle dimension to "distributive justice" that is embedded in Jim Skillen's call for government to recognize and support the roles and responsibilities of non-governmental groups, such as families, businesses, churches and other voluntary organizations. As footnoted in Chapter 4, the Center for Public Justice (CPJ), for which Jim served as founding president, embraces the ideals of "structural pluralism" and "confessional pluralism, both of which aim for 'fair' treatment of all societal groups, governmental and otherwise."

In light of the above brief summary of the broad scope of "doing justice," it is my belief that Christians should foster all of these dimensions of justice, in ways that comport with their Christian faith beliefs[44] However, based on my understanding of the teaching of Jesus recorded in Matthew 25, I sense a special personal responsibility to promote distributive justice to the poor and marginalized members of our society, while applauding those Christians who seek to give expression to the Christian value of justice in other ways.

Shalom

Kevin suggests that Christians should ask the following meddlesome question:

> In this political moment, do [political] parties foster a vision for *shalom*? Do they embody civic practices that leave room for citizens to disagree on weighty issues and still walk away at peace with each other? In the language of this series, do they promote 'respectful conversation' or 'convicted civility'?

It is important that the Hebrew word "shalom" not be confused with the common negative Western definition of "peace" as the absence of conflict or war. In Hebrew the word "shalom" means much more, including a robust positive view of "peace" as living in positive, caring relationships with others, including those who disagree with you, and living in positive relationship with all of Creation.

In commenting on the contentious issue of "bringing the political into the sanctuary" (more about that later), Kevin adds the penetrating insight that "seekers of shalom should start when they gather with each other."

> Church leaders often worry about bringing the political into the sanctuary, and there are compelling reasons for that concern. But is there anything churches should be better

---

44 For example, as a Christian, I reject forms of retributive justice that focus on punishment to the exclusion of rehabilitation. A compelling Christian alternative is the Restorative Justice movement, which attempts to bring about restitution and reconciliation between offender and victim and members of their respective communities. See Zehr, *Changing Lenses* and *The Little Book of Restorative Justice*.

equipped to tackle than disciples who turn their tribes, partisan or otherwise, into an idol? Partisan polarization requires a multifaceted response that matches its complexity. But perhaps seekers of shalom should start when they gather with each other.

Kevin's suggestion that Christians should start practicing shalom when "they gather with each other" points to another pivotal Christian value: "community."

Community

Now is as good a time as any for me to reveal my own political party leanings. I resonate with Jim's perception of a "general" difference between the Republican and Democratic Parties, which he expresses as follows:

I've come to view the Republican Party as generally more concerned about individual rights over community responsibilities, more concerned about government investments to create individual wealth rather than investing to develop community health.

Of course, that is much too simple a generalization. Where I align myself depends on the public policy issue at hand. I support some public policy positions that most Republicans propose, to the chagrin of most Democrats, and I support some public policy positions that most Democrats propose, to the chagrin of most Republicans.[45] But when considering a given public policy issue, my first inclination is to ask, "What is good for the communities of which I am a part?" rather than, "What is good for me or other individuals?" This aligns me more often with Democratic proposals for public policy than with Republican proposals (although I generally then seek ways to find some common ground between the differing proposals because I believe that both individuals and communities are meant to flourish). This admission may raise more questions than it

---

45 To cite two examples, I favor "school vouchers" (generally identified as a Republican initiative) since I believe that parents should be able to decide on the education they want their children to have, provided the school voucher system can be designed to not be detrimental to "public schools" and all schools meet minimal educational standards set by society through its government. And, I am opposed to "abortion on demand" (a position held by many Democrats), while allowing for abortions in cases of "tragic moral choice" such as when the life of the mother is in danger, incest and rape.

answers, but for me to attempt to elaborate would take us too far afield. My point is that in our American culture that seems, at least to me, to overemphasize individualism, I wish to point us to the Christian value of community well-being.

Consistent with this emphasis on community values, Kevin offers the profound insight that our churches can be communities where, by means of our collective worship and other means of loving engagement (like having respectful conversations about our disagreements, I would add) we can model how to overcome the scourge of "tribalism," especially when it comes to disagreements about political issues.

> ... the church makes profoundly 'real' moral claims, and ... its practices—most importantly worship—shape our political lives, even when the church doesn't take partisan sides. I would also argue that the church *ought* to play that role, especially in this age of political tribalism ...

I close this section with a report on how my church in Orange City, Iowa (American Reformed Church) is taking incremental steps to become the kind of loving, Christian community to which Kevin calls us. A criticism that we sometimes hear about our church is that "anybody can go there," which we take as a compliment. Our members are very diverse in their church backgrounds and in their views about controversial issues, like political affiliation and same-sex marriage. How do we handle our disagreements? Not by hiding them, which is the approach favored by those who would settle for an anemic negative view of peace as absence of conflict. Rather, we have created forums where we talk honestly and respectfully about our disagreements as brothers and sisters in Christ who love one another; our way of seeking for shalom.

Differentiation and Complementarity of Roles of Churches and Government

Jim proposes that the "church and government can play complementary roles in addressing one of our country's most significant and challenging issues—our pervasive and ongoing racism."

Angela questions the possibility of such reciprocity. While maintaining that "grassroots democracy" within churches and faith-based organizations can demonstrate "working together across difference to do justice" and recognizing that "serving a community can be a profound blessing to the church" (as noted by Kevin), Angela strongly questions the capability of the political parties to partner with churches to do justice.

> [Parties] ... do not build democratic practices and good citizens; they develop ideologues, partisans and party operatives, and apparatchiks.

But Kevin believes that Angela is too quick to reach that judgment, at least in part because she is "essentializing" the "party pathologies": "[Treating] solvable problems in our party system as rooted in the very nature of party politics."

Contrary to Angela's view, Kevin sees rich potential for reciprocity between the church and government as long as one recognizes a proper differentiation in their respective roles.

> I have no doubt about the evidence that the church is well positioned to address the felt needs of the vulnerable and dispossessed. Churches and other faith-based groups are indeed the backbone of civil society today. Often their work is diaconical and nitty-gritty: stocking food pantries, tutoring kids and adults, offering temporary housing, finding jobs for returning citizens, giving a little benevolence to pay a utility bill, and so on.

> The problem, as I see it, is that Cowser has conflated the role of the parties with the role of the church. If parties do share the role of the church, then it's easy to see why anyone would understand parties as dispensable. After all, the church does a better job than parties at fulfilling the call to do diaconical work in their communities and speak the biblical truth of *shalom* to those in power. But the point is that parties and churches do not and ought not share that role; the comparison is apples to oranges. We shouldn't expect parties to fulfill the diaconical work of the church

or take on the same kind of public witness. Conversely, we shouldn't expect the church to fulfill the work of parties. Parties perform crucial functions as linkage institutions in electoral democracies by connecting elites to the electorate and bringing structure to the lawmaking process. They might do this work poorly—again, Cowser and I agree about that—but it's hard to imagine other organizations fulfilling the same functions.

To differentiate roles is not to seal institutions off from each other.

Hence, Kevin concludes, "the relationship of the church and the broader community is richly reciprocal. It combines attention to felt needs with a formative spirituality and a public witness to shalom."

Despite her concern that political parties, as presently functioning, will not partner with churches in the way that Kevin proposes, Angela does in the end (the last paragraph in her last posting), hold on to the ideal of churches partnering with government.

A measure of justice can happen when congregations realize that we are part of the polis—the people—that the Gospel has reach into all spheres of human life, and that the fundamental purpose of religion (*religio*) is to transform the world. Transforming the world means taking our seat at the tables of significant decision-making in our communities, speaking and organizing as full citizens who've taken up the responsibility of governing—along with business and government.

The nitty-gritty of such attempts at reciprocity between church and government will be addressed in depth in Chapter 10.

Limits to What Politics can Accomplish

Christians, like me, who have a vision for political activity to be an instrument for fostering God's redemptive purposes need to honestly face the limits as to what political activity can accomplish due to human finitude and sinfulness.

Although our conversation partners do not comment directly on the limitations on political accomplishments due to human finitude, recall, from Chapter 2, my call for humility that models that rare commitment of stating my beliefs on a given issue with clarity and conviction at the same time that I acknowledge that "I may be wrong." Such humility may be especially called for when dealing with public policy issues because of the complexity of such issues and the danger of unintended consequences of public policies that have good intentions.

Doug does call our attention to the limits on what politics can accomplish due to "sin." The context for his fair warning is set by his understanding of the principles of "sphere sovereignty" and "subsidiarity," defined as follows:

> **Sphere sovereignty** claims that each sphere of life has distinct responsibilities, authority and competence, standing equal to other spheres and in direct responsibility to God. An all-encompassing God-created order includes topical task-oriented communities, such as those for education, worship, civil justice, economy and labor, marriage and family and artistic expression. No one area is sovereign over another. Particularly, neither institutions of faith (e.g., churches) nor civil justice (e.g., governments) has any particular superiority. Rather, the main job of each level or branch of government, and government as a whole, is to protect the boundaries among the spheres. It is as if government is the internal and external walls of a home, and the really important work happens within the house's many rooms, each room more or less authoritative over what happens in it. In a complementary way, **subsidiarity** argues that the most local competent authority best handles matters of public

concern. It has thick notions of human responsibility and sociability. Localized institutions such as the family, church and voluntary associations link and empower individuals, and assigning duties to them fulfills their callings.

These principles of sphere sovereignty and subsidiarity inform the "both/and" position that I proposed in Chapter 4 relative to the differentiated yet complementary responsibilities of government and non-governmental groups such as families, businesses, churches and other voluntary organizations. Doug also notes how these principles place "limits" on the reach of government and the reach of the church for the purpose of "[maximizing] well-being while minimizing [the effects of] sin."

> The Christian notions of sphere sovereignty and subsidiarity have a variety of government applications, particularly the American version. Both limit government (as well as church) reach, fitting well with American federalism and separation of powers. Based on Christian insights into the nature of human possibility and sin, they serve as strategic guides to maximize well-being while minimizing sin, the latter particularly prone to large institutions such as the church and state organized and operated by well-meaning but still fallen individuals.

As an entry into the next section, Doug suggest another "limit to politics": "Christian politicians and activists" need to avoid the tragedy of being "consumed by their political activity."

> There are three other limits to politics to note. First, partisan political engagement around national issues is not a moral requirement to live a Christian life, even though it has occupied a conspicuous portion of my own. Perhaps writing only to myself, more than 20 years ago,[46] ... I wrote that 'I look for politicians who take the time to pay attention to their families, who have developed outside interests that are not political, who take time off every week, year, or within their careers to cultivate the other areas of life. ... [E]vidence that life is more than politics is crucial. There is something

46 Koopman, "Reformed Christian Citizenship," 41-54.

tragic, even hypocritical, about Christian politicians and activists consumed by their political activity." My voluntary relocation away from Washington, D.C. in the mid-1990s probably was required for me to follow my own advice on that point.

A Christian Calling to do Politics

To those who have read this book up to this point, it should be obvious that "doing politics" is not for the faint of heart. Doug describes his many years of engagement in the political realm as a "calling"; a part of his life that has to be "fully dedicated to God" that he finds "personally interesting, rewarding and comprehensible."

> ... how much moral weight is there to political involvement and partisan choice in the United States today? My simple answer is—far less than the questions imply or that my nearly 40 years of full-time engagement with American politics seems to indicate. I feel personally called to significant political involvement. I also maintain a longstanding preference for the Republican Party. I don't, however, see either choice as morally superior to minimal citizenship activity and support for Democrats. To me, politics is part of a life that has to be fully dedicated to God, and political parties are an invaluable tool in organizing government policies that hopefully move society forward. I find that work personally interesting, rewarding and comprehensible.

Doug also reports on the inspiration he received from the example of Paul Henry, the late U.S. congressman from Michigan, including the way in which Henry's "welcoming personality and skills in listening, balancing and synthesizing made Paul perfectly suited for legislative representation."

> ... a Christian seeking to engage the political system also has to feel deeply called. I believe the call has to be a rather specific one, to a particular type of service and in a particular time in life. After less than four years in my Washington, D.C.

political career, in 1984 I was fortunate enough to connect
to Paul B. Henry in his first campaign for the U.S. House,
and to work in that campaign and in his first years of service
in the U.S. House. After Paul's death in 1993, my colleague
in those adventures, Gary Visscher, wrote with me a short
tribute to Paul in which we note how well-fitted Paul was
to the position of elected legislator. We made the case that
his welcoming personality and skills in listening, balancing
and synthesizing made Paul perfectly suited for legislative
representation, more so than careers in the executive or
judicial branches for which he was also mentioned. It seems
too often that people who claim a call to political service
by seeking a particular office may be masking a more
worrisome will to political power by any means necessary,
misrepresenting a desire to dominate as an eagerness to
serve. The challenging task for a Christian voter is to try to
discern those motivations in the many candidates seeking
such positions and, for the Christian contemplating his or
her own political future, to a thoughtful and thorough self-
examination of both abilities and motivations.

Kevin seconds Doug's suggestion that becoming involved in party
politics can be a "calling" for a "seeker of *shalom*," despite the focus on
"competition," while acknowledging that this can be a "fraught vocation."

... I want to suggest that a seeker of *shalom* can in principle
embrace party politics. Competing and highlighting political
differences are not necessarily morally disqualifying.
Perhaps some Christians even have a special calling to be
salt and light as critical insiders within the parties. But it
is surely a fraught vocation, especially considering how
easily the mobilization of our differences can swerve into
demonization of the other side.

There is much to unpack in Doug's thoughtful reflections, which I will
now attempt, in my own words, in a manner that connects with some of
what you have read in previous chapters (without attributing these closing

reflections to any of my conversation partners for this chapter or previous chapters).

A "calling" that a Christian senses to do politics may well reflect a deep conviction that God intends to redeem all realms of life (Colossians 1:20), including the political realm.

This doesn't mean that every Christian is called to do politics. Biblical teachings about the Body of Christ (e.g., 1 Corinthians 12) suggest that God's redemptive intentions are fostered on earth by each Christian "partnering" with God according to his/her particular gifts and abilities.

And, as the example of Paul Henry reveals, the gifts to "do politics well" include the gifts of providing a welcoming space for those who disagree with you about public policy issues, listening carefully to their contrary views, and balancing and synthesizing in the sense of seeking to find common ground, at best, or ways of living well with one another in the absence of common ground, all of which is noticeably absent in current political discourse.

But one who heeds a calling to do politics must learn to settle for modest redemptive accomplishments due to our finitude as human beings and the brokenness in our world, including our own sinfulness.

My excursions into doing politics are modest, compared to Doug, Jim, Kevin, Angela and many other Christians, limited to my recent political advocacy and work to foster the well-being of my Latino neighbors in northwest Iowa.[47]

My advocacy work has included face-to-face meetings with local and national politicians who have little interest in fostering the well-being of our Latino neighbors (e.g., Steve King, my 4th District of Iowa representative in the U.S. House). I leave such meetings broken-hearted. The only thing that keeps me going is my unswerving conviction that, despite all the contrary evidence, God's redemptive purposes will be fully realized some day; and, in the meantime, I am called to plant tiny "seeds of redemption," even in the political realm, entrusting the harvest to God (Matthew 13: 31-32).

---

47 By means of my involvement with CASA of Sioux County (Center for Assistance, Service & Advocacy), a local nonprofit that "envisions transformed northwest Iowa communities that welcome, empower and celebrate people from all cultures."

6

The Role of Money and Special Interests in Politics

ONE OF THE perceived problems in party politics is that money and special interest groups play an inordinate role in influencing the positions that parties and individual politicians take relative to public policy issues.

In this chapter, Kim Conger and Frank Hill present contrasting responses to the following set of leading questions:

- How have money and special interests influenced politics: for good or for ill?
- What is your position on the *Citizens United* decision of the Supreme Court?
- Should the role of lobbyists for special interests be restricted?
- Should there be stricter conflict of interest rules?

As you read what follows, keep in mind that Kim comes to these questions primarily as a teacher of political science and administrator at a university and Frank considers these same questions primarily from the perspective of a political practitioner with extensive experience in the halls of Congress. This difference in social location may help the reader to better understand the nature of their agreements and disagreements, which I now consider in that order.

Agreements

There are numerous areas where Kim and Frank express agreement.

We need government since we are not "angels"

Frank reminds us that "whenever believers start to think about their role in our modern American democratic republic, they should keep the following three facts in mind": "We are not a theocracy"; "We have a civil government run by imperfect fallen creatures"; "We are not yet living in the city of God but rather the city of Man." He adds that "James Madison recognized the dilemma when he wrote 'Federalist No. 51' and said":

> If men were angels, no government would be necessary. If angels were to govern men, neither external nor internal controls on government would be necessary.

Frank concludes that "we are not all angels and therefore, we do need government."

Kim heartily concurs, asserting that "men are not angels and that's why we need government," but adding the caveat that "we need government to help protect our fundamental rights" (the first hint of an area of disagreement, to be dealt with later).

Frank adds that "Christians have to learn how to play by the rules of the game as they exist today, not as they wish they would be if all they had to do was wave a magic wand and transform the United States into the 'City on The Hill' overnight."

Kim concurs: "I think one of the strengths of Mr. Hill's approach is his recognition of the system and situation as it stands, not a hoped-for utopia. Recognizing that we do not live in a theocracy is important."

Political campaigns do need money

Kim asserts that "campaigns do need money" because "it's expensive to try to communicate your idea to voters in ways that make impact. Many other things are competing for citizens' attention and it's just modern reality that it takes money to get and hold the attention of the people one wants to represent."

Similarly, Frank observes that "from the very beginning of the American republic, some form of 'campaign finance' has been used to help people of one party or the other get elected," adding that this need for "campaign finance" has "been long recognized as part and parcel of that 'freedom of speech' we all hold dear" (more about a possible connection with "freedom of speech" later).

Campaign finance helps voters to gather the information needed to inform their voting

Frank makes a strong case for the need for money for candidates for office to "get their message out to the voters."

> The other component to campaign finance is that it really does get at the heart of freedom of expression, opinion and political sentiment. A person can have well-grounded and sound beliefs about how we should live our collective life together as Americans but unless he or she has a way to convey those great ideas and sentiments to a majority of voters in their state or district, how will we ever know if what they are saying makes any sense or not?

> That is where campaign finance comes in. Candidates have to raise enough money to be able to pay for the newsletters, TV ads, social media campaigns and door-to-door literature drops that allow even the most virtuous Christian to get their message out to the voters who actually have the power to agree with them and put them in office so they can put their great ideas to work in the public square for all of us, or not.

Frank adds that in our broken world, voters need information that "refutes political attacks" and getting such information out requires money.

> It would be nice to believe that all men and women are virtuous, Christ-centered individuals who follow Scripture religiously. In such a world, we would not need any expensive political campaigns because everyone would tell the truth about themselves and their opponents and there

would be no need to refute any vicious political attacks with expensive campaign commercials.

Kim agrees with Frank about the need for voters to have more information to inform their voting, particularly relative to full disclosure of campaign contributions, another area of agreement to which I now turn.

All campaign contributions need to be fully disclosed

Frank makes a strong case for the need for full public disclosure of all campaign contributions.

> Mandate that *all* contributions to any political campaign or effort in support of a party or candidate is *immediately* disclosed through an online reporting portal through the Federal Election Commission for federal races and state board of elections for state and local races.

> But so much of it [support of a party or candidate] today is in 'undisclosed' contributions that can find its way into the 'dark' campaigns that technically do not support the individual candidacy of any particular candidate but 'officially' are considered 'public advocacy' of a general issue, all of which is considered 'free speech' and guaranteed by the First Amendment.

> The best way to shed light on all of this 'dark money' is to bring it out into the open and mandate that any dollar spent on any campaign or advocacy effort must be disclosed immediately online for all the world to see.

Kim strongly concurs.

> *Three cheers for disclosure!* I'm definitely supportive of the kind of comprehensive, real-time donation disclosure Frank Hill suggests. On a practical level, this may be the only way to improve some of the challenges I see in the system, at least in the near term. And I strongly agree with the idea that the solution is found in more information. Disclosure laws with

real teeth certainly give citizens the kind of information they need to make better decisions about who they should support.

Kim adds that in addition to requiring full disclosure, "campaign finance legislation" should also establish "spending limits."

Political corruption is not a major problem

Kim says: "My main concern is not ... with the potential for political corruption that exists in the pursuit of donors and supporters. While this corruption happens, and people are currently in jail for trading votes and other decisions for money or favors, this is only the most visible challenge presented by the role of money and special interests in our system. And I believe literal corruption is actually a relatively minor threat to our democratic system."

Frank concurs: "I ... agree with her [Kim's] statement that 'literal corruption is actually a relatively minor threat to our democratic (republican) system.'"

Money seems to be a problem only when the "other side" gets it

Somewhat amusingly, both Frank and Kim point to the hypocrisy of political parties or politicians only complaining about the role of money in politics when it is the "other side" or political opponent who "gets it."

> Very few people I have ever met in close to 40 years of politics are truly principled when it comes to eradicating the 'scourge of Big Money' in campaigns and politics. It is only 'the other side' that is evil when it comes to campaign finance abuse and detestability (Frank).

> I also strongly agree that most people's opposition to 'money in politics' is opposition to 'money in politics I don't agree with' (Kim).

The effects of money on a politician's decisions are "slim to none"

This agreement may surprise some readers. Kim states this belief most emphatically:

> *First, money does not change a politician's mind. I whole-heartedly agree* [with Frank]. There's very little evidence that any type of campaign contribution or favor impacts decision-makers votes ... we also know that lobbyists actually do not spend a lot of time trying to convince opponents—they spend most of their time with supporters.

Frank acknowledges that elected representatives can sometimes be swayed by "the allure of more campaign money," but, in general, "the impact of campaign money on daily decisions for most elected representatives is slim to none."

> I am not saying that there are not any elected representatives who can never be swayed by the allure of more campaign money coming in from one source or another. History is replete with cases where congressmen and senators and presidents have taken money and then been swayed to vote in a way that was contrary to their core philosophy or goals.

> However, my experience has been that with the speed of modern-day politics and the sheer amount of work that has to be done on a daily basis on Capitol Hill, since that is where my frame of reference is, the impact of campaign money on daily decisions for most elected representatives is slim to none.

Having worked in the trenches of day-to-day politics in the office of former U.S. Senator Elizabeth Dole and others,[48] Frank is able to provide a perspective on why the effect on money on the day-to-day decisions

---

48 Frank indicates that "there are several points of disagreement [with Kim]" that "might result from" his "22 years of working on Capitol Hill, 12 years as chief of staff for a congressman and U.S. senator [Elizabeth Dole] and 10 as a lobbyist ... plus ... four years ... in North Carolina working with the state legislature and governor's office."

is "often overblown" that eludes some citizens and scholars working in academia, as reported in the following extended quote:

> ... 14 years ago when I was chief of staff to former U.S. Senator Elizabeth Dole, we would regularly get 5,000 emails per day in her Senate office, 2,500 fax messages (which are obsolete today), 1,000 phone calls in the various offices from constituents and lobbyists and reporters on *top* of the 10,000 written letters, many handwritten by constituents who were concerned about everything from the Greyhound Racing Act of 2002 to the monumental issues of fighting al-Qaida in Afghanistan to balancing the federal budget.
>
> In addition to working on the legislative agenda for the day and answering all of these emails, faxes and letters, we just didn't have time to wonder who had given how much money to Senator Dole's campaign or not. Every single one of our 49 staff people who handled casework, legislative correspondence and policy issues for the senator had zero idea of who ever even contributed to her campaign, much less in what order of magnitude.
>
> The only people who had any real idea of who had contributed to her 2002 campaign were our campaign manager who lived in North Carolina and only occasionally visited Washington, D.C., and myself and that was only because I was familiar with the large donors from my time with former Congressman McMillan of Charlotte from 1985-1995 and the various lobbyists with PACs who were from North Carolina or who had interests in North Carolina.
>
> It is not a humongous pool to draw from. In fact, in many states, the pool of PACs that represent business interests in the state could be below 10 total.
>
> When it comes to the elected official, in many cases they don't even remember the name of the lobbyist and rely

heavily on staff to tell them who they are about to meet with and why. Movies and the news try to glamorize the cozy relationship between a shifty elected senator and some nefarious lobbyist with a big PAC to protect big interests in their state, but for the most part, that is just Hollywood fiction and storytelling.

Every elected official has their favorite friends and some of those friends might be a lobbyist with a PAC because of shared philosophy on government or perhaps a shared interest in a sports team or maybe they went to college together. Former staff do have a leg up on a relationship with an elected official they might have worked for over the years but that usually means that person has a close relationship with 1 out of 100 senators or 1 out of 435 members of Congress which is hardly a majority of either legislative chamber.

So it would be good for any observer of money in politics to try to separate the fiction from the fact and put a couple of shakers of salt on any story they might come across in the news about some 'undue influence' any lobbyist might have with an elected official.

Often times, it is overblown.

Frank's extended report on his work on the ground in politics should alert us to the dangers of over-generalization. There may indeed be politicians who give into the allure of money from special interest groups. But there are many politicians whose first commitment is to fostering a common good.

But despite this apparent agreement between Kim and Frank that the reported effects of actual cash contributions to the coffers of politicians may be "overblown," a hint of significant disagreement emerges when Kim rejects the idea that "the money spent in politics is just about money." Rather, the problem with money in politics is the way in which it creates "inequality in political representation." I will unpack Kim's suggestion in the course of now considering two major points of disagreement.

Disagreements

Campaign finance as an expression of "free speech"

The first major area of disagreement between Kim and Frank is about the role that the "right" to "free speech" should play in the debate about the role of money and special interests in politics.

Frank argues that "some form of campaign finance" is "part and parcel" of "freedom of speech."

> From the very beginning of the American republic, some form of 'campaign finance' has been used to help people of one party or the other get elected which has been long recognized as part and parcel of that 'freedom of speech' we all hold dear.

As already reported, both Frank and Kim agree that campaign finance helps voters to gather information needed to inform their voting. As indicated above, Frank sees this as an expression of "freedom of speech."

But, while acknowledging the importance of "rights," like the right to "freedom of speech," Kim expresses concern about the "pervasiveness of rights in our political thinking and rhetoric," which reflects an inordinate focus on "individualism" in America.

> One challenge here is the pervasiveness of rights in our political thinking and rhetoric. It is difficult for any American, I think, to sacrifice our individual freedoms for the sake of others' freedom. It runs counter to not only our socialization but also our individual experience in an individualistic system. Recall, however, Paul's instructions on how to use our 'rights.' We are not to use our rights and freedoms as followers of Jesus to cause problems or destroy the consciences of other believers. Namely, we are to love them by giving up our rights so they can enjoy the same freedom in Christ that we do. I find that to be a powerful model of

how Christians might use their own individual political rights in a democratic system. We are not responsible for others' freedom, but we are responsible for our own actions in promoting and protecting that freedom. That sounds like a pretty good basis for creating pervasive political equality.

Note carefully, for later reference, that Kim's concern about the pervasiveness of thinking exclusively in terms of "my rights" is that it doesn't pay adequate attention to the "rights of others," which is called for as an expression of "love" for others and points to a need for "political equality" (much more about "political equality" and the "politics of love" later).

Kim elaborates by reminding us that although our "free speech rights" are very important, such "rights" are "not inviolable."

I very much agree [with Frank] that one of the core challenges in the conversation about money and special interests in politics is one of free speech. As Americans, our free speech rights are among the most comprehensively protected in the world and that is one of the reasons our democratic system has been so long-lived and stable. But it is important to recognize that even our free speech rights are not inviolable. There are situations in which we limit free speech in order to protect public safety. If you yell '**fire!**' in a crowded theater (and there is no fire), that is not protected speech. If you stand on the steps of a state capitol with a gun in your hand advocating overthrow of the government, that is not protected speech. We limit freedom of speech when it is a clear and present danger to the citizens or the political system. And we already limit some kinds of campaign spending and lobbying behavior for these same reasons. Businesses are not allowed to contribute money directly to political campaigns, and former elected and appointed officials have a waiting period before they can lobby their former institutions. This is a recognition that some types of speech are so compelling that other citizens' liberty are threatened by the protection of an individual citizen's rights. That is what I see happening with money in politics, and particularly the equation of money with speech. It is legitimate to limit freedom in order to ensure that freedom can extend to everyone, therefore it is legitimate to limit individual freedom to spend money in order to make sure everyone has an equal shot at representation within the political system.

Once again, Kim gives us a hint here as to something she believes is more fundamental than "free speech rights," which is the "right" to "an equal shot within the political system," which leads us to a second area of disagreement.

Political equality

Both Frank and Kim believe in the need for "political equality." But their views differ as to what constitutes such "political equality" and how to ensure that it is attained.

Frank seems to equate "political equality" with the "right to vote" that every citizen has, while bemoaning the fact that such a low percentage of citizens exercise that "right."

> She [Kim] is right to be concerned about all of our citizens being able to participate equally in our democratic republic. It is always surprising to folks outside of the government or political realm when they find out that perhaps 35 percent of all adults eligible to vote in any election are not registered to vote for whatever reason.

In that light, Frank goes on to propose that the best way to "achieve political equality" is to get everyone to vote.

> The 'easiest' way to achieve political equality is to find ways to get everyone to vote every time in every election in which they are eligible to vote. That would be the purest way to achieve equality and put away any notions that someone is gaining an advantage one way or the other by supporting this or that candidate with hard money, soft money or word-of-mouth campaigns.

Kim expresses her disagreement with Frank's view that "the real problem with unequal representation is low voter turnout" as follows:

> Mr. Hill suggests that the real problem with unequal representation is low voter turnout. I disagree for several reasons. Voting is a blunt instrument—citizens get to choose representatives but not the actual issue and policy positions they espouse. In fact, citizens don't even really get to choose representatives. That choice is already structured by elites in the form of political parties and the state laws that enshrine the two major parties in power. So, true and robust representation in our system has to seek avenues beyond voting. Even with 100 percent voter turnout, this challenge would remain.

What, then, is Kim's position on the meaning of "political equality"? It is in essence that every citizen has an "equal stake" in the political system that includes "majority voices" not ruling "minority voices out of being."

> ... One of the foundational commitments of democratic systems is political equality. This is the idea that within the political system, each person has an equal stake, made practical in terms of voicing one's opinions, voting and access to governmental authority. It is the foundation of popular sovereignty; the basic premise of authority and rule within democratic systems. If citizens are not largely equal in their ability to help rule themselves, then tyranny is a likely outcome, whether in the form of a king, an aristocracy, or simply a long-term concentration of power in just a few individuals or groups. The institutions of our political and governmental system are largely designed with this requirement in mind. Majority rules in the legislative branch while minority rights are protected through civil liberties and the courts. A citizen's issue position may not win the day, but the system protects the right to come back and try again tomorrow. Majority voices cannot rule minority voices out of being. This fundamental principle is embedded in the pervasive checks and balances and

separation of powers in our system. One of the reasons it is so hard to create change of policy or institutions is that our political system is designed to be slow and deliberative, and to ensure the equal participation of citizens and their representatives.

Kim adds that various amendments to the U.S. Constitution over the years have "expanded" our view of "what political equality means."

In the United States, our vision of what political equality means, or more specifically who it pertains to, has expanded over the life of the republic. The Civil War (Reconstruction) Amendments (13th, 14th and 15th), expand both the definition of who deserves political equality and the responsibilities of governmental institutions in extending equal protection of the law to all citizens. The 19th Amendment extends to rights of equal citizenship and political equality to women and the laws passed in the civil rights era again expanded government's responsibility to protect that equality. Political equality is so important that Americans are constantly reevaluating the principal and how well the political culture enables it.

In light of her view of the meaning of "political equality," Kim then points us to the danger of money and special interests in politics." They "buy access" to a politician's "time and attention."

... the activities and strategies used by interest groups and lobbyists ... focus on the two types of currency most important for a decision-maker to stay in office, money and information. In fact, while political scientists have not been able to establish a link between donating money to a campaign and specific policy choices of elected officials, there is a significant amount of evidence that campaign money buys access to a member's time and attention. So, the information, the opinions, and the policy preferences of these interests gets much more airtime on the decision-maker's schedule than the needs of others in their constituencies.

This cannot help but impact the decision of the officials and their staff.

Kim elaborates on this inordinate influence of money and special interests in terms of "representation multipliers": "all the factors that can help an individual, group or business gain a bigger share of representation through dominating the attention of a decision-maker," with these "factors" not just being money but also "information that is relevant and persuasive."

> While many special interests also provide money to campaigns in some way, in many cases their primary multiplier is in the network of information they can provide to a decision-maker. This is why the most successful lobbyists are those who have served in the positions of the people they later lobby. These lobbyists better understand not only what information is relevant and persuasive, but can use their existing networks to provide information on other important player's preferences. For example, a former member of Congress that becomes an important lobbyist is successful not simply because they can steer campaign donations to a sitting member of Congress, but also because they understand the constraints a member of congress operates under and can advise the member about their options and the perspectives of others in their networks. Money seems to be important to get a decision-maker's attention, but keeping their attention requires a long-term beneficial relationship based on other representational multipliers.

Here, then is the fundamental problem with the role of money and special interests in politics that concerns Kim: *Campaign donations buy access and attention.*

> It may certainly be the case that the people Mr. Hill has worked for were paying attention to the marginalized among their constituents ... the preponderance of evidence is that members of Congress are listening more closely to those

that give them money. Campaign donations buy access and attention. This is seen not only in individual decision-makers, but in the larger scope of issues considered by Congress and the executive branch.

Kim adds that she does not see much hope for comprehensive campaign finance reform because "resourced interests" have no incentive to call into question the "status quo."

> The other wicked challenge for political equality is the power of the status quo ... People and organizations who hold power behind the scenes based on their access to representational multipliers are not going to give up those advantages without a fight. Overall, the predicament is complex and wide-ranging and the challenge of special interests in a democracy has plagued us from the beginning. I do not hold out much hope for lobbying reform, let alone a comprehensive campaign finance solution.

> Even when clear opinion exists among voters, there are issues and policies that are never discussed because resourced interests want to preserve the status quo.

From my personal perspective, clear contemporary evidence for Kim's assertion that "resourced interests" keeps certain issues and policies from even being discussed, "even when clear opinion exists among voters," is the obvious way in which the influence of the NRA keeps politicians from grappling with the need for "reasonable gun control measures," despite polling data revealing that the large majority of Americans favor the strengthening of gun controls. I would add that strengthening gun control measures should be in addition to, not in place of, other needed measures related to mental health and addressing the pervasive factors, like the entertainment industry, that contribute to a "culture of violence."

Despite her critique of "representational multipliers," Kim concludes that they are "not necessarily problematic on their own"; they only become problematic when they silence the average voter.

Representational multipliers are not necessarily problematic on their own. Decision-makers are finite beings who genuinely need expert help to manage all the disparate information required to make good decisions on policies. Members of Congress cannot be experts in all the areas about which they are asked to make decisions … So, we can expect that there will always be some disconnect between a representative and their constituents. The concern I have is when these disconnects threaten fundamental political equality.

Political equality is threatened when citizens who desire to make their voice heard in government cannot because they have been crowded out by organizations and businesses whose resources so dwarf the average voter as to make them invisible. Having resources that allow you to catch decision-makers attention is not necessarily bad; using those resources to make sure that no one else gets heard is.

What Kim is asserting is that "political equality" requires that "everyone be heard." I heartily concur. For the sake of emphasis, I now present some of Kim's further reflections on this requirement to prepare the reader for consideration of a possible "Politics of Love" and a proposed "Way Forward."

All Voices Need to Be Heard in the Political Process

Kim is emphatic in her concern about the "voices of average citizens" being "crowded out" by those who have "the money and other resources" needed to "buy an outsized piece of representation."

It's not really about how much we spend, or the fact we have the right to spend it; the point is that money and other resources buy an outsized piece of representation, something that is supposed to be equally distributed among sovereign citizens in a democracy. My concern is less about the money

> itself and more about the crowding out effect it has on the
> voices of average citizens.

> Voices of the average citizen are crowded out by the activities
> of people, organizations, and businesses with the money
> and access to not only make their preferences heard, but to
> drown out the preferences of the other side.

I pause here to interject my reflection on Kim's crucial assertion above, that her concern is "less about the money itself and more about the crowding out effect it has on the voices of average citizens." Recall that both Kim and Frank agree that the influence of money from special interest groups on a politician's decisions may be "overblown." But that doesn't mean that "big money contributions" to politicians are not problematic. What Kim is arguing is that a very significant problem with such "big money" in politics is that (in my words) it severely narrows the political landscape. The voices of average citizens, who do not have adequate financial resources to enable their voices to be heard are, in effect, "made invisible"; their voices are not heard in the quest to identify a common good.

Kim suggests that this "crowding out" of the voices of average citizens makes it impossible for those who disagree with those who have "majority power" in the political process to even express their disagreements.

> Left to our own devices, people would (and do!) try to use
> majority power to not only achieve their policy goals, but
> to make sure that those who disagree can no longer contest
> the issue.

Kim notes that the "loudest, most resourced voices are not always right." Therefore, although "more money can help us make our message *louder*, it doesn't necessarily make that message more true, or more helpful to the larger democratic system."

Kim concludes with the radical suggestion that helping my neighbors to "exercise their voice" is an expression of "love"; speculating that Frank would agree "that democratic politics requires citizens to be able to use their voice," but wondering whether Frank would also see this as an expression of "love."

I don't know if Mr. Hill would share my view that politics is about love, but I do think he shares my opinion that democratic politics requires citizens to be able to use their voice.

Kim adds that the need to express love for others by enabling them to "have a voice" in the political process should be taken with utmost seriousness by Christians because of the "call to love my neighbor" that is central to the Christian faith.

As a Christian living within this democratic system, I think the call to love my neighbor means both acting justly towards them by helping them exercise their voices, but also seeking to change political systems that make it hard for them to speak.

Kim adds that "Christians … need the guarantee that our voice can be heard, no matter how unpopular or under-resourced we are."

Kim's proposal that enabling others to "have a voice" in the political process is an expression of "love" comports well with my proposal, reported in Chapter 2, that it is a "deep expression of love" when I provide another person a safe and welcoming space to express his/her perspective on the issue at hand. Kim refers to this approach to doing politics as the "politics of love," a topic to which I will turn after a brief excursus.

Excursus on *Citizens United*

In *Citizens United v. Federal Election Commission* heard in January 2010, the U.S. Supreme Court held (5–4) that the free speech clause of the First Amendment to the Constitution prohibits the government from restricting independent expenditures for communications by nonprofit corporations, for-profit corporations, labor unions, and other associations.

Frank and Kim were asked to state their respective positions on the Supreme Court decision.

Kim argues for "reversing the *Citizens United* decision" because it has a detrimental effect on "political equality."

... by expanding the idea of the corporate 'person' to include civil liberties and free speech rights, it alters the playing field of political equality, giving collective actors rights beyond the individuals who make them up. This is particularly problematic in the context of the need for political equality. The notion that a corporation, with resources far beyond the means of any individual, should be treated on the same level as an individual citizen goes against the core constitutional principal that gave citizens, not institutions or groups, the right to vote and choose representatives.

Kim elaborates by asserting that "no entities other than individuals and states have political standing in our [American political] system"; "businesses should not have explicit standing to claim political rights."

... I don't think people lose their ability to join the political conversation just because they work for or own a large corporation. I think that corporations shouldn't have the same political rights as citizens. Corporations are made up of people who all bring their individual rights with them. These organizations may be more than the sum of their parts in the economic sphere, but our political system does not recognize organizations of any type for representational purposes. No entities other than individuals and states have political standing in our system.

Other democracies have explicit representation of business within their representative and executive systems. We do not. Treating corporations as individuals with free speech rights introduces special 'super actors' into our representation system that have an unfair advantage in the influence system. Can and should CEOs and the people who work for businesses advocate for that business' interests? Absolutely. They can use their individual rights to advocate for that purpose or any other. But businesses should not have explicit standing to claim political rights.

Frank disagrees with Kim, arguing that "people who work for any organization are still 'people' too. They are all guaranteed the right to assemble and that right to assembly means coming together to work for political goals in their common interest," adding that "they should not be excluded from the public square of debate and dialogue just because they happen to work for a corporation ... "

Agreeing with Kim that "loving your neighbor may be an effective political tool" (more about that in the next section), Frank suggests that rather than trying to reverse the *Citizens United* decision, Christians should devote their energies to organizing "thousands of people ... to effect change in the public square."

> ... there is almost no case I can think of where this ['loving thy neighbor' in the political sense] cannot be better achieved by Christian men and women of deep convicted faith acting out their faith in a productive manner instead of trying to place artificial restrictions on the rights and freedoms of others in the political marketplace by trying to find the 'perfect' piece of legislation such as *Citizens United* (part 2) designed to reverse the decision of the Supreme Court in *Citizens United* (part 1).
>
> It is far too easy to sit on the sidelines and complain about politics and point fingers from afar at big corporations and wealthy individuals for spending their money on political speech.
>
> It is an entirely different thing to make the conscious decision to organize thousands of people for a common purpose to effect change in the public square.
>
> That is what the committed Christian can and should do in our modern American democratic republic.

Although Kim did not respond to Frank's "either/or" proposal, I am guessing that she would argue for *both* trying to reverse the *Citizens United* decision *and* organizing people to effect change in the public square.

The Politics of Love

Kim presents a stark contrast between political conversations that focus on "winning" and doing politics as an expression of love for others: "I think it is correct to say that most conversations concerning politics are about winning, or getting a point across, or achieving an outcome; they aren't about loving our neighbors and fellow citizens." Kim makes it clear that she views the doing of politics as an opportunity to "love others" by fostering the "political equality" that is realized when "all voices are heard" on a "level playing field."

> So, how should a Christian respond inside a system that is not only broken, but seems unlikely to change? I think the most important thing we can do is to remember what politics is for. It is a tool we can use to love our neighbor. In this case, I think loving our neighbor combines both using our own representational multipliers in the service of people who do not have any and working to increase the resources of time, networks, education and money available to those without these multipliers. Political equality can be had by suppressing the excesses at the top of the ladder, but it can be achieved more holistically by helping to bring those with few resources up to a level playing field. This strategy requires an enormous amount of humility on our parts; we have to use our resources to let others' voices be heard, not to convince them to echo our own preferences. There is a great temptation to see our own political work as helping the least without actually taking the time to find out what it is these citizens need and want. But approaching helping our neighbors in terms of political equality, and finding ways in which we can increase its practice, can help remind us that our neighbors are not simply instruments in helping us to create a good society; their participation on equal terms is what pushes toward a good society.

Kim adds that in light of the second great commandment to "love our neighbors" that Jesus gave to those aspiring to be his followers (Mark

12:31), this focus on the "politics of love" places a special responsibility on Christians and goes beyond the hope for "good policy outcomes" to commitment to getting such good outcomes in the "right way."

> This is where I think Christians have a particular responsibility and a particular contribution to conversations about not just money and special interests but about all realms of our political life. Our goal in politics should be not only to get to good policy outcomes, but to get there in the right way. A way that values others above ourselves and takes seriously the notion of a truly common good. This intention takes on particular import in a democracy, where our individual choices matter and where we, at least in principal, have the power and responsibility to govern ourselves.

Kim's exhortation for Christians to seek good policy outcomes in the "right way," which includes enabling all voices to be heard, is an important reminder in our turbulent political times in America that we need to avoid the common fallacy of thinking that any "means" for attaining a policy outcome can be justified because we believe the "end" (the outcome) is good. I believe that Christians need to call into question the legitimacy of seeking policy outcomes they perceive to be good by means of the demonization of opponents and misrepresentation of the "truth" that are rampant in contemporary politics—practices that are antithetical to the Christian faith. Is it possible that the many evangelical Christians who turn a blind eye to the non-loving ways in which many contemporary politicians seek to attain some good goals lack the faith to believe that God can attain good "ends" by exclusive use of good "means," working in "partnership" with Christians, however slow that process may be? I dare to believe that God does not condone seeking to accomplish goals that are congruent with the Christian faith by "means" that are antithetical to the Christian faith.

Kim concludes with a provocative suggestion that the loving engagement with our neighbors that she advocates as a way to do politics can be a "way to create sustained systemic change" within the political system.

> Too many times, calls to religiously motivated political activity focus only on individual rather than systemic change. Particularly in the context of reform within a

democracy, it makes sense to look both at the individual and at how an individual can impact the larger system. There is plenty of historical evidence that suggests that this kind of engagement with our neighbors and those who are less politically equal is a way to create sustained systemic change. Social movements across the political spectrum, most committed to expanding political rights and liberties of an under-resourced group, have been the great engine of increased political equality. Abolitionists, women's suffragists and African-American civil rights activists all successfully broadened our definition of who deserves political equality in our system and what it should look like. In many cases, these were people with representation multipliers of time, energy, networks, civic skills and money, who chose to use those resources in the service of their underrepresented neighbors, not for their own enrichment. We have a similar opportunity to use our representation multipliers in service to building a more just political community.

This suggestion connects well with the proposal from Harry Boyte, reported in Chapter 4, that the "priority" for political activism should be at the "grassroots" level; in the activities of non-governmental groups (e.g., families, churches, businesses, voluntary associations) rather than at the governmental level (the executive, legislative and judicial branches of local, state and national governing bodies). If Kim is correct, then practicing the "politics of love" can be an "incubator" that leads to working toward systemic changes in governmental political systems.

You will recall that Kim wondered whether Frank would share her view that "politics is about love." Frank's enthusiastic agreement with Kim is striking:

The thing I think was the most impactful from the initial post of Ms. Conger was the concept of pulling in the Christian concept of 'loving your neighbor' as a tool for effective politics.

I am not sure that I have ever heard anyone over the past 38 years of being in and out of and around politics and government make that specific connection. Politics is often seen as an 'I win/you lose' game, and occasionally a 'win-win-win' proposition but seldom as a 'love thy neighbor' mission.

Frank brings his point home most emphatically by asserting that "'loving thy neighbor' in the political sense would be as radical and disruptive as any political campaign in American history."

Frank adds that the way that Christians should "love their neighbor as themselves" is to try to help those who are not as fortunate as [they] are," noting some powerful past examples such as the civil rights movement.

American history is rife with examples of religiously-led and inspired people who have entered the public square and achieved great things for their 'fellow neighbor' whom they probably have never met in many cases but have loved nonetheless ...

Southern African-American civil rights leaders formed the Southern Christian Leadership Conference behind the brave actions and words of the Rev. Dr. Martin Luther King Jr. in the 1960s to force the issue of granting justice and equality for millions of black citizens across the nation which went far beyond the needed changes in the South ...

Men and women of faith have always been at the forefront of some of the greatest advancements to civilized society since the time of Christ 2,000 years ago. They were not looking for political advantage or success to begin with; they were seeking to put their Christian faith into productive action and follow the precepts of Christ who told his disciples to 'feed his sheep' and 'take care of the widow and orphans' among us.

Many millions of Americans here in this country and perhaps billions worldwide are disenfranchised in some way, shape or form be it in terms of hunger, lack of resources or education, or not being able to live in a decent form of housing, or have access to adequate health services anywhere nearby.

Christians should 'love their neighbor' as themselves and try to help those who are not as fortunate as we are.

That can and should include forming political action committees for the poor, the homeless, the destitute and the disadvantaged; or by being involved in social media; in the entertainment or sports world or perhaps even by running for office.

A Way Forward:
Balancing Freedom and Political Equality

The above narrative reveals a tension between providing "freedom" and "equality" in the political process. Both Kim and Frank reject an either/or approach to resolving this tension, arguing for a both/and strategy that requires the challenging search for an appropriate "balance." In Kim's words:

> ... it is not necessarily problematic to pursue one's interest in democratic politics. But there is an important tension at the heart of the democratic project, the interaction between individual citizens' freedom and the necessity of citizens' equality before the law and in political terms. Many of the deepest disagreements in our political system spring from the place where freedom and equality meet. How much liberty are we willing to give up to ensure equality and how unequal are we willing to be in order to protect individual liberty? Americans generally recognize that, practically speaking, some individual liberty must be curtailed for the

benefit of the whole, and that overall, people are not equal in their capacities and resources. But there are contexts where this conflict comes into high relief, where providing for one expressly limits the other. This suggests that our solution should likely be one of balance and not control.

Frank concurs, tracing the need to seek a balance between freedom and equality to our Founding Fathers: "Once our Founders recognized the need for government, they also worked to insure basic freedoms we take for granted today."

As already reported, Kim asserts that a central component of the "equality" among citizens that needs to be protected from individual interests is "political equality."

> … we ask our government to impinge on individual rights all the time in order to protect the larger society or the rights of another individual. My primary argument is that ensuring political equality is part of that mandate: We want this system, one we've built and designed to be responsive to citizens, to protect us from other people's drive to use their rights to the detriment of others.

It is important to reiterate Kim's primary concern that the major impediment to "political equality" occurs when special interests that have "overwhelming access to resources" cause the "voices of most ordinary citizens" to be "crowded out."

> It is important to point out that my concern isn't whether these are good interests or whether I agree with them. My concern is that their influence is so pervasive and ubiquitous that the voices of most ordinary citizens are crowded out. Representing one's interest in politics isn't bad, but like so many other things, it has to be balanced with the needs of a good society. No one interest should be able to dominate the conversation or decision-making based on their overwhelming access to resources. In those scenarios we all lose. Political equality is only the most important of the democratic values such dominance threatens.

The quest for an appropriate "balance" between "freedom" and "political equality" raises a final question as to the best means to attain that balance.

Get into the game

Frank proposes that the main "takeaway" from his conversation with Kim should be that Christians need to "get in the game" rather than to just "sit on the sidelines" complaining about politics.

> It is far too easy to sit on the sidelines and complain about politics and point fingers from afar at big corporations and wealthy individuals for spending their money on political speech.

> It is an entirely different thing to make the conscious decision to organize thousands of people for a common purpose to effect change in the public square.

> That is what the committed Christian can and should do in our modern American democratic republic.

But, how should Christians "get into the [political] game"? Frank focuses on the need for Christians to "run for public office," noting that this is the primary goal of The Institute for the Public Trust for which he provides leadership.

> ... we need great new people to run for public office.

> I run The Institute for the Public Trust in Raleigh, North Carolina. Our sole mission is to find, recruit and train the next Jeffersons and Madisons and Hamiltons of this generation and the next to get them to run for public office once again.

> Christians need to seriously think about putting themselves on the ballot and therefore on the direct line where the rubber meets the road of representative democracy.

As you consider Frank's proposal for Christians to "get into the [political] game" by seeking elected office, keep in mind the suggestions of other conversation partners reported in earlier chapters that in addition to, not in place of, such engagement in "governmental" forms of political activism, there are many opportunities to become politically involved through non-governmental entities such as families, businesses, churches, schools, and voluntary organizations. The possibility of such political engagement in churches and para-church organizations will be considered in great detail in Chapter 10.

7

Immigration

BUILDING ON THE reflections in Part One on "Political Discourse" and Part Two on "The Nature of Politics," we now consider the first of three highly contested public policy issues: Immigration—a multifaceted topic that is often in the daily news headlines about which politicians have failed to find much common ground over many years.

This chapter reports on responses given by Matthew Soerens and Robert McFarland to the following set of leading questions:

- Are current immigration laws and deportation practices just? Is so, why? If not, why not and what changes should be made?
- Is there a way for Christians and Christian churches to respond to undocumented immigrants that will avoid harm to both undocumented immigrants and citizens?

Matthew comes to these questions primarily as a practitioner heavily involved in advocating for immigration reform that reflects his experience with immigrants and his understanding of Christian teachings about "justice." As a professor of law, Robert starts with his commitment to the "rule of law" and his understanding of the implications of that rule of law for public policy and practices relative to immigration.

These differing, yet overlapping, starting points led to some initial frustrations, especially relative to lack of clarity regarding the meaning of some key terms (e.g., justice). However, as the conversations proceeded, some significant areas of agreement emerged and disagreements were clarified enough to hold promise for fruitful ongoing conversations among all Christians that may even hold promise for a "Way Forward" in the heated national debate. I start by pointing to important areas of agreement.

Agreements

The first area of agreement is essential, since, without it, further conversation is impossible.

Simplistic rhetoric is a conversation-stopper

Robert makes an assertion that could be a potent advertisement for this entire book, and for all my work in recent years: *Conversations are essential to human well-being.*

Robert adds a plug for my eCircle projects by noting a sharp contrast with perverse uses of social media that tend to isolate us, leading to polarization.

> Oddly, as our world has grown digitally interconnected, it appears that we find in ourselves a growing sense of isolation. And this isolation seems to be polarizing. One cannot spend much time on social media without wondering what is going on there. Perhaps perceived anonymity online causes some to forget that they are talking to (and about) other human beings. And God help us if controversial topics are posted in a friend's status line on the social media feed. Should I 'unfriend them' or block their posts? In this world dominated by tweets, selfies and Instagram posts we are facing real danger of finding ourselves stranded, isolated and alone.

> It is very refreshing to enter a digital space intentionally designed to nourish our humanity by bringing us together in Respectful Conversations.

To emphasize his point, Robert notes that the leading questions I pose are too complex to "answer with a hashtag or in 140 characters or less," adding that such attempts at succinct simplicity relative to immigration issues can, at best, appeal to the passions.

> Rhetoric, not reason … reigns over social media battles regarding immigration. Rather than engaging our minds, many, on all sides of the immigration wars, put passion on display, invoke their preferred catchphrase, minimize or mock their political opponents, and impute to all who disagree asserted biases justifying writing off those who might disagree as bigots. This is the rationalization process of our social media culture used to dismiss those who ask questions and then attempt to answer them with reasoned arguments. Conversation is reduced to catchphrases: the wall; Dreamers; the travel ban; sanctuary cities; and so on. Catchphrases are powerful rhetorical devices. Which is why politicians (of all sorts) deploy them …
>
> Catchphrases stir up passions. Unfortunately, human beings often reason poorly when consumed by passions. Catchphrases may secure votes, but at the expense of finding answers to questions concerning immigration law and policy.

Robert expresses the hope that his conversation with Matthew will help him to "gain more knowledge"; even "wisdom."

> I want to make clear my understanding that the point of this conversation is to move beyond rhetoric in the immigration conversation. Progress in this conversation calls on us to engage reason, and by reasoning together about the questions we've been asked to discuss we just may make discoveries leading us to greater understanding. Along with Matthew, I seek to gain more knowledge in this conversation. As we share our thoughts, informed by the knowledge we have already acquired, in pursuit of greater

understanding of issues pertaining to immigration law and policy the conversation may lead us to discovery ...

What if our conversations regarding immigration led us to wisdom? Wisdom refuses to reduce the conversation to catchphrases. Wisdom refuses to marginalize those who disagree. Wisdom refuses to minimize, always recalling that this conversation is real, and practical, not mere theory. Wisdom refuses to be held captive to passion.

Matthew agrees with Robert that "immigration is a deeply polarized—and often polarizing—topic ... public conversations on this topic seem to be mired in rhetoric and prone to talking past one another," adding that "we [Robert and I] agree that immigration law and policy are extremely complex and not served well by simplistic rhetoric."[49]

Matthew elaborates on his agreement with Robert that "rhetoric has proven problematic in the U.S. debate over immigration" with the added important insight that when the debate over immigration issues is reduced to simplistic rhetoric, this too often leads to a "false choice" between extreme positions, adding that some "realistic possibilities" for immigration policies are "more moderate, far from either pole."

As Robert rightly notes, the national debate over immigration is too often characterized by lazy rhetoric devoid of complexity and nuance. When we get caught up in rhetoric, it's easy for the conversation to become a false choice between the extremes. It's often hard to proceed to discuss the more politically realistic possibilities of policies that combine border security, more market-sensitive visa systems and earned legalization processes because we're so quick to presume there is no common ground.

Advocates of one view or another tend to sniff out the terminology used by others and immediately lump them into one of two opposite poles, but the reality is that the

49 Robert notes that Matthew and Jenny Hwang "rightly observe that there can be no progress in conversations regarding immigration until we move beyond rhetoric" in their book *Welcoming the Stranger*, 2009.

only politically realistic policy proposals are more moderate, far from either pole.

Robert suggests that the tendency to employ simplistic rhetoric regarding immigration issues plagues politicians on both sides of the political aisle.

> ... it is very important to note that rhetoric is deployed on all sides of this debate. Our president has reduced the debate to one word: wall. His opponents have their own: Dreamers.

To illustrate this problem with "simplistic rhetoric" often leading to unacceptable extreme policy proposals. Robert notes that some Christians use the catchphrase "welcome strangers" to "justify jettisoning law." Matthew provides his own example of how some have interpreted his commitment to "welcome the stranger" to mean that he believes in "amnesty," which is not the case; and some have interpreted his reference to Romans 13 to mean that he believes in "mass deportation" and "closed borders" which is also not true.

> ... if I emphasize that the Bible commands us to 'welcome strangers' (which it does: read literally, Romans 12:13 commands us to practice loving strangers, the literal meaning of the Greek word *philoxenia*, or hospitality), many will presume that I believe in amnesty (another wrought word, which I do not believe is a fair descriptor of a legalization process that involves the payment of a fine or other serious restitution) for 'illegal aliens.'
>
> On the other hand, if I emphasize Romans 13's insistence that Christians are to be subject to the law established by governing authorities (which it does), others will presume that I'm for mass deportation and closed borders ...

Matthew suggests that those who embrace the extreme positions regarding "amnesty" and "closed borders" that he rejects, comprise a minority of the American citizenry.

There are, of course, advocates of open borders and amnesty, who believe immigration restrictions of any sort are illegitimate—but actually very few. And there are xenophobes who simply dislike anyone born in another country who want to restrict immigration altogether, who want not *secure* borders but *closed* borders—but they are actually a very small share of the population as well.

Rather, Matthew suggests that "most Christians and most Americans" have more nuanced positions on many immigration issues that avoid the simplistic extremes.

We (and I'm including myself here) tend to look for cues so that we can categorize others into one camp or the other. But most Christians and most Americans actually have nuanced views on this topic: they want secure borders but are opposed to mass deportation of all immigrants in the country unlawfully. They want those who are a public safety threat deported, but would like long-time residents who have (except for their violation of immigration law) stayed out of trouble to be given a chance to make amends and stay lawfully, especially in cases when their deportation would likely divide family units. Most Americans value the contributions of immigrants to the country economically and culturally, both throughout our history and at present, but they are troubled by the erosion of the rule of law that results when our federal government seems to look the other way when individuals enter, overstay a visa, or work illegally.

Matthew further suggests that "most politicians" also "reject the most extreme positions on either side" of the political aisle.

In reality, though, not only do most Americans and most Christians reject the most extreme positions on either side, so do most politicians. There are very few conservative Republicans in Congress who advocate mass deportation and very few liberal Democrats who have ever proposed a mass amnesty that does not include serious fines, a decade-plus process toward permanent legal status and significant expenditures on border security.

Robert summarizes this area of agreement by noting "our agreement that the common good depends on willingness to move beyond rhetoric." What follows will reveal the results of this quest by Robert and Matthew to uncover some more common ground.

A shared commitment to obedience to Jesus

As the following quotes indicate, a second important area of agreement between Matthew and Robert is that they share a "commitment to honor Christ" and they both desire to love their neighbors in response to the teachings of Jesus.

> One of the very special things about this project is the fact that I know I am having a conversation with someone who shares my commitment to honor Christ. We intend to share thoughts regarding an important and challenging topic, and will likely demonstrate that it is possible to disagree respectfully. I hope this conversation enables us (and others) to discover how Christ might be honored through thought, reason and communication (Robert).

> I'm grateful for Robert's tone in this discussion: Whether we ultimately agree or disagree, we can do so, respectful that the other's views are genuinely based on our respective desires to love our neighbors in fulfillment of Jesus' commands (Matthew).

The importance of this shared commitment to be obedient to Jesus cannot be overstated. My experience, especially in my local involvement in conversations regarding potential immigration reform and the hot-button issue of human sexuality, is that Christians who disagree about these volatile issues too easily gravitate toward the view that those who disagree with them are "inferior" Christians (if they are Christians at all) who do not follow the teachings of Jesus and other biblical teachings.[50] That is the

---

50 Recall the observation of Kevin den Dulk, reported in Chapter 5, that "political tribalism" is characterized by an unwarranted extrapolation from saying that the person who

ultimate conversation-stopper. There is hope for a fruitful conversation only if Christians who disagree recognize that the other also aspires to be a faithful follower of Jesus. That Robert and Matthew view each other in that way is of great significance.

Respect for the rule of law

An additional pervasive conversation-stopper when one proposes public policies that will help undocumented immigrants to flourish, is that "you are rewarding those who have broken the law," thereby showing disregard for the "rule of law." I wish I had a dollar for every time I have heard that said by both local citizens and my state and national political representatives. That is simply not true, as later portions of this chapter will reveal. To set a context for that later elaboration, it is important to note that both Matthew and Robert agree that, with rare exceptions (to be noted later), the "laws of the land" ought to be obeyed.

Robert's position on the "rule of law" is unambiguous: "Christians ought to seek to uphold and obey the law."

> Within borders, God has ordained civil government. Romans 13:1-7, 1 Peter 2:13-17, and Titus 3:1 are among the passages teaching that God has chosen civil government as a means of securing justice on earth. Those concerned with thinking biblically must integrate these passages into their thinking about matters such as immigration.

Matthew agrees that "it is appropriate to insist that violation of U.S. law is unacceptable." But, consistent with the concerns of both Robert and Matthew (reported above) about the destructive limitations of "simplistic rhetoric," Matthew's affirmation of the importance of the "rule of law" does not lead to a simplistic conclusion that he favors "amnesty" (which, by definition, means "no penalty" for breaking the law) or "mass deportation" (which he believes is an excessive penalty for breaking the law by entering the country illegally—more about that later).

In noting that Matthew agrees with him that "immigration law is not inherently unjust" (i.e., "justice does not require the elimination of

---

disagrees with you is "wrong" to saying that he/she is immoral or evil. The tendency to view the Christian who disagrees with you about immigration issues as an "inferior" Christian is a manifestation of such political tribalism.

immigration laws"), Robert indicates that this area of agreement is "some-what surprising to [him]" (a pleasant surprise, I gather), adding that he had assumed that "Matthew would be making the argument that immi-gration law itself was a violation of individual rights to migrate rooted in justice" (relieved to discover that this is not what Matthew is arguing— more about exactly what Matthew is arguing later).

Because of this agreement about the importance of the "rule of law," which, as will be seen later, includes laws regarding "borders" and "border security," Matthew suggests that it would *not* be a good use of their time for him and Matthew to talk about the position that some Christians take that calls into question the "entirety of immigration law."

> But, perhaps, it is not immigration law that Christians demanding comprehensive immigration reform really want to discuss. Perhaps Christians (relying on passages regarding hospitality, welcoming strangers and the like) take issue with the entirety of immigration law. After all, by its very nature, legislation pertaining to immigration excludes. Perhaps some Christians (reading the biblical narratives regarding the global unity of the family of God) believe that there ought not be any borders (or walls). If this is the case, then we are not discussing immigration reform— we are discussing a political revolution (Robert).

> Robert suggested that his second essay will focus on the views of Christians who believe 'there ought not be any borders' which would, he says, be 'a political revolution.' I know that there are academics who take this position—I have encountered them—but such a proposal is both a) not my view ... and b) so far from ever being a political reality that it does not seem like the best use of our time to debate (Matthew).

However, for later reference it is important to point out that Robert tempers his belief that "where law exists, there is an obligation rooted in justice to obey the law," with the qualification, "unless the law itself is unjust," adding that where such "civil disobedience" (my words, not Robert's) is called for, such "breaking" of an "unjust law" must be accompanied by a willingness to accept the "penalty for breaking the law."

> ... even here, where Christians determine that the legal requirements violate moral, ethical or other divine requirements, there remains an obligation of fidelity to law. Dr. King addressed this obligation directly in his 'Letter from Birmingham Jail.' There he explained that one breaking an unjust law must do so 'openly, lovingly ... and with a willingness to accept the penalty.'

Although Matthew does not respond to Robert allowing for such rare expressions of civil disobedience, I believe he would allow for such rare possibilities.

While affirming the importance of the "rule of law," both Robert and Matthew acknowledge that laws made by humans are "imperfect," sometimes because they have "unintended consequences."

Robert paraphrases the position of Mark Amstutz[51] that in their "statements and position papers" on immigration issues, many Christians "emphasize biblical morality, but they contain little political science," leading to the result that their proposals for "comprehensive immigration reform" have not adequately taken into account "questions of jurisprudence" such as the "law of unintended consequences." Therefore, Robert adds, when Congress considers proposals for immigration reform, they "ought to anticipate and avoid as many negative unintended consequences as possible."

Matthew concurs by stating that "we [Robert and I] can both acknowledge that policy responses to the challenges of U.S. immigration will be imperfect and almost certainly have unintended consequences."

Robert has an interesting afterthought about Matthew's agreement that U.S. immigration law will be imperfect and may have unintended consequences: Possibly, this means that Matthew is "deferring to democratic resolution of the question of the content of the [immigration] law," adding that if this is what Matthew believes, then "I fully agree with him." We will return later to the question of whether this is what Matthew believes.

---

51 Amstutz, *Just Immigration*. An interesting aside is that Dr. Amstutz was one of Matthew's professors during his undergraduate studies at Wheaton College.

An Unresolved Issue: The Meaning of Justice

The month-long conversation between Matthew and Robert got off to a bumpy start, precipitated by Matthew's assertion (in the first paragraph of his first posting) that "a better question" than whether "our nation's current immigration laws are just" (the first leading question that I posed) would be "how can we pursue *more just* immigration policies, particularly for those of us whose understanding of justice is defined by our Christian faith?"

Robert's concern is that to seek "more just" immigration policies is to presuppose that the meaning of the word "just" is agreed upon. Robert emphatically asserts that this is not the case: "Justice is itself a disputed concept."

> ... a very significant challenge embedded in our first leading question [posed by Harold] ... [is that] many (Christians and non-believers alike) fail to recognize (or acknowledge in conversation) that justice is itself a disputed concept. Before we begin utilizing "justice" as a standard to evaluate the content of law ... [we must identify] ...the nature of justice.

Robert adds that "if Matthew and I do not first identify disputed terms [e.g., "justice"] in our leading questions then we will not be engaged in conversation. We will just be talking at each other, not with one another," further adding that "even worse, open-ended questions tend to invite informal fallacies to join the chat. Rhetoric has room at its table for straw men and *ad hominem* attacks, but truth (and justice) in the immigration debate will not be found there."

In response to Robert's criticism that he has presupposed a shared meaning of the disputed concept "justice," Matthew confesses that he is "guilty as charged," elaborating as follows:

> Robert fairly observed that I effectively 'changed the question,' suggesting that a more practical question was not whether U.S. immigration laws and deportation practices are *just*, but how they could be made *more* just.

I ... agree with Robert that we need to define terms before
we can really dialogue. And I suspect I erred there in my
first post ... Robert spent much more time carefully defining
terms, whereas I jumped right into my views.

However, agreeing that their conversation will not go far if they don't
first address the meaning of the word "justice" does not mean that Matthew and Robert ascribe the same meaning to that word. Since I erred by
not posing a question as to the meaning of "justice" as one of my leading
questions, the postings from Matthew and Robert did not directly address
that foundational question. But, I can glean at least partial responses from
their postings, which I will do shortly. But, first, it is important for the
reader to remember that questions as to the meaning of "justice" also
arose in Chapters 4 and 5, a summary of which I now present to set a
context for me to report my understanding of what Matthew and Robert
mean by that word.

Recall, first, that a general definition of "justice" is to treat everyone
"fairly" or to give everyone his/her "due." Robert traces this general view of
justice within the "Christian tradition" to Augustine and Aquinas.

In the Christian tradition, justice is most often associated
with the thought of Augustine and Aquinas. Although there
are significant differences, both considered justice to be
related to giving to each person what they are due. Both
recognized that justice regards right ordering. Thus, the
just thing to do is the thing that comports with obligations
towards God and others.

This call for "fairness" has at least the following three sub-categories:
Commutative Justice: protecting the rights between one individual and
another individual, as in the expectation that both parties bound to a
contract will honor that contract; **Retributive Justice**: punishment for a
wrongful act that is proportional to the magnitude of the offense; and **Distributive Justice**: fair allocation of goods to all members of society.

Recall also a particular dimension of "distributive justice" that is
embedded in Jim Skillen's call for government to recognize and support
the roles and responsibilities of non-governmental groups, such as families, businesses, churches and other voluntary organizations. As footnoted

in Chapter 4, the Center for Public Justice (CPJ), for which Jim served as founding president, embraces the ideals of "structural pluralism" and "confessional pluralism, both of which aim for 'fair' treatment of all societal groups—governmental and otherwise."

With that as context, here is my attempt to understand the meanings for the word "justice" that can be gleaned from the postings from Robert and Matthew.

Justice focusing on obedience to laws

It appears to me that a particular dimension of the multifaceted concept of justice that Robert focuses on (without suggesting that he ignores other dimensions) is that justice requires "obedience to laws." This is suggested by Robert's proposal to me, before this month-long conversation with Matthew even started, that his conversation with Matthew should begin with their responses to the following "resolution":

Resolved: A nation's failure to enforce its immigration laws is unjust and such failure contributes to moral harm to both immigrant and citizen.

As Robert noted, for good or for ill, I opted to stick with my original more "open-ended" leading questions.

Relative to the taxonomy of the various dimensions of "justice" summarized above, it appears to me that Robert is here focusing on the "retributive" dimension of justice that, rightfully, calls for appropriate punishment, proportional to the offense, when a person disobeys a law; and to not administer that punishment is "unjust."

As already reported, Matthew agrees with Robert on that particular dimension of justice when he indicates his "respect for the rule of law" by asserting that "it is appropriate to insist that violation of U.S. law is unacceptable" (although some disagreement may linger as to the "magnitude" of that punishment when the offense is entering the U.S. without documentation—more about that later).

However, while acknowledging that dimension of justice that calls for obedience to laws, it appears to me that Matthew focuses on another dimension of justice.

Justice focusing on helping the marginalized and vulnerable

While Matthew clearly asserts that "the Scriptures do not prescribe a U.S. immigration policy" (with which Robert concurs), he notes the numerous biblical passages in the Old Testament that point to God's concern for the well-being of the "stranger or foreigner" (which, Matthew suggests, would, today, include the "immigrant").

> The Hebrew word for an immigrant (or, in various English translations, the stranger, sojourner, foreigner or alien), transliterated as *ger*, appears 92 times in the Old Testament alone. By the count of theologian Orlando Espín,[52] 'welcoming the stranger or foreigner (the "immigrant," we could say today) is the most often repeated commandment in the Hebrew Scriptures, with the exception of the imperative to worship only the one God.'

> [I do not] believe that the laws God established for Israel in the Pentateuch should be simply transferred over to U.S. law. The Bible's many descriptions of and teachings regarding the treatment of immigrants, though, reveal a great deal about the unchanging character of God and of how he defines justice, including, specifically, for the immigrant.

> In a relatively short essay, there is not space to review every biblical principle relating to immigration, but I'll mention a few. First, as Old Testament scholar Daniel Carroll R.[53] observes, Christian thinking about immigrants begins with a recognition of their personhood, they are made in the image of God, with inherent dignity (Genesis 1:27). Carroll also notes that many of the most prominent figures in the Old Testament—Abraham, Moses, Ruth, David and Daniel, among many others—lived as foreigners at one point in their respective stories. God is revealed as a God who 'protects immigrants' (Psalm 146:9 Common English Bible,

52 Espín, "Immigration and Some of its Implications," 19-32.
53 Carroll R., *Christians at the Border*.

here and following except as noted) and 'loves immigrants, giving them food and clothing' (Deuteronomy 10:18), with the explicit commandment to the Israelites: 'That means you must also love immigrants' (Deuteronomy 10:19).

When God's justice is described in the Hebrew Scriptures, it is often in the context of protecting the rights of those who were most vulnerable to injustice: the orphan, the widow and the immigrant. 'Do what is just and right ... Don't exploit or mistreat the refugee, the orphan and the widow,' the prophet Jeremiah writes (Jeremiah 22:3). The prophet Zechariah echoes these concerns: 'Make just and faithful decisions; show kindness and compassion to each other! Don't oppress the widow, the orphan, the stranger and the poor' (Zechariah 7:9-10). God also warns those who act unjustly toward the vulnerable that they will themselves face judgment: 'I will be quick to testify against ... those who cheat the day laborers out of their wages as well as oppress the widow and the orphan, and against those who brush aside the foreigner' (Malachi 3:5).

It is important to note Robert's critique of the biblical passages that Matthew cites above as reflecting an "incomplete biblical analysis." He elaborates as follows:

Matthew concedes that the Bible is not a policy manual to be used by legislators, and that Old Testament law ought not be imported directly into the United States code. This concession is necessary, of course, because not all of the Old Testament law would fit comfortably with Matthew's policy preferences. For example, consider Deuteronomy 15:3: This portion of the Old Testament law allowed discrimination between Israelite and foreigner in the payment and collection of debts. Or consider Leviticus 25: 44-46; This portion of Old Testament law permitted Israelites to purchase foreigners as slaves, and to bequeath foreign slaves to their heirs. Other Old Testament passages required obedient Israelites to destroy nations, and the people occupying them. Selectively citing the Old Testament invites questions about passages omitted.

There is a more significant problem in Matthew's argument. He cites the number of references to immigrants in the Old Testament (specifically, the word *ger*). As others have noted, this sort of biblical argument in support of immigration policy preferences is not convincing because the biblical interpretive method is incomplete.[54] The Old Testament uses a number of different terms when referring to citizens of other nations, and these different terms indicate different lawful status for foreign citizens in Israel. Citing one of these terms, but ignoring the others, leads to poor interpretation and understanding.

How can we sort out this disagreement as to the significance of selected Old Testament passages relative to the status of "immigrants" to our country? Although I am not a biblical scholar, here is my modest proposal: Consider the teachings of Jesus as recorded in Matthew 25: 31-36:

> [In the 'judgment of the nations' at the end times] the king [Jesus] will say to those at his right hand, 'come, you that are blessed by my father, inherit the kingdom prepared for you from the foundation of the world; for I was hungry and you gave me food, I was thirsty and you gave me something to drink, I was a stranger and you welcomed me, I was naked and you gave me clothing, I was sick and you took care of me, I was in prison and you visited me.'

I am not competent to sort through the disagreements between Matthew and Robert noted above as to what a "complete analysis" of Old Testament passages would entail. But, I am prepared to state my strong conviction that the teaching of Jesus in Matthew 25 calls all Christians to seek to help the marginalized and vulnerable in society (the "least" of those in our midst, as Matthew 25 goes on to say, v. 45). If, as my local experience suggests, my immigrant neighbors are often marginalized

54 Hoffmeier, "The Use and Abuse."

and vulnerable, this calls me to seek to help them and advocate for others to also help. But that sense of calling does not answer the question as to what particular immigration policies and practices are most helpful to my immigrant neighbors, a topic to which we will soon turn.

But, first, it is very important to note that this dimension of justice on which I (and Matthew) are focusing is an aspect of the "distributive" dimension of justice; which is not to negate the "retributive" aspect of justice on which Robert focuses, that calls for obedience to laws and appropriate punishment for those who violate the laws. Contrary to most of the conversation these days about immigration issues, it is not either/or; it is both/and. (More about that later when we consider some specific, concrete proposals for immigration reform.)

A Foundation for Conversation About Concrete Public Policy Proposals

As suggested above, the fact that people bring differing conceptions of the meaning of "justice" to conversations about whether present immigration laws are "just" makes it difficult, if not impossible, to have a fruitful conversation about whether such laws are "just" or need to be made "more just." This problem is compounded by the fact that those willing to talk often have an inadequate understanding of the "facts" related to current immigration laws.

In our current political climate, in which the bizarre idea of "alternative facts" is advanced, fruitful conversations about immigration will be elusive if politicians and their supporters propagate "misinformation." Consider, for example, the following "untruths" about immigrants that Matthew points out.

> Undocumented immigrants are often scapegoated as responsible for economic malaise, even though most economists (96 percent surveyed by *The Wall Street Journal*[55]) believe they're a net positive force on the economy.

---

55 Annett, "Illegal Immigrants."

Immigrants are blamed for waves of violent crime, though they are incarcerated at rates well below that of U.S. citizens.[56]

To illustrate further how disagreement or misunderstanding regarding the "facts" can impede conversation, consider the following exchange between Matthew and Robert regarding "chain migration."

In his first posting, Matthew makes the parenthetical statement that chain migration is "basically a myth." Robert disagrees:

> Matthew claims that chain migration is 'basically a myth.' This statement is also striking. In fact, ... the family reunification program, also commonly known as chain migration, accounts for 37 percent of all visas presently granted by the United States. The priority of familial reunification in current immigration policy is clearly revealed in government data regarding the number of visas granted over the last several years. Denying that chain migration exists merely confuses policy debate. In fact, the question of whether the United States ought to prioritize visas on the basis of familial status rather than other factors is central to the policy debate regarding comprehensive immigration reform. Obscuring this policy question by claiming that chain migration does not presently exist is not helpful.

In response, Matthew points to his sentence prior to his parenthetical statement: "Contrary to popular misperception, it is not possible to petition for one's cousins, grandparents, or other extended family members," explaining that the "myth" he was referring to was the misperception that "chain migration" means that that "our family reunification laws allow a single immigrant to sponsor 'virtually unlimited numbers of distant relatives.'"

> My understanding of the idea of 'chain migration' is essentially what President Trump stated in his State of the Union Address that our family reunification laws allow a single immigrant to sponsor 'virtually unlimited numbers of distant relatives.' I do not dispute that our immigration laws allow U.S. citizens and lawful permanent residents to

56 Landgrave, "Criminal Immigrants."

petition for particular family members (all relationships I would consider my close relatives: parents, spouse, children, siblings), nor that this is the most common avenue for lawful migration under existing law ... But this is very different than the president's conception of 'chain migration,' which I believe is held by many Americans, that existing laws allow a 'virtually unlimited number' of 'distant' relatives. That conception is what I maintain as 'basically a myth,' since family petitions are limited to those relatives allowed in statute (not cousins, grandparents, etc.). On average, an immigrant to the U.S. petitions for fewer than two relatives in a lifetime, which is far from the exponential growth that a 'virtually unlimited number' suggests.

My point in harping on this apparently minor disagreement between Matthew and Robert is that misinformation or misunderstanding regarding the "facts" can be a "conversation-stopper" (which, fortunately, did not happen in this case). To avoid the conversation ending prematurely, we all do well to embrace Robert's proposal that setting the stage "for a meaningful conversation" about concrete public policy proposals pertaining to immigration issues requires that three pre-conditions need to be met, as follows:

> ... we need to 1) identify the [immigration] law we are discussing with particularity; 2) identify the conception of justice we are employing to evaluate the law; and 3) articulate our reasoning regarding whether the law we've identified is or is not just.

In addition to these pre-conditions for a potentially fruitful conversation about public policy proposals regarding immigration, Matthew and Robert agree on certain background "biblical principles" needed to inform such conversations. Robert's summation of Matthew's presentation of these principles in his first posting is as follows:

- Immigrants are people made in the image of God.
- Many Old Testament figures lived as immigrants.
- God protects immigrants.

- God loves immigrants.
- God commanded the Israelites to love immigrants.
- God's justice is concerned with the treatment of immigrants.

Robert says that "I agree with all of the biblical principles Matthew identifies," elaborating as follows:

> All people (immigrants and nonimmigrants, documented and undocumented) are made in God's image and entitled to respect. God indeed loves the entire world, so much that he gave the entire world His son. Christians ought not, therefore, treat immigrants (whether legal or illegal) as less than human. God's justice is indeed concerned with our treatment of all people, especially those who are often marginalized and forgotten.

But Robert proposes two additional background biblical principles that "make clear that God loves all the world (not just those who live in the United States)," one being that "borders are important" and the other being that "God has ordained civil government."

> Borders are important. This is a principle running throughout the Bible.
>
> Deuteronomy 32:8, for example, explains that 'when the Most High gave to the nations their inheritance, when he divided mankind, he fixed the borders of the peoples according to the number of the sons of God.' Boundaries are referenced in the wisdom literature (e.g., Proverbs 22:28, 23:10-11). And God's deliverance of His people from slavery in Egypt culminated in the entry of His people into the physical borders of the promised land.
>
> Borders make possible cultures, homelands, safety, security and a number of other human goods related to the flourishing of political communities. As Peter Hitchens recently explained, 'without borders, we would dwell in a global parking lot. A reasonable love of where you live, its

customs, landscape, language, and humor, is the basis for all
other communal loves.'[57] Borders enable nations to create
and maintain the conditions necessary for other important
institutions to thrive.

Within borders, God has ordained civil government.
Romans 13:1-7, 1 Peter 2:13-17, and Titus 3:1 are among the
passages teaching that God has chosen civil government as
a means of securing justice on earth. Those concerned with
thinking biblically must integrate these passages into their
thinking about matters such as immigration. There are also
many passages regarding God's desire for the just to live at
peace with all men so far as is possible without disobedience
to God. Living within a nation unlawfully is a situation that
is anything but peaceful. Christians ought to seek to uphold
and obey the law.

As we have already seen, Matthew agrees with Robert's assertions that
"God has ordained civil government" and "Christians ought to seek to
uphold and obey the laws." As we will soon see, Matthew also agrees that
"borders are important." But the looming question remains as the extent to
which these background biblical principles can be translated into concrete
public policy proposals; a question to which we now turn.

Public Policy Proposals for Immigration Reform

The above reflections on the meaning of "justice" will seem to be mere
"theoretical abstractions" to those immigrants whose lives are significantly
affected by current immigration policies and deportation practices. When
recounting his personal experience with three Dreamers who have been
adversely affected by the rescinding of the DACA program (Deferred
Action for Childhood Arrivals), Matthew asserts that "immigration is *personal* and *urgent*," which requires that conversations about immigration
"move from the theoretical and utopian to the concrete."

---

57 Hitchens, "In Praise of Borders."

> My point is that, given the impact of these policies on human
> lives, I think it is vital that we move from the theoretical
> and utopian to the concrete. I'm eager to engage, to have
> my own proposals thoughtfully critiqued (the Lord knows
> I have been wrong before and am very likely could be now),
> but then to reason together toward more just policies.

As already indicated, both Matthew and Robert agree that the Bible
does not prescribe particular immigration policies and practices. As Robert summarizes his agreement with Matthew on this point: "The Bible is
not a policy manual to be used by legislators."

However, I propose that the broad background principles based on the
Bible that were enumerated above, especially the apparently contrasting
views that "justice" should focus on "obedience to laws" (Robert) and
"justice" should focus on "helping the marginalized and vulnerable" (Matthew)—which I will soon argue are not mutually exclusive (it is both/and;
not either/or)—can inform concrete public policies and practices relative
to immigration, which does not mean that these biblical principles are
determinative of such policies and practices.

In that light, let us consider various proposals for concrete reform of
current immigration policies and practices, starting with three proposals
on which Matthew and Robert agree.

Levels of immigration need to be controlled: no open borders

Matthew notes that he and Robert both agree that "borders are legitimate," adding that he "suspects" that "90 percent of Americans and 99
percent of members of Congress" also agree.

Robert adds that this shared belief that "borders are legitimate" means
that "immigration law is not inherently unjust ... nations have good reasons to regulate their borders."

Of course, agreeing that there are good reasons for the U.S. to "regulate"
its borders raises questions as to the content of such regulations. So, to
paraphrase, Robert poses the following specific questions:

- What should the annual ceiling be as to the "number" of
  immigrants?

- How should the number of visas granted annually be "distributed"?
- What will be the "economic impact" of the responses given to the above two questions?

Unfortunately, the month ran out before responses could be given to all these questions (so many questions, so little time). But Matthew did present a concrete proposal, which Robert judged to be "reasonable": "Increase the number of immigrant visas available, not without limit, but to better approximate the needs of the U.S. labor market," adding that "the vast majority of undocumented immigrants would much prefer to have had the opportunity to apply for a visa abroad and come lawfully to the U.S., had such a possibility existed" (a special case of Matthew's assertion that "the single best way to minimize illegal immigration is to facilitate legal migration").

Some readers may object that Matthew's proposal to grant visas in a way that "better approximates the needs of the U.S. labor market" places too much emphasis on fostering a healthy U.S. economy at the expense of fostering the well-being of immigrant families by granting more visas for the purpose of "family reunification" (or "chain migration," depending on which side of the aisle you sit). Matthew refers to this option for lawfully immigrating to the U.S. as "family sponsorship," which he implicitly encourages in his correcting the "false" notion that such sponsorship goes beyond spouses, children, parents and siblings to include cousins, grandparents or other extended family members, and in his lamenting that such petitioning for "family sponsorship" "is far from a fast process." Of course, there is room for disagreement as to the appropriate balance between the number of visas granted to meet the needs of the U.S. labor market and the number granted for "family reunification."

Another concrete regulatory proposal from Matthew, which Robert also finds "reasonable," is that the problem of "visa overstays" needs to be addressed. In Matthew's words:

> We should focus more resources on ensuring that those who enter the country lawfully on a temporary visa comply with the terms of their visa, since most new undocumented

immigrants in the past decade have come through this channel, not illegally across the border.

Robert's way of putting it is to call for a "heightening [of] enforcement of immigration laws in regards to visa overstays."

Improving border security

Implicit in the agreement between Matthew and Robert that there should not be "open borders" is agreement that current measures for "border security" need to be improved. In Matthew's words: "I ... think it is appropriate for our country to take reasonable steps to deter ... unlawful entry to the country." He adds his "presumption" that "we [Robert and I] agree that we should have secure borders."

Of course, this raises another question, now hotly debated, that Matthew and Robert didn't have time to address in detail: What are the best means for improving border security? Is it a wall, or improved electronic surveillance, or more border agents, or some other means or combination of deterrents? Matthew did express his view that "our nation can (and should) find more cost-effective ways to achieve a largely secure border than by dramatically expanding the existing border wall."

Just treatment of undocumented immigrants

The most contentious issue in the current immigration debate is the question of how to deal with the millions of immigrants who currently reside in the U.S. without documentation. It is noteworthy that Matthew and Robert share some significant common ground relative to this question that reflects a good faith attempt to create a both/and scenario (rather than either/or) that synthesizes Robert's focus on justice requiring "obedience to laws" and Matthew's focus on justice calling for "helping the marginalized and vulnerable." I will seek to elaborate.

First, recall Matthew's assertion that "violation of U.S. law is unacceptable." But what should the "penalty" be for such violation of the law? Matthew asserts that the penalty "need not necessarily be deportation," and he proposes what he considers to be a "better solution."

> I ... think it is appropriate to insist that violation of U.S. law is inappropriate ... But the penalty for that infraction need

not necessarily be deportation. A better solution, in most cases, would be to allow those who are unlawfully present to come forward, pay a fine (which is what would distinguish this from amnesty, which is synonymous with forgiveness), and then receive a probationary legal status that would allow the individual to stay and work lawfully in the country. Over the course of time, these individuals could earn permanent legal status if they meet particular requirements, including paying all appropriate taxes and not being involved in serious criminal infractions, and then, like any lawful permanent resident, eventually earn citizenship.

Given that an oft used conversation-stopper in current debates over the status of undocumented immigrants is that anything short of deportation is "amnesty," it is extremely important to note that Matthew is not proposing "amnesty" (which, by definition, means "no punishment"). Rather, Matthew is suggesting that a more appropriate form of punishment may be the levying of "fines." In my local conversations with others about this contentious issue, it boggles my mind that so many citizens lack the moral imagination to envision some appropriate middle ground between no punishment and the devastating punishment of deportation that is tearing apart many immigrant families. And it is more than a bit ironic that many of those failing to exercise such moral imagination are quick to give lip service to "family values."

It is also important to note that despite the quick way that many politicians prematurely end the conversation by playing the "amnesty" card (e.g., Steve King, the member of the U.S. House of Representatives who represents the 4th District in Iowa where I currently live), most citizens have a more "nuanced view," as Matthew notes:

> ... most Christians and most Americans actually have nuanced views on this topic [of how to treat undocumented immigrants]: they want secure borders but are opposed to mass deportation of all immigrants in the country unlawfully. They want those who are a public safety threat deported, but would like long-time residents who have (except for their violation of immigration law) stayed out

of trouble to be given a chance to make amends and stay lawfully, especially in cases when their deportation would likely divide family units. Most Americans value the contributions of immigrants to the country economically and culturally, both throughout our history and at present, but they are troubled by the erosion of the rule of law that results when our federal government seems to look the other way when individuals enter, overstay a visa, or work illegally.

Robert asserts that Matthews's proposal for "adjusting enforcement practices" by "favoring fines followed by pathways to citizenship rather than deportation" is "reasonable," adding that this is a "better proposal than outright amnesty."

I cannot overstate the significance of Robert's judgment that Matthew's proposal of "favoring fines followed by pathways to citizenship rather than deportation" to be "reasonable." Remember that Robert started his conversation with Matthew with the view that "justice" should focus on "obedience to laws," while Matthew's view of justice focused on "helping the marginalized and vulnerable." But, what eventually emerged from their ongoing conversation was acknowledgement that these two foci are not mutually exclusive; it is both/and, not either/or; those who have broken the law can be given suitable punishment (fines rather than deportation), followed by pathways to citizenship.[58] Talking respectfully with someone with whom you disagree can make a difference.

Grant more asylum requests

Matthew posed two more concrete public policy initiatives to which Robert did not respond, no doubt due to the sheer volume of ideas addressed in their electronic exchanges. The first was "respecting our laws" that allow for those immigrants who are fleeing persecution in their home countries to "request asylum" in the U.S.

> Our government can and should enforce the law, but they should do so humanely. And enforcing the law also means respecting our laws which permit someone fleeing a well-founded fear of persecution to request asylum in the United

---

58 Alas, the 2013 legislation that would have implemented such a "both/and" solution was passed by the U.S. Senate, but could not get through the House of Representatives.

States, which accounts for an increasing share of those apprehended at the U.S./Mexico border.

Address deplorable conditions in home countries that drive emigration

Matthew also proposes that attempts at "comprehensive immigration reform" should be expanded to include consideration of ways in which the U.S. government (and non-governmental organizations, such as churches) can address the deplorable living conditions in many countries that "compel individuals to emigrate in the first place."

> I'm concerned that our policy proposals are actually insufficiently comprehensive. They usually do little to nothing to address the situations that inspire or in some cases compel individuals to emigrate in first place, including extreme poverty, conflict, war and environmental degradation. I believe a truly comprehensive approach to immigration would include doing all we can—both governmentally and through local churches and other non-governmental organizations—to make living conditions outside the U.S. more just, so that fewer would feel that emigration was their best option.

The possible role of churches in such initiatives will be considered briefly toward the end of this chapter and in more detail in Chapter 10.

No set of public policy proposals for immigration reform will be perfect

Matthew emphasizes that no set of proposals for reforms of public policy regarding immigration will be "perfect," especially in light of Robert's legitimate concern about "unintended consequences." But his Christian faith commitment compels him to "grapple with the complexity" and advocate for what he considers to be "more just" policies.

> We [Robert and I] can both acknowledge that policy responses to the challenges of U.S. immigration will be imperfect and almost certainly have unintended consequences. We can also agree that the questions and terminology themselves are limited, debating what is meant by a 'just' policy or practice.

But questions of immigration policy are also far more than theoretical: they directly impact millions of people, and my conviction is that my faith compels me to do all within my power to grapple with the complexity and pursue more just policies on behalf of these neighbors whom I'm called to love, even while acknowledging that no changes to U.S. law will result in a perfect (or perfectly just) reality.

At the same time, Matthew acknowledges that "there are many ways in which "our immigration system" "is just and functions quite well," some of which he enumerates.

So, no, I do not believe that our immigration system is fully just. But there are many ways in which it *is* just and functions quite well, in the interest of our economy, our society and also the immigrants who benefit from the system. I've witnessed several naturalization ceremonies where refugees who were invited by the U.S. State Department to rebuild their lives in the freedom and safety of the U.S. pledge their allegiance to the country that has magnanimously welcomed them in as fellow participants in the American democracy. I have seen families reunited through family reunification visas, who then support one another through the process of cultural adjustment and societal integration. I have seen victims of horrific domestic violence, whose abusive U.S. citizen husbands used their lack of legal status to coercively keep their wives from calling the police to report the crimes of which they were victims, be granted legal status through the Violence Against Women Act and find the freedom to report crimes. And I have seen abusers and others who have engaged in violent crime appropriately penalized with deportation.

Matthew concludes this line of thought by asserting that "justice [as he understands the meaning of this word] is "worth pursuing" in light of the calling of Christians to pursue "God's kingdom … on earth as it is in heaven."

Our system has elements of justice and elements of injustice. There are and—this side of God establishing in full his kingdom of justice and righteousness—always will be unjust elements within *every* human system. It's not that I do not believe there *is* a standard of justice, but Robert is right in a sense to say that I think of justice as a sliding scale: I do not believe that perfect standard of justice will ever be achieved short of God's kingdom in its fullness, because all systems of justice are implemented by fallen human beings.

But that does not mean justice is not worth pursuing: We are commanded to pray for (and, I believe, work towards) God's kingdom here "on earth, as it is in heaven" (Matthew 6:10).

DACA and Dreamers

The DACA (Deferred Action for Childhood Arrivals) program allows some individuals, called "Dreamers," whose parents brought them to the U.S. illegally when they were minors to receive a renewable two-year period of "deferred action" from deportation and to be eligible for a work permit. President Obama initiated DACA in 2012 by an executive action when Congress failed to act. In December 2017, President Trump revealed plans to phase out the DACA program. A final decision is pending, waiting on the adjudication of lawsuits and legislative action by Congress.

Matthew emphatically asserts that Dreamers should be provided a pathway to citizenship without any punishment, such as fines, because they have not violated any laws. (It was their parents who violated immigration law.)

> ... I do not think it makes sense to penalize undocumented immigrants who were brought to the U.S. as children: neither the Bible nor any other area of U.S. law would hold children responsible for decisions they did not make. The young immigrants known as 'Dreamers,' many of whom benefitted from the Deferred Action for Childhood Arrivals program under the Obama administration but are now poised to lose those protections under the Trump administration, should

be offered the opportunity to earn U.S. citizenship in an expedited fashion, and without the requirement of fines.

Matthew's strong conviction about providing deportation relief for Dreamers does not only reflect a theoretical concern. His concern is "personal and urgent" based on his friendship with three young Dreamers who have become productive members of society whose lives would be devastated if the DACA program is rescinded and they faced deportation from the only country they have known.

Robert acknowledges that Matthew makes a "compelling point" about the fate of Dreamers, saying that Dreamers ought to be treated "differently" than their parents, who "brought them here illegally."

> One of Matthew's most compelling points, and one of the most pressing present issues, concerns the DACA program. I agree with Matthew's assessment that children who were brought to the United States (and who consider the U.S. home) ought to be treated (as a matter of justice) differently than those who brought them here illegally.

But Robert's acknowledgment that Dreamers should be treated "differently" than their parents begs the question as to the magnitude of the "different" treatment. Does Robert agree with Matthew's proposal that Dreamers should be provided with a pathway to citizenship without any punishment? Robert doesn't answer that question directly. His answer may be implicit in his final reflections on what "justice" may "require" for Dreamers, as follows:

> Who, then, as a matter of justice, caused the instability and uncertainty faced by the Dreamers? First, those who brought them to the United States unlawfully. Matthew's prior essays make clear his agreement with the obligation to obey existing laws. Those who bring children to this country unlawfully are willingly exposing those children to the uncertainties associated with unlawful status.

> Second, the DACA program itself, as a unilateral executive action, is constitutionally questionable ...

Third, those who encourage unlawful entry into the country are responsible, in justice, for contributing to instability and uncertainty faced by those here unlawfully. This includes "public interest" groups, employers, universities and others that may have contributed (for reasons of self-interest) to the problem by encouraging or facilitating unlawful entry into the country.

And ultimately, if there is no natural right or principle of justice entitling the Dreamers to live in the United States, those seeking exemption from existing laws are responsible in justice for the uncertainty and instability they will face in their own lives.

I do not intend here to deny the right and responsibility of Christians to come to the aid of all people. We ought to help Dreamers and citizens alike seek equal justice under law. But I am warning against the danger of justifying violation of existing law on the basis of our desire to achieve other 'good' outcomes. Call your representatives and senators and demand legislative reform, but do not facilitate violations of the law in the name of justice.

I must confess that I cannot draw out the "different" treatment that Robert proposes for Dreamers from these final reflections. It appears to me that Robert is saying that the "instability and uncertainty" experienced by Dreamers is a consequence, however much "unintended," of the decision of their parents to violate immigration law. But that does not answer the question as to whether this violation of the law by their parents should result in some form of punishment for their children. Matthew answers "no." Obviously, more conversation is needed.

Defer to the Democratic Process, or Not?

The above narrative describes some areas of agreement between Matthew and Robert—regarding promising public policy proposals for immigration reform; a possible area of disagreement regarding DACA and Dreamers; and some ideas (e.g., granting more asylum requests) that were not discussed—all of which beg for further conversation. But the huge question then arises as to how to bring about any of these ideas for reforming public policies?

As already agreed upon by Matthew and Robert, the Bible is not a policy manual relative to immigration policies or any other public policies. Its background teachings can inform public policy debates but they do not "determine" the outcome of such debates. Robert brings this point home again by asserting that while he "agrees with all of the biblical principles that Matthew identifies," "These truths ... do not compel agreement with the immigration policies Matthew proposed," noting, for example, that "God's love for immigrants, and His command that we love immigrants, does not *require* that immigrants have easier access to citizenship in the United States."

In this light, Robert considers Matthew's proposals for immigration reform to be "relatively minor prudential adjustments to current law"; "prudential" because "Matthew disclaims the suggestion that justice *requires* the adjustments he recommends."

Of course, it is arguable whether any of Matthew's proposals are "relatively minor ... adjustments" in existing immigration law. (Current heated debate, in Congress and the media, would suggest otherwise.) But Robert's understanding that Matthew does not view his proposals as being "required," combined with Matthew's concession that "even if his proposals are adopted, U.S. immigration law will remain imperfect" and may have "unintended consequences," leads Robert to believe that Matthew is "deferring to democratic resolution of the question of the content of the law." If so, Robert strongly agrees. But, is Matthew deferring to the "democratic process"? Before reporting on Matthew's response to that question, I will report on Robert's strong conviction that the content of immigration law must be determined by the democratic process.

First, Robert affirms that "the starting point for anyone seeking to understand U.S. 'immigration law' is the United States Constitution," with particular emphasis on "the legitimacy of the legislative powers established in the U.S. Constitution" (which Robert assumes Matthew also "affirms"). In other words, also expressed by Robert, "There may be good reasons to change the [immigration] rules … and Congress has the constitutional power to make those changes."

But, as Robert adds, this starting point does not eliminate "complexity," as introduced by factors such as presidential "executive orders," the "rulings of courts" and the "precedents" that such rulings establish, and the "complexity of dual sovereignty in the U.S. legal system—the coexistence of state and federal law."

Robert's response to Matthew's concern that he [Robert] has not offered specific concrete proposals for immigration reform is that he has not had the opportunity to attend legislative hearings about "these difficult [complex] questions," citing as an example the difficult question as to whether "justice requires a specific volume of visas annually."

> I have not offered any specific proposal because I have not attended (nor read) legislative hearings regarding these difficult questions. Unless justice requires a specific volume of visas annually, I would defer to the judgment of our elected representatives (and to the democratic process) to determine the volume of visas to grant. I am not at all opposed to Matthew, or any other Christian, calling his or her elected representative regarding these policy questions.

> My prior essays reflect the fact that U.S. immigration law has been modified numerous times over nearly two and a half centuries. If Congress deems it necessary to modify immigration law by allowing more visas I would not have a principled objection to that conclusion. But nor would Matthew, I take it, have a principled objection to a decision in the opposite direction. Congress strikes a balance and resolves these prudential questions because justice does not require the United States to permit immigration.

Here again, Robert is noting his deference to the democratic process, at the same time that he is not opposed to Christians advocating for particular concrete proposals, which brings us back to the question of the extent, if at all, to which Matthew defers to the democratic process.

Matthew is emphatic in asserting that he does not support subverting "the will of the American people as expressed through our democratic process." But "part of the democratic process" is to "seek to persuade" when we think "a system can be improved," citing again his concrete proposal regarding the "number of immigration visas."

> I'm not advocating that I should be given authoritarian powers to subvert the will of the American people as expressed through our democratic processes, but part of our democratic process is, when we think a system can be improved, to seek to persuade. I affirm that these decisions are prudential: My argument is not that justice—whether defined by the Bible or John Rawls or any other particular philosophy—clearly requires a specific number of immigrant visas, but that it is reasonable to conclude that an immigration policy that more closely matched labor market demands would ultimately lead to a more just outcome.

And Matthew adds, once again, that he is "passionate about these issues" because they affect "close friends of mine," reminding all of us that our system of government is "responsive" to such "advocacy."

> As I argued in my second piece, I'm very passionate about these issues, first and foremost, because they are so personal to me. The individuals whose interaction with our immigration system I would describe as unjust are, in many cases, close friends of mine. I feel a sense of responsibility, given that our system of government is responsive to the advocacy and voting habits of citizens (including me), to at least do my best to propose solutions, even if I acknowledge they will not fully remedy every injustice.

Robert expresses his "appreciation" for Matthew's agreement that "Christians ought to be willing (as citizens in our republic) to thoughtfully

participate in democratic consideration of immigration law and policy."
Robert also agrees with Matthew that "all laws are 'personal' and 'urgent,"
and affirms that he also wants to "support immigration laws that would
enable human flourishing." But, it is precisely because of the impact of
immigration laws on "millions of people" that Robert believes that "deference to democratic judgment regarding the content of the law is so
important."

> ... all laws are 'personal' and 'urgent' in the manner Matthew
> describes. As a lawyer, and a law professor, I could also
> tell many, many stories about the ways in which I have
> personally witnessed law impacting people. Laws shape the
> world in which people live. It is because U.S. immigration
> law impacts millions of people (indeed, our entire nation
> and its relationship to the world) that I believe deference to
> democratic judgment regarding the content of the law is so
> important.

> Matthew describes himself as feeling a 'moral obligation'
> to 'leverage the influence' he has so that those individuals
> potentially denied lawful status can flourish. And it is here, I
> suspect, that Matthew views himself to be acting practically
> (as opposed to theoretically). He wants to do something.

> But I also seek to support immigration laws that would
> enable human flourishing—not just for individuals denied
> access to lawful immigration status, but for everyone. In
> order to achieve such a result I think it is vital that Congress
> consider Matthew's proposals in an effort to secure the
> common good.

The Role of the Church

Matthew proposes that "the church has a key role in advocating for just [immigration] policies." But he also proposes that "the role of the church goes far beyond advocacy," extending to the provision of services to immigrants.

> ... the role of the church also goes far beyond advocacy. I often am approached by church leaders torn between their desire to love, welcome and share the Gospel with immigrants whom they suspect may be in the country unlawfully and their commitment to abiding by the law (Romans 13:1). Fortunately, in most cases, they can do both (with the notable exception of employing someone who is present unlawfully). Churches and the individuals who compose them are free to minister in any number of ways. There is no legal requirement that a private citizen or faith-based institution report someone they suspect of being present unlawfully, nor does the law restrict a church from sharing the Gospel, baptizing new believers, teaching English, operating a food pantry or providing any other spiritual or social good that a church might offer to someone without legal status.

At the same time that Matthew proposes that "Christians have an important voice to contribute toward ... efforts [to help immigrants]," he expresses concern "that many American Christians—particularly white evangelicals like me—have allowed a political narrative to blind us to the Gospel opportunity that I believe God has placed in front of us, missing opportunities to obediently love and serve our immigrant neighbors because we have seen them only as a cultural threat, an economic drain or a political problem, rather than people made in God's image for whom Christ died."

Chapter 10 will discuss in more detail the potential role of churches and Christian para-church organizations relative to "action" pertaining to all political issues, including immigration.

A Concluding Personal Reflection:
It Is Both/And, not Either/Or

Politics is messy, especially when you start dealing with concrete public policy proposals relative to contentious issues, like immigration. As this chapter illustrates, it is sometimes hard to get such conversations off the ground because of misinformation regarding relevant "facts" and differing conceptions of the meaning of "justice."

But the exchange between Matthew Soerens and Robert McFarland reported in this chapter also models to a marvelous degree my main procedural suggestion for doing politics: *Politicians and their supporters who appear to have irreconcilable disagreements about public policy issues, like immigration, will be able to find significant common ground if they are willing to talk respectfully to one another.*

That is not to say that Matthew and Robert now see eye-to-eye relative to all immigration issues. And it is not to suggest that the agreements they have forged relative to some immigration issues are the "final" or "best" solutions to some existing problems with our current immigration system. But they have laid a strong foundation for ongoing conversation between them and their allies that has the potential to lead to more common ground.

It is particularly noteworthy that while Matthew and Robert start with differing foci as to the root meaning of "justice," they find some common ground that embraces both of their foci. Robert's focus on "justice" requiring "obedience to laws" and Matthew's focus on "justice" calling for "helping the marginalized and vulnerable" are *not mutually exclusive.* I cannot overemphasize the importance of this point since my experience advocating for immigration reform in northwest Iowa has been the conversation-stopper that erroneously holds that one cannot be **both** a proponent of obedience to the law **and** an advocate for helping our Latino neighbors who are vulnerable and marginalized in our midst. An adequate broad view of the full meaning of "justice" embraces both of these ideals. It is both/and, not either/or.

This both/and approach to dealing with immigration issues is so noteworthy because it is so contrary to the either/or approach that currently dominates political thinking on both sides of the aisle. Too many politicians and their supporters say "it's my way or the highway." Matthew and

Robert beautifully demonstrate that if politicians and their supporters who have significant disagreements about public policy issues are willing to respectfully engage one another in conversation about their disagreements, they may be able to find some common ground that reflects the best thinking on both sides of the given issue.

That is not to say that proponents on either side of the issue will be entirely happy with the end result. This both/and approach will often mean that you get "half a loaf," not all that you had hoped for, and you may get some things you had hoped to avoid. This is illustrated well in Matthews's reflections on the proposed bill for immigration reform recently proposed by Senators Mike Rounds and Angus King that was rejected by the Senate.

> ... while my view is that our nation can (and should) find more cost-effective ways to achieve a largely secure border than by dramatically expanding the existing border wall, I called my elected officials a few weeks ago urging them to vote **for** the amendment from Republican Senator Mike Rounds and independent Senator Angus King (an amendment which ultimately failed) that would have appropriated roughly $25 billion for a wall and other border security improvements— because it would also allow my friends with DACA to earn citizenship over the course of 12 years if they met all the proposal's requirements. I believe that would have meant, on the net, a more just situation for them and for the country.

This both/and approach to doing politics, far from yielding perfect results in the eyes of those on either side of the issue, is surely better for the well-being of our nation than the political gridlock that has emerged from the political tribalism that has taken over the political realm due to the inordinate influence of extremists and the "hollowing out" of the "middle" group of moderate politicians who are courageous enough to take a both/and approach.

8

Wealth and Poverty in America

WE NOW CONSIDER the second of three highly contested public policy issues: the disparity in the distribution of wealth in America and the related persistence of poverty. This chapter reports on responses given by Steve McMullen, an economist, and Kelly Johnson, a theologian, to the following set of leading questions:

- America is increasingly divided between rich and poor. What are the root causes of poverty and wealth disparity in America?
- Is there a connection between wealth disparity in America and disparities in the rest of the world?
- Is there a biblical and Christian ideal for the distribution of wealth, both nationally and globally?
- How should Christians respond personally and politically to national and global poverty and wealth disparity?

It is important to note at the outset that the agreements and disagreements that will soon be reported often reflect differences in the respective "disciplinary perspectives" taken by Steve (economics) and Kelly (theology).

If one believes, as I do, that the primary distinctive of education from a Christian perspective is to seek to uncover "connections" between knowledge claims in the various academic disciplines and one's biblical and theological understanding,[59] then the results that have emerged from this conversation are a marvelous exemplification of this quest for "integration of knowledge." To set a context for these results, consider first the following reflections from Steve relative to these disciplinary differences.

> It is ... noteworthy ... that our focus is quite different. While Dr. Johnson focuses almost entirely on the theological, cultural and moral dimensions around economic inequalities, I focused instead on economic institutions and policies. This reflects a kind of disagreement, but it is likely a disciplinary difference, not necessarily a political or ideological one. It is not surprising, then, that my reading of her post left me with some large questions.
>
> It is worth pointing out that Dr. Johnson and I offer very different ways in which Christians can contribute to the larger conversation about inequality. She calls us to see the way our culture and history are wrapped up in inequality, and how our Christian tradition should push us to face the injustice. My approach is to zero in on economic institutions and policies, and try to discern how our Christian tradition can help us design a more just system. These are not in conflict, and they clearly reflect different disciplinary priorities. Each approach has natural pitfalls, though. We economists tend to assume that we can approach everything as a kind of amoral technocratic problem to be solved. Theologians can, instead, approach the topic as only a moral problem.

In response, Kelly notes that her view of theology does not comport with the views of some other theologians that theology has "little to offer" beyond the "articulation of values or ideals," which enables her to engage with Steve relative to "particular policy questions."

---

59 My belief about this fundamental distinctive of "education from a Christian perspective" is referred to at Christian institutions of higher education as one aspect of the meaning of "integration of faith and learning." For a few of my own writings on this integrative theme, see Heie and Wolfe, *Reality of Christian Learning*; Heie and Wolfe, *Slogans or Distinctives*; Heie, "Nature of Mathematics," in Migliazzo, *Teaching*, 95-116. See also Hasker, "Faith-Learning Integration," 234-248.

What about the importance of engaging particular policy questions? Dr. McMullen argues that this work is important because it is the principle area of disagreement, because our efforts to craft solutions lead to a better understanding of the problems, and because in the end good intentions simply won't get it done. He argues that theological thinking matters not only in setting ends for the economy, but in helping to determine right means, which is the really juicy question.

I appreciate the compliment paid to the discipline of theology. Too often the presumption, on all sides of the issue, is that theology, properly speaking, stops with the articulation of values or ideals and really has little to offer beyond that. That presumption is rooted in the belief that theology is about ideas rather than historical action or human communities. Some theologians will argue that that is exactly what theology is.[60] I am not one of them. Christian theology is about God as known by a historical revelation and the community that lives by it and through the gift of the Spirit. So for Christian theology, a focus on God is a focus on events, people and a social organization, as well as the texts, stories and principles that animate those people.

Hopefully the report that follows will reveal ways in which Steve and Kelly seek to make connections between their respective disciplinary perspectives on wealth and poverty in America.

Underlying Biblical Principles

In preparation for eventually reporting on Steve and Kelly's positions relative to specific public policy issues pertaining to wealth and poverty, it is important to note their agreement about some foundational biblical principles that will inform consideration of such specific issues.

---

60 Sullivan, "Catholic Theology."

Moral importance

First, Steve and Kelly agree that "economic equality is a first order moral problem" (Steve). In Kelly's words, this means that "the economy is not just ... a 'quasi-mechanical system'"; it "serves an end," something that is discerned as "good" by a community.

> A key area on which we [Steve and I] agree is that questions of poverty and wealth are questions of moral import, political questions in the sense that they require discernment by a community about what is good. The economy is not just a procedure, a quasi-mechanical system; it serves an end. Economic interests do not necessarily create good results, if left to themselves, and some very important goods, particularly public goods, need to be fostered by means other than the market. Such goods are beneficial in ways that have to do both with a good business climate and also with humanity.

Sustaining and including everyone

Steve asserts that what the Bible is teaching about the "economy" is that it should serve a "particular end": "the sustaining of the life of a community, and the inclusion of everyone in that community."

> In the Bible, and the Old Testament in particular, property and wealth are often framed as a blessing that allows someone to provide for their own needs and the needs of those around them. Moreover, the treatment of wealth in the Sabbath laws seems to prioritize the inclusion of everyone in the economic community. Anyone who had more than they needed was obligated to include others by giving loans, jobs or gifts to sustain them. Extraordinary wealth, moreover, clearly gives one the power to include others in the community or exclude others from their calling, a danger that is highlighted throughout Scripture. In the Bible, it seems that the economy is a system that has a particular end: the sustaining of the life of a community, and the inclusion of everyone in that community. In Catholic theology, this

has been summarized in the principle sometimes called 'the universal destination of goods.'

The principle of "the universal destination of goods" that Steve affirms (also called the "universal distribution of goods") is summarized by Kelly as follows: "The goods of the earth are intended to meet the needs of all." Kelly also endorses this principle, adding that it requires that "human need takes precedence over private ownership."

> There is one less well-known teaching I want to introduce into our conversation. The principle, dating back to the Church Fathers and strongly affirmed again by Catholic leadership in recent years is 'the universal distribution of goods': The goods of the earth are intended to meet the needs of all. That is to say, God did not and does not make some people to have plenty while others go without their needs met. When that happens, it happens because humans have made it so, not because it is God's will. The principle does not require that all persons have equal wealth, and it does not forbid private property. But it does require that human need takes precedence over private ownership.

Steve asserts that the "theme of participation in the economy" on which he focuses is "a key element of economic justice," which calls for "people's ability to participate in the process of wealth creation." He adds his concern that "the rules of the economic game can be rigged against those without economic power" and can lead to "an excessively punitive justice system that locks people out of the economy through debt, incarceration or deportation."

> Within the U.S., much of the reward from dramatic increases in production have gone to those who are able to take advantage of international trade, advances in technology and mass markets. Those with little education or those separated from global markets by geography or social standing are left with fewer opportunities and increased international and domestic competition. There is a real long-term danger that, left to current trends, we would find that there is ever less

investment in common public goods, and less investment in those institutions that create broad opportunity. To counter this, Christians should serve their neighbors by devoting their resources and political energy toward sustaining those institutions—like education and health care—that allow us to invest in people's ability to pursue their own calling. We should likewise be careful to limit the ways in which the rules of the economy can be rigged against those without economic power, such as through regulation that favors established corporations, or an excessively punitive justice system that locks people out of the economy through debt, incarceration or deportation.

Steve's assertion that the economy should "sustain and include every-one" is heartily endorsed by Kelly in her reflections on "wealth disparity."

'Wealth disparity' strikes me as a somewhat evasive term. The truth it refers to is not just that people have different amounts of wealth but that some have luxury while others sicken and die, and this not as a result of some crisis but as a long-lasting, ordinary state of affairs. So, when we are talking about wealth disparity we are talking about how people are excluded from what they need for health and for participation in society. The rates of difference vary but the socially, legally, morally accepted reality is that even when there is enough to meet human needs, it is distributed in such a way that many urgent needs go unmet.

Kelly elaborates further by noting that the "love of neighbor" taught in both "the Old and New Testaments" condemn "passivity in the face of need."

There's nothing surprising or remarkable in noting that Christian teaching condemns passivity in the face of need. Both Old and New Testaments require love of neighbor. In the New Testament, the story of the Good Samaritan debunks any claim that 'neighbor' can be defined in a way that excludes someone in need, showing as it does the falsehood of presuming that 'we' are the good guys.

While acknowledging that "a number of New Testament teachings about economic sharing refer to mutual love among Christians, not general altruism" (e.g., Acts 2 and 4 and 1 and 2 Corinthians), Kelly cites research indicating that Christians are not very generous in sharing their money with those inside or outside the Christian community.[61] She adds that this lack of generosity—a failure to express the "mutual love" to which Christians are called—may help to explain why non-believers often conclude that "the Christian story is a false ... [story]."

> If Christians in the U.S. and globally do not imagine that mutual love among them requires urgent action toward both those who are their brothers and sisters in Christ as well as those they hope to welcome as such brothers and sisters, then we cannot be surprised that people tend to think the Christian story is a false one. It is not science or technology or philosophy that raises the great challenge to the truth of Christian convictions in our day: it is the failure of Christians themselves to witness to mutual love.

Expanding on an assertion by Steve that "inadequate regard for economic disparities is deeply woven into our culture," Kelly notes that "America has always been about exclusion, even as it has always claimed to be about opportunity for everyone"; giving some heart-breaking examples pertaining to minority populations.

> America has always been about exclusion, even as it has always claimed to be about opportunity for everyone. The conquest of the Americas, the most fundamental wealth accumulation on this continent, is a story of war and broken treaties, of people driven onto reservations so that others could use the land that was their home. Africans were forced into slavery, and for 350 years they and their children were beaten and raped, bought and sold regardless of family ties and refused access to education. They created much of the wealth of this land and were excluded from its enjoyment.

---

61 Smith, *Passing the Plate*, 3.

That exclusion continued long past the end of slavery, in Jim Crow laws, in exclusion from Depression-era benefits, in redlining and later reverse redlining, in mass incarceration and new forms of voter exclusion. Mexicans, made U.S. citizens after the Mexican-American War, were not given the protections promised in the Treaty of Guadalupe Hidalgo; and in the mid-20th century as in the 21st, when Mexicans and Central Americans come to the U.S. to do hard labor to create value, they are either managed as guest workers (who can only be in the U.S. for a limited time) or left to work in ways that make it easy for them to be cheated by employers and deported by authorities, so that they too are excluded from full participation in the wealth they are creating. U.S. citizens of Puerto Rico can tell their own story of exclusion.

Kelly asks the penetrating question as to "why" it is that "a country that so prides itself on protecting the rights of all people can, generation after generation, ignore so many?" Her response is that a "key issue" that leads to this failure is a view of "freedom in the U.S." as meaning that "each individual may use his or her private property according to his or her own preferences, with minimal regulation ... "

A problem, as Kelly sees it, with this view of "freedom" is that "whatever outcome arises, ... we will call it justice," hoping that it will "reward merit or effort" at the same time that it will "meet needs" (two different views as to the meaning of "justice," I would add). But neither of these aspects of "justice" are "guaranteed." ("We know that they often are not what happens.") But "at least, we tell ourselves, we are free."

Kelly adds that a particular problem with this faulty view of "freedom" is that it is not adequately "attentive to economic realities."

> ... congregations in the U.S. [need] to shift their talk about freedom, especially religious freedom, in a direction more attentive to economic realities ... If instead of the churches carrying a banner for freedom as defined in the Bill of Rights, they argued for freedom as the freedom from sin encountered when participating in the life of Christ, we might be able to identify individualism and consumerism

as obstacles to freedom. We might be able to talk about defense of the common good (as it affects congregations, neighborhoods, cities, the nation and the world) as an act of freedom.

Elaborating further in no uncertain terms, Kelly concludes that this faulty view of freedom leads us to ignore the needs of the sick, the disabled and other members of society whose circumstances prevent them from being "independent and productive," which fails to acknowledge our "interdependence" and need for "solidarity."

> This kind of freedom means that those who have more property have more scope for their freedom, which is to say, they have more freedom, including more power to shape our political life. But it's more than that. This vision of freedom presumes that the subject of freedom will be independent and productive. Those who, for example, are sick, disabled, unable to speak the dominant language, too young, too old or just too fallible seem in this system to be burdens on the independent and productive. For a system focused on allowing efficient producers to have more independence, such persons are problems to be managed, minimized or removed ...

> In short, it's a philosophical mistake, imagining a human freedom that is an escape from creatureliness, from dependence and interdependence, from mortality. It leads to a justice that is mere fairness and a charity that is mere occasional philanthropy, rather than a practice of solidarity, cognizant of our interdependence.

As a bit of personal commentary, it is clear to me that the biblical teaching about "freedom" seriously calls into question the hyper-individualistic view so prevalent in America that "freedom" means you should use what you own (private property and other personal resources) as you please, as long as you stay "within the law" and do not deter the right of others to do likewise. The more robust biblical view of "freedom" is that it provides you with an opportunity to serve others. Consider, for example, Galatians 5: 13-14.

> For you were called to freedom, brothers and sisters; only do not use your freedom as an opportunity for self-indulgence, but through love become slaves to one another. For the whole law is summed up in one commandment, 'You shall love your neighbor as yourself.'

Having now reported on two broad areas of agreement between Steve and Kelly, that "economic equality is a first order moral problem" and that a good economy should "sustain and include everyone," I will now note some different "emphases" as they attempt to work out the implications of these areas of agreement for public policies. These differing, albeit overlapping foci will reveal somewhat the differing disciplinary perspectives of a theologian and an economist that, I argue, must eventually be "integrated" (which I make an initial attempt at later in this chapter). These differing perspectives can be introduced by reporting on three alternative, albeit overlapping, narratives presented by Steve regarding "domestic wealth inequality." As you read summaries of these narratives, pay close attention to alternative views as to the meaning of "justice" embedded within them and how each narrative plays the "blame game."

The Stories We Tell About Inequality

Under the above title, Steve tells the following three stories about economic inequality.

Rich people are productive risk-takers, poor people have chosen poverty

> If we believe that people who are wealthy got to their position, most of the time, through hard work, talent and delayed gratification, then it is easy to see them as heroic figures. Similarly, if we believe that people who are wealthy usually get that way by providing valuable goods that people need and want, then wealth creation is pro-social and laudable. Along the same vein, if we believe that the primary reason

why people are poor is that they have made poor choices,
it is easy to dismiss their hardship. This combination
of assumptions will usually lead to the conclusion that
inequality is not a moral problem. On the contrary, it might
be the sign of a just system. To be consistent with this
narrative, the rapid inequality in growth over the last [years]
is usually explained by social breakdown in the U.S. among
those with low income and education. While it is rare for
this kind of story to be told in a form this blunt outside of
the pages of an Ayn Rand novel, many of the arguments
of economic conservatives in the U.S. follow this kind of
narrative.

Note that in this story, it is primarily the "poor people" who are to
blame for economic inequality. Also embedded in this story is a view of
"justice" as "receiving what you have earned."

Rich people are corrupt, poor people are exploited victims

If on the other hand, we flip the script, and make those who
are rich the villains of the story, it is easy to argue, instead,
that the richest Americans, usually those in finance or in
the leadership of large corporations, have worked to rig the
economy in their own interests, and against the interests
of the working class. Poor people, on the other hand, are
painted as the victims of this corrupt capitalism, with little
bargaining power and few advantages in a winner-take-all
game. In this story, income inequality is a sign of injustice.
Under this narrative, the domestic rise in income inequality
is likely to be explained by political and economic victories
by those who serve the interests of the wealthiest citizens.
While, again, the narrative is not always painted this starkly,
a story of this type is often told by those most economically
progressive.

In this story, the "bad guys" are the "rich people" who exploit "poor people," which is viewed as "unjust." This assumes a view of "justice" as calling for an "equitable distribution of goods."

Structural economic changes have caused economic inequality to increase

> The last kind of story we tell about inequality is that there is some large shift, largely outside of our control, that has changed the economy and caused increased inequality. For example, some have explained inequality in terms of broad trends in education and technology, arguing that technological developments have tended to reward those with the right set of skills and education, and have replaced workers with less education. Sometimes described as 'skill-biased technological change,' this explanation is exemplified in a 2010 book by two Harvard economists.[62] Other stories in this genre include references to increased international competition, immigration, the rise of Internet commerce and declines in aggregate productivity as explanations for the rise of economic inequality. This kind of story about inequality is usually favored by economists, and it tends to leave issues of justice outside of the story altogether.

In this story, it appears that "no one is to blame" for economic inequality; it is the result of impersonal forces "outside of our control." Questions about what it means to "do justice" are, therefore, irrelevant.

Which is the better story?

As Steve points out, "all three of these narratives about inequality are true, in some respect, and all of them are also problematic." For example, considering the first two narratives, Steve notes that "there are plenty of anecdotes and statistics to support both stories, and so it is easy to fall into one camp or the other and assume that the other side is horribly mistaken." But a particular problem with both of these narratives is that they give

---

62 Goldin, *The Race*.

.

politicians and their supporters, "on the right or the left," ammunition for identifying "clear heroes and enemies."

> Part of the temptation of these kinds of narratives is that they each give convenient cover for a political program, either on the right or the left, and they identify clear heroes and enemies. People on the right can dismiss concerns of those on the left as being motivated by envy; people on the left can, in turn, assume that the concerns of those on the right are motivated by privilege and greed.

Steve indicates that his leaning is toward the third narrative in light of the "big structural changes in the economy," which may reflect his perspective as an economist.

> While I find all three stories convincing on different days, I usually lean toward the third kind of narrative. In the midst of our ideological battles, it is easy to miss that there are big structural changes in the economy that are slowly pushing us toward inequality. Moreover, we can usually have a more productive conversation about how to address inequality if we avoid the kind of characterizations in the first two stories, and pay close attention to broader economic forces.

However, Steve also points us to the danger in the third story: a tendency to view economic inequality as "merely a technical problem" that ignores stories of "hardship, discrimination, ... crime, exclusion for community and culpable opulence" that point to the "substantial moral questions at stake" (which, I would add, point to some of the "truths" in the first two narratives).

> The danger in this third kind of story is that it allows scholars to pretend that inequality is merely a technical problem, and ignore the fact that these broad trends are made up of smaller story arcs about hardship, discrimination, luck, lifetimes of hard work, unemployment, crime, exclusion from community and culpable opulence. That is to say, there are substantial moral questions at stake.

Relative to the first narrative, Kelly points out that people who are poor are often risk averse, but that is a result of poverty, not a cause of it. They are often risk averse because "even a modest loss could be devastating for them." As to the second narrative, she points out the danger of generalizing about "rich people" or "poor people."

> As to the second story, dishonesty and manipulation are human characteristics, and no class has a monopoly on them. People who have superfluous wealth are not necessarily evil geniuses, any more than people lacking in what they need are necessarily always honest and caring.

> ... every person who is poor has a story, and those may involve foolish choices, a lax work ethic or taking one step too many on the road to addiction. So may the stories of those who have plenty, for whom such choices have less drastic effects.

However, Kelly finds the claim in the third narrative that "structural economic changes" are to blame for economic inequality "less than convincing."

> ... The appeal of this [third] story, intellectually, is that it avoids simple good guy/ bad guy plot lines. Sometimes, things just happen. Economics, after all, specializes in unintended consequences.

> In that way, then, the story indicates that technology and its social impact are in some sense out of human control. There's good reason to say that: technology has a logic within itself, and our claims that we can control it, that we can use it for our own good, have repeatedly been shown false. We are creatures caught in 'the technocratic paradigm,'[63] thinking initially that we are seizing control of natural power so that it would serve us, only to find after a time that we ourselves are the ones being controlled.

---

63 Pope Francis, *Laudato Si,* Chapter 3.

What I want to flag here is that saying this was not a matter of human control is no consolation. There were human decisions, human actions involved. Sometimes we find ourselves in a moment of moral tragedy, where we have no good option. In such cases, honesty about our limits and courage in facing the results of our actions may be the best we can do. That is mitigation, but it is not exoneration. Since those who had the power to make the choices that had hard-to-predict or impossible-to-avoid consequences are not the poor who suffer from them, I find the claim that story No. 3 is about something that is no one's fault less than convincing.

Despite the appearance that "no one is to blame" in the third narrative, Steve acknowledges in his summary statement that, in effect, "we all are to blame" [my words, not his] because "it is the responsibility of every-one to politically manage the rules of the economy to favor inclusion and opportunity."

[In my first post] I offered three overly-simplistic stories that we tell about economic disparities. Dr. Johnson was right to note that the difference between the three stories is the answer to the question 'who is to blame?' Dr. Johnson's response to these was thoughtful, though I fear I left the point underdeveloped. Too often, when we talk about the economy, we end up falling into predictable patterns of one kind or another. Conservatives tend to lionize entrepreneurs and blame poverty on the poor; progressives tend to lionize activists and blame inequality on those with wealth. Economists, I noted, when they don't fall into these other patterns, tend to focus only on larger impersonal social forces.

The first two narratives are powerful because there are true stories that validate each. There are many cases of wealth that come from innovation and frugality, just as there are cases of people gaining wealth through corruption. Similarly, the poor can be victims of injustice and they can also be poor because of particularly destructive choices. If one of these stories dominates our narrative about the economy, however, then we can too easily split the world into good guys and bad guys and put up political or economic barricades. I cannot give a clear path out of these ideological pitfalls, but I try to discipline myself to avoid getting too comfortable with a narrative that allows me to easily assign blame to a person. Moreover, it takes real work to push back against the myths that poor people are lazy, or that businesspeople are greedy, or similar stories targeting politicians or minorities ... Even if all of our worst fears are true, when we focus on these stories, we create two problems. First, we make it harder to be charitable toward those with whom we disagree. Second, we stop looking for the institutional elements that can drive the outcomes we care about.

For this reason, when I noted that trends in education and technology provide the best explanation for rising domestic inequality, I recognize that this argument has its own pitfalls. As I noted, and as Dr. Johnson argued, this kind of explanation makes it easy to ignore the moral significance of the increased inequality. This does not mean, as Dr. Johnson argues, that, in this line of argument inequality 'is no one's fault.' It does change the nature of the responsibility, however. Rather than the rising inequality being the fault of those who are rich and those who are poor, it is the responsibility of everyone to politically manage the rules of the economy to favor inclusion and opportunity.

It is important to note from Steve's summary statement that he reiterates his concern, as noted earlier, with which Kelly agreed, that "the economy should sustain the life of a community, and include everyone in that community." He describes that as "economic opportunity" which will require "broad investments in the whole population."

Sometimes, when we imagine a 'land of opportunity' we immediately jump to inspiring rags-to-riches stories. I would like to conclude by reiterating that the rising inequality among a population measured in the hundreds of millions cannot be explained by the virtues or vices that make up these kinds of stories, however, and instead probably reflects a growing divergence of opportunities and higher stakes across the board ... I fear that people are less able to participate in society in a reasonably secure and healthy way because of these changes, and that the power and position of the wealthy will only become more pronounced. We can make choices that will counter this trend, but they require a political consensus behind paying the price for broad investments in the whole population.

What about the Christian story?

As if an attempt to sort through these three narratives isn't complicated enough, Kelly wishes to introduce two elements of the "Christian story" that differ from Steve's "reading of Scripture and tradition in two significant ways." First, Kelly wishes to place greater emphasis on the church addressing the wealth disparity within its own community.

> ... Scripture [is] ...in the first place the church's book, a book about the life of the church in the world. And so I give greater attention to the question of wealth disparity within the community of faith and as a matter of evangelical witness to the world. I take that approach not so much because I see something wrong with considering global economic relations without reference to the church, but because it is so rare to see anyone identify economic inequality as an ecclesial matter. It is, and for those of us who hold that the church lives from God's presence with it, that that presence is a ministry for the sake of the world, the frustrations and vast possibilities of the church are at the center of the story.

We will return to this emphasis on the church later in this chapter. A second area for which Kelly perceives a difference with Steve's interpretation of Scripture has to do with the "language of blessing and stewardship."

She first asks Christians to be honest about the "morally mixed," way, "at best," by which "private property in the U.S. is accumulated."

> My first priority as a theologian is to try to speak truthfully about the Gospel and about ourselves. For example, what are Christians hiding from themselves when they speak of the personal wealth as 'blessings entrusted to them by God' given that private property in the U.S. is accumulated through a morally mixed, at best, historical process? Should Christians reclaim the category of 'filthy lucre,' and if so, how can we use it well, given the complex networks of economic relationships we find ourselves in? For what should we be grateful and for what should we be penitent?

Kelly's elaborates, including her view that "the Bible certainly does not assume that all wealth is a blessing given by God."

> Dr. McMullen points out, rightly, that land, herds and children are counted as blessings in the Old Testament. They are distinguished by their ripple effect, their expansion to foster more life, more relationship, and the laws of the Torah (like the Jubilee) promote redistribution to ensure poverty does not become generational.

> But the Bible certainly does not assume that all wealth is a blessing given by God. It can be wrongfully gained, and it can be related to vices of envy, hatred and luxury.

> ... I criticize 'stewardship.' As a term Christians used to describe responsible ownership of wealth, stewardship took off during the English reformation, and from the beginning, it was a way of ensuring people that the wealth they had gained in questionable ways could be put to good use anyway. Whatever good that terminology may have done—and it may have done some real good in encouraging people to think of their ownership as limited by God's more fundamental authority—it has conveniently displaced other Christian claims, such as the community of goods in Acts, the call to

leave all and follow Christ, the penitential redistribution of Zaccheus, and the communal feasting required in the Torah.

Interestingly, the universal destination of goods is not the language used when my church calls for my contributions. The reason, I'm sorry to say, seems to be that the universal destination of goods is less liable to comfort and flatter those who have superfluous wealth.

Not all wealth has been gained unjustly. Not all business ventures are exploitative. But until the church is able to talk honestly and hopefully about real injustices, historical and present and looming into the future, it has not yet awakened the full moral sensibility needed to address our reality in boldness and joy.

A Public Policy Proposal for Tax Reform

To set a context for considering a concrete public policy proposal for tax reform, it is important to return to Kelly's assertion that she is not one of those theologians for whom theology does not go beyond the "articulation of values or ideals." Despite this assertion, Steve presses Kelly to focus more on ways to "fix" economic inequality, acknowledging that in doing so, he is "following a well-worn track in challenging a theologian to provide some clear policy prescriptions," based on the fact that "economists have a practice of evaluating particular alternatives, rather than just pointing out problems, or appealing to an impossible standard."

Steve explains in some detail three reasons why it is important to go beyond "values and ideals" (which can be viewed as "goals") to concrete public policy proposals.

First, our political disagreements often revolve around differences in policy, not differences in goals. It is easy to get people to agree that poverty and racism are bad and that education is good. The disagreements really gain momentum once we try to help the poor, reform schools, or implement affirmative action. Economic inequality is this kind of problem. Until we agree on a solution, we have not really agreed on much.

Second, thinking about solutions can reveal big differences in how we diagnose the problem. Or, alternatively, different stories about what causes inequality lead us to very different conclusions. If you believe that inequality is due to immigration and trade, and that ordinary working Americans have been hurt by globalization, then it might appear that building a wall and renegotiating NAFTA is a good idea. On the other hand, if you believe that inequality is the result of a shift in bargaining power, with weaker unions and more concentrated firms, then the solution might be higher minimum wage laws and strict anti-trust enforcement. Or, to push it further, if you believe that inequality is the result of fast technological change and stagnating education growth, then the solution might be a radical new investment in education programming and funding, or more generous social programs.

Finally, it is really important to talk about solutions because good intentions are not enough for good policy. One recent example will make the point here. There was a big push in recent years to find ways to improve opportunities for those leaving prison and reentering the labor market. Unfortunately, those with a criminal record have a very difficult time finding an employer willing to hire them. Many lawmakers moved to prohibit employers from asking about an applicant's criminal record prior to hiring. This 'ban the box' movement gained significant ground, and was partially implemented by the federal government as well. A couple of recent studies, however, make a strong case that this policy ended up doing substantial harm.[64] Employers ended up engaging in more discrimination against African-American

---

64 For example, see Doleac, "Ban the Box."

and Hispanic men when they were not able to ask about criminal records. Because they were not able to distinguish between those with a criminal record and those who did not, employers engaged in statistical discrimination, and increasingly favored white job candidates.

Steve concludes that "identifying the problem is not even half the battle," adding that "often the difference between a moderate progressive and a moderate conservative is not in the identification of the problem, it is in the willingness to accept the imperfections of a particular policy agenda. Those on the left may be willing to trade some economic growth and accept some bureaucracy in order to provide more public goods and a more generous safety net. Those on the right may be willing to accept some corporate malfeasance and greater inequality in exchange for fewer restrictions and faster economic growth."

Within this context of establishing the importance of going beyond "goals" to considering concrete proposals for reaching such goals, Steve presents a concrete proposal for tax reform, deeply informed by his biblically based conviction that "we cannot claim absolute authority or ownership over our property."

Steve prepares us for his tax proposal by noting the tension in our market economy between rewarding people ("with income") who do something that people find "valuable and scarce" and helping "people being left behind despite hard work," adding that he is especially concerned about those who are "left behind" (consistent with his already reported focus on "participation [of everyone] in the economy," with which Kelly concurred).

> What we call 'capitalism' or a 'market economy' is a way of doing two things at the same time: it is a method of allocating people, technology and resources to create things that people value, and it is also a way of distributing the wealth that is created. It is tempting to separate these two: leave the market in charge of making stuff, but let the government step in when it comes time to distributing the gains, so that the result is more equal. The problem, of course, is that one of the reasons that our economic system is so good at making goods and providing services, is that we tend to reward

people (with income) as a result of doing something that people find valuable and scarce. This means that sometimes when we redistribute wealth, we also end up decreasing the total amount of wealth there is to share. We fight, politically, about which is more important: creating more valuable goods and services or equalizing the distribution of rewards.

Given my concern about participation in the economy, I tend to be most concerned about people being left behind despite hard work. It may be that creating institutions of opportunity is not enough. Even among those with an education who work full time and who obey the law, there is still rising inequality. Unfortunately, there is no guarantee in economics that trends in technology and trade will always bend toward rewarding hard work. I tend to think, then, that in the U.S., we should move toward more redistribution in the economy, following two principles.

The first principle for "redistribution" of wealth that Steve proposes is that "survival of the fittest" should apply only to "products and production methods," not to "people," elaborating as follows:

While we count on competition to make sure that resources are used efficiently, and to drive the development of new and better processes, too often the casualties of this competitive process are people, not just bad ideas or obsolete organizations. If we are going to embrace market competition, and fast-changing technologies, then we should also embrace a robust safety net for the individuals whose lives are turned upside down. In addition to our current programs, I would like to see universal health care coverage, cheaper college education and training, as well as a more robust guarantee against hunger.

Too often, our political efforts flip this principle, trying to save corporations and industries rather than people. Our current administration, for example, seems intent on saving the coal industry, despite the fact that the decline of coal is well-warranted in the face of cleaner and ever-cheaper energy alternatives. This is a really inefficient way to help coal workers, since propping up this industry will only delay the transition to other industries that could serve these people much better.

The second principle for "redistribution" of wealth that Steve proposes is "progressive taxation," starting with his "premise that material wealth has a purpose, and that those blessed with wealth have a calling to support and care for creation and the people nearby. Those who have an abundance of wealth and who are not using it to support those in need, therefore, are not 'owning' their property properly. The moral claim that they have on their property is weaker." Based on that premise, Steve proposes a "three-fold justification of progressive income or wealth taxation, when combined with a generous charitable giving exemption."

- Those with greater income or wealth have a greater ability to contribute to taxes without suffering comparable loss.
- Those with greater income or wealth, if not putting it to good use, have a weaker moral claim to their wealth, and thus can be taxed more.
- Progressive income or wealth taxation pushes against inequality, even if it does not address the underlying causes.

Steve argues that these three points "rule out, in principle, the kind of individualism that sours into ambivalence toward those in need."

Finally, Steve proposes maintaining an "estate or inheritance tax," arguing as follows:

> The other large check in our tax system on economic inequality has traditionally been the estate or inheritance tax. It is only in recent years that this has become the target of conservatives, to the point where the estate tax is much lower than it had been. While there can be a legitimate debate about whether people should have a protected right to leave large amounts of wealth to their children, the estate tax on large estates is preferable to other methods of taxation,

for two reasons. First, there is a lower efficiency cost to this kind of tax than there is a comparable tax on income, since people are less likely to adjust their productivity and earnings because of the estate tax. Second, this tax can limit people's ability to become wealthy solely through birth. When comparing those who earned and saved their money to those who inherited it, the former has a stronger moral claim.

Steve summarizes his proposal for tax reform as follows: "A high estate tax, a progressive income tax and comparable taxes on income-generating assets, therefore, are good ways to fund the kind of redistribution of wealth that makes up a reliable social safety net and investment in public goods."

Kelly's reflections on Steve's proposals for tax reform are as follows:

His [Steve's] initial proposals for tax reform ... seem to me not only smart but also driven by a proper sense of the common good and human dignity. I could write a fine account of why I think that is so, with an eye to Catholic social teaching ... Once, moral theology and political economy were not distinct disciplines. What are they now? In a secular U.S. economy, the work of sustaining a community of Christians who engage in discernment and organization on their own terms, which is to say in their own kind of politics, is the long-term struggle where I think theology can and should have legs.

Some Areas of Disagreement

The above narrative reveals some significant areas of agreement between Steve and Kelly. But they also had some disagreements that were not resolved—a topic to which I now turn.

The benefits and limits of a market economy

As a follow-up to their conversation about "international inequality" (more about that below), Steve notes that this is "one of a couple of places where Dr. Johnson expresses real skepticism about market economies and profit," adding that "I have fewer broad concerns there." Steve attributes this disagreement to Kelly and him having "fairly different starting assumptions about the economy, even if we end up agreeing on many things." He elaborates on their differing "starting assumptions" as follows:

> Dr. Johnson, I believe, would argue that business is not necessarily bad, but that the system is fundamentally flawed. I am more likely to approve of the system overall, but to be concerned about specific problems. Even if this leaves us in general agreement about tax policy, perhaps, it reflects a deeper disagreement about what progress would look like.

Steve goes on to note some of the things about "market economies" that he "appreciates" that are "easily taken for granted."

> I would like to suggest that ... there are many things to appreciate about market economies that are easy to take for granted. In some ways markets are a lot like democracy. I complain bitterly about the people who get elected, but I would never imagine creating a system in which people are not able to vote. The analogy is not perfect, but it will help explain, perhaps, how I can spend a career writing about the failings of market economies (I have written about animal ethics, environmental sustainability, consumer waste, virtue formation, technology replacing workers, inequality and poverty) while still being generally optimistic about our ability to shape a market economy in ways that will make things better.
>
> In the area of inequality particularly, I am optimistic about our ability to create an inclusive market economy because we have done it before, albeit imperfectly. We have good examples, even if they are all too rare, of rich community organizations, radical investments in education, integration of previously marginalized communities, and innovation oriented toward the common good. Inequality is a particularly persistent problem, and even in a society with

constant vigilance there is the likelihood of abuses of power and injustice. This should not prevent us from working hard to build consensus around opportunities for reform.

Kelly is more skeptical about the benefits of a "market economy" than Steve, observing that "producers are incentivized to produce what will sell for as profit, and that does not necessarily mean they are incentivized to produce what is actually good for human life."

> Does our market economy create value and distribute wealth? As Dr. McMullen might point out, the answer is only partly yes. It's the way the system is set up, to encourage production of goods people will buy, so that producers, by competing with each other, become more efficient and also earn profit. But that is theory, and the evidence in reality is far from that rosy. Producers are incentivized to produce what will sell for a profit, and that does not necessarily mean they are incentivized to produce what is actually good for human life. Schemes of planned obsolescence are one illustration; the existence of Cap'n Crunch would be another. Goods are sold and payment is made in return, but that is not to say that human needs are met, certainly not efficiently or prudently for the long term.

> In fact, insofar as the great economic problem is no longer that we have to encourage production in order to meet needs but that we produce so much that we have to stoke demand among those who have means to buy, it can be more accurate to say that the market economy has to create desires that can be profitably met in the short term. We can call that 'creating value.' But it that isn't the same thing as filling human needs.

> ... Dr. McMullen has been clear that he recognizes the limits of the market, that there are public goods and human needs that cannot be met by the market. Obviously, I agree. I think where we differ is that I don't see how we can

maintain a system where those are only a margin around a material order that is in the main organized by this system. Fundamentally, I worry that relying on the logic of growth to serve human well-being seems like relying on a cancer to sustain health.

Alas, we ran out of time before Steve and Kelly could continue this conversation about the benefits and limits of a market economy.

Addressing income equality or addressing poverty

Steve makes an important distinction between the problem of addressing "material deprivation" (or "poverty"), which he views as "a first-order moral concern for Christians," and "economic inequality," which he views as "less obviously a problem." To clarify this distinction, Steve proposes a question as a "thought experiment."

> As a thought experiment, if we discovered and implemented a perfect solution for material need, so that all basic necessities were guaranteed for everyone, and yet there was still substantial inequality between the middle and top of the income distribution, would inequality be a pressing moral problem?

Steve presents two reasons why "this question matters."

> First, the answer to this question determines how we measure progress, or success. If we are primarily concerned about poverty, then we should focus our attention on quality of life and economic participation for those in the bottom half of the income distribution, and ignore the rising gap between the top 20 percent and the top 1 percent. Second, the answer to this question changes the kinds of policies we need to think about. If we are only worried about poverty, then social safety net programs, education, and the entry-level job market are the area to focus on. If we want to worry about inequality more broadly, then there are a host of other concerns about technology and market power that become more important.

Most importantly, though, I think the answer to this question matters because there are many who find it easy to be concerned about poverty but not inequality.

Steve asserts that he is concerned about both "poverty" and "inequality" because each represents a "different kind of injustice" and he is concerned that we not lose sight of the way in which "economic inequality can, by itself, be a sign of injustice." He elaborates on such "injustice" in the following ways.

First, inequality undermines solidarity and social cohesion. Or perhaps inequality is a sign that solidarity and social cohesion has already broken down. Either way, the political and social interests between two communities diverge sharply when there is a $50,000 gap in average incomes between groups. With different political priorities, different complaints and different experiences, building a political consensus is harder, and leaders can scapegoat one or the other community for political gain. Providing funds for public services becomes harder if the beneficiaries or need are all clustered in one community.

Second, inequality can undermine social mobility. There is good evidence that in times and places with more economic inequality there is more limited opportunity for a person to improve their economic position ... Moreover, recent evidence indicates that the unequal distribution of income directly harms the opportunities of young people, when compared to their parents. Most people's intuitions about economic justice in the U.S. revolve around opportunity and mobility. The sad truth is that we are not building an economy in which there are real opportunities for everyone, and rising inequality is tied up in this problem.

Even more importantly, inequality can point to specific kinds of injustice. Dr. Johnson highlighted the fact that our country has been built, too often, around opportunity for some and the exclusion of others. We are only starting, as a nation, to come to terms with the ways that racism is and has been built into the way the economy functions. African-American men, with the same family structure, income, education and wealth still have substantially lower upward mobility than do white men. Moreover, the evidence for labor market discrimination against African-American job candidates is very strong. When you add in the history of racism in housing, education and law enforcement, it becomes clear that building just economic systems must include a substantial reckoning with the way that our institutions have often excluded or failed to invest in minorities. This element of inequality is clearly an injustice that is independent of inadequate generosity or poverty.

Finally, and perhaps most generally, the dramatic increases in inequality over the last 40 years make it harder to maintain that the way our market institutions distribute rewards is just. Many economists have begun to build the case that concentrations of market power are holding down wages, limiting competition and increasing returns for the largest companies … With the decline in union bargaining power over the last 50 years, a rise in the market power of large firms will allow employers to give a smaller share of new wealth to employees.

Steve summarizes his main point here by asserting that "the particular ways in which economic inequality can point to injustice is essential for the next step [of going beyond "simple solutions" to economic problems]."

Kelly notes that she finds "Dr. McMullen's reasoning about the civic importance of attention to the growing gap between the middle class and the wealthy quite compelling," elaborating as follows:

I mentioned earlier the variety of studies[65] that have shown a negative correlation between wealth and empathy, and the results of that alienation writ large indicate a profound civic

---

65 Robinson, *Real Wealth*.

problem. I have to revise my view in light of that. What is hidden by the frequent appeals for support for the middle class is the need not only to support those living in poverty as well as those being driven from the middle class into poverty. It is also the necessity of addressing the moral and social sickness of excessive wealth, particularly the damage it does to the persons who have it, to the society fascinated by it and to the civic order that suffers from the alienation it produces.

But Kelly expresses a deep concern that whereas "fighting for [economic equality] for the middle class [in comparison to the wealthy] is a winning cause; fighting to end poverty is not," elaborating as follows:

We cannot seem to make addressing poverty a political or moral priority. My emphasis on poverty is a function of my concern that no political party in the U.S. is seriously campaigning to address poverty. Fighting for the middle class is a winning cause; fighting to end poverty—to address food insecurity, lack of funding for educational systems in areas with lower property values, housing and medical care as human rights, a living wage, the rights of low wage workers to organize and environmental justice—is not. In fact, it seems we have come to a situation where poverty is such a matter of shame that even people of good will prefer to talk about policies that will support the middle class rather than policies that support people living in poverty. Being a member of the middle class who is being driven into poverty is honorable, and trying to assist such a person in keeping and advancing that hard-won place is an appealing struggle. Being poor just doesn't have the same cache.

Global economic progress or not

Steve and Kelly disagree as to the benefits, or not, of participation in a global economy on "economic equality" on "poorer parts of the world." Steve contends that whereas "inequality in the U.S. has increased by a variety of measures since the early 1970s," "globally, inequality has been diminishing and there has been faster economic growth, on average, in historically poorer parts of the world than in historically richer parts." He adds that "since the 1980s, there have been consistent declines in absolute poverty and improving circumstances for the many of the poorest parts of the world."

Kelly demurs. She notes that while she is "aware of the numbers showing a significant reduction in extreme poverty in India and China," there are "rather different results in sub-Saharan Africa and Latin America." Therefore, she is "skeptical" about concluding that "opening to the global economy reduces poverty" (A story that Steve "did not embrace," but which he also "didn't repudiate"). Kelly presents three reasons for her skepticism.

First, climate change will make it impossible for "global trade" to "continue as it has."

> In particular, fossil fuels ... are doomed to extinction, though they are dug in and clinging for all they are worth. While alternative fuels are ramping up, it is far from a given that global trade will be able to continue as it has, for the simple problem of transporting goods over great distances without fossil fuels. And poverty, driven by, for example, rising sea level, extreme weather, ocean acidification and drought, seems doomed to rise. Factors outside the usual economic indicators will have a grave effect on the safety and longevity of humans in the next century.

Secondly, Kelly is concerned that a global economy is not particularly good at promoting "locally-controlled sustainable business," which is unfortunate since "good work, in which people have not only a wage but some access to power so that the control of that work is in local hands, is key to ending poverty and honoring human dignity." Because of this, the global economy actually contributes to greater domestic poverty and inequality.

Finally, Kelly argues that there are "qualitative issues involved" that are "part of human flourishing," suggesting that "the damage done by the global economy credited with reducing poverty is soul-deep, insofar as to profoundly transform our relationships to our producing and to other producers, to our land and to our desires." She concludes that "further growth of the global consumer economy is not good news, including for many of those in poverty, whose families and traditions and home places may be their last wealth."

In his last posting, Steve responds to Kelly's three concerns about the global economy. Relative to her concern about "climate change," Steve acknowledges the adverse effects of climate change and the fact that "much of the cost of climate change will fall on the poor, both because of the regional distribution of climate effects, but also because those with more wealth are better able to adapt to the changes that are likely to come." This points to the "essential" need to "invest quickly in the kind of development that will give a more stable foundation to the livelihood of those that will be affected [by climate change], even as those in the richer parts of the world make rapid changes to our system and lifestyle to minimize climate change-contributing emissions."

Relative to Kelly's second concern that "the same system that has produced declining global inequality has produced increased domestic inequality," Steve acknowledges this problem, noting the example of China, where "as poverty has declined, inequality has probably risen substantially." He adds that "all over the world, in fact, we have seen increased inequality within countries and decreased inequality globally." However, Steve's "instinct is that the declines in absolute poverty are far more significant [than increased inequality within countries]."

As to Kelly's third concern, Steve "admits" that it "sounds serious," but he is not "sure what it means." He says that "while I understand the reluctance of theologians to make peace with capitalism, I am not sure what soul-deep damage is being referenced here."

Unfortunately, we ran out of time before Steve and Kelly could further sort through their agreements and disagreements regarding the benefits, or not, of a global economy.

The role of the church and the role of government

Recall that Steve and Kelly agree that "we cannot claim absolute authority or ownership over our property," and, therefore, the "Christian story" calls Christians to assist those living in poverty. But how should Christians provide such assistance? Kelly draws on the well-known work of Reinhold

Niebuhr[66] to call into question the extent to which "social bodies" can be influenced by "Christian ideals" [such as assisting those in poverty].

> ... Reinhold Niebuhr ... made a very persuasive case that such Christian ideals [such as assisting those in poverty] may influence individuals sometimes, but are useless in social ethics, as social bodies operate quite differently. Needing to protect their own, relying on the encouraging feedback from others in their group, social bodies will not be able to give up anything of their own power, unless they are forced to do so. After Niebuhr, the naïve hope that Christian ideals could renew the world became the domain of the pious and ignorant. Real social ethics abandoned that path.

Kelly observes that "the evidence on Niebuhr's side is impressive. On the whole, he was right to identify the way self-interest and self-deception operate in social groups." But Kelly suggests that churches may be the "exceptions."

> The exceptions are those cases in which Christians have acted as social bodies that are the corporate body of Christ. Christianity is not an individual calling, to be exercised in such limited ways as might be possible within 'reality,' which is not Christian. It is a corporate calling, to be a different people.

While not denying the role the church plays to "share with ... neighbors," Steve argues that Christians need to do more than model such sharing within the church; they need to also advocate for "justice" by means of "political reform."

> I see Dr. Johnson exhibiting a deep hope in the power of God's work to transform the way we think and live, particularly in the church. I also see a skepticism about the ability for Christian ethics to reform broader economic practices and institutions. Without a full endorsement, she cites Niebuhr's argument that worldly institutions follow their own logic and are insulated by the self-serving incentives of those

---

66 Niebuhr, *Moral Man.*

with power from all but the strongest challenges. I see the argument, and I agree in principle. However, I cannot move from this description of the world to the conclusion that 'the naïve hope that Christian ideals could renew the world became the domain of the pious and ignorant.' There have been too many examples of real change, small and large in scale, that were helped along by individuals who pushed for justice because of their hope regarding God's work in the world.

If we fall too readily into a separation between Christian ethics and political reform, it becomes easy for Christian ethics to become something that only applies to *us*, and only *among us*. This line of thinking tempts people to share with their neighbors, certainly, but to abandon hope for reforms that would help bring about a more just world. While Dr. Johnson does not shy away from connecting Christian ethics to politics, many Christians do.

In response to Steve's call for Christians to advocate for reforming public policies regarding poverty, Kelly says she does "not despair of influencing U.S. policy," but the rules of "fair procedure" in the "democratic process" fall short of the "standard" of "justice" and "it is certainly not the Gospel."

Engaging U.S. policy questions theologically is a different project altogether than engaging ecclesial policy ... The U.S., while always overwhelmingly Christian in number, has never been Christian in principle. Policies in the U.S. are formed by what we like to hope is a fair procedure, a representative democratic process (aka sausage-making) in which consent of the majority is the functional standard. To be clear, that means the standard is not justice, and it is certainly not the Gospel.

Furthermore, Kelly is concerned that for Christians to advocate for reforming public policies to assist those living in poverty can, in our current political environment, make faith captive to the U.S. political system (what has been called "politicizing the faith"), leading to a "dividing [of] our ecclesial communities ... for the sake of party politics."

> Will we make the theological argument to those who might be persuaded by it, in hopes that they can become an interest group or a voting bloc big enough to advance the agenda? In that case, we have to face the accusation of politicizing the faith, dividing our ecclesial communities for the sake of judgments on which there can be conscientious disagreement. Given how polarized Christian communities already are, it's probably more accurate to say that we would be making use of the divisions that clearly already exist, for the sake of party politics. Some of my colleagues have gone this route, doing conscientious, brave and hard work, hoping to use political struggle to address injustice and awaken Christian conscience. I cannot bring myself to embrace that approach when I see the damaged Body of Christ, torn ever more by our attempts to fit the Gospel into the alternatives currently available.

It is for these reasons that Kelly says she is "highly skeptical of theological attempts to circumvent the work of discernment, formation and organization within Christian communities themselves," adding that "the route" she "favor[s] for influencing U.S. policy is to work on healing the church ... so that it can better play its role, for the life of the world and even for the life of the U.S. That role would involve economic creativity in practice, energetic work to analyze and address the causes of poverty affecting the church around the world, and a fresh encounter with the good news." We now turn to Kelly's proposals for how the church should play this role.

Redistributing Wealth Within the Church

In light of the disparity of wealth among members of a church, Kelly proposes that church should replace a focus on "stewardship" of wealth to "redistribution" of wealth.

... First, in lieu of stewardship programs, churches should have offices of redistribution, their work reenvisioned in line with that title. The error of treating, in theory and in practice, the property of Christians as given to them individually by God and under their sole authority (before God, who is not on hand and therefore needs stewards) has to be confronted. Wealth can and should be identified as an ecclesial question: Some members of the Body of Christ have far too much and some have far too little.

But, how should such a redistribution of effort be implemented within a church? In contrast to efforts of the "state," which "has the power to compel," the church needs to focus on "catechetical, homiletic and sacramental efforts" to "create a culture [of] ... mutuality."

Who will have the authority to lead this process, and what sorts of pressure would be used to bring about wealth transfer? The state has the power to compel. The church will be wise to follow a quite different approach, through catechetical, homiletic and sacramental efforts, working structurally and intentionally to create a culture in which mutuality is constitutive of the joy of the Gospel. One wise teacher of mine liked to say that when a person joins a Christian community, a step in admission should be disclosing his or her income and wealth. That would not require you to divest yourself of any of it, but it would be a necessary step toward communal discernment of what those who share in the Body of Christ ought to do about disparity of wealth in their midst.

Kelly acknowledges that such redistribution efforts within a church could lead to "conflict" and may not always be successful, but "failure would be better than ... current practice," which leaves questions about "material sharing" to "the individual believer."

Such local policies would make other kinds of ecclesial action more imaginable and more substantial. They could be associated with congregational-level work to understand the causes of poverty and to commit to collective work to address those causes. Such judgments, no doubt, will not always be easy to reach. They will open up conflict within congregations, requiring practices of conflict resolution. When reached, they may not be wise. The actions they lead to will not always succeed. Nevertheless, failure would be better than our current practice, which is leave all such questions to the preference of the individual believer, to leave our shared life at a superficial level, and to neglect the Scriptural witness that calls for mutual love and material sharing among those who are members of the one body.

For those Christians who feel overwhelmed by this call for "mutual sharing," Kelly shared this exhortation from Dorothy Day, drawing on the encouragement from St. Therese to work in "little ways."

Work patiently with people, in all their slow, odd inconvenient humanity. Act directly, personally, locally in the way in front of you, no matter how small or imperfect the effect. Take the time (and oh, how much time it takes) to be a human creature among other human creatures.

In conclusion, Kelly expressed hope that when churches "get their own houses in order" (my words, not hers) relative to wealth disparity, they would then be better situated to "be encountering those not in their own congregation who are also struggling to get by."

Likewise, once such local policies are in place and congregations are encountering wealth disparity in their midst ... and examining its causes, they will be better situated to be encountering those not in their own congregation who are also struggling to get by. In fact, the pagan emperor Julian complained that in his day all of the poor were becoming Christian because Christians were more generous in their efforts to address poverty than the pagans were. What if all of the poor of the U.S. began to turn to Christian communities, wanting to join them because of their generosity? This would be a fantastic problem to have.

Although Steve didn't have time to ask a follow-up question, I will ask it: Is it conceivable that if churches effectively modeled such "mutual sharing" of wealth within their congregations, they could begin to influence U.S. policies in the same direction (even if attempting to do so in the democratic political process is like "making sausage")? This radical idea leads me to conclude this chapter with some personal reflections that point to possible directions for integrating the cogent insights of both Steve and Kelly.

Both Mutual Sharing Within Churches and Political Reform

Kelly notes that she and Steve could have "fruitfully engaged a number of other questions related to wealth disparity," such as "the logic and effects of war, ... the operation of debt (student debt looming large on the horizon), the Christian tradition of voluntary poverty (and its relation to peacemaking) and the language of hospitality," adding that "we have only touched on questions of power, especially labor organizing, and of state boundaries, as in questions of migration." Alas, six brief postings over just one month barely scratches the surface of the complex issues related to wealth and poverty in America. But, in light of a primary purpose of this book to model respectful conversations among Christians who have strong disagreements regarding political issues, it is important to note the following mutual expressions of appreciation.

> Dr. McMullen's challenges to me have helped me to articulate and reexamine fundamental intellectual and vocational convictions. A strong challenge like that is an accomplishment and a treasure. I am grateful to him for this engagement (Kelly).

> In the contentious political environment that we currently occupy, it is too easy to retreat from political disagreement and instead seek the security of agreement or avoidance. It is a rare pleasure, therefore, in contrast, to be able to discuss economic inequalities in this forum ... Dr. Johnson raises a

collection of important arguments, and has identified some areas where we see things differently. Her depth of reflection about the way theology can inform public life has challenged me to think very carefully about things that I care deeply about. This is a great gift (Steve).

I would like to conclude my part of this conversation by highlighting what I found most helpful and illuminating in Dr. Johnson's contributions. Her clear passion for ensuring the genuine well-being of others is evident, and it is reflected in her scholarship and language. *Given my interests and training, I am very used to thinking about inequality as an aggregate systemic problem, and an individual problem. Dr. Johnson points out that it is also a problem for community, and particularly for the church.* I appreciate her insistence that the church can live out its calling as a community by sharing burdens and pointing toward practices of justice. I also admire the way she models a commitment to living with hard truths, recognizing hardship and injustice, especially when it is born by others. It is too easy to become defensive in discussions about injustice when the beneficiaries look like us and the victims look different. These habits of thought position her to naturally experience and reveal God's heart for the marginalized. I hope that others will read her words and learn from them as well, and that our dialogue will be edifying (Steve, italics mine).

But, coming full circle in this chapter, there remains the "integrative task" seeking for connections between the Steve's insights as a Christian economist and Kelly's insights as a Christian theologian. Kelly notes Steve's reminder that "an appeal to disciplinary specialization is not ... adequate." How can the agreements and disagreements expressed by Steve and Kelly be connected in a coherent manner? It is my hope that Christian economists and theologians will continue that conversation. In the meantime, here are my brief preliminary reflections, presented with some fear and trembling since I have no formal training in either discipline.

It appears to me that three primary overarching integrative threads shared by both Steve and Kelly are that "Christians can't claim absolute authority or ownership of their property"; "the goods of earth are intended to meet the needs of all"; and the goal of any economic system should be "the sustaining of the life of a community and the inclusion of everyone in that community."

Another integrative thread that I perceive is that there is "enough blame to go around." To be sure, some wealthy people are corrupt and/or have no concern for the needs of those living in poverty; and some poor people are living with the negative consequences of past poor choices. But no generalizations can be drawn. And, besides, to focus on "blaming the other" is to avoid something for which we are all to blame: Our failure to manage our economy in ways that foster opportunity for participation and inclusion for all.

So, if one embraces these integrative threads, how are economists and theologians, and other citizens to proceed? The huge task of fostering participation and an inclusion of all members of American society into our economic system calls for "all hands on deck," allowing for different foci for individuals and groups having differing gifts and expertise, without calling into question the foci of others. Therefore, economists need to focus on reforming economic structures and institutions, economists and politicians (and citizens who support politicians) need to work together on reforming economic public policies, theologians, pastors and other church leaders, and "persons in the pews" need to work together to call into question the "moral lapses," individually and collectively, that contribute to poverty and to enable churches to model "mutual sharing" of wealth.

Of course, that is much easier said than done, especially given that so many citizens live in "fragmented silos," thinking that the particular task they are committed to doing based on their respective gifts and areas of expertise is "the" solution to the problems associated with poverty. This leads me to conclude by reminding readers of an important difference in emphasis between Steve and Kelly regarding the best means to address poverty in America that draws on the quotation from Steve that I italicize above: *"Given my interests and training, I am very used to thinking about inequality as an aggregate systemic problem, and an individual problem. Dr.*

Johnson points out that it is also a problem for community, and particularly for the church."

Steve and Kelly have differing, albeit overlapping views as to the respective roles of the church and the democratic political process in addressing the needs of those living in poverty. Kelly's proposals focus on the church modeling the "mutual sharing" of wealth. She does not suggest that government can play a significant role in alleviating poverty.

Steve expressed appreciation for Kelly's focus on the community of believers in a church addressing problems of disparity of wealth within their congregation, in contrast to his tendency to think about "inequality as an aggregate systemic problem, and an individual problem." But, Steve, unlike Kelly, also envisions government playing a significant role in alleviating poverty by means of "political reform" regarding economic public policies. Steve proposes that Christians need to do more than model mutual sharing within their churches; they also need to be advocates for political reform.

9

Health Care in America

THE THIRD AND final contentious public policy issue that we now consider is the status of health care in America. This chapter reports on the views of Clarke Cochran and Jeff Hammond in response to the following set of interrelated leading questions:

- Is health care a public good that everyone has a "right" to (and therefore government has a role to play in securing that "right" for everyone) or is health care a private good; a "privilege" that is primarily the responsibility of each individual with minimal governmental assistance?
- What are the problems with the health care system in America?
- How can the present health care system be improved?
- Is there a Christian perspective that can inform such improvement?

The complexity of health care issues in America boggles the mind. This leads both Jeff and Clarke to express caution as to what can be expected to emerge from their one-month conversation.

> It's impossible to identify all the problems in the American health care system in 9,000+ words (Jeff).

> To no one's surprise, our conversation about health care
> in America ends inconclusively. The topic is too large for a
> month's discussion ... The United States is on a long journey
> of health care reform; it may end well; it may not. The end is
> not in sight (Clarke).

Clarke identifies some of the factors that make health care issues in
America so complex.

> We're considering a system that accounts for 20 percent of
> the entire economy and that touches every person. It is both
> highly technical and deeply personal. A mix of government
> (at all levels), of private, for-profit institutions and of not-
> for-profit, often faith-based organizations.

In light of this complexity, Clarke suggests that whereas there is "little
disagreement that health care in the United States is broken," there is "little
understanding of how and why" and "no consensus on a fix or fixes."

In an attempt to sort through this complexity, this chapter will first
report on some of the problems that Clarke and Jeff perceive in the current health care system in America, followed by an enumeration of some
foundational "Christian principles" that could inform attempts to address
these problems that will lead to some concrete public policy proposals.

Problems With Health Care in America

Both Clarke and Jeff perceive some significant problems with the current health care system in America (as does Julie Kuhl, an interested reader
employed in health care administration who submitted some thoughtful
comments throughout the month-long conversation).

Insufficient access

Clarke observes that the United States is "alone among modern, wealthy
and democratic nations" in leaving "major swathes of population without
adequate access to medical care," suggesting a number of reasons for this
inadequacy.

The main reason is lack of health insurance. At this writing, approximately 12 percent of the population remains uninsured. Health insurance in a modern, expensive, highly technological medical complex is essential to effective recovery from illness and injury and to reentry into participation in the full life of community. Even when persons have insurance, barriers to care are frequent: the complex, stratified and fragmented organization/disorganization of the health care system itself, lack of income for co-pays and deductibles, inflexible hours, poor education and information and racial and ethnic prejudice.

Clarke views this insufficient access to adequate health care for all as an instance of "injustice" (an assertion to which we will soon return).

It is not simply that access to health care is unevenly distributed, which is true in every health system internationally, but that health care in the United States is highly *unjustly* distributed amounting to unjust rationing, excluding millions of persons from full participation in the common good and insulting their dignity.

Excessive cost and quality underperformance

Clarke also expresses concern about the high cost of health care in America, compared to other nations, without commensurate better "health outcomes."

The cost of health care in the United States is the highest in the world, whether measured in absolute dollars, spending per capita or percent of GDP (currently about 18 percent of GDP, with most other similar nations spending around 11 percent). That cost *might* be justified if health outcomes were better. However, the U.S. performs no better than other developed nations on most measures of quality of care; exceeds them in a few; and lags on many.

Clarke suggests that "the clearest causes" of such "high cost and quality underperformance" are "higher prices paid in the United States for drugs, equipment, supplies and salaries of medical professionals; high administrative overhead related to the complexity and fragmentation of the system; and high reliance on technology."

Jeff prefaces his perceptions of problems with the American health care system with an elaboration of the many ways in which "the American health care system has never failed [him]" (always "coming though for him"), because "I, my wife (when first married), or my father (during my growing-up years) have all had excellent jobs with even better fringe benefits, including comprehensive health insurance."

In that light, Jeff suggests that "the best way to 'grow the pie' of access to quality health care" is to "grow the economy so that more people can find good jobs with good benefits," noting that his plan "does not depend on the government starting a new program or expanding an existing one." We will return to that suggestion later. In the meantime, it is important to note Jeff's admission that "I would probably think twice about the 'excellence' of my health insurance if I had an illness that far outstripped my family's ability to cover what insurance did not."

Therefore, Jeff is not discounting the plight of "those people who don't have great (or good enough) jobs and therefore don't have good health insurance," and he acknowledges four "structural defects in the American health care system that impose burdens on less well-insured Americans ... 1) the sub-optimal care at times provided by the Medicaid program; 2) the "charge master" phenomenon of billing the uninsured prices for hospital-provided goods and services orders of magnitude more than those with insurance; 3) the aggressive collection practices of some hospitals (even some nonprofit hospitals); and 4) the difficulty experienced to access reliable and effective bankruptcy proceedings for those with overwhelming medical debt."

Administrative complexity, overregulation and incompetence

Based on her on-the-ground work in health care administration, Julie Kuhl has found "government sponsored health care" to "be a mess, to say the least," which leads her to wonder why we would "want to hand over more to the government to mess up."

> Here is my No. 1 issue with government sponsored health care. Working in health care administration, the government programs of Medicare and Medicaid take the majority of administrative and billing time. It's a *mess* to say the least! So *why* would we want to hand over *more* for the government to mess up?

Julie adds that she doesn't even want to "start on the VA [Veterans Affairs]," since "we have all heard what a mess this is."

Clarke's response to Julie's concern about the "mess" in administering "government sponsored health care" is qualified agreement, noting, based on his extensive experience in the private health care sector, that overregulation, complexity and incompetence are also present in "private health insurance companies."

> My response is to agree ... partially. Of course, Medicare, Medicaid, the VA and other government programs are overregulated, complex and staffed by incompetent people. However, we forget that ... so are private health insurance companies.

Clarke adds the theological point that the need for regulations in both the governmental and private health care sectors reflect the "fallenness" of all humankind: "... regulations exist because somewhere, at some time, someone in private health care delivery either messed up big-time or stole lots of money. Government reflects the fall, but so do you and I. I'm not aware of any evidence that government is more fallen than other institutions."

Clarke concludes that the need to have government involved in health care is not because governmental employees are "more competent than others in health care." Rather, government needs to be involved because of government's special responsibility relative to "the common good and to justice" (an assertion that we will soon consider in some detail).

> ... I don't believe that government and its elected or appointed officials are more competent than others in health care. I believe only that government (especially federal and state governments given our constitutional system) have essential

functions related to the common good and to justice. No
other institution bears public accountability for the social
good.

Emergency room overload

Julie also notes the significant problem with ER departments being "sat-
urated with Medicaid patients using them for primary care due to health
care providers not accepting more Medicaid patients."

Underlying Christian Principles

The above litany of problems with current health care in America is far
from an exhaustive list of perceived inadequacies. Is it possible that Christian teachings can inform attempts to address these thorny problems?

Jeff points out that while he seeks guidance from the Bible for how to
live well, he finds that the Bible is silent as to whether there should, or
should not be, "large-scale, top-down provision of health care services" to
any given population.

> I am working with the famous aphorism attributed to Karl
> Barth: I have my Bible in one hand and a newspaper in the
> other. I try, however imperfectly, to make the Word of God
> the rule for my life in all things. As I read it, I find precious
> little guidance as to how a government should structure
> the services it provides to its citizens. In particular, I find
> nothing, either approving or disapproving, large-scale, top-
> down provision of health care services to a polity.

For future reference, Jeff does note that the teachings of Jesus recorded
in Matthew 25 call Christians to take personal responsibility to help people who are suffering, including the sick. But this differs from asserting
that government bears that responsibility (much more about that later).

> I find a strong injunction in the New Testament to give of
> *myself* for the benefit of my fellow suffering human being,
> who Jesus likened to himself in Matthew 25. I am to visit the
> prisoner, feed the hungry, and yes, care for the sick. Indeed,

what's sobering about this little parable in Matthew 25 is that Jesus seems to say that the Christ follower's salvation depends on how conscientiously he attends to the physical needs of others. This parable is a biblical personification of the little ditty, "If it is to be, it is up to me." If the sick are to be cared for, it is up to me. It's not another's responsibility. It's *my* responsibility. If I am to demonstrate my faith in Jesus, well, I really have to do it and get out there find some sick people to minister to. I don't mean that I can curry God's favor by doing good deeds. What I do mean is that I show Christ himself and the world that I am truly his disciple if I get down to peoples' suffering where they are.

Clarke agrees with Jeff about "the 'thinness' of Scripture when it comes to health care policy prescriptions," and he agrees with Jeff that there is nothing in Scripture that approves or disapproves of "large-scale, top-down, provision of health care services to a polity," adding that "I want to agree with Jeff's point about the limits of the Bible when it comes to the provision of modern, curative and preventative health care, about which it is understandably silent."

But then Clarke raises the important question as to "what to do in the face of such silence?" He suggests the need to develop "social principles" that "transcend partisan and ideological binaries" (more about such transcendence later), citing the examples of what has been done in the Protestant Kuyperian theological tradition and in the Catholic theological tradition which he embraces.

> What to do in the face of such silence? Fortunately, some Christian traditions (I am thinking particularly, but not exclusively, about the Kuyperian and Catholic traditions with which I am most familiar) have developed social principles that allow faithful thinking about policy issues in ways that transcend partisan and ideological binaries.

As an aside, it should be noted that Clarke is pointing to the need to go beyond "these are the words of the Bible" to developing a "theology" that seeks to interpret the entirety of the biblical record in a coherent manner.

Clarke then accepts his own challenge by enumerating "certain Christian social principles" that "determine his understanding of our broken health care system and how it might be fixed," as follows:

Human dignity—all persons are created in the image and likeness of God and thus bear a fundamental dignity that can never be forfeited and that health care must respect and nourish.

Participation—because of that dignity, all persons have the right and the responsibility to participate in decisions and structures that affect their life and human flourishing.

Justice—as a social institution, health care must be structured justly/fairly; that is, the health care system must be so organized and operated as to meet everyone's reasonable need for care within the limits of the resources socially available for health and healing.

Stewardship—as Christians we are responsible to manage and conserve the resources God has given for our well-being. There are limits on our wants and desires. No part of society should be allowed to claw essential resources from other sectors.

Common Good—the principal duty of government is to defend, nourish and advance the common good of the community for which it is responsible. Because the common good is fundamentally related to human dignity, participation and justice, government has the duty to protect and advance health care justice, dignity, and participation while stewarding the ensemble of spheres of life that constitute society.

It is in light of these underlying Christian social principles that Clarke summarizes a number of the problems with health care in America that were enumerated above.

> Far from being the "greatest health system in the world," ...
> our health care is badly shattered. It is rife with injustice and
> violations of the common good. It, too, often insults rather
> than upholds human dignity. It costs far too much, draining
> resources from other sectors of society. Quality of care is
> often suboptimal.

Clarke proposes that these five underlying Christian principles "morph
into more specific policy principles: universal access, equitable access,
affordability, quality and choice," which he describes as follows:[67]

> **Universal and equitable access** can be described in terms
> of rights; however, my preference is the language of justice,
> with deep roots in Christian faith. Fairness or justice in
> health care requires that each person receives the treatment
> he/she needs without resort to begging. 'No health care
> beggars' seems a pretty good Christian slogan. Moreover,
> the governing principle is *need* for care, not one's economic
> resources to pay for care (thus, no queue-jumping). Justice
> also entails that physicians, nurses, dentists, therapists
> and other medical persons receive a fair return on their
> investments of time and resources. There is pretty good
> evidence that in the U.S. most of these receive a premium
> *above* their investment.
>
> **Affordability** is both social and individual. Effective
> government ensures that health care remains in balance
> with other social goods (the common good is the criterion);
> individuals accept limits on their health care *desires* and on
> what is possible for meeting even their *needs*. The value of
> participation means that patients also take responsibility by
> being accountable for their own health to the degree which is
> within their power. Providers take responsibility for limiting
> their own demands for income and for the latest and greatest
> equipment—they accept limits on their capacity for cure. As

67 In addition to his description of these "specific policy principles," Clarke cites a
"Catholic version" (Bouchard) and a "secular version" (Gostin). See Bouchard, "Ethics,"
and Gostin, "Five Ethical Values."

former Colorado governor Richard Lamm put it: No citizen can expect all the health care possible; no nation can give a blank check to the Hippocratic Oath; and no physician can expect to be an unrestrained advocate for his/her patients.

Within the limits established by these first two principles, we want a system that provides the highest *quality* of care possible and the most patient *choice* possible among hospitals, physicians and other providers of care (italics mine).

Relative to "affordability," Clarke adds that "universal coverage/access need not be free," but any cost should not become "burdensome" to "poor and low-income workers" in America.

... universal coverage/access need not be free. Many nations with national health insurance systems have a variety of premiums and of fees at the point of care. A U.S. reform that guarantees access could also include copayments, deductibles and insurance premiums. Indeed, my own proposal for a form of the current employment-based insurance system at its center implicitly includes these features. However, the major problem with fees is inability to pay (leading to delayed care). The United States' high proportion of poor and low-income workers and our deep economic inequality make these more burdensome than other nations with better income support and greater equality.

In light of these "specific policy principles," Clarke presents the following concrete proposals for reforming health care in America:

The current systems of Medicare, Medicaid, Veterans Affairs and military health should be retained and reformed according to their particular strengths and weaknesses.

The rest of the population receives coverage under employment-based insurance, the individual insurance market and a fragile "safety net" of hospitals and clinics for the uninsured.

My own approach would be to require all employers to cover all employees (full- and part-time) with an insurance package of defined benefits covering most health and medical needs. Payments for covering part-time employees would be prorated among each employer of these persons. All employees would be charged a modest premium and would be required to purchase the insurance or to pay a tax penalty. Both employers and employees would be eligible for income- or payroll-based public subsidies. Individuals 55 and over could choose to enroll early in Medicare (and pay an adjusted premium), and low-income individuals could choose to enroll in Medicaid (at a small premium). Finally, a highly regulated and subsidized individual insurance market (plus Medicaid for low-income persons) would be available to all persons not currently employed. These requirements would cover all persons in the United States (other than visitors), both citizens and non-citizen immigrants.

Responses to Clarke Cochran

Clarke has given us much to think about in his statement of "underlying Christian principles" and the concrete public policy proposal that emerges from those principles. I start by suggesting that embedded in his Christian principles is a call for a change from "rights" talk to "common good" talk.

Seeking the common good

Both Jeff and Clarke have a problem with thinking of health care for an individual as a "right," albeit for different reasons.

While Jeff acknowledges that "prolonged physical suffering is suboptimal and having no way to pay for it is even worse," he asserts that this unacceptable state of affairs "does not necessarily mean that the federal government should provide (pay) for that care, particularly as a claim of right."

Jeff explains his position in terms of a distinction between the proper idea of a "right" as a "limitation on government power" rather than an

inadequate idea of a "right" as pointing to a "demand for that which the
government *must* do for you," citing as an example the constitutional
"rights" to limitations on federal power, such as those enshrined in the Bill
of Rights.

> ... a 'right' is that which you and the government recognize
> that it *cannot* do to you, because what you seek to do is bound
> up in what it means to be a free human being. For example,
> the government cannot abridge your right to worship God
> as you choose because humanness, by its nature, entails the
> person's choice to render obeisance (or not) to a god or gods.

> Bound up in the idea of a 'right' is a corresponding limitation
> on government power and not necessarily a demand for that
> which the government *must* do for you.

> The genius of the American experiment in liberty is that the
> best of our constitutional rights are *recognized* in the text
> of the Constitution. Thus, these rights are pre-political and
> not created. The rights originally found in the Constitution
> (free speech, free exercise, due process, etc.) are not small
> carve-outs from vast expanses of government power. Rather,
> they are bulwarks and barriers—capacious buttresses from
> a government that otherwise seeks to aggrandize authority
> and control for itself.

> So, no, I do not believe that health care is a 'right,'
> constitutional or otherwise which *must* be provided by the
> government.

In a later posting, Jeff reiterates his view that "our constitutional rights
are negative rights" that do not place demands on what government "must
do" relative to health care, while adding that his view still acknowledges
the importance of the principle of "human dignity" that Clarke (and he)
embraces and he suggests that his view places the burden of helping those
with health care needs on "Americans of good will (whether Christian
or not)" and "the church and other Christian-affiliated organizations" to

exercise their "freedom" in ways that assist those who do not have the means to obtain adequate health care (much more about that later).

... There is no doubt that each human being, by virtue of their creatureliness, has a worth that cannot be measured or even approximated. Simply, each person bears the *imago Dei*, the image of God.

... However, I am not sure that an appreciation of a person's majestic humanness translates to a *right* to a certain quantum of health care that *must* be provided by the state. It certainly means, at the very least, that I must affirmatively do nothing to mar that image borne by other human beings.

... our constitutional rights are *negative* rights: those things that the government cannot do to you by virtue of your citizenship (or presence) in America. Because we have a charter of negative rights, theoretically, at least, Americans have a maximum amount of freedom. With that maximum amount of freedom comes a realization that the government's role in any one person's life is limited. If our freedom is maximized, then that which any of us can demand or expect from the government is limited. To me, this should nudge Americans of goodwill (whether Christian or not) away from thinking about an omni-competent government that provides everything that a person needs into a society where needs, including needs for health care, are provided by the pillars of civil society, including the church and other Christian-affiliated organizations.

... to ... accurately track with our founders' intent, such a right would have to go through the laborious process of amending the Constitution. It is a process that is designed to fail, because it requires super-majorities in the House and Senate and the states to approve the amendment. So, I think that we can make a simple and obvious conclusion: At no time did the framers contemplate that the government (through Congress' Article 1 legislative powers) provide intimate, personal care type of benefits to citizens.

Clarke also eschews "rights-talk" when it comes to health care, but for different reasons than those proposed by Jeff.

In brief, Clarke believes that "rights claims … are too blunt and too binary (my rights limit your freedom) to work as the primary Christian political principle."

> Jeff and I agree in principle on the limits and dangers of "rights talk." … Although rights claims have their place, especially in the legal/constitutional realm that Jeff describes, they are too blunt and too binary (my rights limit your freedoms) to work as the primary Christian political principle.

While recognizing how difficult it is to "move beyond binary thinking," Clarke's concern with such binary thinking about health care (and other public policy issues) is that it causes "political and policy conversations" to "degenerate into either/or confrontations" (in sharp contrast to his experience of his "respectful conversations" with Jeff and Julie). He wants to "find a health care language beyond liberal and conservative, and beyond rights versus responsibilities."

To help all of us to move beyond binary categories when discussion health care, Clarke starts by calling into question the "binary" wording embedded in the first leading question that I posed: *Is health care a public good that everyone has a "right" to (and therefore government has a role to play in securing that "right" for everyone) or is health care a private good; a "privilege" that is primarily the responsibility of each individual with minimal governmental assistance?* In summary form, Clarke encourages us to move beyond the "public good" versus "private good" binary distinction to embrace the concept of a "common good" that comports better with "a communitarian view of human persons more in line with biblical and historical Christianity." His extended argument is as follows:

> … I believe that the language of 'common good' is better than 'public good' for understanding the role and responsibilities of government, individuals and civil society. I think it better for Christians to speak about the 'common good,' rather than

public or private goods. Public versus private is a function of the development of classical economics in the last few centuries, predicated on a highly individualistic view of human persons. The common good, on the other hand, has a long history in Christian theology and ethics grounded upon a communitarian view of human persons more in line with biblical and historical Christianity.

However, even if one accepts the economic constructs of public and private goods, health care has features of each. Health care in modern societies is essentially communal, contributing both to the human flourishing of individual persons, but also to the health of the body politic ... Suffice it ... to say that health care has *some* features of a classic public good. (In economics, a public good is one that is both non-excludable and non-rivalrous in that individuals cannot effectively be excluded from use and where use by one individual does not reduce availability to others. Clean air is one example; national defense is another.) Classic public health measures (vector control, water and sanitation, air quality regulations, infectious disease monitoring and intervention and anti-smoking campaigns) have all or most of the features of a classic, economic public good.

Other features of our health care system also suggest a relationship to the whole society and its flourishing—that is, to the common good. An extensive body of research documents the social determinants of health. Poor social health in a community (racism, poverty, economic inequality, high crime rates, addictions and so forth) produces poor mental and physical health. Communities with low rates of social dysfunction have better health than other communities. The common good of the whole society thus intimately relates to the health of that community. And the reverse is true: Healthy citizens are more able to contribute to the flourishing of the entire community; healthy citizens are productive economically and engaged civilly.

Some medical interventions are indeed economically 'private' health goods. (That is, excludable and perhaps rivalrous. The best oncologist in a community is physically unable to treat every cancer patient in the community.) However, even these "private" health goods contribute to the common good. Healing interventions repair and even restore human dignity. A healing touch is a powerful expression of love and a vital builder of community. Making health interventions available to all who need them is an expression of Christian community, solidarity and belief in the dignity of all persons. Persons who receive healing interventions are more able to participate fully in the life of the community—that is, contribute to the common good— than those who need medical care, but do not receive it.

Finally, some health care goods are common goods; that is, their production and maintenance depend upon mutual effort and cooperation. Medical training requires community: education resources, organizational structures and funding that no one person or small group of persons possesses. Medical knowledge and technology are webs of connected intelligences, organizations and institutions.

Clarke concludes that "because health care is a constitutive part of the common good, because it is a common good, and because it contributes to the common good, *government* has a role and responsibility to regulate the health care system in ways that shape it toward, rather than away from, the common good."

Different conceptions of justice related to an American ethos of individualism

As the above narrative reveals, Jeff embraced Clarke's underlying Christian principle of "human dignity," but he disagreed with Clarke's suggestion that this principle calls for extensive governmental involvement in providing health care. Relative to Clarke's Christian principle of "justice," the disagreement is much more pronounced. Clarke and Jeff appear to have different conceptions of the very meaning of "justice," or, at least, different views as to what the large majority of Americans view as "doing justice" in the area of health care.

Before sorting through the views presented by Clarke and Jeff relative to this issue, my view is that Clarke's talk about seeking a "common good" relative to health care (or any other societal issue in America) mostly falls on deaf ears among Americans due to an ethos of hyper-individualism in America that is more concerned about what is good for me (and mine) than what is good for all of us. But I had better let Clarke and Jeff speak for themselves.

Jeff's stark reflection on the American ethos of individualism is as follows:

> As I understand it, America is built on the idea that her people can make of themselves what they want without the government's goodies softening the blow if they fail or have some calamity happen to them.

A concrete example of such individualistic thinking is the demise of the "individual mandate" in the Affordable Care Act (ACA), which Clarke wishes to reinstate in his concrete proposal (above). Jeff's explanation for the demise is that "many Americans recoil at the idea of being forced to buy something they don't want to buy" and "perhaps that is borne out of the strident individualism that pulses though America." However, Jeff acknowledges that "there will have to be a way to force Americans to jump into insurance pools to prevent those pools from 'death spiraling' into destruction."

My way of expressing this acknowledgement from Jeff is that there will be no way to provide for health care for those sick and elderly citizens who cannot afford it if those young and healthy citizens who may not presently need much health care are not willing to help pay for the health care needed by others (which comports with Clarke's focus on developing a health care system that fosters the "common good").

While not denying that many Americans think in individualistic terms when it comes to health care, Clarke is emphatic in his assertion that "the

claims of the Christian faith" are "less individualistic and more solidaristic," expressing deep regret that "suspicion of the common good seems ...
a too-frequent symptom of American Christianity's subtle absorption of
liberal individualism."

How is this all related to differing conceptions as to the meaning of
"justice"? As Jeff points out, there is a tension between thinking of justice
in terms of "merit" in contrast to viewing justice in a "distributive" sense.

> It seems to me that ... most regular Americans think of
> justice as something of *merit* rather than that of a *grant*. In
> other words, most Americans consider justice as a reciprocal,
> binary relationship in which each person (in the words of the
> old saw about justice) 'renders' his fellow man's 'due,' and is
> likewise 'rendered' his 'due' by his companion. In this vision,
> justice is a matter of *even relationships*. This is best seen
> in the criminal context. If I commit a crime, I am due—I
> *deserve* punishment. In essence, the punishment is what
> I've earned because I committed that crime. And equally
> important, once I complete that punishment, my standing
> in the community—my relationships—theoretically, should
> be restored.

> Americans have a much harder time thinking about justice
> in the *distributive* sense—in which goods and services are
> parceled out *from* those who currently enjoy those goods
> and services to those who currently do not have them. This
> is in no small part because the practical implementation of a
> system of distributive justice usually means raising taxes on
> those who have means in order to purchase benefits for those
> who don't have means. [Witness, for example, the special
> Medicare payroll tax that was included in the Affordable
> Care Act to pay for some of the act's many initiatives.] And
> raising taxes usually implicates matters of *earning* and
> *desert*—for taxpayers at least. To be frank, many people
> resent having their taxes raised for government services
> that do not tangibly and directly benefit them. [Witness,

for example, in the city and state in which I live there is a
great reticence to raise property taxes in order to improve
the public schools. People who do not have children in the
public schools seem very reluctant to raise the taxes needed
to improve schools because their children have graduated or
attend private schools.]

In my own words, those who embrace the ethos of individualism in
America tend to view justice in terms of "merit" (which is an aspect of
"retributive" justice when dealing with those who have broken the law),
while those who embrace Clarke's focus on seeking for a "common good,"
which would include paying taxes to support public schools that your children do not attend and paying health care insurance premiums that help
to provide health care to those citizens who otherwise could not afford
such care, view justice more in a "distributive" sense (while not necessarily
denying a "merit" or "retributive" sense in certain areas, like the criminal
justice system).

Clarke expresses appreciation for Jeff's "helpful discussion of justice, in
both its retributive and distributive forms," adding that "I agree with him
fully that Americans are more comfortable with retributive than distributive justice," and further noting agreement with Jeff's assertion that "We
are ... living 'in a society that is as individualistic as Cochran suspects and
not nearly as communitarian as Cochran wants.'"

However, Clarke goes on to assert that this agreement with Jeff does
not "doom (as Jeff believes) appeals to distributive or social justice that
ground my Christian understanding, analysis, and public advocacy for
health care reform," giving four reasons:

1. There are areas of life in which Americans are (or at
least have been until recently) very communitarian and
solidaristic in policy preferences. For example, Americans
strongly support comprehensive education for all (even
through at least some post-high school years). Social Security
and Medicare are highly popular, solidaristic policies.

2. It turns out that Americans do support the general 'right'
to health care for all. Public opinion surveys for the last

four decades find broad and deep support for the notion that everyone (at least every citizen) should receive the best possible needed health care. We are more communitarian than we sometimes think.

3. Why should reality trump Christian principle? Faced with opposition in principle and in practice to expanding health insurance to all persons, we can throw up our Christian hands in despair, or we can move forward toward justice and human dignity by whatever small steps our action, organizations and advocacy create. I like to think that my own reform proposals are both realistic enough (they build on what exists) and radical enough (they depend on root Christian principles) to enable another step on the journey.

4. When push comes to shove, Jeff himself employs social justice vocabulary to support public policy changes! I am puzzled by his objection to distributive justice principles in health care reform, because he has a lengthy and enlightening discussion of the 'gross injustice' of the uninsured paying full price for care. This practice is grossly unjust. However, if it's up to individual Christians and the churches to provide care for those who need it, why is it not up to them to pay the unjust bills of the uninsured? What I want to understand is why Jeff believes that Christians should advocate reform based on distributive justice to change unjust billing practices, but should not advocate changes to the larger system toward greater justice?

Cochran concludes that he is "ultimately confused by Jeff's objections to 'social justice' and the 'common good' as orienting Christian principles for health care reform. If exorbitant medical bills shock the conscience enough to create room for reform, should not the plight of uninsured health care beggars equally shock the conscience?" I will try to address this confusion later in this chapter.

So, given the above reflections, the two looming questions are: Where does that leave us? And: Where do we go from here?

A Communitarian Social Ethic

At this juncture it is extremely important to note that Clarke's focus on "Seeking a common good" and the "distributive" aspect of justice (in the two sections above) can be summarized as his call for a "communitarian social ethic" that he views as most consistent with his understanding of the Christian faith, in sharp contrast to the "individualistic" ethos that is so prevalent in American culture. In that light, we do well to consider the following reflections from Martin Luther King Jr., delivered during a Lenten sermon at the National Cathedral in Washington, D.C.:

> We are tied together in the single garment of destiny, caught in an inescapable network of mutuality. And whatever affects one directly affects all indirectly. For some strange reason I can never be what I ought to be until you are what you ought to be. And you can never be what you ought to be until I am what I ought to be. This is the way God's universe is made; this is the way it is structured.[68]

Of course, this raises the question as to the extent that Americans will embrace a communitarian social ethic, a topic to which we now turn.

Recapitulation of Where America Is Relative to Health Care

Jeff expresses agreement, "in principle," with Clarke's "communitarian" approach that views providing health care for all as a "common good." But he emphatically asserts that such a "communitarian social ethic does not presently exist in America," nor does it have "a realistic prospect of existing in the near future."

Cochran's definition of common goods as those which are a part of, foster, or enhance a communitarian social ethic is

---

68 Quoted in Meacham, *The Soul of America*, 245.

fine *in principle*. Where it is not fine, it seems to me, is the positing of a communitarian ethic without proof that such an ethic does exist or has a realistic prospect of existing in the near future.

... Let me be plain: I think we live in a society that is as individualistic as Cochran suspects and not nearly as communitarian as Cochran wants ... I agree with Cochran: If there ever comes a time that America pivots toward a communitarian society, then it can be rightly argued that health care for all is just as much of a common good as clean air and clean water are. Until then, it doesn't seem to accomplish much to say that health care is a common good. For as a matter of living in the political community, traditional Americans seem to be unenthused about paying for their fellows' health care needs (many of which are based on the person's choices).

It seems to me that Cochran has a *foundational* problem (a problem? a realization?) that American society is not Christian enough, or at least not receptive enough at this point to his fundamental pillars (justice, human dignity, access, etc.), that adequate health care for all can be secured.

In a later posting Jeff reflects on why in America it is unrealistic to think that Americans will soon embrace a "true universal system" for providing health care, similar to what is provided in Britain. He attributes this to the lack of agreement as to a "common purpose," which reflects the enormous diversity among Americans as to what constitutes the "common good."

While matters of mandates, taxes, costs and execution are important problems that any person advocating a universal-type of system must overcome, the most vexing issue that Cochran and other advocates of this type of system must answer for is the lack of bona fide common purpose or esprit de corps in America that is found in other nations with a true universal system. America is made up of over

330 million people with many different attitudes, opinions, financial situations, desires, dreams, and most importantly for our purposes, visions of the common good. We are a huge, populous country with many ideas of what it means and what it takes to be a good American.

... Let's be frank. In the 'wilderness' that is modern American life, the opinions and beliefs about who is deserving of care and protection in the form of health care insurance coverage varies wildly.

Jeff adds the additional question as to whether "the conditions" for a "universal-type system" of health care should ever "be right."

... My point is this: The conditions are not right for a universal-type of system. It's unclear whether they ever will be right. Further, we should ask if they *should be* right. We should seriously consider whether the American system (such that it is) is the best that America can do given our cultural and political polarization and Americans' affinity and demand for (relatively) low taxes.

A Possible Way Forward

As recapitulated above, there is serious question as to whether the ethical stances of most Americans are presently, or will ever be, sufficiently "communitarian" to embrace the view that government may need to play a significant role in providing adequate health care for all as a "common good." If that is the case, where do we go from here?

Jeff presents the following considerable challenge to Clarke:

It is ... incumbent on Cochran, as one who wants to change the status quo, to demonstrate the path to transforming America into a society communitarian enough so the satisfactory health care for all Americans can be secured.

Of course, such a transformation of American society would require many "changes in heart" prior to consideration of possible changes in public policies; a task well beyond the scope of political activity. Since that is not on the horizon, what are the options for a Way Forward? The conversation between Jeff and Clarke suggest two possibilities: incremental change through the political process; and collaboration between individuals, government and non-governmental sectors of society.

Incremental political change

Jeff eschews the option of resigning himself to the health care system "never changing."

> If I'm right about this realization [that American society is not Christian enough, or at least not receptive enough at this point to his fundamental pillars (justice, human dignity, access, etc.), that adequate health care for all can be secured], then there are two ways to respond. One is to throw up one's hands in surrender and resign oneself to the system never changing. The second is to slowly, surely and methodically attack the besetting problems of our health care system. I choose the second response.

While reaffirming his earlier suggestion that "growing the economy" will "multiply" "good jobs with good [health care] benefits," Jeff suggests that, due to the complexity of the health care system, addressing the "besetting problems of our system" will require an incremental approach, rather than an attempt to "unify the system."

> America's health care system is really a 'system of systems': a payment system (composed of government and commercial payers and the uninsured, and many ways of paying, including HMOs, PPOs, cash payments, etc.); a delivery system; a training and education system; and a technology development system, among many others.
>
> Unifying this system will be very challenging, if not impossible. There will need to be a catalyst to do so. Note, that I'm not endorsing such a catalyst. It's just my opinion that one will be necessary in order to unify the system.

... I ... think change to the system in which more people get more access will come by 'blocking and tackling'—making one change at a time to one problem at a time.

In that spirit, Jeff does propose four incremental changes in the current healthcare system and Julie adds another proposal for incremental change.

The Chargemaster Problem

Jeff asserts that "there is a gross injustice involved with the uninsured paying full retail prices based on hospitals' chargemasters, while insured patients have their deeply-discounted bills paid for by a third party (the insurer)," elaborating as follows:

A "chargemaster" is a hospital's master spreadsheet of prices it charges for every good and service it provides. The hospital's charges are compared (in the spreadsheet) with the prices it receives from insurers with which it contracts for those same goods and services. Because of the negotiated, contractual relationship insurers have with hospitals (and because insurers bring a certain volume of patients who will use the hospital's services), insurers always pay hospitals significantly less than the "full" chargemaster price for a good or service. Thus, many full retail prices on a hospital's chargemaster are orders of magnitude higher than the most generous insurance reimbursement for the same good or service.

... It is ... flummoxing, perverse and disturbing to me in the extreme that patients who are least able to pay the top charges from hospitals and other health providers are charged full-freight.

What can be done about this? How about Congress passing a bill that says the following: No hospital will charge an uninsured person more than any particular insurer pays the hospital.[69]

69 In a later posting, Jeff did submit a "correction" to this proposal, noting that "the Affordable Care Act and the administrative regulations published thereto prevents

... let me mention just briefly one other item that would greatly benefit uninsured hospital patients charged full chargemaster prices. We can hope and pray for a groundswell of judicial decisions favorably applying the contractual doctrine of "unconscionability" to exorbitant medical bills. Unconscionability is one of the traditional common law defenses to the making of a contract. It has "procedural" (how the contract is made) and "substantive" (the terms of the contract) elements. You can see how both elements would apply to high hospital bills. The patient (or family member) is "forced" to sign an authorization for treatment whereby the patient (or responsible party) promises to pay for the treatment the patient receives in the hospital. On the front end, the patient or family member has no idea how much the services will cost, because prices aren't posted and no one, including the treating doctor(s) or hospital has a good idea all of what the patient will need. The substantive element involves the high prices themselves. Usually, this doctrine hasn't been successful for patients (or families) trying to spring themselves from outrageously high medical bills. Let us hope and pray for just the right welter of cases that would allow this doctrine to be applied to uninsured patients. Further, let us hope and pray that these cases will work just results for the patients *and* the hospitals involved.

The Fee-for-Service Problem

Jeff expresses concern that "the main parts of our health care system are fee-for-service (FFS) based." In particular, he hopes for a "change" in "Medicare's basic delivery and payment model" that "introduce(s) value and outcome reimbursement, hoping to displace FFS."

Based on her extensive experience in health care administration, Julie Kuhl seconds Jeff's push for more "outcome-based care models," elaborating as follows:

---

not-for-profit hospitals from charging the uninsured more than what certain forms of insurance would reimburse to the hospital."

> A physician/hospital gets the same reimbursement from a heart catch that was scheduled and routine as it does for an emergent situation where the patient's life is at risk. The reimbursement is the same if the patient lives or dies. Human nature talking here … take the money for the least amount of work.

Clarke concurs with Julie's observation, noting that this lack of emphasis on outcomes has been called the "ring the bell" model.

> One of the chief medical officers I used to work with called the current model 'ring the bell.' Providers by and large receive payment for each procedure (each ring of the bell), so the incentive is to keep ringing.

Clarke implicitly proposes a change in the "ring the bell" model to an outcomes-based model "one where payment comes from: a) keeping patients well and then, b) helping them get well successfully when 'a' fails." However, Clarke observes that "the route to achieving that goal ['for the last two decades'] has been long, arduous and scattered with the wreckage of unsuccessful experiments (accountable care organizations, upside and downside risk, health maintenance organizations, medical homes, capitation and salary payments and many, many more)."

The lessons that Clarke takes from these failures are that "changing incentives is more difficult than anyone can imagine" and, "such reform must include a major role for government" (a contentious proposal to which we will soon return).

Providing More Preventative Care and Education

Julie proposes a need for more "preventative care and education," adding that "as a Christian, to educate myself and children on nutrition, exercise, warning triggers for common diseases, etc. is a low(er) cost option [than providing cures]. In short, proactive, not reactive."

In response to Julie, Clarke agrees with the need for a person to take preventative measures, like exercising regularly, eating properly and taking medicines as prescribed, but he indicates that his "agreement is qualified," cautioning against setting up a "false binary" between "entitlements and personal responsibility."

In short, my argument that the common good requires a system of national health insurance (which would 'entitle' people to coverage for health needs) does not and need not preclude ways in which such a system might encourage personal responsibility. My own experience with good health insurance is like Jeff's, but I'm guessing that, despite this good health insurance, both he and I try to exercise regularly, eat properly and take medicines as prescribed.

My agreement is qualified. Of course, prevention is important. I hope that I follow Julie's recommended practices. These, plus recommended screenings (mammogram frequency at certain ages; regular endoscopy if one has Barrett's esophagus and so forth), are an essential part of health care. Moreover, evidence-based and medical panel recommended screenings should be included in universal coverage at no or little cost to the patient.

Too often, however, prevention is oversold as a cure for our expensive health care system. Yet, prevention in the form of health education is not cost free. In many cases, a very large population must be educated to prevent a relatively small disease incidence. This is not an argument against education; only a caution that a cost-savings analysis might not reveal monetary savings. Moreover, screenings are also not free and may not be cost-effective. Again, not an argument against them. Catching an early cancer is very important. But screenings entail false positives that may encourage postponed attention to symptoms or false negatives that may lead to unneeded and costly interventions. Enhanced attention to prevention will not reform the health care system.

The next major section of this chapter will return to the complex issue of the relationship between taking responsibility for caring for oneself health-wise and governmental provision of health care, as well as possible responsibilities for non-governmental organizations, like churches and taking personal initiatives to care for one another.

The Emergency Room Problem

Jeff's proposal for addressing the "emergency room problem" stems for his long term "fascination" with "the EMTALA law—the law that mandates that a person cannot be turned away from receiving a 'medical screening exam' or 'stabilizing treatment' when that person seeks care in an emergency room." Jeff observes that "because emergency rooms must provide patients a modicum of evaluation and treatment, those without health insurance have come to realize that they can receive non-emergency care there." Since this creates the problem of overcrowding of emergency rooms, Jeff presents a proposal for legislative consideration.

> ... Congress would do well to reconfigure the EMTALA law to allow hospitals to build and open to the public urgent care types of clinics near emergency rooms so that non-emergent patients can be diverted from the emergency room and treated there. These urgent care clinics would be required to accept Medicaid patients (and perhaps required to accept uninsured patients or state-insured safety-net patients). Congress might consider sweetening the reimbursement for these clinics with special subsidies, etc.

Jeff acknowledges that his proposal is limited in that "it really does nothing for uninsured patients who have genuine emergency conditions. These patients will be faced with substantial, and for all practical purposes, unpayable bills related to their care in the ER (and whatever follow-up care they might require)."

Low-Cost Proposals for Making Health Care More Accessible

Based on her experience as a health care administrator, Julie proposes several "little things we can do to make health care more accessible without a huge cost offset," including the following:

- Create more flexible office hours for doctors.

- Require doctors to keep appointment times with their patients.
- Expand opportunities for family caregivers to provide home care.
- Increase the use of volunteers to assist health care providers.
- Simplify the financial aspects of health care.
- Improve clinical documentation.

Who bears responsibility for providing health care for all?

While Jeff and Clarke agree on the need for some incremental changes in the American health care system (e.g., addressing the "ring the bell" problem), they have some fundamental "big picture" disagreements regarding who the primary actors should be in American society toward the goal of providing health care for all. In particular, what are the proper roles for individuals, churches (and other private non-governmental entities) and government? To summarize what follows, Clarke and Jeff seem to agree that all Americans should have "good access to the health care needed for them to flourish." But, as Clarke observes, "Where we disagree is which actors are responsible for guaranteeing that access. Jeff seems to exclude government (perhaps until he sees society evolving sufficiently toward social solidarity) and to include the church. My case is for a partnership of government and private (including church) actors." I will now elaborate on this disagreement.

It is clear that Jeff assigns primary responsibility to individual Christians (and others) and churches. For Jeff, the "Christian social principles" of human dignity and justice enumerated by Clarke imply that "first and foremost, Christians have personal obligations to care for the sick," adding that "this obligation sounds in justice and emanates from each person's incalculable worth as a creature made in God's image."

However, Jeff "wonder(s) if in the environment we live in today, that means a Christian ought to sacrifice his/her hard-earned money for the care of his less well-off fellows," adding that "just because Christians and the church may have obligations to care for the sick does not necessarily mean that the state has similar obligations."

While indicating that he "find(s) a strong injunction in the New Testament to give of *myself* for the benefit of my fellow suffering human being, who Jesus likened to himself in Matthew 25," Jeff reports that he "can find no similar instruction by Jesus or Paul or any other New Testament writer for kings, rulers or governments to take care of the sick of their kingdoms," adding that "I suspect that such an instruction would sound discordant to Jesus' original disciples or the first Christians and downright silly if it ever made it back to Herod, Caesar or any other first-century ruler."

Jeff goes on to bemoan the fact that "what started as individual and congregational care for the infirm has slowly morphed over the centuries into Christian denominations organizing not-for-profit hospitals or hospital systems, all of which collect fees for goods and services provided to patients. It is rare indeed when those hospitals or hospital systems charge significantly less than their for-profit or secular nonprofit peer facilities or systems. It's also rare when these hospitals or systems do not have a policy that they enforce regarding collection of unpaid fees. In other words, our Christian-affiliated hospitals look much like their secular counterparts in aggressive pricing of health care services and collection practices."

Clarke acknowledges a significant role for the church in providing for health care, including caring about "health care reform," in light of the church's "commitment to justice, fairness, personal dignity, participation and the common good," observing that "one of the chief health care players is the Catholic church through its network of hospitals, clinics, physician practices and other institutions."

But, where Clarke disagrees with Jeff is in asserting that government must play a significant role in providing health care because "no other institution bears public accountability for the social good." "I believe only that government (especially federal and state governments given our constitutional system) have essential functions related to the common good and to justice." Clarke elaborates as follows:

> Christians and others of goodwill cannot deliver fair, accountable and dignified health care without substantial government involvement. In the first place, as discussed above, since health care is deeply related to justice and the common good, government's role as an arbiter of justice and as custodian of the common good makes its role indispensable. In addition, certain features of health care produce what economists call 'market failure'; that is, a situation in which the market cannot regulate itself toward

fair outcomes. When markets fail, governments must step in to regulate. Features of market failure in health care are: 1) medical care is not a commodity like other commodities (it deeply involves moral principles and public goods in the strict sense); 2) health insurance creates 'moral hazard' (the existence of the product creating demand for the service insured against); 3) 'adverse selection' that incentivizes insurance companies to exclude or price out of the market those who most need health insurance; 4) asymmetric information between providers and patients; 5) significant barriers (financial and licensure, for example) to entry into the market; and 6) the large presence of nonprofit entities in the health care market (the Christian organizations described above, among others).

But Clarke is not asserting that the provision of health care is the sole responsibility of government. Rather, he is proposing a collaborative effort between government and non-governmental sectors of society (like churches) that "reinforces" the "current joint public-private system."

> ... The bottom line ... is: Both the Christian community and government must be part of the reform of the U.S. health care system. Christians enter the health care policy space with an intent to build a more just, personal, participatory and communal health care system.

> My proposal is *not* for single-payer health care; *nor* is it for a 'government-run' system. I champion reinforcing the current joint public-private system. Government **provides** some services directly (VA, military health and Indian Health Service); **finances** some services through Medicare and Medicaid and some state-based payments for indigent persons; and **regulates** most of the system through a complex of federal and state laws. There are some government-owned providers (country hospitals, for example), but most providers (whether hospitals, nursing homes, rehabilitation facilities or physician practices) operate in the private sector,

and many are Christian in origin and orientation. All must follow public health and safety and anti-fraud regulations, but they are private. Private for-profit and nonprofit insurers furnish most employment-based insurance.

Clarke reminds us that his concrete proposal for reforming health care in America (enumerated above) "keeps all the private parts intact, as well as retaining the main parts of government delivery, financing and regulation." He notes that he is "not calling for more government in health care," explaining as follows:

> My own recommendations include retention of Medicare and Medicaid and the VA and military health systems (all 'government run,' but in very important different ways). But its centerpiece is the private health insurance system. And private hospitals, clinics, nursing homes and physician and dental practices remain just that: private.
>
> My principal [proposed] changes [in the current health care system] are few, but vital. First, as a matter of justice … government must require and guarantee that all persons have health insurance. Second, Medicare becomes open for purchase through individual premiums by persons 55 and older unable to afford private insurance. Medicaid becomes available to younger, low-income persons who are temporarily unemployed or who work part time. Third, the federal government specifies a few standard packages of insurance coverage, thus simplifying the ability of individuals to understand their benefits. Fourth, I am open to reducing government regulation of various parts of the health care system. Which procedures and processes government should regulate are prudential matters, rather than matters of principle.

Medicare for All?

Note that Clarke is *not* calling for "single-payer health care," and he is *not* calling for a "government-run" system. Rather he calls for improving the current "joint public-private system." Clarke's brief comment on why he is *not* proposing a "'single-payer' or 'Medicare for all' system" is that it "would, I believe, too radically disrupt 18 percent of the economy."

Relative to a possible public-private subdivision of responsibility for providing health care, Jeff allows for elements of governmental involvement in providing health care. But his clear focus is on the role of the private sector, especially churches. Therefore, the "single-payer" option is not something that Jeff would endorse.

But the "single-payer" option is "on the table" in current public conversations about possibilities for health care reform, especially among the Bernie Sanders wing of the Democratic Party. Therefore, a conversation about "health care in America" is truncated if this option is not given some consideration. In that light, during the eCircle conversation between Jeff, Clarke and Julie, I took the liberty of asking Dr. Timothy Johnson, former medical news editor for ABC News, for his reflections on health care reform, knowing full well that he favors a "single-payer" system,[70] by which is meant a health care system that is fully financed by taxes that covers the essential health care costs for all persons, with all payments for health care services paid by a single public authority (the government).

What follows summarizes Tim's reflections, as received in a private email exchange that was not published on my eCircle and excerpts from his book *The Truth About Getting Sick in America.*[71]

First, Tim believes that adequate health care is a "right, not a privilege."

> I ... believe there is a moral imperative to achieve universal health insurance coverage in our society. I believe health care fits into the category of basic rights like police and fire protection which is why I often refer to health care as 'health protection.' Think about it: It is very difficult to achieve 'life, liberty and the pursuit of happiness' without good health.

70 In the interest of full disclosure, I report that "Dr. Tim" is a good friend from our many years worshiping together at Community Covenant Church in West Peabody, MA.
71 Johnson, *The Truth.*

Which is why I believe that health care should not be viewed as an optional commodity like cars, homes or giant TVs, but as a basic right needed by all of our citizens.

Tim's take on the current "American health care system" is as follows:

Every time I hear someone—especially a pious politician—lauding our 'American health care system,' I want to shout out that there is no such thing as an American health care 'system' in the sense of a national program to make sure that all our citizens have health care insurance.

What we have instead is a hodge-podge of private and public insurance plans with cracks between them so large that 30 million Americans have fallen through and still have no health insurance.

The question, of course, is how best to provide universal health insurance—*like every other developed country in the world has done.* I find it incredibly embarrassing that we are the wealthiest country in the world, yet we are the only one that has not been able to figure out how to achieve universal health insurance. How can that be?

While acknowledging the "reasons" given by "experts" for America's failure to achieve universal health insurance, such as "our vast and varied population and geography, our national history of rugged individualism, our fear of 'government control,'" Tim believes "the time has come to admit our failures and think big." As a context for Tim's "big" proposal, I start with consideration of the three characteristics that the majority of Americans desire for their health care in general and their health insurance in particular: **high quality, easy access and low cost.**

In a meeting of residents of northwest Iowa interested in discussing health care issues, Marty Guthmiller, CEO of Orange City Area Health System, made the provocative claim that you can't have all three of these desired characteristics. At best, you must decide on which two you will settle for.

Along these lines, Dr. Tim suggests that there is a "big problem" with what most Americans want:

> To put it bluntly, most of us want a gourmet platter of care and services at a blue-plate-special price. And all too often, we expect top-notch results without any personal effort to improve what we can about our health through such proven techniques as regular exercise or improved nutrition.[72]

To restate Tim's concern in terms of the triad addressed by Guthmiller, most Americans want high quality and easy access, with the expectation that they can get this at low cost, which is an unrealistic expectation given our current health care system.

While desiring to provide high quality health care, Tim suggests that health care reforms are needed to ensure easy access and reasonable costs. As to "access," his proposal for a "national health insurance program" is as follows:

> Any good national health insurance program should be consistent and available no matter where you live or work. (i.e., It should not change with circumstances beyond your control such as sudden job loss, the need to relocate or preexisting conditions.) And when it comes to health insurance in particular, it is very helpful to have experts negotiating cost and coverage on our behalf—versus trying by ourselves to pick between various complicated options.

Tim's strongest recommendation is that easy access and high quality can be provided only if our current health care system can be reformed in two ways that will prevent costs from skyrocketing. The first is a need to reinstate the "individual mandate" for health insurance that was enacted by President Obama's Affordable Care Act (which has subsequently been eliminated under President Trump's administration).

> In order to keep the costs as low as possible for everyone, the risk of having to use the insurance should be spread as wide as possible. The basic concept is that people who don't currently need insurance help pay for those who do,

---

72 Ibid., xi.

recognizing that when it comes to health insurance, it is likely that eventually we will all need it.

Tim's second cost containment proposal is to seriously call into question the current means for paying doctors and hospitals for their services (echoing the concerns of both Jeff and Clarke regarding the "ring the bell" approach that characterizes the current FFS model).

> Our present health care reimbursement systems are based primarily on paying for procedures rather than results or outcomes ... To put it bluntly, our current payment system boils down to a simple yet ultimately disastrous financial incentive: *The more you do, the more you make.*

> I have come to believe that the most critical factor in true reform will depend on the success we have in changing the way we pay our doctors and hospitals.[73]

> The *most basic reform needed is a change in the way we pay providers.* We need to remove the incentive to simply do more to pay more—which is what the current fee-for-service payment system encourages.[74]

Tim's strongest recommendations for cost containment relate to how doctors get paid: "Ultimately, I believe we must pay all our doctors by salary ... And a key component of that salary should be based on outcomes,"[75] adding that "salaries have the advantage of eliminating the inherent conflict of interest in our FFS system, which provides a direct financial incentive to do more."[76]

Providing a ray of hope, Tim observes that "some of our best health care facilities, such as the Mayo and Cleveland Clinics, pay their doctors by salary in order to free them from making decisions based on how much more money they could make."[77]

73 Ibid., 17.
74 Ibid., 61.
75 Ibid., 18.
76 Ibid., 21.
77 Ibid., 18-19. For interested readers, Tim also proposes cost containment measures related to paying for other hospital services, drugs, medical devices and insurance, and for reforming our current malpractice system that is "both immoral and intolerably inefficient," 23-28.

So, in light of Tim's recommendations, where can we go from here? Tim prepares us for his "big proposal" by observing that we currently have a health insurance program available in America that meets his proposed basic requirements for health care insurance, Medicare— but "you have to be over 65 to get it." He notes that "Medicare is classic 'single payer,' meaning the federal government does the financing, collecting the money via taxes and paying the bills after negotiating much lower prices with doctors and hospitals than we could ever do on our own," while still allowing us "to pick our own doctors and hospitals, no matter where we live, no matter what our health status is" (unlike the "socialized medicine" in Britain where the government does the financing as the single payer, but also owns and operates the doctors and hospitals).

Hence, Tim's "thinking big" is to propose "Medicare for all."

What are the obstacles to "Medicare for all"? They appear to be insurmountable. For starters, Tim suggests that one major obstacle is that "the private health insurance industry in this country has Congress in their pocket and will fight it to the death." Tim's response to making the idea of "Medicare for all" more "appealing" is to point to "the huge overhead costs of private health insurance—including marketing and profits," and the eventual possibility of "dramatically lower administrative costs of a single-payer system."

Adding my own commentary, it appears to me that another major obstacle is the resistance on the part of many Americans to the "individual mandate" for health insurance that is central to Tim's proposals for cost containment. As already pointed out by Jeff, in our individualistic American culture, the "communitarian" idea of healthy people paying taxes for health insurance that helps to cover the health care needs of those who are sick and cannot afford adequate health care is anathema to many Americans.

In light of these obstacles to "Medicare for all," Tim notes another "pathway to universal health insurance coverage": a hybrid model used by many other developed countries, meaning the preservation of private insurance companies *but* under the tight control of the federal government in terms of cost, quality and access."[78] While acknowledging that this hybrid model "might be more palatable politically," Tim expresses "very

78 Tim points us to the exemplary hybrid system that currently seems to work very well in Germany. Ibid., 40-45.

little faith that government and the private sector can pull this off given our present political climate."

Tim closes with his prediction for the future of health care in America:

> So, given the current political gridlock in this country, my prediction is that we will limp along in continuing political dysfunction—trying one Band-Aid solution after another—until the costs of health care reach such a critical point that there will be an 'emergency meeting in Washington'—like the banking crisis—at which point we will go to either a single-payer or hybrid system in order to get the spending pipeline in one place. And unless some kind of political miracle occurs to make it happen sooner, I predict it will take about 10 years for that to happen!

In terms of Marty Guthmiller's suggestion that you have to "pick two out of three," it appears to me that Tim's prediction amounts to saying that Americans will not sacrifice high quality health care that is easily accessible, with the result that eventually the cost will become so prohibitive that Americans will reluctantly consider the possibility of paying increased taxes to provide health care insurance for all, the healthy as well as the sick.

Of course, a possible fatal flaw in that prediction is the lack of a widespread communitarian social ethic that calls for Americans to care for one another by having the healthy pay more taxes to care for the sick. This means that Christians should advocate in the public square for such a communitarian ethic, based on the teachings of Jesus recorded in Matthew 25. But isn't that calling for Christians to impose their ethic on those Americans who do not share their Christian faith commitment? No, but it does allow for Christians to attempt "persuasion" in public discourse. This raises a final question as to whether such attempts at persuasion based on a religious commitment should be allowed in public conversations about health care.

Should Christian Voices Be Heard in the National Debate About Health Care?

In response to Clarke's "fundamental social principles," Jeff poses a fundamental question about the relationship between religion and politics:

> I would ask Cochran to answer what I believe to be the most fundamental question of religion and politics: Are there areas of our common politics that are not or should not be governed by religious, or even Christian principles? That is, why is health care so special that it deserves to be analyzed through the prism of Christian thought? Are there areas of legal or political concern that are off-limits to religious influence, analysis, or understanding? If so, why?

Clarke responds:

> The simple answer, I think, is that there are no significant policy arenas that should be off-limits to Christian understanding, analysis and persuasion, so long as the issues concern all or most citizens, there are moral principles at stake, and Christians approach them with humility, without insistence that our principles and understandings should determine public policy.

On a personal note, I concur wholeheartedly with Clarke's response. The views of anyone in any area of human discourse, including politics, are deeply informed by the person's beliefs about the ultimate nature of reality, whether religious or secular. No one comes from nowhere. We all bring our worldview beliefs to the public square. It is a myth that "religious people" bring their religious beliefs to public discourse while secularists are "neutral." In that light, public discourse needs to exemplify an "even playing field" where all voices are heard and no one seeks to coercively impose his or her views on others.[79]

---

79 For my argument for allowing religious perspectives in the academy, see Heie, "Dialogic Discourse."

This Conversation Was Respectful.
But Who Was Left Out?

Anyone who reads the original electronic postings by Jeff, Clarke and Julie will be impressed by the respectful manner in which they talked about their disagreements. Jeff comments on this in his reflections on Clarke's postings:

> I'm particularly struck by Dr. Cochran's generous and conciliatory tone. Throughout his essay, Dr. Cochran maintains a posture of what I will call firm civility. At no time does he compromise his hard-won and long-considered positions, yet, he makes his case in a respectful and moderate tone. In what is best about religiously-based discourse, Dr. Cochran writes with a genuine Christian meekness, and that is much appreciated.

> Dr. Cochran represents what is best about dialogue concerning hard problems. He is civil. He is clear. And, in what is best about *Christian* engagement with difficult conundrums, he presents his interlocutors' positions with charity. It's been a pleasure 'conversing' with him this month. I hope we'll have a chance to think together again about the place of Christian conviction as it relates to the American health care system. Cochran is obviously an expert, and his ideas and positions are well worth reading.

But who has been left out of this conversation? Julie poses a few legitimate and unsettling questions:

> Have we **really** wrestled with health care if we have truly never been on the receiving end of being without it? Do we really know what it's like to not seek care because we cannot afford it? Do we really know what it's like to not be able to fill a prescription? …

I think we do a huge disservice to the entire conversation by looking at it from such a limited scope. There are so many outliers that have to be considered ... The *only* way to account for the full scope of the project is to talk to the end user.

I ... think we need to step back and see who else can be brought into this conversation to hear the entire story ... It's not a matter of us vs. them ... We are *all* wonderfully and fearfully made [in "God's image"] ... are we truly inclusive in our conversations?

So, once again, a theme emerges from this conversation that crops up frequently in all my work, past and present, seeking to orchestrate respectful conversations about divisive issues. We need to stop talking "at" or "about" people whose lives are deeply affected by the topics of our conversations. We need to talk "with" them.[80]

---

80 This theme emerged in a powerful manner in my eCircle on human sexuality, which led to my book *Respectful LGBT Conversations*. See especially my proposal that there is no "Way Forward" in the current contentious debate among Christians regarding LGBT issues until we start listening to the stories of our LGBT brothers and sisters in Christ, 265-266.

Case Studies:
Christians and Churches
Doing Politics

WE RETURN NOW to the question raised in Chapter 4 as to the extent to which individual Christians, church congregations and denominations, and Christian para-church organizations should be "politically active." Recall Harry Boyte's view that while political activity at the governmental level can be of value, the "first priority" should be political activism on the part of non-governmental organizations such as churches, families, businesses and voluntary organizations. Jim Skillen seconded the importance of political activism within the non-governmental sector, but gave more credence than Harry to the importance of Christians being politically active within local, state and national branches of government.

In this chapter, we consider case studies of the extent to which two church congregations and one Christian para-church organization have, or have not, encouraged or facilitated political activity on the part of their constituents. The particular churches/organization involved and the leading questions posed to their leaders were as follows:

Case Study 1: Kalamazoo (Michigan) Mennonite Fellowship—
A church that encourages its members to become involved in social service ministries that serve persons in need (e.g., the homeless, the hungry); that has church-wide social service ministries; but does *not* take church-wide political positions or initiatives.

Leading Questions:

- What kind of social service ministries does your church provide?
- How do you encourage your members to become involved in social service ministries?
- Do you encourage your members to be politically active, and why or why not?
- What are your reasons for *not* taking church-wide political positions or initiatives?

Conversation Partner: Will Fitzgerald, senior pastor, Kalamazoo Mennonite Fellowship.

Case Study 2: First Congregational Church, Kalamazoo (MI)—A church that encourages its members to be politically active and involved in social service ministries that serve persons in need (e.g., the homeless, the hungry); that has church-wide social service ministries; and *selectively* takes church-wide political positions or initiatives.

Leading Questions:

- What kind of social service ministries does your church provide?
- How do you encourage your members to become involved in social service ministries?
- What are your reasons for selectively taking church-wide political positions or initiatives?
- What types of issues have you selected and on what basis did you make that selection?

Conversation Partner: Nathan Dannison, senior pastor, First Congregational Church, Kalamazoo.

Case Study 3: Christian Reformed Church (CRC) Office of Social Justice and Hunger Action—A Christian para-church organization that believes that reforming/redeeming the political realm is an important activity for Christians; that Christians should carry out social justice ministries that serve persons in need; and that provides resources and other assistance to help its church constituent members and their congregational members to carry out these responsibilities.

Leading Questions:

- How do you encourage individual Christians and your church constituent members to become involved in political activities that reform/redeem the political realm and in social service ministries that serve persons in need?
- What kind of resources do you provide for such individuals and churches? What has worked well? What hasn't worked well?

Conversation Partner: Kris Van Engen, Congregational justice mobilizer for World Renew and the Christian Reformed Church Office of Social Justice and Hunger Action.

In what follows, I will first present extended excerpts from the initial postings from Will, Nathan and Kris; excerpts chosen to give the reader a glimpse of the "passion" of the leader, not just his responsibilities. I will then conclude the chapter by reporting some of the reactions of each partner to the initial postings of his partners and inserting my own attempt to make coherent sense of it all.

Kalamazoo Mennonite Fellowship

Kalamazoo Mennonite Fellowship is a small house church in Kalamazoo, Michigan. Fewer than 20 people, including kids, attend on a good day. We are part of the Indiana-Michigan Conference of the Mennonite Church USA, the largest, at least for now, Mennonite denomination in the United States. I say, "at least for now" because difficult questions around Scripture, human sexuality and politics have led many congregations and even whole conferences to leave. The very idea of having respectful conversations is critical to institutional survival, but it is also critical to our spiritual growth and obedience to God's command to be "quick to hear, slow to speak, and slow to anger" (James 1:19).

Even though we are a small church, we believe that God gives us the gifts that we need, as Paul writes in his first letter to the Corinthian Church (1 Corinthians 12:7 and *passim*). If this is true, then when we do *not* have a particular gift, it is at least likely that God has decided we don't quite need it yet. The charism of a small church is intimacy and a certain ease: we don't need to do everything; we lack time and resources.

As a church, we have exactly one social service ministry per se: almost every Thursday night, people (almost always women) gather to make comforters which are then distributed by the Mennonite Central Committee in Syria, the Democratic Republic of the Congo and elsewhere. This small and faithful cadre makes about 65 comforters per year.

However, we have no paid staff and no building to maintain, and so when we donate money to "the church," almost all of that ends up going to others. We don't really have a budget, but about 90 percent of our money ends up going to others. The "social service ministries" we supported in 2017 included:

- Mennonite Disaster Service—despite its awesome name, works to respond to disasters rather than to create them.
- Mennonite Central Committee—despite its rather boring name, does interesting relief and development work throughout the world.
- Anabaptist Disabilities Network—works to support people touched by disabilities and to integrate them into church life.
- Kalamazoo Loaves and Fishes—the main emergency food network in our city.
- Community Homeworks—helps low-income home owners to maintain their homes.
- The Colossian Forum, a sister organization to the Respectful Conversation project—helps the church practice virtue in the midst of conflict.

Several of our members work in social services, including a chaplain at a local hospital, the education director of Community Homeworks and the president of The Colossian Forum. Another member is a librarian, one of the most important social services around, although libraries are so much a part of the warp and woof of our society, it's easy to forget this.

We try to be a place of welcome: "Welcome the stranger," and, "Welcome one another, therefore, just as Christ has welcomed you, for the glory of God," as Paul wrote in Romans.

As a church, we agreed to look for ways to be more involved in welcoming immigrants. Some of us attended protests and demonstrations of support that started to happen in our downtown park. (At one, I stood on the stage with Nathan Dannison, one of my co-discussants.) These demonstrations and protests, as important as they may have been, didn't especially connect with our desire to welcome.

One of our members, Carlie, volunteered to contact Bethany Christian Services and see what would be involved in sponsoring a refugee or immigrant family. The branch director, Joel Bell, came to our church to talk through what this would mean. When we looked around at who we were, and what this entailed, we realized it was more than we could realistically offer. Other churches that are bigger than ours have support groups for refugee families.

It did introduce us to Joel Bell. My wife, Bess, learned that he and his family welcomed 10 members of a refugee family into their home for six weeks. Bess said, if they could do that, so could we. So, we offered our home for emergency housing. Through Joel and Bethany Christian Services Refugee & Immigrant Services, we have been able to welcome a lively Egyptian family for a couple of weeks, and a young Rohingya man, fleeing genocide in Burma.

Joel came to us with a bigger ask: a longer term commitment to a young man from Guatemala named Helder, who came as an unaccompanied minor to the U.S., was taken under Bethany's care, and was about to age out of their services.

This has been fortunate for us—both our family and our church. It's great to have a sweet, kind young man in the house, who is handy and tells a good story.

Having these folks in our homes has taught our church many things, including:

- Gratitude for the gift they are, in and of themselves.
- Gratitude for the programs that state, federal and local agencies have in place to welcome immigrants and refugees. (It's not *all* bad.)
- Anger at the ways immigrants and refugees are exploited by unscrupulous family and so-called sponsors.
- Anger at the ways immigrants and refugees are often scapegoated in the current political climate.

- Anger at some of the piss-poor services offered to immigrants, borne by the public, but often flowing to private, for-profit organizations.
- Acceptance of our limits of what we can realistically do.
- Spanish vocabulary because we're learning words we never knew in Spanish.

I did not grow up in the church, but my father was what came to be called a Reagan Democrat. He strongly believed that participation in civic life, especially voting, was the duty of every citizen. This duty was strongly engrained in me. It came as some surprise to learn that the traditional—or at least one traditional—belief of the Anabaptists was to not participate in politics, even to vote.

Mennonites form one of the historic "peace churches" (along with the Church of the Brethren and the Quakers). And, historically for Mennonites, that meant being *nonresistant* in the face of violence. And, because "the sword" is reserved for those in government service, we should not, therefore, participate in government as office holders, or even as voters.

The current confession of faith used by the Mennonite Church USA expands and erases some of this historic understanding. The idea of *nonresistance* is expanded to include *peace and justice*. Jesus, as the confession says, "has called us to find our blessing in making peace and seeking justice." We are still not to resort to violence, and we call on our members to conscientiously object to military service. But influencing and participating in the secular political process is not forbidden, and is even encouraged.

Some more traditional Mennonites and other Anabaptists maintain the more traditional nonresistant position. Other conservative Mennonites have joined the general trend of conservative evangelicals in supporting politicians and policies set forth by political conservatives.

There's a bit of an open secret about Mennonite history that's relevant, too. A large strand of the Mennonite and Anabaptist movement in Europe was German-speaking ... With the rise of Hitler and Nazism, many Mennonites saw the Nazis in a positive light, supporting their German culture and their religion; and the Nazis saw the Mennonites as good Aryan *Volk* and possible partners in a greater Germany ... The open secret is that some Mennonites, in living memory, were Nazis or Nazi sympathizers. I have friends who have great-uncles or grandparents who were.

The sweep of Anabaptist history has tended towards non-involvement in politics and non-resistance to violence. Over time, these ideals have been lost and compromised (as in the case of Nazi collaboration), or changed and enhanced to include a focus on social justice and social peacemaking, as in the official confession of the Mennonite Church USA.

As a pastor, I have been very wary of encouraging people to identify their political convictions with their Christian beliefs. I've even hesitated to suggest people vote, which I'm sure causes my union-going Democratic father to spin in his grave. In the end, during the 2016 presidential election, I did encourage our church to vote, not for one candidate or another in mind, but to vote … On Facebook, on my personal page, I encouraged people to vote for Hillary Clinton, trying to make it as clear as possible that I was not speaking for anyone but myself, and definitely not for our local fellowship. I encouraged people to do so because, at the time, and to this day, I view the presidency of Donald Trump as an existential threat.

I do not, and probably would not, encourage our little fellowship to take "church-wide positions or initiatives" for a number of reasons. A very important one is simply time and resources.

Another, related reason is that we have church members involved in social justice, care and peacemaking, and supporting them in their work seems more valuable than working on causes directly. Often, that means loving them as they parent their children, working through the frustrations of their jobs and encouraging their spiritual lives, all of which makes it *possible* for them to be more effective in their ministries. Of course, we try to do the same for anyone, and we don't value a career doing social justice over a career doing accountancy. But we also put our money where our heart is, and support agencies and advocacy groups like the ones listed above.

Frankly, I am wary of official church positions for a number of reasons. We have seen in our Mennonite history how some members of a comfortable church, frightened by real dangers, ended up making extremely bad decisions about their place as part of Hitler's *Volk*. And I have viewed with increasing skepticism the capture of the American evangelical church by Trumpism. It's a foolish conceit that *we* are going to make *just* the right call, when others, not really any worse or stupider than we, did not. I also recognize that sometimes we just need to take the risk, though the church worldwide and through history has not had a great track record, especially when the church has been in places of privilege.

[The book of Romans contains a] description of what Paul thinks a healthy church should look like: mutual love and honor, a common life of virtue, prayer, generosity, hospitality and so on. All of these things are about what it means to be in, and extend, the Kingdom of God. Jesus promises that those who hunger and thirst for righteousness will be satisfied, and that peacemakers will be called God's children. It's not an either/or thing; it's not a choice between a common life of virtue, and fighting for a more just world.

I mentioned previously the *charism* of our church. Of course, I have no illusions that we are the perfect model of a church, no illusions whatsoever. And I can affirm that other churches have other gifts or a calling to do something different. Much of what we do has grown organically (in a vine-like way, I hope) out of our own size, resources and abilities. I might want to post warning signs about getting too cozy with powers and authorities, but I don't assume that other churches making policy pronouncements are necessarily in bed with Beliar.

It's hard to do a good job at being the church; it's difficult to make decisions for ourselves as individuals, much less a common life of people at different stages. One way to engage in respectful conversations is to recognize, with humility, that we might be wrong and others might be right (and so are called to learn a new way of virtue); or that we might be right and they might be wrong (and so are called to extend grace); or that we might both be right (and so can praise God for a divine gift of diversity). Of course, the most likely thing is that we are both wrong, but in different ways. So we need to throw ourselves on the grace of God, and the promises of God, and remember that "underneath are the everlasting arms."

First Congregational Church of Kalamazoo

Recently I was asked by a frustrated Christian how I might respond to the imprecation, "keep your damned politics out of my church." I asked her to allow me think on this, as it is something that I have wrestled with in my personal ministry but have rarely spoken about in a pastoral context. Comforted by the promises of Jesus Christ in Matthew 10:20 and Luke 12:12, I offered the following encouragement.

I riffed on the famous quip by German novelist Thomas Mann. I said, "Everything is politics. And nobody goes to church on Sunday to feel bad." On balance, these two counterweights have informed nearly every sermon I've ever preached and my efforts at encouraging fellow pilgrims to repair this broken world and build upon it the Kingdom of God.

I serve as the 29th senior pastor of a church that is nearly two centuries old. Our congregation is older than the city in which we reside. Kalamazoo is a marvelous town of roughly 80,000 inhabitants and we view our mission focus as a principally local concern. We are descendants of Puritan stock and take seriously Winthrop's words that we ought to establish ourselves as a "city upon a hill." Communalism is a deep-rooted theological constant among traditional Congregationalists. As Puritans, we are also thoroughly intolerant of sin. As we view sin through the biblical lens of the oppressive actions of "powers and principalities," it is incumbent upon us to use the capacity of our body (the Body of Christ) to confront, condemn and ultimately exorcize the demonic forces of systemic sin (racism, sexism, homophobia, ableism, etc.)

Historically, our church has sheltered refugees from every war involving U.S. military engagement since 1835. In the 1850s, we willfully and publicly violated the Fugitive Slave Act in order to provide cover, accommodations and supplies to Americans fleeing the state violence of chattel slavery. Sojourner Truth preached in our pulpit. Today, we manifest these core, theological values by advocating spiritually and materially for marriage equality, support for the immigrant and wanderer, ending the unnatural abomination of homelessness and providing radical hospitality in our current house of worship. Each of these issues stems from a biblical mandate.

To be absolutely clear, we are not liberals. We do not "celebrate" or "endorse" any political party. In our affiliated denomination, the United Church of Christ, you will often hear it said: "We aren't liberal. We're just early." Most, if not all, of the positions we stake on Scriptural grounds (i.e. the abolition of slavery, the ordination of women, persons of color and LGBTQ individuals, the enfranchisement of women, opposition to wars of aggression, marriage equality) typically become "common practice" in the greater church within a generation or two after adoption by our independent churches.

Our reasons for selectively taking church-wide positions on ministry are typically the culmination of a great deal of prayer, the study of God's Word and advice from the individuals directly affected by the issue. Recently, we voted to become a public sanctuary church and are now protecting a 63-year-old woman from deportation at the hands of the U.S. Immigration and Customs Enforcement (ICE). We share the use of our campus with over 130 different community justice, arts and support organizations and nearly 14,000 unique visitors passed through our doors last year. We have revitalized the traditional practice of hosting town hall meetings in congregational churches. **We share our building completely free of cost or expectation.** Our church's benevolence provides direct cash assistance to those in need, minus the red-tape of our bureaucratic government or the Kafkaesque process of "proving need" established by other social service agencies. We donated the use of our chapel to another church that was at risk of closing.

These and other actions are preceded by a need, a call for action, critical reflection on God's Word and typically conclude with a congregational vote.

Are these ministries "political" by nature? If we define political as, "having to do with a particular political party or party agenda," then the answer is, "no." If, on the other hand, we adopt a more traditional definition of politics as, "concerning public affairs and public well-being," then they are certainly political issues. Our concerns stem not from loyalty to some political party or figure—but rather from God's high expectations for the practicing Christian. I gave a sermon in which I channeled the words of a preacher I greatly admire, lightly admonishing a few parishioners (which led to some outrage): "Some of you are willing to knock on doors for

Bernie Sanders but you refuse to knock on doors for Jesus Christ—and this tells me a little bit about where you believe the real power in the universe resides." For all I know, in another century we may be lambasted as backward, conservative relics. Our so-called "liberal" identity is a manufactured product of a secular culture responding subjectively to a church tradition that predates modern liberalism by almost 300 years.

But what does this mean for parishioners who are frustrated or disagree with our common ministries? Our congregational votes are rarely unanimous. Congregationalists speak their mind and vote their conscience. By this measure, we are a remarkably healthy church. Our members know that if they stand and voice an opinion, no matter how unpopular, they will never be shunned or held to a separate standard than the dissenting majority. We are, after all, a body made of many members. While our church does enforce church discipline, our disciplinary procedures are reserved for abusive or criminal behaviors. We would never consider exercising church discipline to punish a member for a differing opinion— political or otherwise. Thankfully, God has provided us with the gift of worship and praise by which we can be made whole, regardless of our diversity of thought and behavior.

Every single Sunday morning is a celebration. Every Sunday morning is a little Easter. Every Sunday we rise with dawn and exalt our creator and the work accomplished through the empty tomb by our Risen Savior. On Sunday morning, it no longer matters where we reside on the political or economic spectrum ... The message from the pulpit may rage against the criminal injustices of sinful systems and oppressive regimes—but it is only all the more in order to rejoice over their coming collapse and the ultimate reign of God's shalom. There is nothing that we cannot accomplish through our faith in Jesus Christ and our fealty to the Bible.

I have received no small measure of impatient criticism from my peers within my denomination and elsewhere regarding our excessive, exuberant joy on Sunday morning ... We do the painful, critical work of understanding our role in powers and principalities six days a week. On Sunday, however, we rejoice without ceasing. Because, ultimately, nobody goes to church on Sunday morning to feel bad. And after a sufficient amount of suffering, even the most stalwart Christian would prefer to simply sleep in.

Our journey into the Word of God is going to naturally challenge our personal politics. You cannot get very far on the Jesus path without acknowledging God's preferential option for the poor ... When we begin and end in the very body of our Lord Jesus Christ, we can have a spiritual clarity that defies the raging world and all its many voices and turns, instead, to the still, soft voice of God and obediently follows wherever it leads.

We have no politics but the politics of Jesus Christ. Throughout the week we study, pray, meditate, interview, protest and converse over shared meals. Occasionally, we reach a conclusion. Regardless, on Sunday morning we rejoice, and rejoice, and rejoice always.

Office of Social Justice and Hunger Action of the Christian Reformed Church

Before presenting extended excerpts from Kris Van Engen's initial posting, it is important to describe a context that sets the work of the CRC Office of Social Justice and Hunger Action (OSJ) apart from the work of individual CRC churches (and their members).

As Kris indicated in a private communication,[81] the OSJ is not a stand-alone agency that takes its own initiatives. Rather, the OSJ seeks to assist churches, other CRC agencies and the CRC synod in their implementation of initiatives they have decided to undertake. In Kris' own words, "We [OSJ] really want our work to be an extension or added capacity to the *work that is already happening* through congregations and larger CRC agencies ... Our mandates from [the CRC] synod make those same connections, grounding their recommendations in the relief and development *work that is already happening* ... [which leaves] the OSJ more in the background of the broader efforts" (italics mine).

This collaborative work is guided by a number of foundational statements, the first few of which are CRC synodical statements that are, in Kris' words, "a call to be agents of change in the political realm."

---

81 Email received on July 19. 2018.

Our World Belongs to God Article 52

We obey God first; we respect the authorities that rule, for they are established by God: We pray for our rulers, and we work to influence governments—resisting them only when Christ and conscience demand.

Our World Belongs to God Article 53

We call on all governments to do public justice and to protect the rights and freedoms of individuals, groups and institutions so that each may do their tasks. We urge governments and pledge ourselves to safeguard children and the elderly from abuse and exploitation, to bring justice for the poor and oppressed, and to promote the freedom to speak, work, worship and associate. We call on our governments to work for peace and to restore just relationships.

Charge to Deacons, CRC Ordination Liturgy

Be prophetic critics of waste, injustice and selfishness in our society, and be sensitive counselors to the victims of such evils.

Heidelberg Catechism Q&A 107

Q. Is it enough then that we do not murder our neighbor in any such way?

A. No. By condemning envy, hatred and anger God wants us to love our neighbors as ourselves, to be patient, peace-loving, gentle, merciful and friendly towards them, to protect them from harm as much as we can and to do good even to our enemies.

A second level of foundational statements is found in the Mission Statement and Mandate that the CRC synod has given to the OSJ. The stated mission of the OSJ is that it "exists to lead and equip the CRC in carrying out its transforming mission to pursue God's justice and peace," as stated in its Denominational Mission/Vision Statement.

The Mandate given to the OSJ is quite detailed.[82] It states that, "The OSJ is mandated to encourage and assist the CRCNA (Christian Reformed Church in North America)—its leaders, agencies, institutions, and members—to better 'live justly, love mercy and walk humbly with God (Micah 6:8),'" focusing "primarily on the systemic causes of poverty, hunger and powerlessness, as well as those social injustices to which synod or the board of trustees (BOT) has directed it," including calls to "raise awareness and educate ... about issues of justice that relate to root causes of poverty, hunger, powerlessness and those social justice issues that synod or the BOT have identified as priorities" and to "raise the voice of the CRCNA in advocacy for and with those who suffer injustice, through action alerts to our members, participation in advocacy coalitions and public statements when appropriate."

The mandate then goes into great detail relative to "criteria" for "selecting justice issues" that should be addressed, which include addressing the questions: "Is this an issue or action that is important to the integrity, faith and life of our church and our society?" and, "Does this issue arise from a biblical theme?"

Within the context of these foundational statements, we now turn to extended excerpts from Kris' first posting, the most pivotal of which is his stating that the focus of the work of OSJ is "transformational advocacy."

> I wouldn't describe the OSJ's work as 'redeeming the political system' because politics isn't our focus but I would say we are seeking, along with CRC congregations and ministries, to be faithful actors within the system; especially when it comes to standing in solidarity with groups whose voices are being marginalized. Neighbors and members of the church have experienced oppression throughout her history in various forms and that marginalization continues to this day—so we advocate for change. Micah Challenge, of whom the CRC is a member organization defines transformational advocacy as, 'Challenging ourselves and leaders to change

---

82 www.crcna.org/sites/default/files/2011_agenda.pdf, 75-76.

attitudes, behaviors and policies that perpetuate injustice and deny God's will for all creation to flourish." Because the church is a body of people with so many backgrounds who have such a range of experiences of privilege and oppression, we are in a unique position to be examples of how to engage in the public square. Hopefully, our transformational advocacy work leads to systems of human flourishing and brings a value added of faithfully demonstrating the value of political engagement that amplifies voices from the margins.

As described in the following extended quotes, Kris provides four examples of such OSJ advocacy: Refugee protection from deportation, the Kimberly Accords, immigration reform and climate change.

Refugee protection from deportation

The pastor of the Highland Park Reformed Church in New Jersey came to the OSJ with a plea for assistance with the efforts of his church to help members of an Indonesian congregation who shared their building to avoid deportation. This prompted the OSJ to "coordinate hundreds of letters to Congress, urging legislation that would allow these Christians, who came to the U.S. fleering persecution, to gain legal permanent status in the United States." As indicated by Kris in the following extended account of the history of these collaborative efforts, they have not yielded a "permanent solution."

> Highland Park Reformed Church started sharing their building with an Indonesian congregation in the late 1990s—not for immigration sanctuary but as a shared space where both congregations could worship. Members of the Indonesian congregation had recently left their predominantly Muslim country at that time and arrived in the U.S. on tourist visas which were offered as means of quick escape from the danger they were in as members of a minority religion in their home country. Once in the U.S., they had a year to apply for permanent asylum but many say they were unaware of the necessity of that crucial step. Because they never adjusted their status, when their first

year ended they were living here illegally and the window for a chance at permanent legal status was officially closed.

Later in 2002, after the September 11 terrorist attacks, male foreign visitors, mostly from predominantly Muslim countries, were asked to register with a program called the National Security Entry-Exit Registration System (NSEERS). Since Indonesia was on the list, the men from this church consulted with their own pastor and the pastor of the Highland Park church and made the decision to come forward and be registered. They believed this could be an opportunity to repair their legal status but that didn't happen. Instead they found themselves on the radar of immigration enforcement. ICE raids were carried out and dozens of members of the church were deported. Leaders from both congregations met together to make a plan to try to find a way to stop the deportations.

They managed to work out an agreement with ICE to allow undocumented Indonesians with no criminal record to live and work in the community if they checked in regularly, but that was a temporary solution and within months the deportation raids started again. The only permanent solution would be an amendment to U.S. immigration law that would allow them to apply for asylum even though they were outside of the one year window. Without that change to the law, there could be temporary waivers and discretion by ICE to not prosecute certain cases, but they would still be a precarious situation without true legal status.

Attorneys from the church drafted sample legislation that their congressperson could introduce to the House of Representatives. The Highland Park pastor shared the story throughout the U.S. and brought more churches on board to join in doing advocacy and raising awareness about the situation. Church members, including followers of the OSJ, sent letters and set up meetings with their own members of Congress and dozens of representatives joined to cosponsor the legislation. Unfortunately, the legislation was never adopted and a permanent solution still hasn't been enacted, so the New Jersey church continues to show hospitality and to advocate for justice. The Highland Park congregation made a decision to stand with the Indonesian congregation and to this day they are continuing to share God's love by sharing both their building and their voices of influence.

The Kimberly Accords

The work of the OSJ on what became known as the "Kimberly Accords" originated when the staff of the Christian Reformed World Relief Committee (now known as World Renew) and Christian Reformed World Church Missions (now known as Resonate Global Mission) reported on the ways in which 15 years of their "integrated community development work in Sierra Leone" was being "destroyed."

In brief, these CRC agencies "were using the latest in community development theories and practice and they were seeing real results in terms of increased ag yields, increased savings for families to survive through lean years and decreasing rates of poverty and hunger." But that work was now being "destroyed," largely by "a corrupt global diamond marketing system ... that was fueling West African warlords' greed for money and power." It became clear that without stopping the illicit trade in diamonds there would be no peace, no development and no CRC church-planting in Sierra Leone.

In response, "missionaries who were once on the ground in Sierra Leone now placed themselves on the ground in Washington, D.C. They lobbied members of Congress and testified before committees." At this point in time, the newly formed OSJ stepped in to assist as one of its first advocacy projects: "Over the two-and-a-half year campaign to bring our governments to agreement on what was called 'The Kimberly Accords', the CRC [through the OSJ] repeatedly used its small but strategic influence to help. Several small groups of church members visited their local diamond stores to simply ask: 'Can you assure us that the diamonds you sell do not come from illicit sources? Are not 'blood diamonds'? How can you be sure? Visits like this soon turned the diamond industry into allies and our lone CRC congressman from western Michigan, Vern Ehlers, became a champion of the Kimberly Accords in the U.S. House of Representatives."

This advocacy work had a good outcome, but there is still much work to be done.

> Following implementation of the Kimberly Accords, the entire country of Sierra Leone experienced progress beyond what the CRC was originally able to accomplish in those individual communities where they had started working.

> ... the Kimberly Process is losing effectiveness due to lack of enforcement but the progress that was made cannot be undone. Sierra Leone and other countries like it had the time to institute their own internal controls on diamond mining. There is still work to do on other abused commodities, such as precious metals in the Congo, but if we are willing to learn from the lessons of our own short history we could use our influence to push back on the unchecked abuse of power by those who control these resources.

Comprehensive immigration reform

After noting that "The CRC has also made statements on specific biblical justice issues that intersect with the realm of politics" that "include the sanctity of human life, religious persecution, immigration and climate change," Kris describes the efforts of OSJ advocating for "comprehensive immigration reform."

> On the topic of immigration, synod directed the OSJ to create educational resources for churches and to advocate for comprehensive immigration reform. Even though immigration is a topic that makes headlines there tends to be a lack of awareness about how the immigration system works and what it takes to immigrate legally to the U.S. To overcome this lack of awareness the OSJ does immigration simulation workshops with interested congregations. The simulation gives participants the bio of an individual who

hopes to live and work permanently in the U.S. With their bio in hand the participants walk around the room to try to find a visa for which they could successfully apply. For everyone who hasn't had a lot of experience with our immigration system there are usually light-bulb moments. They discover the connections between the broken spots of our immigration system—like the fact that 70 percent of all U.S. farm workers do not have legal status—and how the system actually works, in this case how it is nearly impossible for a potential immigrant farm worker with a job offer in the U.S. to meet the requirements needed to earn a visa. This first step doesn't always result in a consensus on solutions but it does lead to more civil conversation and more respect for immigrants because people are speaking from the same set of facts.

Like any workshop that exposes a previously unknown crisis, participants then ask, 'What can I do about this?' The OSJ's response to that question goes back to the statement on immigration from synod and back to that deeper call to be a people who expose injustice. Along with faith-based coalitions like the Evangelical Immigration Table and Interfaith Immigration Coalition, we share resources to empower members of the CRC to advocate in the public square for immigration reform that keeps families together. There are strong opponents to calls for more humane immigration laws so progress is a challenge but every time we see significant reforms come close to clearing the final hurdle we also see our numbers grow. When we started working on immigration in late 2010 we did about 15 workshops in one year and advocacy alerts would get about 50-100 people sending a message to their congressperson. This year we've convened over 50 workshops, advocacy alerts have had over 1,000 participants and we've had several in-person meetings between CRC members and their elected officials.

Climate change

Relative to advocating for addressing problems caused by climate change, Kris notes that unlike the work of OSJ empowering CRC congregations, OSJ worked more directly with "individuals in congregations."

> Our climate change work takes a similar approach [as advocacy for comprehensive immigration reform] but engages more directly with individuals in congregations who are then empowered to set their own course for their church's activity. Individuals sign up to be part of a campaign called the Climate Witness Project (CWP). Then, when a congregation has three or more people signed up, regional organizers from CWP connect with those individuals to share resources and ideas based around four main pillars of the project: 1) worship, 2) education, 3) advocacy and 4) energy stewardship. We also send out a monthly newsletter with updates and we organize national level advocacy opportunities that all CWP members can get involved with on their own or as a church.

Kris presents an apt summary description of the nature of the OSJ "transformational advocacy" efforts as a much needed extension of the maxim "give a fish and eat for a day, teach to fish and eat for a lifetime," referring to "a third movement in the theory of giving a person a fish— give a fish and eat for a day, teach to fish and eat for a lifetime *unless there is no access to the pond*" (italics mine). OSJ advocates for the marginalized people in our society to have "access" to the opportunities and benefits that the rest of us have, as a matter of "justice."

Common Ground and Lessons Learned

The responses of Will, Nathan and Kris to the initial descriptions of their respective ministries reveal some significant common ground, along with a few disagreements, out of which some important insights emerged relative to the future of possible political initiatives on the part of churches and para-church organizations.

Different models for being church

Will expresses great appreciation for the ministry of its sister church in Kalamazoo, the First Congregational Church, noting that the size of a church affects the possible scope of ministry.

> ... First Congregational Church, in addition to its main sanctuary, has a sizable chapel. Their welcoming hearts extended to North Presbyterian, and North meets in their chapel, without charge. North has been able to continue to meet because of the generosity of First Congregational. Isn't that a bit amazing?
>
> I heartily admire their stance of welcome. "Welcome" appears on their church's home page eight times, and the link http://allwelcome.church/ leads you there ... I am delighted that they have decided to be a public sanctuary church and take in Saheeda Nadeem as part of that welcome, as we have welcomed immigrants into our own home/church.
>
> As the pastor of a small church, I am grateful that some churches have enough time, talent, buildings and money to put on larger events that we can participate in ...

Note that implicit in Will's expressions of appreciation for the ministries of Nathan's church is the recognition that different churches can have differing ministries. Will then refers back to his earlier assertion that his church has particular gifts, as a small church,[83] adding his appreciation that Nathan's church exercises differing gifts of a "progressive" nature.

> In my [first posting] ... I stated my belief that individual churches have different gifts, or charisms, and I believe it is First Congregational Church's charism to be a progressive Christian church, and I am glad they are who they are.

---

83 Recall Will saying that "even though we are a small church, we believe that God gives us the gifts that we need, as Paul writes in his first letter to the Corinthian Church (1 Corinthians 12:7 and *passim*). If this is true, then when we do not have a particular gift, it is at least likely that God has decided we don't quite need it yet. The charism of a small church is intimacy and a certain ease: we don't need to do everything; we lack time and resources."

Nathan returns the compliment, even going so far as to suggest that "small churches likely represent the future of churches in America."

> ... I have an immense amount of respect for small church ministry—I cut my teeth doing ministry in small group settings. I have found that the smaller the church, the more intense the relationships and the deeper the discipleship. It is incredibly challenging to get more than a handful of Congregationalists to agree on nearly anything. Small churches likely represent the future of the church in America and we ought to live into their example.

It is important to note that this mutual appreciation for the different ministries of the Kalamazoo Mennonite Fellowship and the First Congregational Church of Kalamazoo comports well with the teachings of 1 Corinthians 12 (as pointed out by Will; see footnote 83) that, in my own words, God's redemptive purposes are fostered by different Christians, and (Will and Nathan and I would add) different churches, exercising their particular gifts.

But Will and Nathan are not completely on the same page. Will suggests that the First Congregational Church may have some blind spots that reflect a lack of humility, adding reflections on two areas where they may not have "gotten everything just right."

> ... the claims [of Nathan] that 'we have no politics but the politics of Jesus Christ' and, 'We aren't liberal, we're just early' are a bit disingenuous. I would prefer them to acknowledge with a bit more humility what they are about. I don't know much about the history of First Congregational Church. It really is wonderful that they worked as abolitionists during the Civil War and invited Sojourner Truth to speak to the congregation. But any church with a history of nearly 200 years has closeted skeletons and the legacy of some of those problems. Even acknowledging that they were 'early' to the right position or stance implies there was a time when they were wrong. It's hubris to believe there they've gotten everything just right.

I will suggest two such areas where they might be wrong; they are just suggestions, and barely rise to the level of criticisms. First, are questions of what some Catholic theologians call a 'seamless garment' ethic of life, including the life of the unborn. Nothing in Nathan's essay, or the First Congregational Church's website, mention the unborn or abortion. Is it at least imaginable that, one day, First Congregational Church will look back and wonder why they did not care for 'the least of these.'

Second, I wonder whether we will look back and ask why progressive churches spent so much time on *identity politics* implied in Nathan's list of 'the demonic forces of systemic sin (racism, sexism, homophobia, ableism, etc.).' I don't really know what the reality at First Congregational Church is, but it takes up an inordinate amount of energy in some of the church circles I am in. Will there be some new insight that comes along which dethrones *power dynamics* as the central concern of the progressive church? I see Nathan's leadership in joyful worship as a possible hint.

Nathan essentially agrees with Will's expression of concern, adding a significant shortcoming of his church that Will didn't mention.

Will suggests that our congregation, despite her firsts, has likely missed the mark in her two centuries of Christian labor. I completely agree! I will give one absolutely glaring example. I am the 29th senior minister. I am a white man— as has been **every single** senior minister to come before me. This is a product of the biases of the congregation—because it is certainly not a product of a lack of qualified candidates who identify as women or persons of color.

But Nathan does "push back" a bit regarding Will's concern that the First Congregational Church is too involved in "identity politics," based on the teaching in Matthew 25: 40 that Christians should "identify" with "the least of these."

I do want to gently push back against Will's concern over our activity in 'identity politics.' Many in our congregation were created by God with identities that, like the Ethiopian eunuch, or the hemorrhaging woman or the Gerasene demoniac, are considered 'unclean,' or 'undesirable,' or, worse, 'criminal' by our larger society. Their identities can occasionally get them killed. So we view identity politics through the lens of Matthew 25:40.

The commonality that emerges from this exchange between Will and Nathan is that different churches can exercise differing gifts, but no church has it all right.

Both seeking justice and rejoicing without ceasing

Nathan poses an insightful and meddlesome question as to the relationship between "participating in church" and "living a Christian life."

A concern that I have for all churches (large and small) that is highlighted by the articles posted by my peers is as follows: What is the substantial difference between *participating in church* and *living a Christian life*? In other words, is church membership sufficient for transformational ministry or is it merely a supplement to following the Way of Jesus? Our identity as a Congregationalist church can become a hindrance when we selfishly fail to address the larger reality of the greater church in the world.

An exchange between Nathan and Will reveals that an enthusiastic point of agreement is that an either/or response to this question is inadequate; it is both/and. Recall first Nathan's observation that "we [members of the First Congregational Church] do the painful, critical work of understanding our role in powers and principalities six days a week. On Sunday, however, we rejoice without ceasing. Because, nobody goes to church on Sunday morning to feel bad."

Will heartedly applauds this both/and approach that allows for a "sense of joyful worship on Sunday in the midst of a politically engaged congregation," indicating that he will visit the First Congregational Church during a sabbatical to "rejoice with them … and learn from them."

Here's something I really do want to learn from First Congregational Church: that sense of joyful worship on Sunday in the midst of a politically engaged congregation. In fact, I'm taking a short sabbatical this summer, and I hope to join my sisters and brothers at First Congregational Church for worship, both to rejoice with them, but also to learn from them. There is so much dourness, depression and discouragement in our current moment, and in our past. It sounds refreshing to join in a large group of people in joyful worship. I want to learn more viscerally that 'nobody goes to church on Sunday morning to feel bad,' and what to do about that.

Nathan adds the cogent observation that following six days of laboring for justice with a day of "rejoicing without ceasing" challenges "underlying assumptions about where power really lies." Nathan sharply contrasts the "power" that emerges from "rejoicing without ceasing" with the attempts of "untrained pastors and celebrities attempting to seize power by 'othering' other Christians."

I conclude this section with an important word of caution from Kris related to a previous proposal in Chapter 4 that politics should be broadly defined to include forging a common life together in the midst of lack of agreement as to a common good.

I also appreciated Nathan's thoughts on the inescapableness of politics wherever we are, including in worship, combined with the idea that worship is a place where people are looking for healing and assurance and not a place to, as he said, feel bad about themselves. The challenge with this expectation, as Will and Nathan both mentioned in their own ways, is that if we are talking about healing and assurance at a surface level, my 'feeling good' might be in conflict with yours. Faith and politics intersect on the level of speaking for justice in a given moment, like in the case of the family separations, but they also intersect in the sense that the church's response will influence deeper value systems that will shape politics into the future—obviously sensing these shifts can be a source of discomfort.

My understanding of Kris' caution is that what makes me "feel good" during worship on Sunday morning may differ from what makes you "feel good," possibly in light of the results of our respective attempts to seek justice during the previous week. So be it! This suggests that a church might do well to schedule a time directly after a Sunday worship service to enable members to talk about possible connections of the sermon or homily with their attempts to promote justice during the other six days.

However, from my own hard-earned experiences with such post-sermon conversations at my home church in Iowa,[84] I extend a word of caution about such conversations. Great care must be taken to ensure that members reflect on the sermon or homily in light of their "Christian lenses" rather than in light of their "political lenses" as members of a particular political party. This caution warrants a few words of personal elaboration.

A "Christian lens" trumps a "political party lens"

Recall Will saying that, "I have been very wary of encouraging people to identify their political convictions with their Christian beliefs." I have found this problematic "equation" to be rampant. I am dismayed at how quickly discussions about public policy issues among Christians deteriorate into political posturing. This is not an abstract assertion. I have seen it happen in too many conversations in which I have been involved. The first knee-jerk response to a given public policy question too often is: "What does my political party say about that?" While I am a registered Democrat, that is not my first question. My first question is: "What does my understanding of the Christian faith say about that?"

The way Nathan expresses my concern is powerful: "If all theology is usurped by political posturing we've made a hash of a wonderful gift—namely, the living Bible." It is important here to return to Nathan's earlier response to the question as to whether the various "social justice" ministries of the First Congregational Church of Kalamazoo are "political."

If we define political as 'having to do with a particular political party or party agenda,' then the answer is, 'no.' If,

---

84 In an Adult Discipleship class offering at American Reformed Church (Iowa) titled "Text to Turf."

on the other hand, we adopt a more traditional definition of politics as, 'concerning public affairs and public well-being,' then they are certainly political issues. Our concerns stem not from loyalty to some political party or figure—but rather from God's high expectations for the practicing Christian.

I couldn't agree more. This points to the importance of Christians addressing public policy issues from their "Christian lenses," rather than from the lenses provided by a particular political party or politician.

Your pastor is a citizen, too

Although it may seen like a minor lesson to be learned, Will has something to teach all of us when, as reported above, he says that "on Facebook, on my personal page, I encouraged people to vote for Hillary Clinton, trying to *make it as clear as possible that I was not speaking for anyone but myself, and definitely not for our local fellowship*" (italics mine).

Will makes an extremely important distinction. When a church has decided not to take a church-wide position relative to a given public policy issue, it is obvious that the pastor should not present his position as that of his church. But your pastor wears many hats. He/she is not only your pastor. He/she is also a citizen of the United States. And in that role, your pastor should not be silenced, anymore that you should be silenced in your role as a citizen.

Jeff Sessions and Romans 13

Moving beyond the abstract nature of some of the above narrative, Will, Nathan and Kris have an interesting exchange regarding Attorney General Jeff Sessions' appeal to Romans 13 to justify the "zero tolerance" policy for immigrants at the border. Will starts the exchange by sharing a sermon he gave at his church, noting that this was an "unusual sermon" for him "in that it's a bit more 'political' (that is … responding to a political issue in the news) and much less exegetical (we usually follow the lectionary, and I usually preach from one of the lectionary passages)." In his sermon Will summarizes what has happened as a result of this "zero tolerance" policy as follows:

As attorney general, Brother Jeff has cracked down hard on what he sees as violations of immigration laws and policies. Most recently, he has led the effort to detain adults crossing into the United States without permission, and even the detainment of adults who are seeking asylum in the U.S. He's also come out strongly in favor of limiting which kinds of asylum seekers will even have their cases heard. The detainment of adults has meant that children who have come with those adults have been separated from their families. We have reliable news reports that over 2,000 children have been taken away from their parents in a recent six-week period, and this is ongoing. This happened to some extent even under the previous administration, but then, asylum seekers were allowed to remain in the community, with their children, while they awaited hearings. That policy has been derided by the current administration as 'catch and release,' and stricter, harsher policies put in place.

It is significant that Will identifies Mr. Sessions as "Brother Jeff." Will explains as follows:

> ... I call him 'brother' because he is my, our, brother in Christ. He is a member in good standing at the Ashland Place United Methodist Church in Mobile, Alabama. He professes to follow Jesus, and it's always been important to me to take, at least usually, people at their word.

As we'll soon be seen, Will believes that "Brother Jeff" is all wrong, especially in his interpretation of Romans 13. But being "wrong" about something cannot be equated with "not being a Christian." If that were the case, all of us who profess to be Christians would be in big trouble.

Will summarizes Brother Jeff's "simple argument" as follows:

> Brother Jeff justified the taking away of children from their parents by quoting the 'wise words' of the Apostle Paul in Romans 13 were that we should 'obey the government.' In Brother Jeff's mind, it seems to be a fairly simple argument: People should not seek to enter the United States illegally,

or perhaps even seek asylum here. We don't want 'em; and if they come, they'll suffer the consequences of being separated from their children. It's not our fault, but theirs. If they would just do the right and lawful thing, they would be OK. (The attorney general and the president blame the Democrats, for what it's worth.)

Suggesting that "there are so many things wrong with Brother Jeff's exegesis," Will focuses on his faulty interpretation of Romans 13.

… to think that Paul's 'wise words' are a statement to obey the government in all cases is ridiculous on its face. Paul is writing to the church in Rome, but it's important to remember that many of his letters were written from Rome, while under arrest from Rome. Even Paul didn't heed Paul's wise words. Which is to say, they can't mean what Brother Jeff claimed they mean. Elsewhere, Paul says we should try to live peaceably if we are able, and he and the other early Christians showed, by their example, the importance of disobedience at times. And, as we saw in the example of Jesus a few weeks ago, Jesus broke the law by 'working' on the Sabbath. Jesus said the Sabbath was made for humanity, not humanity for the Sabbath. And I think it's a good natural extension to say that laws and government are made for humanity, not humanity for laws and government.

As Will points out in no uncertain terms, the glaring error in Brother Jeff's interpretation of Romans 13 is to believe that this passage in Scripture exhorts Christians to "obey the government in all cases." To be sure, Romans 13 exhorts us to be obedient to a government that governs well. But Christians ultimately answer to a "higher law" than that imposed by their government and when the "laws of the land" violate the teachings of the Christian faith, Christians first have an obligation to seek to change those laws, and, in those rare cases where such changes are not made, Christians have an obligation to "disobey," accepting the consequences (the "civil disobedience" that Christians practiced during the civil rights movement in the 1960s is a recent example, but the history of God's dealings with humankind are replete with numerous other examples, including that most famous example of the biblical story of Daniel and the den of lions[85]).

In effect, what Will is asserting is that there is a question that is prior to the question of whether a government's policies are being obeyed. That prior question is whether "those policies ... are justified." In his own words, Christians must always ask whether a government's "policies and enforcement actions are justified."

> ... when Brother Jeff was asked to justify the government's actions, he did not justify the government's actions, but put the burden on immigrants to obey. He is the policy maker and policy enforcer. Even if it were the case that we should always obey the government (and, as we have seen, it is not), if one is in a position to set policy and set enforcement, the question really is to ask whether those policies and enforcement actions are justified. Brother Jeff, like us, seeks to serve a Lord who was wrongly crucified under cruel enforcement of government policy. Jesus was 'obedient unto death,' but woe to those who set the policies and enforced those policies that led to his death!

That Will believes the government's "zero tolerance" policy and its mode of implementation are "not justified" is obvious from the following five steps that he believes members of his congregation and his church can do in response (italics mine):

> One small thing we can do is to *simply state, as a church*, that we stand with immigrant parents and children, and against those who would tear them apart.
>
> Another set of things we can do is to contact our representatives in Congress, and the White House, and state our position to them. I have a sheet of paper to pass out with *steps you can take*, if you are interested.

---

85 For a compelling reflection on the story of Daniel, recorded in the Old Testament book of Daniel, see Brueggemann, *God, Neighbor, Empire*. Whereas King Darius promulgated "the law of the Medes and the Persians" that cannot be changed (Daniel 6:12), Daniel chooses to obey the "law of his God" (Daniel 6:5) as an expression of commitment to a "higher law," 108.

Thirdly, we might explore *taking some more steps, as a church*, to welcome and stand with immigrants. I have some ideas about that, such as contacting our friends at Bethany Christian Services and perhaps the local organization called *Movimiento Cosecha* to see what kind of monetary support might be useful to flow through them. If anyone has time and energy and a vision for this, please let me know.

We also can pray for the children and parents who have been caught in this terrible situation. And we should pray for our brother Jeff Sessions and for the president for a change of heart. Honestly, I don't have much faith in doing so (it's not even mustard-seed size), but we are called to do so anyway.

Finally, we can be a community of gratitude. Truly grateful people are protected, at least somewhat, from the despair of living in a terribly broken world. Truly grateful people can open themselves up in welcome to neighbors and strangers in need because they know they will be cared for. Truly grateful people provide an alternative to the fears of missing out, of being cheated, of not getting what we need.

It is important to note (from the italicized portions in the above quote) that Will is recommending **both** actions on the part of individual members of his church **and** actions to be taken "as a church," which does not appear to fit well with his earlier assertion that "I do not, and probably would not, encourage our little fellowship to take church-wide positions or initiatives" (more about that in my conclusion to this chapter).

In response to Will's reflections on Jeff Sessions and his interpretation of Romans 13 relative to the "zero tolerance" policy, Kris notes the contrary views of a number of "faith organizations."

Pastor Will wasn't the only person to take notice of Sessions' Romans 13 comment. The Franciscan Action Network along with the Interfaith Immigration Coalition also joined together to organize a statement with dozens of faith institutions signing on. Their statement, below, picks up on some of the same sentiments as Pastor Will:

Let us be clear; the administration's border enforcement tactics are, immoral, inhumane and unnecessary. It is an affront to religious faith that administration officials are using the Bible to rationalize and validate these immoral actions. As it was in the eras of slavery and legal segregation, this perverse misuse of sacred Scripture once again appears to be designed specifically to single out people of color.

Children should not be forcibly taken away from their parents; they and their parents should not be subject to inhumane conditions ... We are called to 'welcome the stranger' and to 'love our neighbors,' and as a nation of immigrants we should be ashamed. The Bible is unambiguous in the call to love God and love our neighbor as St. Paul's Letter to the Romans tells us: 'Love does no harm to a neighbor. Therefore love is the fulfillment of the law.' (Romans 13:10 New International Version, passim).

Nathan also notes the beliefs of a wide array of "Christian denominations" that the "zero tolerance" policy and its mode of implementation are not justified.

... the leadership of Christian denominations as diverse as the Roman Catholic Church, the Southern Baptist Convention, the Church of Jesus Christ of Latter-day Saints and my own beloved denomination, the United Church of Christ, have each independently released statements decrying the inhumane treatment of children on our southern border by the agents of the U.S. Immigration and Customs Enforcement.

Kris includes in his response an interesting and provocative suggestion that it is appropriate for people of faith, like Jeff Sessions, to play a role in debates about public policies.

... I especially appreciated the post in reference to Jeff Sessions' application of Romans 13 because it demonstrated the idea that faith institutions aren't merely inserting themselves into politics from the outside but elected officials themselves are often people of faith, acting on instincts handed down from prior generations. The Romans 13 citation from Sessions also highlighted that there is an expectation that Scripture and faith traditions have something to contribute to policy decisions and that they can play a role in shaping debates.

I concur, with the understanding that people of "all faiths, or none" should have a voice in such public debates, with the hope that such public conversations will help all conversation partners to sort out truth from error, including judgements as to the most adequate interpretations of relevant passages from various Holy Books.

Conclusion: Don't Box in the "Spirit of God"

Recall that in a previous section ("Different Models for Being Church"), I reported on an exchange between Will and Nathan which concluded that "different churches can exercise differing gifts, but no church has it all right."

But the exchange between Will, Nathan and Kris regarding "Jeff Sessions and Romans 13" also reveals that even for a given church (or para-church organization) there can be an evolution in the church's discernment as to the extent, if any, to which the church should take a church-wide position relative to a given public policy issue rather than just leaving that decision to individual members. Will hints as to the possibility of such "evolution" (my word, not his) when he says that "much of what we do [the Kalamazoo Mennonite Fellowship] has grown organically (in a vine-like way)." In fact, Will's postings point to such an "evolution" in his own thinking and the thinking of his congregation.

As noted previously, whereas Will originally indicated that "I do not, and probably would not encourage our little fellowship to take church-wide positions or initiatives," he is ready to make an exception in response to what he views as egregious governmental enforcement of a "zero tolerance" policy at the border. In his own words, "One small thing we can do is to *simply state, as a church,* that we stand with immigrant parents and children, and against those who would tear them apart" (italics mine—the word "probably" saves Will from contradiction).

The moral of the story is that not only may different churches be exercising differing gifts, but in the history of a given church, there may well be an evolution to the extent to which its members, and the church, "as a whole" discerns a calling to address perceived injustices, even by political means. "One-size-fits-all" is not an adequate way to think of political activism on the part of churches. And, my report on the work of the CRC Office of Social Justice and Hunger Action also reveals some "dynamic flexibility" as it decides when and how to contribute to the "work that is already happening through congregations and larger CRC agencies." In theological terms, there are no neat formulas for how the "Spirit of God" will lead.

It is fitting to conclude this chapter with Kris' observation that "how the church interacts in the political realm ... [is] extremely important."

> The learning that I'm taking away from this conversation is that our choices on how the church interacts in the political realm are extremely important because they have long consequences—both on people's freedom from injustice now and on who the church will be as a people of God in the future.

Steps Toward Reforming American Politics

HAVING JUST REREAD first drafts of all the preceding chapters, I have a feeling that the title I have chosen for this chapter promises much more than I can possibly deliver. But here goes anyway.

What follows is my proposal for a possible "Way Forward" that draws heavily on the insights of my 23 conversation partners while not embracing everything they say (since they have some significant disagreements in the midst of their agreements).

My proposal does not reflect any formal education in political science, since that is nil. But, in addition to drawing on the insights of my conversation partners, my proposal also reflects some hard-earned personal lessons I have learned in the local political trenches as I have worked over the past eight or so years as an advocate for comprehensive immigration reform as a member of CASA of Sioux County (Center for Assistance, Service and Advocacy).[86] I take full responsibility for the content of this chapter.

I organize my proposal in three sections: Current problems with politics in America; Christian values that could be the basis for addressing

---

86 The vision of CASA is for "transformed northwest Iowa communities that welcome, empower and celebrate people from all cultures." For more details, go to www.casasioux-county.org.

these problems; and some concrete suggestions for applying these Christian values toward reforming American politics.

Current Problems With American Politics

My conversation partners point to multiple problems with how we do politics in America.

Political rancor and the scourge of tribalism

In Chapter 1, Jeff VanDerWerff and Kim Van Es lay bare a number of problems with political discourse among Americans, including personal attacks that demonize persons who disagree (not only are they wrong, they are immoral/evil); blurred lines between news and commentary/opinion; redirection (changing the subject); no time, patience or interest in nuance and deliberation about complex issues (especially on social media); and confirmation bias (listening only to an echo of yourself).

It is confirmation bias that has the most destructive long-term effects because it feeds the tribalism that is increasing in American society, as explained forcefully and eloquently by Kevin den Dulk in Chapter 5. In my own words, here is the scourge of tribalism:

It is human nature to gravitate toward those who are like us. Where that tendency becomes very destructive in politics (and elsewhere) is when we will not give careful consideration to the views of those who disagree with us. We create an "us vs. them" mentality that effectively silences "them." (They are wrong, we are right, so why should we even listen to them?)

As Kevin points out, such tribalism, which he labels "affective polarization," reflects a deep emotional attachment to the in-group and a visceral reaction against the opposition—the out-group. In light of that emotional attachment, there is no incentive to have a conversation with "them" to discuss and evaluate whatever reasons each side may have for their contrary beliefs.

As Kevin has also noted, tribalism becomes extremely destructive when an unwarranted extrapolation is made from a belief that the other is "wrong" to a belief that the other is "untrustworthy, immoral and dangerously threatening."

Former Secretary of State Madeleine Albright paints the dangers of tribalism even more starkly—noting how it leads to "contempt" for the "other" that invites the power grab of a demagogue.

> At many levels, contempt has become a defining characteristic of American politics. It makes us unwilling to listen to what others say—unwilling, in some cases, even to allow them to speak. This stops the learning process cold and creates a ready-made audience for demagogues who know how to bring diverse groups of the aggrieved together in righteous opposition to everyone else.[87]

I have seen such tribalism in action in some of my failed attempts to get local residents together in the same room to talk about immigration issues. After a local newspaper published a letter to the editor that criticized our county sheriff for not honoring ICE detainers, I extended a county-wide invitation, via the local newspaper, for those on both sides of this issue to meet together to talk about their disagreements. A few persons who supported the sheriff's position accepted my invitation. No one who opposed the sheriff's position, including the persons who wrote the letter to the editor, was interested in talking.

Political inequality

In her exchange with Frank Hill on the role of money and special interests in politics, Kim Conger points us toward what I believe is an enormous problem with politics in America: political inequality.

Although denying or suppressing the right to vote for any citizen is an egregious sign of political inequality, the problem that Kim highlights is deeper than that. In Kim's words, the deep political inequality problem is that not everyone has an "equal stake" in the political system; majority voices too often rule out minority voices. Particularly problematic is the extent to which "campaign donations buy access and attention," which too easily leads to silencing the average voter (not to mention the marginalized members of our society).

In my own words, this deep problem is lack of an "even playing field" in which every American citizen, independent of his/her resources or status

---

87 Albright, *Fascism*, 235.

in society (majority or minority) is able to participate equally in the political process, well beyond voting, by being given a voice.

Structural problems

Our conversation partners point to numerous, seemingly intractable structural problems with American politics, a number of which contribute to the political inequality noted above.

One problem is the partisan gerrymandering of voting districts, which in the words of Angela Cowser, "fosters noncompetitive districts, deepens partisan divides and impoverishes civic conversation." Kevin den Dulk notes the pernicious way in which gerrymandering is related to tribalism: "The resulting seats are almost always 'safe' ... Because incumbents don't need to moderate their views to cast widely for votes, they are liberated to govern from one side of the polarized extremes."

Another significant structural problem is the practice of holding closed primaries, where voting is limited to registered party members who must declare their party affiliation. What happens in practice, whether intended or not, is that such closed primaries tend to attract extremists in both parties, thereby excluding more moderate voices.

An element that is common to both of these structural problems is a "hollowing out of the middle" caused by favoring the extreme elements of both parties, thereby contributing to the political inequality of an uneven playing field.

Two of our conversation partners point to what may be even deeper structural problems in politics. Jim Skillen suggests that the very Constitution of the United States is problematic in that "it was built on the presumed priority of state government and states' 'rights,'" thereby not adequately recognizing that "the United States has become a national polity and is no longer merely a coalition of state polities."

Jim also sees a problem with the very nature of "electoral representation," arguing for some type of "proportional representation" where seats in the House of Representatives are allocated according to the proportion of votes each party receives statewide rather than by means of winner-takes-all district elections. Kevin den Dulk expresses sympathy for this approach, suggesting that it would have the benefit of "opening the door wider to more [political] parties," although he views the possibility of such a radical structural reform as "quite dim."

The politics of Donald Trump

By my choice of leading questions, I carefully avoided making my eCircle a referendum on the presidency of Donald Trump. A few of my conversation partners did slip in a few criticisms of Trump, but that was not a prominent feature of any of their postings.

However, in my personal reflections in this chapter, I need to state, and explain, my strong belief that the manner in which Donald Trump carries out his presidential responsibilities is a major problem with American politics and is antithetical to the Christian faith.

The context for my concern about the presidency of Donald Trump is that I am an evangelical Christian[88] who is not among the 80-plus percent of evangelicals who voted for Trump in 2016. Before presenting my reasons for not supporting President Trump, it is important to note that it is not possible to create a simple cause and effect relationship between the words and actions of President Trump and the present dysfunction in American politics. It has reasonably been argued that the manner in which President Trump is exercising his presidential powers has emerged from the political dysfunction that predates his candidacy; he is not the cause of that dysfunction. To whatever extent that is true, however, I believe that his words and actions, as both candidate and president, have significantly added to that existing dysfunction and are antithetical to my understanding of the Christian faith in at least the following five ways (for each of which I will pose a question for his consideration and for consideration by his evangelical supporters).

Self-giving service to others: It is not my business to pass judgment on President Trump's motives and intentions. They are known only to God. But from the outside looking in, it appears to me that President Trump is fixated on what is good for him. And when he seeks to do something that he perceives to be good for others (e.g., tax cuts), he does so within the context of the hyper-individualism that is prevalent in American culture. How is this consistent with the teaching of Jesus that greatness lies in

88 My understanding of my commitment to being an "evangelical" differs radically from views held by many other self-proclaimed evangelicals and, especially, the distorted views propagated by the media. See Heie, *American Evangelicalism*, 1-20.

self-giving service for others (Matthew 23:11), which calls a Christian to move beyond what is good for me to care for and help others?

Truthfulness: It is indisputable that President Trump has often said things that are untrue. To give just one recent example, after appointing Matthew Whitaker as acting attorney general after the firing of Jeff Sessions, President Trump went on the record to say that he "did not know Whitaker." Yet a few months earlier, he publicly stated that he "knew Whitaker." Obviously, one of these two statements is untrue. How is this consistent with the indisputable fact that truthfulness is a Christian value,[89] as specifically stated in the biblical exhortation to "speak the truth in love" (Ephesians 4:15)? Not only does President Trump often fail to "speak the truth," but when he speaks, there is little evidence that he does so "in love," as noted in my next concern.

Respect and love for those who disagree: My area of concern that is most pertinent to the content of this book is with the manner in which President Trump talks at or about those who disagree with him. He typically demonizes and vilifies them, showing very little, if any, respect and love. How is this consistent with the neighbor-love taught by Jesus; not only love for those who disagree with us, but even for those we consider to be our enemies (Matthew 5:44)?

Overcoming evil with good: I address this concern primarily to those evangelicals who are supporters of President Trump. I have often heard it said that many evangelicals are willing to overlook things that President Trump says and does that they agree are antithetical to the Christian faith (like the three concerns that I express above) because of the "good" that may eventually emerge (e.g., the appointment of conservative Supreme Court justices who may eventually help to overturn *Roe vs. Wade*).

Although Kevin den Dulk has reported that some recent research suggests that the "subset of white evangelical voters" who voted for President Trump for this reason "was quite small" (the more significant reason being "polarization"), it is important to point out that the problem with this reason is that, even if one believes that a "good end" will result, that does not justify an "evil means." As Nigel Biggar has pointed out, Christians should

---

89 I personally find President Trump's failure to adhere to the Christian value of "truthfulness" to be particularly problematic since in my long career as a teacher and administrator at Christian institutions of higher education, the "quest for truth" has been my primary goal.

"not resort to evil means of combating evil."[90] How does support for Donald Trump comport with the clear biblical teaching, which I grant sounds outrageously unrealistic, that "evil is to be overcome with good" (Romans 12: 21)?

I insert my own personal response to this meddlesome question by repeating what I asserted in Chapter 6.

> I dare to believe that God does not condone seeking to accomplish goals that are congruent with the Christian faith by "means" that are antithetical to the Christian faith.

Another perspective on the fallacy of thinking that an evil means is justified by a good end is related to the Apostle Paul's listing of the "fruit of the spirit" as "love, joy, peace, patience, kindness, generosity, faithfulness, gentleness and self-control" (Galatians 5:22-23). Paul is **not** suggesting that these Christian virtues are normative for followers of Jesus *except* in cases where their violation can accomplish a good end. Christians are called to give expression to the "fruit of the spirit" at all times and in all places.

Real power is love: Bob Woodward quotes presidential candidate Donald Trump as saying "real power is … fear."[91]

After outbreaks of political violence, like the October 2018 murder of 11 Jewish worshippers in Pittsburg, President Trump tells American citizens that our country needs to be "united." But I believe it is accurate and fair to say that in his unscripted comments, especially at campaign rallies, his overarching political strategy is to gain support for his ambitions by "dividing" us[92] and his primary tactic for creating such division is to sow "fear."

Of course, there are legitimate fears. I fear the current assault by President Trump on the checks and balances that our founders had the wisdom to build into our Constitution. But I do not fear those many persons from Central America who, as I write these words, are marching through Mexico, fleeing violence in their home countries and hoping to find asylum in America.

---

90 Biggar, *Behaving in Public*, 40.
91 Woodward, *Fear*, Epigraph.
92 Jon Meacham asserts that "Trump is determined to be a force for division, not unity" in his essay, "When Leadership Fails." *Time*, November 12, 2018.

Therefore, Christians need to distinguish between fears that are founded in commitment to underlying Christian values (more about that later) and fears that feed on a rejection of such Christian values.

But the question I pose to those evangelicals who are supporters of President Trump is even more meddlesome. How does one reconcile President Trump's claim that "real power is fear" with the clear biblical teaching that "there is no fear in love, but perfect love casts out fear" (1 John 4:18)? As outrageous as it may sound to the modern ear, "real power is love."

Christians as part of the problem

I must frankly say that I am utterly dismayed at the extent to which so many who claim to be followers of Jesus contribute, and even exacerbate a number of the problems with American politics that are enumerated above. Three areas of complicity come to mind.

Political rancor and tribalism: Many Christians have gleefully joined the chorus of nastiness in political discourse, demonizing their political opponents and exhibiting extreme forms of us vs. them political tribalism. (We Christians are right; the rest of you are wrong.) As Jeff VanDerWerff says about those Christians who consider themselves to be evangelicals: "Evangelicals seem to have let the world press them into its mold of political practice."

Political inequality: Based on my experience with local political advocacy, complicity in this area is more subtle. Many Christians give lip service to everyone having a voice in the political process. But, my local experience suggests that few proactive initiatives are taken by Christians to help everyone to have a voice in the political process or to "speak out" on behalf of those who have little nor no voice.[93]

For example, in my local advocacy work on behalf of our immigrant neighbors, I find that very few Christians go out of their way to talk *with* their immigrant neighbors, but rather just talk *about* them. Until we (and our local politicians) listen carefully to their stories of pain and anguish as they strive to help their families flourish in an environment that is

---

93 That Christians should "speak out" for "those who have little or no voice in the political process is suggested by Proverbs 31:8-9: "Speak out for those who cannot speak, for the rights of all the destitute. Speak out, judge righteously, defend the rights of the poor and needy."

generally indifferent or hostile, we have not provided them with political equality.

Support for Donald Trump: I am dismayed at the high percentage of evangelical Christians who supported candidate Trump and now support President Trump. As I hinted at above, I can understand that level of support on the part of some evangelicals because the "ends" that President Trump is seeking to accomplish line up with their Christian beliefs (even though many of them admit to not being comfortable with the "means" he employs).

But, as I have already indicated, the crucial question then is whether what is perceived as a good end justifies any means toward accomplishing that end, even means that are acknowledged to be antithetical to the Christian faith. I have already suggested that the clear, yet seemingly impractical, biblical teaching that evil cannot be overcome with another evil—evil can only be overcome with good—precludes resorting to means that are antithetical to the Christian faith. Since that seems to be an outlandish suggestion in our broken political world, I will return to it later.

Why this complicity of many Christians with these current problems with American politics? In addition to my suggestion that this complicity reflects the mistaken notion that any means can be justified by a hoped-for good end, my local experience suggests that this complicity is fueled by first looking at issues from the lens of a particular political party rather than from a "Christian lens."

Substituting a political party lens for a Christian lens

I had a painful experience when I tried to facilitate a conversation in an adult discipleship class at my church devoted to seeking a "Christian perspective" on current issues dominating the news headlines. Sparing you all the gory details, it didn't take long for the conversation to become "politicized." It quickly became obvious that for many attendees, their response to the given issue was primarily informed by "what my political party [my tribe] says about the issue."

With all due respect, I had to tell the attendees that I was not asking what their political parties said about the issue; I was asking them to share what they believed the Christian faith had to say about the issue. In other words, I was asking them to trade in their "political party lenses" for their

"Christian lenses." Given the current political environment, that is a challenging thing to ask for in any group of Christians, especially since many Christians spend a lot more time viewing a single cable TV channel that echoes the views of their political party than spending time reflecting on the implications of biblical teachings for public policy issues.

Jeff VanDerWerff's way of encouraging us to put on our "Christian lenses" when considering public policy issues is to emphasize that our "ultimate loyalty" to the "Kingdom of God" must take precedence over our "loyalty to a political party."

So, what is an appropriate "Christian lens" for looking at the current problems with American politics enumerated above? I will now seek to respond to that question by focusing on my understanding of certain non-negotiable "Christian values."[94]

Underlying Christian Values

There are a number of "Christian values" that have the potential to inform concrete steps that Christians can take to address the many current problems with politics in America. A number of these values are "virtues" that Christians have embraced throughout history, at least in their rhetoric.

Love

No Christian I have ever met denies that Jesus has called all who claim to be his followers to love their neighbors (Mark 12:31). So far, so good. But there is considerable disagreement, even among my conversation partners, as to how to give expression to such neighbor-love.

My respectful conversation projects focus on one oft-neglected expression of neighbor-love. The premise behind my eCircles, and much of my work over many years, is very uncomplicated and easy to state. (It isn't rocket science, at least to state; it is much harder than rocket science to do.)

Providing someone who disagrees with you a safe and welcoming space to express that disagreement and then to talk respectfully about your disagreements is a deep expression of love.

---

94 Recognizing that a number of these values are shared by other religious traditions and some secular traditions.

A corollary of this premise is: **You don't love someone whom you have silenced.**

Humility

Even though I am somewhat of a political news junkie, I have very few recollections of a politician or staunch supporter of a particular public policy position saying: "I may be wrong."

As human beings, the particularities of our social locations inform our views on public policy. The position taken by someone who disagrees with me may be deeply informed by particularities, such as gender, socioeconomic status, race, sexual orientation and elements of personal biography, which may enable this person to see things that I miss. Likewise, my particularities may enable me to see things that this person misses. And since we are both finite and fallible human beings, we cannot claim that either of our partial glimpses captures the full truth on the matter, as only fully understood by God. In addition, I can be blinded when I succumb to the temptation to sin by thinking, "It's all about me and those who agree with me." As Scripture teaches, we all "see through a glass darkly" (1 Corinthians 13:12).

It is hubris—a gross failure to exemplify an appropriate attitude of humility—for me to assume that I have a God's eye view of the truth about a given public policy issue. It takes genuine humility for me to express my beliefs with clarity and conviction while acknowledging that "I may be wrong." The ideal of humility that I aspire to can be summarized as *my acknowledgement that however strongly I hold to my beliefs and express them with deep conviction (and, yes, even with deep emotion and passion), I may be wrong.*

Note that such humility does not mean being wishy-washy about your beliefs. Rather, it involves you holding in tension that very rare combination of embracing and expressing your beliefs with clarity and deep conviction at the same time that you publicly acknowledge that you may be wrong.

Both Ian Barbour and Richard Mouw have given eloquent expression to the nature of this rare combination. In his book *Myths, Models and Paradigms*,[95] Barbour proposes the following definition of "religious maturity":

---

95 Barbour, *Myths, Models and Paradigms*, 136.

It is by no means easy to hold beliefs for which you would be willing to die, and yet to remain open to new insights. But it is precisely such a combination of commitment and inquiry that constitutes religious maturity.

In his splendid book *Uncommon Decency*,[96] Richard Mouw draws on Martin Marty in highlighting the importance of "civility" in living out this rare combination of commitment and inquiry, calling for a "convicted civility":

> One of the real problems in modern life is that the people who are good at being civil often lack strong convictions and people who have strong convictions often lack civility ... We need to find a way of combining a civil outlook with a 'passionate intensity' about our convictions. The real challenge is to come up with a *convicted civility*.

Openness to the beliefs of others without commitment to your own beliefs too easily leads to sheer relativism. (I have my beliefs, you have yours, end of conversation.) Commitment to your own beliefs without openness to listening to and respectfully discussing the beliefs of others too easily leads to fanaticism, even terrorism. (As C. S. Lewis has observed, to which past and recent world events tragically testify, "Those who are readiest to die for a cause may easily become those who are readiest to kill for it.")[97] *One of the most pressing needs in our world today, is for all human beings, whatever their religious or secular faith commitments, to embrace, and hold in tension, both commitment and openness; giving living expression to "convicted civility."*

Courage

One of my invitees to be a conversation partner for my previous eCircle on human sexuality declined my invitation, explaining that if he went public with his views on same-sex marriage, he would be "painting a bull's-eye on his back." Sometimes we need the courage to paint bull's-eyes on our backs.

---

96 Mouw, *Uncommon Decency*, 12.
97 Lewis, *Reflections*, 28.

A precondition for actualizing a respectful conversation about signifi-cant disagreements is the virtue of courage—the willingness to "speak out" my understanding of the truth relative to the issue at hand—even if nega-tive consequences result from my doing so.

Exemplifications of courage are often missing in the political realm. Too often, politicians do not express their deepest convictions for fear of what their constituents will think, and the possibility that they may be punished for such honesty on the next election day—a symptom of the inordinate focus on winning in politics.

I have personally witnessed such lack of courage in face-to-face con-versations I have had with some local elected officials as I have advocated for the well-being of my immigrant neighbors, documented or undocu-mented. A specific example involves my advocacy for Iowa state legislation for temporary drivers' licenses for all immigrants, which, in my estimation is a win-win-win situation (good for public safety, employers and immi-grant families). The response of one member of the Iowa legislature in a face-to-face meeting was, in effect, that he agreed with the need for such legislation and would support it if it were proposed by others (jumping on a bandwagon), but it would be too politically risky for him to take the initiative to propose such legislation.

Relative to the August 2017 tragedy in Charlottesville, I am not in a position to know or to pass judgment on the motives of others. But I encourage politicians who have remained silent about President Trump's equivocation regarding the moral culpability of the protestors and anti-protestors at Charlottesville to examine their motives. Is it possible that such deafening silence reflects a failure in courage?

Respect

Are there not limits to the extent to which we should respect others? Should I respect those white supremacists, neo-fascists and members of the KKK who marched in Charlottesville chanting "Jews will not replace us"? It depends on what you mean by "respect."

As reported in Chapter 2, I embrace the distinction that Stephen Darwall has made between two kinds of respect.[98] *Appraisal respect* is a positive evaluation of somebody's achievements or virtues. *Recognition*

---

98 Darwall, "Two Kinds of Respect," 36-49.

respect is elicited by the worth someone has simply because he/she is a person, independent of his/her achievements or virtues. As Clarke Cochran said in his reflections on "human dignity": "All persons are created in the image and likeness of God and thus have a fundamental dignity that can never be forfeited."

In my own words, all persons are of worth, deserving "recognition respect," because they are "beloved by God" and have been created in the image of God, however distorted that image has become. Therefore, I recognize the worth of those who practiced bigotry while marching in Charlottesville at the same time that I believe that their beliefs and actions are deplorable (not granting them "appraisal respect"). And that means that I would be willing to engage them in respectful conversation about our disagreements, if they so desire.

Truth

When you dig all the way down, it is my quest for truth that is the foundational reason for my passion for seeking to orchestrate respectful conversations among people who have strong disagreements—in the political realm and elsewhere.

This passion has emerged from a continuous integrative thread in my life since my early teaching days: my insatiable search for truth at the cognitive level and my aspiration to live out that truth one day at a time.[99]

The ultimate authority to which I am committed is not to be found in the pronouncements of church leaders, the pope or anyone else, or to the interpretations of Scripture and doctrines of any particular Christian tradition or denomination, for no person or Christian tradition/denomination has a corner on God's truth.

Rather, my ultimate authority is the truth as God fully knows it. *The fact that I am not God presents a considerable challenge.* Since I only have a partial glimpse of the truth, at best, it is important for me to engage with love, humility, courage and respect in conversations with those whose glimpses differ from mine, so that, together in conversation, we can gain better approximations to that truth.

I have received some pushback along the way because of my unswerving commitment to seeking the truth. When I announced my eCircle on

99 For a marvelous story about the importance of "putting in good minutes, one at a time" rather than focusing on an unknown future, see Pirsig, *Zen*.

human sexuality, I became suspect in the eyes of some Christians in high places. The fact that I would give a voice to those who questioned the traditional view of marriage was a cause for suspicion.

In my conversations with some of my critics, I noticed a strange omission. As has been my practice for many years in talking to others about what I perceive should and should not be done (like in my days advising undergraduate students when I was a teacher), I always try to dig down beneath the surface of decisions that need to be made to identify the underlying values that ought to inform those decisions (as I am trying to do in this chapter). In my conversations with those who criticized my human sexuality eCircle, it soon became apparent that we were motivated by a different set of values. All I heard was talk of values like "acceptance" or "affirmation" by others in Christendom or the larger culture, and concern about how "supporters of our work" might withdraw their support if they found out that "we were even talking about such things." Not once did I hear the word "truth" spoken. Nor do I recall any mention of the Christian virtues of love, humility, courage and respect.

Because of misunderstandings that have arisen in some of my conversations with others who are as committed as I am, if not more so, with orchestrating respectful conversations among Christians who disagree strongly about some contentious issues, I need to make clear my understanding of the relationship between facilitating such respectful conversations and the quest for better approximations to the truth.

Some of my friends who share my vision for facilitating respectful conversations are concerned that if you prematurely focus on disagreements about the truth relative to the issue at hand, your conversation will quickly reach a dead-end. You first need to help conversation partners to develop loving relationships characterized by mutual understanding, respect and trust for each other as brothers and sisters in Christ. I agree 100 percent, as will soon become apparent. But to say that this foundational work must be done first, does not preclude the need, eventually, to get to difficult questions as to which beliefs about the issue at hand are true and which are false.[100]

100 Matthew Kaemingk presents an excellent practical example of the importance of starting with the development of personal relationships of mutual understanding and trust in his book *Christian Hospitality*, when he reports on a sewing group in Rotterdam (the Netherlands) composed of Christian and Muslim women. As one Christian participant reported, "When you get to know them, you get to see that they are not that different

Shalom, community and freedom

I consider this triad of Christian values together because of their close interconnections. As will soon be seen, it is with respect to these three values that I find the greatest disconnect between the hyper-individualism that pervades American culture and a communitarian Christian call to care for the well-being of others.

Shalom: As indicated in Chapter 5, It is important that the Hebrew word "shalom" not be confused with the common negative western definition of "peace" as the absence of conflict or war. In Hebrew, the word "shalom" means much more: a robust positive view of "peace" as living in positive, caring relationships with others—including those who disagree with you—and with all of Creation.

But before proceeding to this broad view of shalom, it is important to dwell a bit on the negative aspect of shalom as the absence of conflict. A pressing question is whether this aspect of shalom precludes the use of violence.

Recall that, as recorded in Chapter 2, Gregory Williams and I had differing responses to that question. I agreed wholeheartedly with Greg that "Christian love requires that I actively seek to foster the flourishing of poor, marginalized and oppressed peoples." But where Greg and I disagreed was relative to the means for such activities.

Dwelling on the need to address injustices perpetrated against "workers" by some "owners" in our capitalist economy, Greg proposed that violence may be necessary, in the form of "occupations," "blockades" and "sabotage." Where I disagreed is that I view such means as crossing the line into violent behavior. I have no problem with resistance to injustice in the workplace provided that the means of resistance to injustice are nonviolent—with my position on this heavily influenced by the profound example of Martin Luther King Jr. on the necessity and efficacy of nonviolent resistance to injustice.

---

from you and me" (240). As Kaemingk concludes, "Achieving what no government program could, this little sewing group is producing a rare social phenomenon in Dutch civil society—inter-ethnic, interfaith friendship and affection" (240). In my own words, "questions of truth can come later." But, my point is that this foundation of "friendship and affection" can facilitate eventually dealing with important questions about truth.

But whatever position you take on whether nonviolence should be a norm for all Christians at all times,[101] it is the positive aspect of shalom that I believe has the most profound implications for how Christians should do politics, a subtopic to which I now turn.

Community: A central element of the positive aspect of shalom calls for Christians to live in positive caring relationships with others. As I indicated in Chapter 5, this means that when considering a particular public policy issue, my first inclination is to ask, "What is good for the 'communities' of which I am a part?" rather than, "What is good for me or other atomistic individuals?"

To ask such a question is surely swimming upstream in American culture, which is too often characterized by a hyper-individualism that too often focuses exclusively on, "What is good for me and mine?"

Among our conversation partners Clarke Cochran in his position on health care issues, is most emphatic on the need for Christians to embrace a "communitarian social ethic" that seeks for a "common good" (e.g., adequate health care for all). To get more specific, that is why I personally support the "individual mandate" that was part of "Obamacare," which would require the cohort of healthy young Americans to purchase health insurance that they may not need to enable older, less healthy citizens to have the insurance coverage they need. That the individual mandate has been scuttled under President Trump is consistent with the reigning hyper-individualism that pervades American culture.

Freedom: To suggest that Christians should take steps to foster the well-being of others appears, on the surface, to violate the cherished American value of "freedom." But that is only the case if you assume that your freedom should be unbounded[102]; you should be free to do as you please.

---

101 Recall my acknowledgement in a footnote in Chapter 2 that full consideration of nonviolence as a possible norm for all Christians is too complex to deal with in this book (taking us into the controversial question as to whether Christians should ever participate in war); although I did cite Chapter 21 (Tragedy, Just War and Peacemaking) in my book *Learning to Listen, Ready to Talk*, where I address this thorny issue.

102 In reaction to the legalistic nature of my Christian upbringing, where the ethical preoccupation was on a long list of "dos and don'ts," a question that I have struggled with for many years is: "What is the relationship between law and liberty in a Christian ethic?" The "integrative thread" that has emerged in my response to that question is that Christian living (and even the doing of mathematics) should be guided by the concept of "freedom within bounds." For elaboration, see my essay, "Mathematics: Freedom Within Bounds," 206-230. I call this an "integrative thread" because it reflects my major attempt to make "connections" between my biblical/theological understanding and one of the

Although the reflections of some of our conversation partners seem to be perilously close to such a radical view of the meaning of freedom, I believe that such a view is antithetical to a biblical understanding of what freedom means.

My understanding of the biblical view of freedom is stated most succinctly and eloquently by the Apostle Paul in Galatians 5:13:

> For you were called to freedom, brothers and sisters; only do not use your freedom as an opportunity for self-indulgence, but through love become slaves of one another. For the whole law is summed up in a single commandment, 'You shall love your neighbor as yourself' (New Revised Standard Version).

I leave to biblical scholars the question as to the adequacy of this NRSV translation. The alternative translation that I find more helpful is the New International Version (NIV): "You, my brothers or sisters, were called to be free. But do not use your freedom to indulge the flesh; rather, *serve one another humbly in love*" (italics mine).

Whatever translation may be best, the core message is clear and simple (to say, if not to do). Christians are called to exercise their freedom in ways that contribute to the well-being of others.

Justice

The Christian value that was most prominent in the many postings for this eCircle was "justice." But that raised some challenges because not every conversation partner was using that word in the same way. Robert McFarland noted this challenge most directly in his conversation with Matthew Soerens regarding immigration when he noted that Matthew was assuming that the meaning of the word justice was agreed upon, when, in Robert's view, "justice is itself a disputed concept" (more about that later relative to the immigration issue).

So, to clear out some underbrush, it is first necessary to note various aspects of the multifaceted concept of "justice."

At a very general level, "justice" means to treat everyone "fairly," or to give everyone his/her "due." But, as will soon be seen, there is much room

---

academic disciplines—mathematics (the search for such "connections" being a core component of the meaning of "integration of faith and learning" that I believe is the most fundamental distinctive of Christian higher education).

for disagreement as to what is fair or what a person is due in a given situation. To complicate things further, there are multiple dimensions to justice, three of which were appealed to in some way by one or more of our conversation partners.[103]

Retributive justice: Punishment for a wrongful act that is proportional to the magnitude of the offense.

Distributive justice: Fair distribution of goods to all members of society.

Justice for different organizations: Allowing for both government and non-governmental entities/organizations to exercise what they take to be their responsibilities.

There are differing views as to how three forms of justice are to be implemented. For example, punishment for the violation of the laws of government as an expression of retributive justice can too easily be viewed as a transaction involving only the offender and government. My own more expansive view of retributive justice is deeply informed by the restorative justice movement,[104] which, committed to the Christian value of shalom, has a strong focus on rehabilitation of the offender in the context of attempts to restore positive relationships between the offender and the victim as well as healing the harm done within the communities in which the offender and victim are embedded (more about that later).

Relative to the postings of my conversation partners, the following three views were either explicitly or implicitly taken relative to what is "fair" in implementing the distributive justice principle.

Distribution according to "merit": It is fair for you to receive the goods that are due to you because you have earned them by something meritorious that you have done.

Equal distribution of "opportunity": It is fair for everyone to have the same opportunity to obtain the goods of society, although the results of such equal opportunity may differ from person to person.

---

103 One facet of justice that was not addressed by our conversation partners is "commutative justice," which involves protecting the "rights" of two individuals or organizations in a transaction, as in the expectation that both parties in a contract will honor that contract.

104 Much of the pioneering work for the restorative justice movement was done by Mennonite scholar Howard Zehr. See Zehr, *Changing Lenses* and *The Little Book*. My daughter-in-law, Tammy Krause Heie, served as a teaching assistant for professor Zehr at Eastern Mennonite University.

Distribution that promotes "human flourishing for all": Some goods are so necessary for human flourishing (e.g., adequate health care) that it is fair for these goods to be provided for everyone, independent of circumstances.

How do I sort through these disagreements about the nature of distributive justice in light of my understanding of biblical teachings? I believe there are elements of truth in all three views. But, I believe that both testaments of the Bible point to Christians having a special obligation to foster human flourishing for all, with emphasis on helping the poor, marginalized and oppressed members of society to flourish. Consider the following teachings from the prophet Isaiah and Jesus:

> Is not this the fast that I [God] choose; to loose the bonds of injustice, to undo the thongs of the yoke, to let the oppressed go free, and to break every yoke? Is it not to share your bread with the hungry, and bring the homeless poor into your house; when you see the naked, to cover them, and not to hide from your own kin? (Isaiah 58:6-7)

> Then [in the Judgment of the Nations at the End Times] the King [Christ] will say to those at his right hand, 'Come, you that are blessed by my Father, inherit the kingdom prepared for you from the foundation of the world; for I was hungry and you gave me food, I was thirsty and you gave me something to drink, I was a stranger and you welcomed me, I was naked and you gave me clothing, I was sick and you took care of me, I was in prison and you visited me' (Matthew 25:34-36).

As will be seen in the next major section of this chapter, when I seek to apply the Christian principles enumerated in this section toward a reformation of American politics, one central aspect of this emphasis on fostering the human flourishing of the "least of these" (Matthew 25:40) is that, "All relevant voices must be included in political discourse, especially those marginalized populations that have been systematically excluded from conversations that could have a significant effect on their well-being."

The next major section will also reveal the problems that can arise when a binary choice is forced between the retributive and distributive dimensions of justice for the immigration issue.

Patience and hope

I save these two Christian values for last because they are the basis for my response to those evangelicals who support Donald Trump and believe that the ends he pursues comport with Christian beliefs, even if they acknowledge (as many do) that the means he has chosen to pursue those ends are antithetical to the Christian faith.

To set a context for the importance of patience and hope, I reiterate something I said in Chapter 2: "I can imagine some of my readers rolling on the floor laughing: 'Harold, you are living in la-la land; totally out of touch with political reality.'" It is hopelessly naïve to think that a significant number of politicians and their supporters will soon be embracing the Christian values that I have enumerated in their engagement with political opponents. Commitment to such values is in short supply, even among those, like Christians, who pay them considerable lip service.

I acknowledge the force of this objection. But I have not hosted my current eCircle on politics because I envision being successful in changing how Americans do politics. I embarked on this eCircle because I aspire to be faithful to my understanding of how followers of Jesus are called to lovingly and respectfully engage those who disagree with them in politics (and all other areas of public discourse).

However, I do have this wild dream, that I can only envision through the eyes of faith, that if my eCircle models respectful conversation in an effective manner and readers see that it can even lead to some good public policy positions, they will sit up and take notice and give it a try (continuing the conversation). But I say that knowing that there is a fine line between faith and stupidity and I am not always sure on which side of that line I am walking.

Throughout my life, I have been driven by dreams that seem impossible. What has sustained me is the parable of the mustard seed told by Jesus, as recorded in Matthew 13:31-32:

> The kingdom of heaven is like a mustard seed that someone took and sowed in his field; it is the smallest of seeds, but

when it is grown it is the greatest of shrubs and becomes a tree, so that the birds of the air come and make nests in its branches.

In ways that far exceed my limited understanding, the "Kingdom of God" inaugurated by Jesus "is here but not yet." In our broken world, we see only faint intimations of the eventual fullness of the Kingdom of God to come, something like the early morning sunrise provides a hint of the full noonday sunshine to come. In the meantime, I am called to plant tiny seeds of redemption, entrusting the harvest to God. Therefore, it is only through the eyes of faith that I can envision my trying to live well in the political realm bearing any redemptive fruit.

But what does all of that have to do with **patience** and **hope**? A great deal. James Calvin Davis helped me to see that in my reading of his marvelous book *Forbearance*.[105]

For starters, Davis says that, "Perhaps a sufficient definition of patience might be 'waiting for the fulfillment of God's purposes for ourselves, the church and the world, without complaint or *destructive reaction in the meantime*'" (italics mine).[106]

I submit for your consideration the possibility that those evangelical Christians who support Donald Trump are condoning destructive actions (actions antithetical to the Christian faith), which reflects a lack of patience with God, who will work out redemption of our world "in time" and in ways that comport with the Christian faith.

Of course, that remains a hope that imagines a different future; a hope that can only be envisioned through the eyes of faith. In the meantime, all of us needs to respectfully engage one another about our disagreements. Davis beautifully captures the nature of this "patient hope" as follows: "Patient hope invites us to give our differences the gift of time."[107]

My call for patience and hope should not be misinterpreted as a call for passivity. God's redemptive activities do not preclude human agency. Followers of Jesus are called to partner with God in fostering God's redemptive purposes. Therefore, Christians who embrace some of President Trump's

---

105 Davis, *Forbearance*. The Christian values/virtues for dealing with disagreements within the Christian church that Davis elaborates in this book significantly overlap with the Christian values that I enumerate in this chapter..
106 Ibid., 48.
107 Ibid., 64.

ends, such as reducing or eliminating abortions or appointing more conservative judges to the Supreme Court, should give voice to those beliefs
in the public square. Where I draw the line, however, is that their advocacy
should not include means that are antithetical to the Christian faith, such
as insulting and demonizing those who disagree with them. Rather, they
should engage those who disagree with them in respectful conversations
as a deep expression of love.

Applying Christian Values to American Politics: A Way Forward

In the midst of many disagreements among my conversation partners regarding the complexities of American politics and how Christians
should navigate this minefield, I have been able to discern some practical
advice on how Christians can plant tiny seeds of redemption as a "Way
Forward" within the political process. The advice I give will include proposals for three primary strategies for how Christians and others can take
initial steps toward reforming American politics.

My sharing this advice will read like I am preaching to you, the reader.
Be assured that I am preaching to myself, since despite my aspirations, I
often fall far short of the advice I now give.

Do politics everywhere but don't politicize

Thanks to the insights of Gregory Williams, a new Christian friend I
have never met, I now embrace a broad definition of politics as not only
a quest for a common good but also as "the attempt to forge a flourishing
life together in the midst of lack of agreement about a common good."

This means that you are doing politics whenever you are seeking to
foster a flourishing life together with others—whether in your home, your
church, your school, your community, your place of employment; or in
the executive, legislative or judicial branches of local, state or national
government.

But as you do politics everywhere, don't "politicize." Whatever the issue
at hand. Don't start with a "political party lens," promoting the position

that your political party embraces or the positions taken by the pundits on your favorite cable TV news channel.

Start rather with your "Christian lens," seeking to discern how a follower of Jesus should view the issue, starting with your understanding of foundational Christian values.

Dig down deep to your Christian values

I have always tried to avoid making decisions based on what others will think,[108] or what is likely to gain me acceptance or accolades in the broader culture, which has made life challenging for me at times. I have always aspired to be clear about the Christian values that I embrace and I have sought to make decisions based on those value commitments.

As Angela Cowser has cogently pointed out, there is no consensus among Christians as to any list of "Christian values." I have laid bare my commitment to the bedrock values enumerated in the previous section. You need to do the same, and when doing politics, wherever, you should put on that "Christian lens" as you seek to shape your position on the issue at hand.

Develop personal relationships of mutual understanding

The **first primary strategy** that I propose for Christians and others to take initial steps toward reforming American politics is: **You must develop personal relationships of mutual understanding by listening to and talking with those who disagree with you.** This strategy is the centerpiece of most of my work in recent years, especially in my hosting of three major eCircles on my website.[109] It follows from what I believe is an oft-neglected dimension of the Christian virtue of love that all Christians embrace, at least in words.

As I have said, the premise underlying all my eCircles is that providing someone who disagrees with you a safe and welcoming space to express that disagreement and then to talk respectfully about your disagreements is a deep expression of love.

---

108 Using the distinction that David Riesman made between being "inner-directed" or "other-directed," I am inner-directed to a fault. See Riesman, *The Lonely Crowd*.
109 For my elaboration on this advice that emerged from my eCircle on "human sexuality," see Heie, *Respectful LGBT Conversations*, 279-282.

I have said what follows in many different ways on my website, in previous books, earlier in Chapter 2 and in this current chapter. I don't know how many different ways I can say it. But, since this is so important, here goes once again.

A person who disagrees with you about any given issue is not coming from nowhere. She has what she considers to be good reasons for her beliefs, reasons that are deeply informed by her particular story, which includes the elements of her biography, such as the religious or secular tradition in which she was brought up or is now embedded, as well other elements of her social location, such as gender, race, sexual orientation and socioeconomic status. And she has fears and hopes reflecting her story that you need to listen to.

It is a marvelous and rare gift of love to let her know that you want to hear her story and listen carefully to her reasons for her beliefs and her fears and hopes. Such careful empathetic listening, before you do any talking, will break down barriers and will be the first steps toward developing a personal relationship of mutual understanding that will make ongoing conversations possible, as friends rather than as adversaries. It is amazing how much your views of other persons and their beliefs can change when you get to know them.

In a meeting I attended, Richard Mouw gave some excellent practical advice as to how to initially respond to someone who expresses a point of view with which you disagree: Rather than starting with, "I disagree with you"; start with, "Help me to understand what you are saying."

Move from understanding to trust

When you get to know the person who disagrees with you sufficiently to build a relationship of mutual understanding, you have taken a significant step toward building trust. You may discover that while you still disagree, the other person also has good intentions and your belief that he/she is "wrong" does not mean that he/she is evil or immoral. You will begin to breach the walls built by an us vs. them tribal mentality. You will begin to see that "they" may even have some good ideas that you can incorporate into your thinking (much more about that later).

Convene respectful conversations and expect civility

Persons who have strong disagreements can develop personal relationships of mutual understanding only if they are willing to talk to one another. Such conversations can take place electronically or face-to-face.

My eCircle on "Reforming Political Discourse" reported on in this book was an electronic conversation. Although readers of my website will have to judge, I believe it is fair to say that my 23 conversation partners modeled respectful conversation to an admirable degree. But that result didn't emerge "by chance."

Before being accepted as a conversation partner, each invitee had to agree to provide a welcoming space for respectful conversation by aspiring to the following ideals:

- I will try to listen well, providing each person with a welcoming space to express his/her perspective on the issue at hand.
- I will seek to empathetically understand the reasons another person has for his/her perspective.
- I will express my perspective and my reasons for holding that perspective, with commitment and conviction, but with a noncoercive style that invites conversation with a person who disagrees with me.
- In my conversation with a person who disagrees with me, I will explore whether we can find some common ground that can further the conversation. But, if we cannot find common ground, I will conclude that "we can only agree to disagree"; yet I will do so in a way that demonstrates respect for the other and concern for his/her well-being and does not foreclose the possibility of future conversations.
- In aspiring to these ideals for conversation, I will also aspire to be characterized by humility, courage, patience and love.

Since I view the providing of such a "welcoming space for respectful conversation" as a deep expression of love, and I view the above ideals for conversation as the essence of "civility," this approach to my eCircle is my expression of the position taken by both Mark Douglas and Tony Carnes (as reported in Chapter 3): that Christians should promote both civility and neighbor-love.

So, my recommendation to the Christian reader is that, in your sphere of influence, you seek to orchestrate respectful conversations among those who disagree with one another about contentious political issues, whether electronically or face-to-face, as a deep expression of the neighbor-love to which Jesus has called you, and that when you do so, you make clear up-front the ideals for civil discourse by which you expect all participants to abide.

But a discerning reader may ask, "Is not the 'imposition' of such guidelines for civil discourse a violation of 'freedom of speech'?" No! I will seek to elaborate, drawing on the reflections of Mark Douglas reported in Chapter 3.

First, recall my suggestion earlier in this chapter that the biblical teaching on "freedom" is that freedom is not license to do as you please. "Freedom" has boundaries. Christians should not exercise their freedom in ways that are destructive of Christian values. And, as Mark Douglas has pointed out, this means that "free speech" must be "restrained" to "avoid violence"; to "avoid silencing critics"; and to "avoid tribalism." Mark elaborates by proposing that speech can be "restricted or prohibited" when persons wish to use "speech" in one of the following ways:

- Where speech is used to incite, encourage or valorize violence.
- Where speech is used to end conversations, to silence critics, to shut down unpopular positions, to harm through deception or to reject diversity of voices.
- Where speech is used to categorize people, to generalize and then demean people, to reject and then to dehumanize people.

Therefore, as you convene respectful conversations about contentious issues as expressions of love, dare to state at the very beginning your expectations for how you will talk to one another, indicating, graciously but firmly, that those not willing to abide by these ideals may be happier if they spend their time doing something else.

I close this section with a few words of advice to those readers who accept my challenge to convene respectful local face-to-face conversations about contentious issues, political or otherwise. This advice flows, in part,

from two failed attempts on my part to orchestrate face-to-face conversations about some contentious issues in my local community of Sioux
County, Iowa.[110] *Don't try to recruit local conversation partners by placing
blanket impersonal invitations in local venues, like newspapers or church
bulletins. Rather, take a "personal approach," working through a local network of friends to identify two persons, one on each side of the controversial
issue, who may be willing to participate in such a face-to-face conversation.
Extend those two individual personal invitations—also asking them to identify a few others who share their perspectives—to whom you and they can
also extend personal invitations. All of these invitations should make clear
the expectation that accepting the invitation entails an agreement to aspire
to abide by my "ideals for conversation."*

I came by this bit of advice the hard way. In Sioux County, reported to
be the second most politically conservative county in America, I found
that those local residents with "liberal leanings" are much more anxious
to talk than those with more "conservative leanings." So, if you want a reasonable balance between "liberal" and "conservative" participants in your
face-to-face conversation, which you should strive for, it is best to enlist
one member in each "camp" to collaborate with you in extending personal
invitations to those who agree with them.

*If you serve as the moderator of such a face-to-face conversation, strive
to be impartial, facilitating a conversation between those who have strong
disagreements, without appealing to your position on the issue at hand.*

I am encouraged by comments from a few readers of one or more of
the four books that have emerged from my eCircles that my reports on the
conversations between two partners who have strong disagreements have
not revealed a bias on my part for either position (despite the fact that I
do personally hold to a particular position). That has seemed to work well
in my attempts to orchestrate electronic conversations. The same attempt
must be made when facilitating face-to-face conversations.

As of this writing, I have successfully recruited eight local residents to
discuss the topic "President Trump and Visions for America." My eight
conversation partners are equally divided between those who would classify themselves as "general" supporters of President Trump and those who

---

110 For elaboration, see the Musing on my website: http://www.respectfulconversation.
net entitled "Pivoting From Respectful Electronic Conversations (eCircles) to Face-to-
Face Conversations: A Big New Challenge."

would classify themselves as "general" non-supporters. (I use the word "general" to indicate that many will take a position that is more nuanced than "all for" or "all against.") In recruiting my eight participants, I followed my first bit of advice above. I will serve as the moderator for this conversation, which will begin in April 2019, during which I will work as hard at following my second bit of advice as I did for my eCircles.

Reach across the aisle (or table) seeking both/and positions

One of the pernicious results of tribalism is the view that my tribe has the truth, the whole truth and nothing but the truth about the issue at hand. And "they" are wrong about all of it. This tendency is rampant in the tribalism exhibited by extremists in both major political parties. What is typically missing is any attempt to identify elements of truth embraced by politicians and their supporters on both sides of the aisle or table and, where these elements are in tension, to forge an appropriate "balance."[111]

The most powerful way to overcome the scourge of political tribalism, albeit the most difficult to implement, is to reach across the aisle or table to respectfully listen to and talk with those who disagree with you, toward the goal of reaching a both/and position.

To avoid misunderstanding, I need to clarify the nature of this both/and goal. It is **not** to eliminate all disagreements about the issue at hand. That will generally be impossible. Rather, the goal is to find enough areas of agreement to forge a coherent position that captures the best insights of those on both sides of the aisle or table, even if neither side receives the "full loaf" they were hoping for.

To go beyond such abstract talk about this both/and goal, I note the concrete marvelous example of the conversation on immigration between Robert McFarland and Matthew Soerens, as reported in Chapter 7.

---

111 This need for forging a "balance" between differing political views on both sides of the aisle was a major theme that emerged from my first significant foray into political discourse; my first eCircle project on the topic "An Alternative Political Conversation," which led to my book *Evangelicals on Public Policy Issues*. The examples presented in that book included seeking appropriate balances for the following policy areas: Gun control—balancing the need to address mental health and culture of violence issues with some commonsense gun control measures; Health care—balancing the need to provide health care for those not having adequate health insurance with the need to reduce the spiraling costs of health care. Federal budget—balancing the need for cuts in certain expenditures with the need for increased revenues. For a summary of these and other examples, see pp. 139-142.

Both Robert and Matthew appealed to the "concept of justice," albeit focusing on two different dimensions of that "contested concept." Jeff focused on the retributive dimension of justice; arguing that those immigrants who have entered the country illegally ought to be punished. Matthew focused on the distributive dimension of justice, arguing that undocumented immigrants ought to be provided a pathway to citizenship.

At first, there appeared to be an impasse. But Matthew overcame that apparent impasse by proposing a both/and solution that provides a pathway to citizenship while also punishing those who have entered the country illegally by means of appropriate fines, rather than the draconian punishment of deportation that is tearing apart many Latino families.

Robert found Matthew's proposal to be "reasonable," adding that this is a "better proposal than outright amnesty." (Matthew's proposal does not call for "amnesty" since it includes punishment in the form of fines.)[112]

So, in only three brief electronic exchanges, Robert and Matthew, despite a bumpy start because of differing views as to the appropriate focus of justice, arrived at what appears to be a both/and solution that both find to be "reasonable"(at least reasonable enough to be the basis for ongoing conversation, keeping in mind my hope that the all-too-brief postings on my eCircle will be just the beginning of an ongoing conversation).

Now this progress toward an acceptable both/and position occurred because Robert and Matthew were willing to respectfully listen to and talk to each other about their agreements and disagreements regarding immigration. Contrast that with what happened in the halls of the U.S. Congress in 2013.

In 2013 a bipartisan "gang of eight" senators collaborated to forge a comprehensive immigration reform bill (the Border Security, Economic Opportunity, and Immigration Modernization Act of 2013) that reflected

112 My own view is that Matthew's proposal is much more than "reasonable"; it is "essential." To defend this assertion would take me too far afield. Suffice it to say here that his proposal "begins" to wed both the distributive dimension of justice (by providing a pathway to citizenship for undocumented immigrants) and my "restorative justice" slant on the retributive dimension of justice (see footnote 104). I say "begins to wed" these two dimensions of justice because more needs to be added to Matthew's proposal in light of the "restorative justice" focus on restoring positive relationships among all persons and communities affected by immigration without appropriate documentation. For example, in addition to suitable fines for undocumented immigrants accompanied by a pathway to citizenship, steps must be taken to foster the flourishing of those on a pathway to citizenship and to build positive relationships between the immigrant community and their Anglo neighbors.

the best thinking of representatives of both major parties. It included both improved border security and an arduous pathway to citizenship that includes the imposition of fines for having entered the country illegally (like Matthew's proposal). The Senate passed this bill by a vote of 68-32.

This comprehensive immigration reform bill was not considered by the House of Representatives. While the reasons for the House not acting on this bill were complex and multifaceted, I can't help but wonder whether the House would also have approved this bill, or a variation thereof, if they too had formed a bipartisan group of representatives to talk about the possible contours of a comprehensive bill that would be found acceptable on both sides of the aisle.

The willingness of Robert and Matthew to seek a both/and position on immigration reform inspires my **second primary strategy** for Christians and others to take initial steps toward reforming American politics: **In your political activities, always seek for a both/and position relative to any public policy issue that reflects a balanced synthesis of the best insights of those who have disagreements, and encourage political representatives on both sides of the aisle to do likewise.**

Note the sequence and synergy between this second primary strategy and my first proposed primary strategy of "developing personal relationships of mutual understanding by listening to and talking with those who disagree with you." It is by first building a foundation of mutual understanding by careful listening and talking that you open up the possibility of these conversations leading to balanced both/and positions agreeable to all.

In addition to my elaboration above as to how the conversation between Robert and Matthew exemplified the quest for a both/and position, it is important for me to point out that a number of the other conversations in my eCircle also modeled the search for both/and solutions to current contentious problems, rather than the either/or solutions (it's my way or the highway) typically embraced by us vs. them tribal extremists in both major political parties.

Poverty in America: As an economist, Steve McMullen focuses on systemic problems that contribute to poverty, like recent technological developments rewarding those with certain skills and levels of education, which replaces workers with less education.

In an apparent contrast, Christian ethicist Kelly Johnson focuses on the failures of Christian churches to seek to alleviate the poverty of some of their members, proposing concrete means for doing so.

However, as both Steve and Kelly acknowledge, it doesn't have to be either/or. The best insights of Christian economists and ethicists can be integrated to forge a both/and comprehensive approach to addressing poverty.

Freedom and political equality: In the conversation between Frank Hill and Kim Conger about the role of money and special interests in politics, Frank focuses on the freedom accorded to political actors as an expression of the free speech guaranteed under the U.S. Constitution, which leads him and his political organization to view political equality in terms of an equal right to vote.

Kim views political equality in terms of an equal ability for everyone to participate in the political process beyond voting, with special emphasis on giving a voice to the poor and marginalized members of American society who cannot contribute much to the coffers of those who run for political office. In this view, the freedom of well-resourced political actors may need to be restricted to ensure the political participation of those with negligible resources.

Yet again, why take an either/or position? An adequate view of freedom requires appropriate restraints that prevent you from just doing as you please. There is room for forging a both/and position that creates an appropriate balance between highly valued—but not unbounded—freedom, and enabling all members of society to participate equally in the political process.

Limits to civil discourse and free speech: In the conversation between Mark Douglas and Tony Carnes as to whether there are limits to civil discourse and free speech, Mark argues that free speech should be restricted, or prohibited if necessary, to avoid violence, to avoid silencing critics, and to avoid demeaning or dehumanizing people

Tony argues that neighbor-love demands more than negative restraints on free speech; it calls for proactive initiatives as exemplified by the parable of the Good Samaritan told by Jesus. Mark agrees, leading to another both/and position: An expansive view of the type of neighbor-love that will promote civil society requires both appropriate restraints on your freedom of speech and positive expressions of love for those who disagree with you, including your enemies.

Governmental and non-governmental political activity: In the conversation between Harry Boyte and Jim Skillen on the relationship between governmental political activity (the work of the executive, legislative and judicial branches of local, state and national government) and political activity on the part of non-governmental entities (such as churches, schools, businesses and voluntary social organizations), Harry argues that "first priority" should be given to political activity on the part of non-governmental actors.

Jim agrees with Harry about the importance of political activity on the part of non-governmental actors, but doesn't prioritize such activity over direct political activism at the governmental level. Despite the considerable challenges that Jim enumerates for doing politics at the governmental level, Jim argues for strong involvement on the part of Christians in governmental politics as part of a both/and strategy.

Why do I report these many examples of where my conversation partners were able to find both/and positions? Because they give compelling support to the main point I wish to make in this book:

> *Building relationships of mutual understanding by listening well and talking respectfully about initial disagreements has the potential to bridge apparently irreconcilable differences. Please go and do likewise!*

But, again, that is easier said than done. I conclude this section with a report on the local challenges I have faced in trying to reach across the aisle or table seeking both/and positions.

My intentions have been good. In my local political activities, I always seek for a both/and synthesis when I can get people who disagree into the same room, and I start my conversations with others by first listening well to develop personal relationships of mutual understanding (as per my first proposed strategy) that will lay the foundation for continuing conversations.

However, as I have already reported, I have had trouble getting persons who disagree about contentious issues into the same room.[113] (Maybe I

---

113 It was also a challenge to recruit my 23 conversation partners for this eCircle on my website. I extended about 110 invitations before I obtained my full cohort of partners.

need to change my deodorant.) I believe this difficulty primarily reflects the scourge of tribalism.

In my local community, I am considered to be a "Liberal." That puts me in the category of "one of them" in a county that, I am told, is the second most "politically conservative" county in all of America. So, whereas some of my Liberal friends are happy to talk (we used to meet in a phone booth, but we can now fill an entire room), my "Conservative" neighbors don't rush to accept my invitations.

But my difficulty in getting local people who disagree about contentious public policy issues in the same room is a "Sunday school picnic" compared to the apparently insurmountable obstacles to getting elected politicians to talk respectfully about their disagreements toward the goal of seeking both/and solutions to societal problems (even when they are forced to be in the same room).[114]

There is no easy way to overcome these obstacles at the level of governmental politics. These obstacles reflect the deep structural problems with our political system that I have already noted (e.g., gerrymandering and closed primaries) that contribute to a "hollowing out of the middle," which gives inordinate voice to the extremists in both major parties.

So, the only further advice I can give relative to that portion of my second primary strategy dealing with governmental political activity is to encourage you to persist in encouraging your elected political representatives to listen carefully and respectfully to the views of those on the other side of the aisle in the quest for both/and solutions, at the same time that you endorse and support more middle-of-the-road candidates for office. If there is any political endeavor where the Christian values of patience (and persistence) and hope are needed, that is it.

---

114 I finalized this paragraph two days before that eventful day when the Judiciary Committee of the U.S. Senate interviewed Christine Blasey Ford and Judge Brett Kavanaugh. An amazing thing that happened a day later is that Republican Sen. Jeff Flake and Democratic Sen. Chris Coons, who had to be in the same room, left that room, motivated by their friendship, to try to reach a compromise agreement to delay a full Senate vote on the confirmation of Judge Kavanaugh as a justice of the U.S. Supreme Court for one week, to give time for an FBI investigation of professor Ford's allegations. As Sen. Coons reported that evening in a CNN interview with Chris Cuomo, Sen. Flake said the following to him: "We have to do something to show that we [Republicans and Democrats on the committee] can hear each other." I can think of no more powerful example of the need for politicians to genuinely "listen" to each other as they sort through their disagreements. For my further reflections on this momentous event, see my Musing on my website: http://www.respectfulconversation.net entitled "Friendship Trumps Tribalism."

As testified to by the length of this section, it is fair for the reader to conclude that I see little hope for reforming American politics until politicians reach across the aisle to seek both/and policy decisions that reflect the best thinking of both parties. I conclude this section with words of support for my conclusion from an unexpected source—Jared Kushner—offered in an unlikely place—a White House staff meeting.

As reported by Bob Woodward,[115] in a White House staff meeting held on July 20, 2017 that was devoted to immigration issues, Stephen Miller presented a "shopping list of issues," saying that "we need to select the winning issues ... the ones that are bad for the Democrats." As reported by Woodward, the following exchange ensued:

> Kushner strongly disagreed with Miller's strategy. We need to focus on bipartisan, constructive things, and even find things we could give the Democrats ... 'a few of our priorities, a couple of theirs.' He wanted 'a path forward so we can actually get something done.'

> [Reince] Priebus disagreed with Kushner. 'I know the Hill, I know what's going to be good in terms of these messaging votes.' A real estate developer from New York City like Jared didn't know much about politics.

> Jared protested. 'I know how to get things done and be constructive and take people with disagreements and get them in the same place.'

Hope for the future of American politics lies with the views expressed by Jared Kushner, not with the views expressed by Stephen Miller and Reince Priebus.

Help the poor, voiceless and marginalized to flourish

I am very attracted to Catholic social teachings, especially the "preferential option for the poor." Granted there are multiple dimensions to the meaning of justice, all of which are important. It is my judgment that at this particular time in history, Christians need to take special initiatives to promote a view of distributive justice that seeks flourishing for all who

115 Woodward, *Fear*, 217-218.

are poor as well as others who are marginalized in society and voiceless in governmental politics. The tendency for the "haves" to marginalize or ignore the "have nots" has never been greater in my lifetime in America and many other parts of the world.

So, I encourage all who claim to be followers of Jesus to pay special attention to his teachings in Matthew 25.

In that dimension of political activity carried out by government at the local, state and national levels, commitment to the teachings of Jesus in Matthew 25 demands adherence to a view of political equality that goes beyond an equal right to vote—as important as that is.

As was cogently argued by Kim Conger, an adequate view of the meaning of political equality is that all citizens have an "equal stake" in the political system; the voices of the marginalized should not be drowned out or ignored in the political process. Politicians should not be making legislative decisions without first seeking input from those who will be most affected by their decisions.

I have seen the painful results of my Latino neighbors being rendered voiceless in the political process in northwest Iowa. In meetings I have attended featuring Rep. Steve King and Sen. Charles Grassley, when immigration issues have arisen, none of my Latino neighbor were there to tell their stories.

It was at a meeting in my home church a number of years ago that I heard the heartbreaking story told by a Latino mother of how her daughter would cry before going to school every morning because of her fear that when she returned in the afternoon, her mommy would not be there because she had been taken away for deportation. Would Rep. King think twice about his toxic demeaning of his Latino constituents if he took the time to get to know them by listening to their stories?

This suggests that whatever initiatives you take to advocate with your elected political representatives, you should include advocacy for them to talk with their constituents who will be significantly affected by their legislative decisions, especially those who have been marginalized and have little or no voice in the governmental political process.

Not all Christians will have the opportunity to engage in conversations in the governmental sector of politics. But in our churches and other community organizations, whenever a topic is broached that has implications for the well-being of others, especially those who are marginalized and voiceless, take steps to ensure that they are invited to the table. Believe me, making such a suggestion will not always be welcomed with open arms. But it is the right thing to do.

Focus on the importance of "community"

Your efforts to help the poor, voiceless and marginalized members of society to flourish and to play a significant role in the governmental political process are a deep expression of the importance of "community," as a much-needed antidote to the hyper-individualism that is prevalent in American society.

Whenever you are involved in conversation about any public policy issue, go beyond the common question of, "What is good for me and those close to me?" to the question of, "What is good for all of those who are members of the particular communities that we are a part of?" and always encourage others to ask that same question.

Present a Christian perspective in public political discourse

There are two reasons why this advice seems totally unrealistic in contemporary American culture. First, there are many Americans who believe that there is no place for religious perspectives in public discourse in our pluralist society. The perceived problem is that Christians, like me, bring their value commitments to public discourse. Yes! And so does everyone else. For some, these values flow from particular religious commitments. For others, their values flow from secular views about the nature of reality and their places within that reality.

As I asserted in Chapter 2, this fact that the public square is not value-neutral means that political discourse should be characterized by a level playing field, where all perspectives, religious or secular, should be given a hearing; an approach that has been called "dialogic pluralism," where each perspective is **not** evaluated on the basis of its genesis (e.g., Did it come from a Christian, a Muslim, a Jew, an atheist, or from a Republican, a Democrat or an Independent?), but, rather, on the basis of the extent to which the perspective being proposed can lead to public policy that fosters the common good or help us to live well together in the midst of disagreements as to a common good.

A related second objection to Christians having a voice in public political debates is the undeniable empirical fact that too many Christians, especially those who consider themselves to be evangelicals, have a horrid track record as conversation partners, showing disdain and contempt for those "pagans" who disagree with them.

My response to that objection, as this entire book should make obvious, is that all Christians should model respectful conversation with those who disagree with them as they engage in public political discourse. That would be a marvelous public witness to the Christian faith in our fragmented and polarized society. And it would be amazing if those who do not profess commitment to the Christian faith would take notice of the benefits of such civil discourse and seek to do likewise.

Be an agent for nonviolence

I have noted my commitment to restricting or prohibiting "free speech" if that is necessary to "avoid violence." But my commitment to nonviolence goes further than that. I will seek to elaborate.

As I have already noted above, I am committed to the Christian value of shalom, which goes beyond a negative definition of peace as the absence of conflict and war. I embrace an expansive view of shalom as living in positive, caring relationships with others, including those who disagree with you, and living in a positive relationship with all of Creation.

But it is important not to minimize the negative view of peace as the absence of conflict and war, which, in my estimation, means that with possible extremely rare exceptions, Christian should not resort to violence.

I have already reported how my conversation partner Greg Williams and I disagree about this issue. Whereas we agree that Christians should actively seek to foster the flourishing of poor, marginalized and oppressed peoples, Greg proposes that to accomplish this goal, Christians may at times, have to resort to violent means, such as resorting to "occupations," "blockades" and "sabotage" when some "owners" in our capitalist society treat their workers "unjustly."

While I leave open the question as to whether Christians should resort to violence in certain extremely rare circumstances (as proposed in just-war theories),[116] I do not believe that such rare exceptions include the

---

116 See footnote 101.

examples that Greg presents.

Embracing the example of Martin Luther King Jr., I believe I should always seek for nonviolent means to address injustice. I recognize that this commitment could lead to a "cross." There is ample historical evidence that persons who will not resort to violence may be crushed by people in power who have no compulsion to resorting to violence (to the list of my heroes who could testify to that reality, I add the names of Mahatma Gandhi, Nelson Mandela and Jesus).

Let one thousand churches bloom

I am amazed at the gracious exchange on my eCircle between the pastors from two churches in Kalamazoo (MI) that are as different as any two churches could be: Will Fitzgerald, pastor of a small Mennonite Fellowship, a house church that numbers "fewer than 20 people, including kids, on a good day"; and Nathan Dannison, pastor of the large First Congregational Church that is nearly two centuries old, at which Sojourner Truth spoke in the 1850s.

A beautiful thing about the exchange between Will and Nathan is their deep mutual appreciation for the unique gifts and ministries of each church, contrary to the view that all churches are and do the same thing. A few of their reflections are worth repeating.

> Even though we are a small church, we believe that God gives us the gifts that we need ... when we do *not* have a particular gift, it is at least likely that God has decided we don't quite need it yet. The *charism* of a small church is intimacy and a certain ease: We don't need to do everything; we lack time and resources (Will).

> In my [first posting] ... I stated my belief that individual churches have different gifts, or charisms, and I believe it is First Congregational Church's charism to be a progressive Christian church, and I am glad they are who they are (Will).

> I have an immense amount of respect for small church ministry—I cut my teeth doing ministry in small group settings. I have found that the smaller the church, the more

intense the relationships and the deeper the discipleship. It is incredibly challenging to get more than a handful of Congregationalists to agree on nearly anything. Small churches likely represent the future of the church in America and we ought to live into their example (Nathan).

Note especially Will's appreciation for the "progressive" nature of the First Congregational Church, apparently in contrast to his more conservative church. At first glance, this difference that Will is referring to reflects the fact that whereas both churches encourage its members to be politically active, the First Congregational Church selectively takes churchwide positions on some public policy issues, while the Mennonite Fellowship has *not generally* taken any churchwide positions.

The words "not generally" italicized above are important. For, as Will's successive postings reveal, the Mennonite Fellowship has recently taken a churchwide position in opposition to the draconian separation of Latino children from their parents at the border in light of the "zero tolerance" policy of the Trump administration. An important lesson for churches emerges from this exception.

Not only do churches differ in their particular gifts and ministries, but any given church can evolve in its sense of calling to ministry. Relative to political activism, this means that in the history of a given church, there may be an evolution in the extent to which its members and the church (as a whole) discerns a calling to address perceived societal injustices. "One-size-fits-all" is not an adequate way to think of political activism on the part of churches. This conclusion is consistent with the report from Kris Van Engen on the variety of ways in which the Christian Reformed Church Office of Social Justice and Hunger Action works with individual CRC churches to support initiatives that these churches have already decided to undertake.

But, it is extremely important to note that Will, Nathan and Kris emphatically reject the idea that a church should take a churchwide position that endorses a particular political party or party agenda, or a particular candidate for elected office. Rather, using a broad view of politics as seeking to live well together in the midst of both agreements and disagreements as to a common good, churches should feel free to take churchwide positions to address social injustices. But this should be done using a "Christian lens," not a "political party lens." As Nathan so eloquently put it: "Our concerns [to foster "public well-being"] stem not from loyalty to some political party or figure—but rather from God's high expectations for the practicing Christian."

Based on the above reflections, my dream (hope!) is that 1,000 Christian churches in America will make a new commitment to churchwide political activism that addresses injustices in American society, especially injustices experienced by the poor, voiceless and marginalized among us, not as a substitute for traditional ways of worshipping together as a congregation, but as another form of worship—another both/and scenario where, as Nathan describes the First Congregational Church of Kalamazoo: "We do the painful, critical work of understanding our role in powers and principalities six days a week. On Sunday, however, we rejoice without ceasing."

It is also my hope that if numerous Christian churches, in addition to their individual members, can faithfully and effectively model a deep commitment to churchwide political activism that addresses injustices in American society, that will inspire many other persons and groups in our society to do likewise. (Hope springs eternal!)

Discern and use your particular gifts for political activism

As a context for my proposing a third major strategy for Christians and others to take initial steps toward reforming American politics, I remind the reader of my previous embracing of an expansive view of political activism.

Politics is everywhere if you take a broad view of it as seeking to live well together in the midst of both agreements and disagreements for a common good. So, one can do politics both in a governmental setting (the executive, legislative and judicial branches of local, state and national government) and various non-governmental settings (e.g., churches, schools, businesses voluntary organizations).

This expansive view of doing politics does not mean that you wear a particular "political party lens" when you do politics in a non-governmental setting. Rather, if you are a Christian, you wear a "Christian lens" (while others wear their particular religious or secular worldview lenses). I even go so far as to say that even when doing politics in governmental settings, your first loyalty is to be faithful to your "Christian lens," within your political party affiliation (recognizing tensions that can result between these two loyalties, which you need to resolve, which could mean switching parties or becoming an Independent).

Within this context, what contribution should you make to political activity? As preparation for my positive advice, I will suggest what you should **not** do if you are a Christian. You should **not** let other Christians tell you that political activity that focuses on one area of redemptive work is more important than redemptive work that focuses on another area.

For example, I still remember with sadness a pronouncement a few years ago from the leader of a Christian organization focused on an anti-abortion agenda that the new work of the National Association of Evangelicals (NAE) on promoting environmental responsibility was "a distraction." Nonsense! If you believe, as I do, that God intends to redeem all aspects of Creation, then efforts in one area are no more or less important than efforts in another area. It is all important. But no one Christian or Christian organization can do it all, which leads me to my positive suggestion.

My understanding of the biblical teachings on the "Body of Christ," as in 1 Corinthians 12, is that God intends for each Christian to contribute to the accomplishment of God's redemptive purposes in accordance with his/her particular God-given gifts. Therefore, you need to **discern where your gifts lie and, based on that discernment, choose those political activities that best fit your gifts** (my **third proposed primary strategy** for contributing to the reformation of American politics).

Doug Koopman presented an excellent example of this strategy in his reflections on how the giftedness of Paul Henry, the late U.S. congressman from Michigan, fit so well with the responsibilities of being a political legislator: "[His] welcoming personality and skills in listening, balancing and synthesizing made Paul perfectly suited for political representation." My appreciation for this example reveals my view that Christians who embrace hyper-partisanship are not a good fit for doing legislative politics.

I close this section, and this book, with a personal reflection, from my own experience, of how this attempt to fit one's gifts with one's understanding of the redemptive work that God intends to accomplish in the political realm (broadly defined) is a dynamic, evolving process.

As I have already mentioned, I have been involved for a number of years in the work of CASA of Sioux County to help our Latino neighbors to flourish. My initial efforts focused on political advocacy in the form of seeking to influence the views of elected political representatives, including face-to-face meetings with Rep. Steve King, Sen. Chuck Grassley and a few Iowa state legislators. Frankly, I have not seen much progress toward immigration reform as a result of my political advocacy efforts, either because of the intransigence of our political representatives or my lack of giftedness for this type of advocacy work, or a combination thereof.

As a result, I have made a recent adjustment in my CASA efforts, working on a major initiative to encourage local churches to declare themselves as sanctuary churches for undocumented immigrants who have received deportation orders, as places to live while their cases are adjudicated in the legal system. We have seen some progress in that a few local churches have declared themselves sanctuary churches, albeit for a rather narrow target audience (Latino members of their own churches or members of one local Latino church). However, at some churches, including my own, these efforts have gone nowhere, primarily because (in my estimation) too many local churchgoers have immediately politicized the issue, substituting a "political party lens" for the "Christian lens" they should be wearing.

My point in introducing this personal example is that as you seek to discern the match between your giftedness and your understanding of how God can use you to foster the Christian values that you believe are the foundation for the redemptive work that God is doing in this world, you need to be attentive to what is happening around you and adjust accordingly.

Whatever adjustments you may need to make during the course of your Christian pilgrimage, it is my hope and prayer that you will take some of the steps recommended above to contribute to a reforming of American politics that will comport with your understanding of foundational Christian values.

Bibliography

Albright, Madeleine. *Fascism: A Warning*. New York: HarperCollins, 2018.

Amstutz, Mark. *Just Immigration: American Policy in Christian Perspective.* Grand Rapids, MI: Eerdmans, 2017.

Barbour, Ian. *Myths, Models, and Paradigms: A Comparative Study in Science and Religion*. New York: Harper & Row, 1974.

Biggar, Nigel. *Behaving in Public: How to Do Christian Ethics*. Grand Rapids, MI: Eerdmans, 2011.

Bouchard, Charles, OP, STD. "Ethics—Is There A Catholic Policy on Health Care Reform?" *Journal of the Catholic Health Association of the United States*, January/February 2018.

Brooks, David. "Our Elites Still Don't Get It." *The New York Times*, November 16, 2017.

Brueggemann, Walter. *God, Neighbor, Empire: The Excess of Divine Fidelity and the Command of Common Good*. Waco, TX: Baylor University Press, 2016.

Carroll R., M. Daniel. *Christians at the Border: Immigration, the Church, and the Bible,* Second Edition. Grand Rapids, MI: Brazos Press, 2013.

Cech, Erin. "Culture of Disengagement in Engineering Education?" *Science, Technology & Human Values*, September 13, 2013.

Darwall, Stephen L. "Two Kinds of Respect." *Ethics, 88*, (1), October 1977.

Doleac, Jennifer L. "'Ban the Box' does more harm than good." *Brookings*, May 31, 2016.

Dovere, Edward-Isaac. "Obama, opening his foundation's first summit, calls for fixing civic culture." *Politico*, October 31, 2017.

Dreher, Rod. *The Benedict Option: A Strategy for Christians in a Post-Christian Nation*. New York: Penguin Random House, 2018.

Goldin, Claudia and Katz, Lawrence F. *The Race Between Education and Technology*. Cambridge, MA: Harvard University Press, 2010.

Gostin, Lawrence O. "Five Ethical Values to Guide Health System Reform." The JAMA Forum, November 8, 2017.

Hasker, William. "Faith-Learning Integration: An Overview." *Christian Scholar's Review, 21*, (3), 1992.

Heie, Harold. "Mathematics: Freedom Within Bounds." *The Reality of Christian Learning: Strategies for Faith-Discipline Integration*, Harold Heie and David L. Wolfe, eds. Grand Rapids, MI: Eerdmans, 1987.

————. "Developing a Christian Perspective on the Nature of Mathematics." *Teaching as an Act of Faith: Theory and Practice in Church-Related Higher Education*, Arlin A. Migliazzo, ed. New York: Fordham University Press, 2002.

————. *Learning to Listen, Ready to Talk: A Pilgrimage toward Peacemaking*. New York: iUniverse, 2007.

————. "Dialogic Discourse: Christian Scholars Engaging the Larger Academy." *Christian Scholar's Review*, Spring 2008.

————. *Evangelicals on Public Policy Issues: Sustaining a Respectful Political Conversation*. Abilene, TX: Abilene Christian University Press, 2014.

————. *A Future for American Evangelicalism: Commitment, Openness, and Conversation*. Eugene, OR: Wipf & Stock, 2015.

————. *Respectful LGBT Conversations: Seeking Truth, Giving Love, and Modeling Christian Unity*. Eugene, OR: Cascade Books, 2018.

Heie, Harold and King, Michael A., eds. *Mutual Treasure: Seeking Better Ways for Christians and Culture to Converse.* Telford, PA: Cascadia Publishing House, 2009.

Heie, Harold and Wolfe, David L., eds. *The Reality of Christian Learning: Strategies for Faith-Discipline Integration.* Grand Rapids, MI: Eerdmans, 1987.

Heie, Harold and Wolfe, David L. *Slogans or Distinctives: Reforming Christian Higher Education.* Lanham, MD: University Press of America, 1993.

Hitchens, Peter. "In Praise of Borders." *First Things*, October 2017. www.firstthings.com/article/2017/10/in-praise-of-borders.

Hoffmeier, James K. "The Use and Abuse of the Bible in the Immigration Debate." Center for Immigration Studies, December 1, 2011. https://cis.org/Use-and-abuse-Bible-Immigration-Debate.

Jacquet, Jennifer. *Is Shame Necessary? New Uses for an Old Tool.* New York: Vintage Books, 2015.

Johnson, Tim. *The Truth About Getting Sick in America: The Real Problems with Health Care and What We Can Do.* New York: Hyperion, 2010.

Kaemingk, Matthew. *Christian Hospitality and Muslim Immigration in an Age of Fear.* Grand Rapids, MI: Eerdmans, 2018.

King, Michael A. "Conversations on Homosexuality as a Quest to Love Enemy Prejudices." *Mutual Treasure: Seeking Better Ways for Christians and Culture to Converse*, Harold Heie and Michael A. King, eds. Telford, PA: Cascadia Publishing House, 2009.

Kuhn, Thomas. *The Structure of Scientific Revolutions*, Fourth Edition. Chicago: University of Chicago Press, 2012.

Koopman, Douglas L. "Reformed Christian Citizenship in America." *Reformed Review, 50,* (1), 1996.

Landgrave, Michelangelo and Nowrasteh, Alex. "Criminal Immigrants: Their Numbers, Demographics, and Countries of Origin." *Immigration Research and Policy Brief No. 1*. CATO Institute, March 15, 2017.

Lewis, C. S. *Reflections on the Psalms*. New York: Harcourt, Brace & World, 1958.

Lukacs, John. *Outgrowing Democracy: A History of the United States in the Twentieth Century*. New York: Doubleday, 1984.

Mann, Thomas E. and Ornstein, Norman J. *It's Even Worse Than It Looks: How the American Constitutional System Collided with the New Politics of Extremism*. New York: Basic Books, 2012.

Marty, Martin E. *By Way of Response*. Nashville: Abington Press, 1981.

Meacham, Jon. *The Soul of America: The Battle for our Better Angels*. New York: Random House, 2018.

_____. "When Leadership Fails." *Time*, November 12, 2018.

Migliazzo, Arlin A., ed. *Teaching as an Act of Faith: Theory and Practice in Church-Related Higher Education*. New York: Fordham University Press, 2002.

Mill, John Stewart. *On Liberty*. USA: Dover Publications, 2002.

Mouw, Richard. *Uncommon Decency: Christian Civility in an Uncivil World*, Second Edition. Downers Grove, IL: InterVarsity Press, 2010.

Niebuhr, Reinhold. *Moral Man and Immoral Society: A Study in Ethics and Politics*. Whitefish, MT: Kessinger Publishing, 2010.

Nyden, Philip. "Public Sociology, Engaged Research, and Civic Education." *Civic Studies: Approaches to the Emerging Field*, Peter Levine and Karol Edward Soltan, eds. Washington, D.C.: Bringing Theory to Practice, 2014.

O'Neill, Thomas P. "Frenemies: A Love Story." *The New York Times*, 2012. http://campaignstops.blogs.nytimes.com/2012/10/05/frenemies-a-love-story/?mcubz=3.

Pirsig, Robert. *Zen and the Art of Motorcycle Maintenance: An Inquiry into Values*. New York: HarperCollins, 1999.

Pope Francis, *Laudato Si': On Care for Our Common Home*. Vatican City: Libreria Editrice Vaticana, 2015.

Putnam, Robert D. *Bowling Alone: The Collapse and Revival of American Community*. New York: Simon & Schuster, 2000.

Robinson, Angela and Piff, Paul. "Wealth can make us selfish and stingy. Two psychologists explain why." *World Economic Forum*, October 2016.

Ronson, Jon. *So You've Been Publicly Shamed*. New York: Riverhead Books, 2016.

Schultze, Quentin. *An Essential Guide to Public Speaking: Serving Your Audience with Faith, Skill and Virtue*. Grand Rapids, MI: Baker Academic, 2006.

Schrock-Shenk, Carolyn. Foreword. *Stumbling Toward a Genuine Conversation on Homosexuality*. Michael A. King, ed. Telford, PA: Cascadia Publishing House, 2007.

Skillen, James. *Recharging the American Experiment: Principled Pluralism for Genuine Civic Community*. Grand Rapids, MI: Baker Books, 1994.

_____. "The Bible and the State." *Churches and the Rule of Law*. Stephen Brown, ed. Geneva, Switzerland: John Knox International Reformed Center, 2013.

Smith, Christian, Emerson, Michael O. and Snell, Patricia. *Passing the Plate: Why American Christians Don't Give Away More Money*. New York: Oxford University Press, 2008.

Soerens, Matthew and Hwang, Jenny. *Welcoming the Stranger: Justice, Compassion & Truth in the Immigration Debate*. Downers Grove, IL: InterVarsity Press, 2009.

Sullivan, Meghan. "The Practice of Catholic Theology: A Modest Proposal"? *Commonweal*. September 22, 2016.

Woodward, Bob. *Fear: Trump in the White House*. New York: Simon & Schuster, 2018.

Zehr, Howard. *Changing Lenses: Restorative Justice for our Times*. Harrisonburg, VA: Herald Press, 2015.

_____. *The Little Book of Restorative Justice*. Brattleboro, VT: Good Books, 2015.

Recommended Readings

The following is a composite list of recommendations for further reading from the conversation partners.

Askin, Elisabeth and Moore, Nathan. *The Health Care Handbook: A Clear and Concise Guide to the United States Health Care System*, Second Edition. St. Louis: Washington University in Saint Louis, 2014.

Black, Amy E. *Honoring God in Red or Blue: Approaching Politics with Humility, Grace, and Reason*. Chicago: Moody Publishers, 2012.

Black, Amy E. and Gundry, Stanley H., eds. *Five Views on the Church and Politics*. Grand Rapids, MI: Zondervan, 2015.

Bonhoeffer, Dietrich. *The Cost of Discipleship*. New York: Touchstone, 1995.

Boyte, Harry. *Awakening Democracy through Public Work: Pedagogies of Empowerment*. Nashville, TN: Vanderbilt University Press, 2018.

Bretherton, Luke. *Resurrecting Democracy: Faith, Citizenship, and the Politics of a Common Life*. New York: Cambridge University Press, 2014.

Carnes, Tony. "Sympathetic Objectivity Parts 1-4." *A Journey Through NYC Religions*. https://www.nycreligion.info/sympathetic-objectivity-part-1/.

Carroll R., M. Daniel. *Christians at the Border: Immigration, the Church and the Bible*. Grand Rapids, MI: Baker Academic, 2008.

Cavanaugh, William. *Being Consumed: Economics and Christian Desire*. Grand Rapids, MI: Eerdmans, 2008.

Coates, Ta-Nehisi. "The Case for Reparations." *The Atlantic*, June 2014. https://www.theatlantic.com/magazine/archive/2014/06/the-case-for-reparations/361631/.

Danforth, John. *The Relevance of Religion: How Faithful People Can Change Politics*. New York: Random House, 2015.

Davis, James Calvin. *Forbearance: A Theological Ethic for a Disagreeable Church*. Grand Rapids, MI: Eerdmans, 2017.

Davison Hunter, James. *To Change the World: The Irony, Tragedy, and Possibility of Christianity in America*. New York: Oxford University Press, 2010.

den Dulk, Kevin. "Isolation and the Prospects for Democracy: The Challenge for the Alienated." *Comment*, summer 2018.

Dionne, E. J., Jr. *Our Divided Political Heart: The Battle for the American Idea in an Age of Discontent*. New York: Bloomsbury, 2012.

Douglas, Mark. *Believing Aloud: Reflections on Being Religious in the Public Square*. Eugene, OR: Cascade Books, 2010.

Fea, John. *Believe Me: The Evangelical Road to Donald Trump*. Grand Rapids, MI: Eerdmans, 2018.

Gerson, Michael. "The Last Temptation." *The Atlantic*, April 2018.

Gerson, Michael and Wehner, Peter. *City of Man: Religion and Politics in a New Era*. Chicago: Moody Publishers, 2010.

Gilens, Martin. *Affluence and Influence: Economic Inequality and Political Power in America*. Princeton, NJ: Princeton University Press and the Russell Sage Foundation, 2012.

Goldin, Claudia and Katz, Lawrence F. *The Race Between Education and Technology*. Cambridge, MA: Harvard University Press, 2008.

Habermas, Jürgen, Blair, Tony and Debray, Régis. "Secularism's Crisis of Faith." http://kenan.ethics.duke.edu/religion/files/2017/04/Habermas-Notes-on-Post-Secular-Society.pdf.

Harper, Lisa Sharon and Innes, D.C. *Left, Right & Christ: Evangelical Faith in Politics.* Boise, Idaho: Russell Media, 2011.

Hicks, Douglas A. *Inequality and Christian Ethics.* New York: Cambridge University Press, 2000.

Hill, Frank. "If You Are Upset About the Level of Money in Politics, You Should Support Radical Tax Reform." *Telemachus,* October 4, 2017. http://www.telemachusleaps.com/2017/10/if-you-are-upset-about-level-of-money.html.

Hough, Douglas E. *Irrationality in Health Care: What Behavioral Economics Reveals About What We Do and Why.* Stanford: Stanford University Press, 2013.

Inazu, John. *Confident Pluralism: Surviving and Thriving Through Deep Difference.* Chicago: University of Chicago Press, 2016.

Johnson, Kelly. "Blessings, Curses, and the Cross." *Ex Auditu: An International Journal of the Theological Interpretation of Scripture, 27,* 2011, 82-99.

King, Martin Luther, Jr. *Strength to Love.* Minneapolis, MN: Augsburg Fortress, 2018.

Lee, Justin. *Talking Across the Divide: How to Communicate with People You Disagree with and Maybe Even Change the World.* New York: Penguin Random House, 2018.

Levin, Yuval. *The Fractured Republic: Renewing America's Social Contract in the Age of Individualism.* New York: Basic Books, 2016.

Lysaught. M. Therese and Kotva, Joseph V., Jr. (with Stephen E. Lammers and Allen Verhey), eds. *On Moral Medicine: Theological Perspectives in Medical Ethics,* Third Edition. Grand Rapids, MI: Eerdmans, 2012.

Margolis, Michele F. *From Politics to the Pews: How Partisanship and the Political Environment Shape Religious Identity.* Chicago: The University of Chicago Press, 2018.

Mill, John Stewart. *On Liberty*. Elizabeth Rapaport, ed. Indianapolis: Hackett Publishing, 1978.

Mouw, Richard. *Uncommon Decency: Christian Civility in an Uncivil World*, Second Edition. Downers Grove, IL: InterVarsity Press, 2010.

Mutz, Diana A. "Status threat, not economic hardship, explains the 2016 presidential vote." *Proceedings of the National Academy of Sciences of the United States of America 115*, (19), E4330–E4339, May 8, 2018. https://doi.org/10.1073/pnas.1718155115.

Mutz, Diana C. *Hearing the Other Side: Deliberative versus Participatory Democracy*. New York: Cambridge University Press, 2006.

Norris, Kristopher and Sam Speers. *Kingdom Politics: In Search of a New Political Imagination for Today's Church*. Eugene, OR: Cascade Books, 2015.

Palmer, Parker J. *Healing the Heart of Democracy: The Courage to Create a Politics Worthy of the Human Spirit*. San Francisco: Jossey-Bass, 2011.

Putnam, Robert D. and Campbell, David E. *American Grace: How Religion Divides and Unites Us*. New York: Simon & Schuster, 2010.

Reichley, A. James. *The Life of the Parties: A History of American Political Parties*. Lanham, MD: Rowman & Littlefield Publishers, Inc., 2000.

Reid, T. R. *The Healing of America: A Global Quest for Better, Cheaper, and Fairer Health Care*. New York: Penguin Press, 2010. See also video of Reid presenting his findings: https://www.youtube.com/watch?v=nfqBNNAgopY.

Rovner, Julie. *Health Care Policy and Politics A to Z*, Third Edition. Washington: CQ Press, 2008.

Sargent, Greg. *An Uncivil War: Taking Back Our Democracy in an Age of Trumpian Disinformation and Thunderdome Politics*. New York: HarperCollins, 2018.

Schattschneider, Elmer E. *The Semisovereign People: A Realist's View of Democracy in America*. Boston: Wadsworth, 1975.

Sherratt, Timothy. *Power Made Perfect? Is There a Christian Politics for the Twenty-First Century?* Eugene, OR: Cascade Books, 2016.

Skillen, James W. *The Good of Politics: A Biblical, Historical, and Contemporary Introduction*. Grand Rapids: Baker Academic, 2014.

Skillen James W. and McCarthy, Rockne M., eds. *Political Order and the Plural Structure of Society*. Atlanta: Scholars Press, 1991.

Smith, James K. A. *Awaiting the King: Reforming Public Theology*. Grand Rapids, MI: Baker Books, 2017.

Snowe, Olympia. *Fighting for Common Ground: How We Can Fix the Stalemate in Congress*. New York: Weinstein Books, 2013.

Soerens, Matthew, Yang, Jenny, and Anderson, Leith. *Welcoming the Stranger: Justice, Compassion & Truth in the Immigration Debate*, Revised Edition. Downers Grove, IL: InterVarsity Press, 2018.

Soper, J. Christopher, den Dulk, Kevin R., and Monsma, Stephen V. *The Challenge of Pluralism: Church and State in Six Democracies, Third Edition*. Lanham, MD: Rowman & Littlefield Publishers Inc., 2017.

Sowle Cahill, Lisa. *Theological Bioethics: Participation, Justice, Change*. Washington: Georgetown University Press, 2005.

Sundquist, James L. *Dynamics of the Party System: Alignment and Realignment of Political Parties in the United States*, Second Edition. Washington, D.C.: Brookings Institution Press, 1983.

Thompson, Mark. *Enough Said: What's Gone Wrong with the Language of Politics?* New York; St. Martin's Press, 2016.

Wallis, Jim. *On God's Side: What Religion Forgets and Politics Hasn't Learned About Serving the Common Good*. Grand Rapids, MI: Baker Publishing, 2013.

Wolterstorff, Nicholas and Audi, Robert. *Religion in the Public Square: The Place of Religious Convictions in Political Debate*. Lanham, MD: Rowman & Littlefield Publishers Inc., 1997.

About the Authors

Harold Heie is a senior fellow at The Colossian Forum. He previously served as founding director of the Center for Christian Studies (now the Center for Faith and Inquiry) at Gordon College and as vice president for academic affairs at Messiah College and Northwestern College in Iowa, after teaching mathematics at Gordon College and The King's College. He holds a doctorate in mechanical and aerospace sciences from Princeton University and served as a trustee of the Center for Public Justice and as a senior fellow at the Council for Christian Colleges and Universities (CCCU).

Harold's website, www.respectfulconversation.net, is devoted to encouraging and modeling respectful conversations concerning contentious issues about which Christians have strong disagreements. The eCircle on "Reforming Political Discourse" that is the basis for this book is the fourth major eCircle he has hosted on his website, the first three of which resulted in books: *Evangelicals on Public Policy Issues: Sustaining a Respectful Political Conversation* (2014); *A Future for American Evangelicalism: Commitment, Openness, and Conversation* (2015); and *Respectful LGBT Conversations: Seeking Truth, Giving Love, and Modeling Christian Unity* (2018).

Richard Mouw was president of Fuller Theological Seminary from 1993 through June 2013, and presently serves on the Fuller faculty as Professor of Faith and Public Life. Prior to joining the Fuller faculty in 1985, he taught in the Philosophy Department at Calvin College. Mouw has also served as visiting professor at several institutions, including the Free University in Amsterdam. A graduate of Houghton College, Mouw studied at Western Theological Seminary and earned a master's degree in philosophy at the University of Alberta. His PhD in philosophy is from the University of Chicago. Mouw is the author of 20 books, and has received several awards, including Princeton Theological Seminary's 2007 Kuyper Prize for Excellence in Reformed Theology and Public Life, and the Shalom Award for Interfaith Cooperation from the American Jewish Committee. He served as president of the Association of Theological Schools, and co-chaired for six years the official Reformed-Catholic Dialogue.

Conversation Partners

Harry Boyte worked for Martin Luther King Jr. during the civil rights movement in the 1960s as a field secretary in the Citizenship Schools. He has published 10 books on political theory, community organizing and democratic practices and traditions. He is also the founder of the international Public Achievement civic education initiative and architect of the civic engagement concept called "public work." His new book, *Awakening Democracy through Public Work: Pedagogies of Empowerment* (Vanderbilt, 2018) recounts and analyzes stories of the public work movement around the world.

Tony Carnes is the founder and editor of the online magazine *A Journey through NYC religions*. His books include *New York Glory: Religions in the City*, edited with Anna Karpathakis and *Asian American Religions: The Making and Remaking of Borders and Boundaries*, edited with Fenggang Yang, both published by New York University Press. His "Asian American Religions" was recently published in the *Oxford Research Encyclopedia on American Religions*. Some of his ideas were developed in discussions at the Columbia University Seminar on Contents and Methods in the Social Sciences.

Clarke E. Cochran was ordained a deacon in the Catholic Church in 1981. He serves at St. Peter Church in Charlotte, North Carolina. He taught religion and politics and health care policy at Texas Tech University from 1970-2007 and served as vice president, Mission Integration, with Covenant Health from 2008-2013.

Kimberly H. Conger teaches political science and public administration at the University of Cincinnati. She is a national expert on religious activists in state level politics and the past president of the Religion and Politics Research Section of the *American Political Science Association*. Her current projects examine the policy influence of religious political advocacy, and the role of religious activism in reducing political inequalities in the U.S.

Angela Cowser is associate dean of Black Church Studies and the Doctor Of Ministry Programs, and associate professor of Black Church Studies at Louisville Presbyterian Theological Seminary. She was previously assistant professor of the Sociology of Religion and director of the Center for the Church and the Black Experience at Garrett-Evangelical Theological Seminary in Evanston, Illinois; and lead organizer for a 75-member congregation community organizing group called Tying Nashville Together (TNT) in Nashville, Tennessee.

Nathan Dannison currently serves as the 29th senior minister of the First Congregational Church of Kalamazoo, Michigan. He is a graduate of the Chicago Theological Seminary and an ordained minister in the United Church of Christ and the Christian Church (Disciples of Christ).

Kevin R. den Dulk is the Paul B. Henry professor of political science and the executive director of the Henry Institute for the Study of Christianity and Politics at Calvin College. An award-winning teacher, his scholarly work focuses on the intersection of faith and democratic citizenship. He has co-authored or co-edited several books, including *The Challenge of Pluralism: Church and State in Six Democracies* (2017), *Religion and Politics in America* (2018), and *The Church and Religious Persecution* (2015). He writes regularly for *Comment* magazine and the Center for Public Justice.

Mark Douglas is professor of Christian Ethics and director of the Master of Divinity Degree Program at Columbia Theological Seminary in Decatur, Georgia. His most recent book is *Believing Aloud: Reflections on Being Religious in the Public Sphere* (Cascade, 2010), and he has a new book,

Christian Pacifism for the Environmental Age, coming from Cambridge University Press in 2019.

Will Fitzgerald is the lay pastor of Kalamazoo Mennonite Fellowship in Kalamazoo, MI. He is licensed for special purposes in the Indiana-Michigan Mennonite Conference of Mennonite Church, USA. He is also a Staff Security Engineer at GitHub, Inc, and has a Ph.D. in computer science from Northwestern University.

Jeffrey B. Hammond is an associate professor of law at Faulkner University's Thomas Goode Jones School of Law in Montgomery, Alabama. His teaching and scholarship focus on constitutional law and the intersections of law and Christian theology and American health law and policy. He is particularly interested in constructing Protestant theories of laws and conscience and in free exercise and establishment clause theory.

Harold Heie is a senior fellow at The Colossian Forum. He previously served as founding director at the Center for Christian Studies (now the Center for Faith and Inquiry) at Gordon College and vice president for academic affairs at Messiah College and Northwestern College in Iowa, after teaching mathematics at Gordon College and The King's College.

Frank Hill ran for Congress in 1984 at the age of 28 in NC-2 (North Carolina's 2nd Congressional District) and became chief of staff to former U.S. Rep. Alex McMillan of Charlotte, NC (NC-9) for a decade. He later was Senator Elizabeth Dole's first chief of staff. Frank is the director of The Institute for the Public Trust in Raleigh, NC, which recruits and trains top-flight new candidates to run for public office. Frank is a graduate of The University of North Carolina at Chapel Hill and the Fuqua School of Business at Duke University.

Kelly Johnson is associate professor in the Department of Religious Studies at the University of Dayton and author of *The Fear of Beggars: Stewardship and Poverty in Christian Ethics*, a historical critique of modern thought on private property and particularly the church's language of stewardship. She has a doctorate in theological ethics from Duke University. She is a founding member of the Ekklesia Project and serves on the editorial board of the Journal of Moral Theology. Her intellectual work grapples with the role of grace in contemporary moral discourse.

Douglas Koopman is professor of political science at Calvin College. His academic specialties are American political institutions and religion in American politics. Koopman joined the Calvin faculty in 1995 after 15 years working in national politics. He has interrupted his academic work at times for assignments in politics, government and higher education leadership. Koopman has co-authored college texts in his specialty areas and written about the federal faith-based initiative and how to integrate Christian faith in politics.

Robert L. McFarland is the associate dean of external affairs and an associate professor of law at Faulkner University's Thomas Goode Jones School of Law in Montgomery, Alabama. He and his colleague Adam MacLeod have co-authored the textbook *Foundations of Law*, and he has authored numerous essays and articles for various legal journals.

Steven McMullen is an associate professor of economics at Hope College in Holland, Michigan, a fellow at the Oxford Centre for Animal Ethics, and executive editor of the journal *Faith & Economics*. His areas of research include education policy, animal/environmental ethics and theology. He received his doctorate in economics from the University of North Carolina in 2008.

James W. Skillen was the founder and then director of the Center for Public Justice from 1977 to 2009. He taught political science and philosophy at three Christian colleges from 1973 to 1981. He earned his doctorate in political philosophy, international relations and Christian ethics at Duke University. Now retired, he continues to write, speak and mentor students and public servants. He is the author of *The Good of Politics* (Baker Academic, 2014) and a forthcoming book of biblical interpretation, *God's Sabbath with Creation.*

Matthew Soerens serves as the U.S. director of Church Mobilization for World Relief. He is co-author of *Welcoming the Stranger: Justice, Compassion & Truth in the Immigration Debate* (InterVarsity Press, 2018) and *Seeking Refuge: On the Shores of the Global Refugee Crisis* (Moody Publishers, 2016).

Jim Talen is currently serving his tenth two-year term as a Kent County Commissioner, representing parts of Grand Rapids, MI. He serves on the boards of the Grand Rapids Downtown Development Authority and Network180, a local mental health oversight authority.

Kim Van Es has been an English educator for over 25 years, most recently at Northwestern College in Orange City, Iowa. She presents at conferences affiliated with the National Council of Teachers of English, often on the irresistible subject of grammar. Kim has a passion for using words well, an aspiration she pursues as a freelance writer and editor. As vice-chair of the Democratic Central Committee in the most conservative county in Iowa (Sioux), she believes that dialogue among those who differ can be both honestly robust and completely civil.

Jeff VanDerWerff is dean of the social sciences at Northwestern College (Iowa), where he has taught courses in American government and public life for nearly two decades and continues to wrestle with the political theology of engaging democracy as a faithful follower of Jesus. After a brief stint as the administrative director for Mission Year (formerly Kingdom-works), he pursued his doctorate from the Department of Government at the University of Kansas prior to returning to his undergraduate alma mater.

Kris Van Engen is an ordained minister in the Reformed Church in America and is the Justice Mobilizing team leader for World Renew and the CRC Office of Social Justice. Kris is the assistant editor of the book *Live Just.ly* and co-creator of the Church Between Borders immigration workshop. He also serves on the advocacy steering committee for The Alliance to End Hunger in Washington, D.C. and is a board member with Lighthouse Immigrant Advocates in his hometown of Holland, MI.

Gregory Williams is a doctor of theology student at Duke University, specializing in Christian theology and ethics, historical theology and critical theory. He is a member of the prison abolitionist group Inside-Outside Alliance, and serves as organizing coordinator for the Raleigh-Durham branch of the Industrial Workers of the World. His research focuses on radical discipleship and social movement work in the United States. He is a reformed Protestant, a baptized Jew of Ashkenazi heritage and an anarcho-communist.

Acknowledgments

I first want to thank the 23 "conversation partners" who contributed postings to the electronic conversation (eCircle) on "Reforming Political Discourse" (RPD) that was the basis for this book. They modeled in an admirable way that Christians who have strong disagreements about controversial issues can engage in respectful conversations about their differences. They are the persons who made this book possible.

I want to thank Luke Bretherton from Duke Divinity School for his marvelous assistance in helping me to design the agenda of subtopics and leading questions for my RPD eCircle.

A special word of thanks goes to Rob Barrett, director of forums and scholarship for The Colossian Forum (TCF) and to Michael Gulker, the president of TCF, for their steadfast support of this project. It was under Michael's leadership that TCF agreed to pay most of the costs associated with managing my website during the 11 months of the RPD eCircle. This project would not have happened if it were not for this generous financial support, for which I am extremely grateful. Rob has been a constant source of encouragement and sage advice as we create welcoming spaces for respectful dialogue in our respective spheres of influence. It is an honor for me to serve as a TCF senior fellow since their mission to "create hospitable space for conversations about divisive issues" comports so well with my commitment to facilitate "respectful conversations" about contentious issues.

Brian Workman and Dan Hefferan of the 5 espressos web design and development company served with distinction as my web managers leading up to and during the RPD eCircle. I thank them for the extremely competent, efficient and gracious manner in which they managed my website.

I thank David Crumm, cofounder and editor of the Read the Spirit Publishing House for his willingness to publish this book under their Front Edge Publishing (FEP) imprint. I also thank Dmitri Barvinok, the director of production at FEP, for the professional and efficient manner in which he brought this book to publication.

I want to express my deep appreciation to Richard Mouw for writing the Foreword for this book. For many years, Richard has set a marvelous example for me and countless others on how to effectively engage in gracious and respectful conversations with those committed to other religious and secular faiths. It is an honor and a source of great encouragement to have a Christian statesman of his stature and reputation express appreciation for this book.

Finally, I want to thank Jim Skillen, to whom this book is dedicated. Little did I know when we both came to teach at Gordon College in the fall of 1975 that Jim would have a profound influence in expanding my view of God's redemptive purposes for all of Creation, including the political realm. That was the start of a lifelong friendship that has been a constant source of encouragement and inspiration for me.

CPSIA information can be obtained
at www.ICGtesting.com
Printed in the USA
FFHW021818170519
52512533-57944FF